RITUAL SITES AND RELIGIOUS RIVALRIES IN LATE ROMAN NORTH AFRICA

In *Ritual Sites and Religious Rivalries in Late Roman North Africa,* Lander examines the rhetorical and physical battles for sacred space between practitioners of traditional Roman religion, Christians, and Jews of late Roman North Africa. By analyzing literary along with archaeological evidence, Lander provides a new understanding of ancient notions of ritual space. This regard for ritual sites above other locations rendered the act or mere suggestion of seizing and destroying them powerful weapons in inter-group religious conflicts. Lander demonstrates that the quantity and harshness of discursive and physical attacks on ritual spaces directly correlates to their symbolic value. This heightened valuation reached such a level that rivals were willing to violate conventional Roman norms of property rights to display spatial control. Moreover, Roman Imperial policy eventually appropriated spatial triumphalism as a strategy for negotiating religious conflicts, giving rise to a new form of spatial colonialism that was explicitly religious.

Shira L. Lander is the Director of Jewish Studies at Southern Methodist University, where she holds a faculty appointment in Religious Studies. She previously served as the Anna Smith Fine Senior Lecturer for the Program in Jewish Studies at Rice University, where she also directed the Boniuk Institute for Religious Tolerance. Her publications focus on Jewish-Christian relations, including the commentary on 1 Corinthians in Oxford University Press's ground-breaking publication, the *Jewish Annotated New Testament*. She co-edited *A Most Reliable Witness: Essays in Honor of Ross Shepard Kraemer* for Brown University's series in Judaic Studies.

RITUAL SITES AND RELIGIOUS RIVALRIES IN LATE ROMAN NORTH AFRICA

SHIRA L. LANDER

Southern Methodist University

CAMBRIDGE
UNIVERSITY PRESS

CAMBRIDGE
UNIVERSITY PRESS

University Printing House, Cambridge CB2 8BS, United Kingdom

One Liberty Plaza, 20th Floor, New York, NY 10006, USA

477 Williamstown Road, Port Melbourne, VIC 3207, Australia

4843/24, 2nd Floor, Ansari Road, Daryaganj, Delhi – 110002, India

79 Anson Road, #06-04/06, Singapore 079906

Cambridge University Press is part of the University of Cambridge.

It furthers the University's mission by disseminating knowledge in the pursuit of education, learning, and research at the highest international levels of excellence.

www.cambridge.org
Information on this title: www.cambridge.org/9781107146945

© Cambridge University Press 2016

First published 2016

Printed in the United States of America by Sheridan Books, Inc.

A catalog record for this publication is available from the British Library.

Library of Congress Cataloging in Publication Data
Names: Lander, Shira L., author.
Title: Ritual sites and religious rivalries in late Roman North Africa / Shira L. Lander.
Description: New York: Cambridge University Press, 2016.
Identifiers: LCCN 2016026404 | ISBN 9781107146945 (hardback: alk. paper)
Subjects: LCSH: Africa, North – Church history. | Church history – Primitive and early church, ca. 30-600. | Christianity and other religions – Judaism. | Judaism – Relations – Christianity. | Jews – Africa, North – History – To 1500. | Africa, North – Antiquities, Roman.
Classification: LCC BR190.L36 2016 | DDC 276.1/02–dc23
LC record available at https://lccn.loc.gov/2016026404

ISBN 978-1-107-14694-5 Hardback

*To my loved ones, teachers, and colleagues
for their support, guidance, and inspiration*

CONTENTS

ILLUSTRATIONS

PREFACE

This project originated in the course of writing my dissertation at the University of Pennsylvania under the direction of Ross S. Kraemer, Robert A. Kraft, Brent D. Shaw, and E. Ann Matter. While examining the role of martyr veneration rituals in reconfiguring social arrangements of late antique North Africa, time and again the importance of ritual sites surfaced. That project afforded neither the time nor space that this significant issue demanded, and I embarked on a study that took me deeper into the fields of archaeology and cultural geography. Throughout the decade that I was researching ancient conflicts over religious sites, the world repeatedly witnessed attacks on religious buildings and monuments around the globe. Most recently the temple of Baalshamin in Palmyra and its chief of antiquities, Khaled el-Asaad, were annihilated by ISIS militants under the guise of religious precepts. The persistence of spatial contestation as a strategy for negotiating power provoked questions about the significance of space and place in the human imagination, questions that I address in this book.

Along the way I have been fortunate to share these questions with wonderful colleagues who have provided opportunities for fruitful dialogue and critique. Many of the methodological issues I wrestle with emerged from a 2004 panel of what was at that time known as the *Europe and the Mediterranean in Late Antiquity Group* of the American Academy of Religion. I delivered a paper entitled "'The Word Made Flesh': Case Studies of Confluence and Conflict in the Shrines of the Terebinths of Mamre and the Maccabean Martyrs in Daphne, Syria." One of my fellow panelists, Georgia Frank, was working on similar issues, and our respondent, Patricia Cox Miller, challenged us to consider how the "material turn" influenced our work. Frank went on to publish numerous articles exploring the relationship between sacred objects and memory, and Miller published her analysis of the "thingness" of saints' bodies in *The Corporeal Imagination: Signifying the Holy in Late Ancient Christianity* (2009). One of the participants, Christine Shepardson, asked me to think further about

issues posed by cultural geographers, and informed me that she, too, was studying spatial contestation in Antioch. At that point my research was not geographically specific, yet the value of such a project became clear to me in my
ongoing encounters with Shepardson's work and I focused my research on
North Africa.

Brent Shaw then published his monumental study of North African
conflict, *Sacred Violence. African Christians and Sectarian Hatred in the Age of
Augustine* (2011). His richly delineated history of North African violence in
the post-Constantinian century reframed and expanded much of what I had
learned from him as his doctoral student, and confirmed the usefulness of this
type of regionally focused study. In order to deepen current understanding of
the North African conflicts and to shed light on the strategy of spatial contestation more broadly, I chose to examine the material dimension of those battles.

Many people have made this book possible. My loving and nurturing
family and friends have given me the wherewithal and humor required
to stay the course. My wise and erudite teachers, most exceptionally Ross
Kraemer, have simultaneously supported and challenged my work. Along
the way, various versions of this project have received helpful suggestions and critique from my wonderful colleagues at Rice and Southern
Methodist Universities, the *Europe and the Mediterranean in Late Antiquity
Group* of the American Academy of Religion, and the *Religious World of Late
Antiquity* and *Violence and Representations of Violence among Jews and Christians*
sections of the Society of Biblical Literature. I am grateful to Ross Kraemer,
Christine Shepardson, and the anonymous other readers for their careful
perusal of the manuscript.

ABBREVIATIONS

Note: Abbreviations follow *The SBL Handbook of Style* unless otherwise noted below. All translations are mine unless otherwise noted.

Act. pur. Fel.	*Acta purgationis Felicis episcopi Autrumnitani*, ed. C. Ziwsa, CSEL 26 (Vienna, 1893), pp. 197–204 = Optatus, Appendix 2 to *de schism. Don.*
Act. Mun. Fel.	*Acta Munati Felicis* in the *Gesta apud Zenophilum*
Conc. Gall.	*Concilia Galliae a. 314–506*, ed. C. Munier, CCL 148 (Turnhout, 1963), pp. 9–24
Conc. ep. Arel.	*Concilium episcoporum Arelatense ad Silvestrum papam*, ed. C. Ziwsa, CSEL 26 (Vienna, 1893), pp. 206–208 = Optatus, Appendix 4 to *de schism. Don.*
CJZC	*Corpus Jüdischer Zeugnisse Aus Der Cyrenika*. Tubinger Atlas Des Vorderen Orients. Ed. Gert Lüderitz, with an introduction by Joyce M. Reynolds. Wiesbaden: L. Reichert, 1983.
de schism. Don.	Optatus, *de schismate Donatistarum*, *Optat de Milève: Traité contre les Donatistes* 1: Livres I et II, ed. M. Labrousse, SC 412 (Paris, 1995) and *Optat de Milève: Traité contre les Donatistes* 2: Livres III à VII, ed. M. Labrousse, SC 413 (Paris, 1996).[1]

---

[1] Most editions use the title *de schismate Donatistarum*, yet Mandouze preferred *contra Parmenianum Donatistam* ("Optatus," PCA 1: 795–7). Paul Monceaux noted that neither title was preserved in ancient manuscripts; the Codex Remensis has *ad Parmenianum schismaticorum auctorem*. See Monceaux, *Histoire littéraire de l'Afrique Chrétienne depuis les origines jusqu'a l'invasion arabe*, 7 vols. (Brussels: Impression Anastaltique. Culture et Civilisation, 1901–23: 1966) 5: 248. I will use the conventional *de schism. Don.*

Ep. Const. Aelaf.	*Epistula Constantini Aelafio*, ed. C. Ziwsa, CSEL 26 (Vienna, 1893), pp. 204–206 = Optatus, Appendix 3 to *de schism. Don.*
Ep. Const. Cels.	*Epistula Constantini Celso*, ed. C. Ziwsa, CSEL 26 (Vienna, 1893), pp. 211–212 = Optatus, Appendix 7 to *de schism. Don.*
Ep. Const. episc. cath.	*Epistula Constantini episcopis catholicis*, ed. C. Ziwsa, CSEL 26 (Vienna, 1893), pp. 208–210 = Optatus, Appendix 5 to *de schism. Don.*
Ep. Const. episc.	*Epistula Constantini episcopis*, ed. C. Ziwsa, CSEL 26 (Vienna, 1893), pp. 210–211 = Optatus, Appendix 6 to *de schism. Don.*
Ep. Const. episc. Afric.	*Epistula Constantini universis episcopis per Africam*, ed. C. Ziwsa, CSEL 26 (Vienna, 1893), pp. 212–213 = Optatus, Appendix 9 to *de schism. Don.*
Ep. Const. Zeu.	*Epistula Constantini Zeuzio, Gallico, Victorino et. al.*, ed. C. Ziwsa, CSEL 26 (Vienna, 1893), pp. 213–216 = Optatus, Appendix 10 to *de schism. Don.*
Gest. Zeno.	*Gesta apud Zenophilum*, ed. C. Ziwsa, CSEL 26 (Vienna, 1893), pp. 185–197 = Optatus, Appendix 1 to *de schism. Don.*
JIGRE	*Jewish Inscriptions of Graeco-Roman Egypt*. ed. William Horbury and David Noy. New York: Cambridge University Press, 1992.
MiAg	*Miscellanea Agostiniana*. Vol. 1. *Sermones post Maurinos reperti*. ed. G. Morin. Rome: Tipografia Poliglota Vaticana, 1930.
Pass. Dat. Saturn.	*Passio ss. Dativi, Saturnini presb. et aliorum* (*Acts of the Abitinian Martyrs*), P. Franchi de' Cavalieri, "La Passio dei martiri Abitinensi," in *Note agiografiche 8* = *Studi e Testi 65* (Città del Vaticano, 1935): 3–71.
PCA	*Prosopographie chrétienne du Bas-Empire. Études d'antiquités africaines*. ed. Henri Irénée Marrou and Jean-Rémy Palanque. Vol. 1. "Afrique." ed. André Mandouze. Paris: CNRS Editions, 1982.

PLRE   *The Prosopography of the Later Roman Empire.*
                            Vol. 1. ed. A. H. M. Jones, J. R. Martindale, and
                            J. Morris. Vol. 2. ed. J. R. Martindale. Cambridge:
                            Cambridge University Press, 1980. Cambridge:
                            Cambridge University Press, 1971.

PLS   *Patrologiae cursus completus. series Latina. Supplementum.*
                            ed. A. Hamman. Paris: Garnier, 1958–1974.

INTRODUCTION: SCAFFOLDING

IN THE FOURTH–SIXTH CENTURIES, THE URBAN LANDSCAPE OF THE Roman empire, with its vaunted architectural achievements, underwent profound transformation. North African city centers at the intersection of their main arteries shifted, old buildings were refurbished for new purposes, new buildings rose from grounds once considered unsuitable, and walls were built that redefined the city limits. Once seen by modern scholars as an abrupt change, a direct consequence of the collapse and Christianization of the Roman empire, this transformation has more recently been understood as a far more gradual process prompted by economic and demographic changes. Yet early Christian historiographers construed the customary mechanisms of spatial transformation – imperial largess, disuse, reuse, use of spolia, changes in ownership, architectural alterations, to name just a few – in religious terms. Why did they characterize these nonviolent spatial activities as hostile takeovers and intentional destructions? Christian literary sources from this period construe spatial transformation as the defeat of Judaism and what they refer to as "paganism." Christian leaders seized the opportunity afforded by temple abandonment and synagogue decline to promote their imagined interpretation of the shifting landscape, the victory of Christianity. This imaginal map was useful for securing imperial support, asserting authority, as well as negotiating and patrolling group boundaries.

To explore these issues, this book examines ancient notions of place and explores the spatial relations between religious competitors in the late Roman provinces of North Africa. The examples of Christians, practitioners of traditional Roman rites, and Jews suggest that not only did places of communal religious assembly serve as focal points for religious competition, but Christian writers claimed that the changing landscape of Late Antiquity augured their triumph. I argue that the rhetoric of spatial contestation was a key component in negotiating religious identifications that underwent seismic shifts over the course of the third through fifth centuries. I contend that what made this possible was a particular conception of religious place that anthropologists have termed "place identity." Place identity is the constellation of ideas, behaviors, emotions, and values that people associate with a particular location in their physical environment. Those associations are called "place meanings." By exploring what certain places meant, what they symbolized to their audiences, we are better able to determine why these sites were targeted for negotiating group boundaries and identification. With church buildings increasingly portrayed and perceived by late antique North Africans as loci of authority and divine forces, their symbolic power grew. The acts of seizing, damaging, or destroying them thereby acquired their own symbolic power from these buildings' place meanings and from the place identities related to them.

By focusing on one particular part of the Roman empire, this study aims to take seriously regional variation while also attempting to redress its omission from previous treatments of spatial conflict. The recent study of Antioch by Christine Shepardson is a superb example of this kind of regional work. My choice of North Africa rests on two foundations: First, it is understudied.[1] Second, and more importantly, spatial contestation plays out somewhat differently in this region than in the eastern part of the empire, where religious motivations more directly "altered the cityscape," as Shepardson has demonstrated.[2]

Christian writers described architectural transformations using terms related to violence and power because spatial control correlated to dominance, and spatial boundaries could be associated with boundaries of group identification. In North Africa, these narratives took their cues initially from intra-Christian struggles for spatial control and subsequently applied the paradigm to relations with non-Christians. The idea of triumph was concretized by capturing or destroying the symbol of an adversary's power, or that which was regarded as most "sacred" or "holy."

The terms "sacred (sacrum)" and "holy (sanctus)" reproduce ancient modifiers used to describe material objects that were differentiated from other objects by their use for religious ritual and their association with divine power. "Sacra" appears in inscriptions describing rituals, while "sanctus" appears in inscriptions describing objects dedicated by devoted donors.[3]

---

[1] This is undergoing reversal in the past decade (see the recent works of Stern, Shaw, Rebillard, Dessey, Leone, and Burns and Jensen).

[2] Christine Shepardson, *Controlling Contested Places: Late Antique Antioch and the Spatial Politics of Religious Controversy* (Berkeley, CA: University of California Press, 2014), p. 241.

[3] ILAlg 1 506 = CIL 8.20903, a mosaic pavement from the late fourth-century chapel built by the bishop Alexander in Tipasa: *Omnis sacra canens, sacramento manus porrigere gaudens*

Literature goes beyond these attributions, assigning the adjectives to ritual sites themselves.[4] Augustine, the bishop of Hippo, refers to churches as "consecrated places" (*locis ei sacratis*).[5] The functions and associated meanings of these edifices enabled both users and observers to distinguish them from their surroundings and to recognize their ascribed value.[6]

In addition to conveying dominance, spatial boundaries were useful tools for creating and reinforcing social boundaries. As Maijastina Kahlos has demonstrated, Christian polemicists, apologists, and shapers of Christian culture used spatial separation – both rhetorically and physically – to identify particular types of difference and thereby define the boundaries between themselves and others. This strategy is challenged by Faustus of Milevus, a Manichean teacher, in his dispute over the genealogy of religious groups with Augustine, a former practitioner of Manichaeism himself:[7]

> You are indeed a schism from your parent group, having nothing different except your place of assembly. … Hence, it is clear that you and the Jews are schisms from the gentiles. Holding their faith and rites, though slightly changed, you think that you are sects [i.e. distinct groups] only because you meet separately.

Faustus claimed that Christians and Jews were "gentile" offshoots (i.e. non-Christian, non-Jewish) because the rites they practiced were similar to those of gentiles, despite their apparent claims to the contrary, claims

---

(Rejoicing in every sacred singing and extending the hands for the sacrament; see discussion in Paul Monceaux, "Enquête sur l'épigraphie Chrétienne d'Afrique," *Revue Archéologique* 4.8 (July–December 1906): 297–310, 297–300), and also in epitaphs of consecrated virgins (CIL 8.27915 = ILAlg I 3430 = ILCV 1702); ILCV I 1824 = CIL 8.20914, a mosaic pavement dedicating renovations of the St. Salsa cemetery basilica in Tipasa: *Munera quae cernis quo sancta altaria fulgent* (The benefactions that you see, by which the holy altars shine).

[4] *Reg. Eccl. Carthag. Excerpta* (401) c. 60 (CCSL 149: 196): … *in natalibus beatissimorum martyrum per nonnullas civitates et in ipsis locis sacris* (in some cities on the birthdays of most blessed martyrs, and in the very sacred places themselves).

[5] Aug. *Civ. Dei* 1.3.41.

[6] This understanding of "sacred" space relies on Jonathan Z. Smith, *To Take Place: Toward Theory in Ritual* (Chicago, IL: University of Chicago Press, 1987), pp. 11–26.

[7] Faustus apud Aug. *c. Faust.* 20.4.1, tr. Roland Teske, slightly modified, *The Works of Saint Augustine* (4th Release). Electronic Edition. Answer to Faustus, a Manichean. Vol. I/20 (Charlottesville, VA: InteLex Corporation, 2014) (CSEL 25.1): *estis sane schisma a matrice sua diversum nihil habens nisi conventum … quare constat vos atque iudaeos schismata esse gentilitatis, cuius fidem tenentes et ritus modice quamuis inmutatos de sola conventuum divisione putatis vos esse sectas.* For the most thorough examination of Augustine's relationship to his Manichaean past, see Jason BeDuhn, *Augustine's Manichaean Dilemma*, 2/3 vols. (Philadelphia, PA: University of Pennsylvania Press, 2009 and 2013).

substantiated by the fact that their assemblies met in separate locations.[8] This line of argument, even if it was not entirely convincing, illustrates that space was recognized in antiquity as a feature of group identification.

Ancient writers like Augustine used the paradigm of spatial conflict and conquest, which I term "spatial supersession," to represent one Christian group's dominance, or victory, over those portrayed as opponents, whether they be other Christians, practitioners of Roman traditional religion, or Jews. Their rhetorical inventions were so successful that they contributed to a widespread perception, repeated by scholars over the decades, that such "temple closures" and "synagogue destructions" accurately described the predominant relation between Christians and the sacred places of their neighbors, namely "pagans" and Jews.[9] Until recently, historians took at face value the discourse of ancient historiographers and polemicists. There are several problems with this historical pattern of reconstruction: first, such assessments do not distinguish between events and their interpretation or rhetoric; second, these evaluations rarely consider archaeological evidence, and when they do, they focus on inscriptions; and, finally, little attention has been paid to intra-Christian spatial conflicts. This study attempts to redress these omissions.

Background

Of all the achievements for which Roman civilization is known, architecture – particularly city-building – is among the most significant. The history of Roman architecture is often included in architecture curricula because later western architecture builds on its foundations, both theoretically and literally. Despite historians' embrace of the term "late antiquity" to refer to the period spanning the third–sixth centuries, archaeologists have been slow to adopt corresponding vocabulary. "Archaeologists," as Luke Lavan points out, "have generally preferred to remain as Roman, Early Medieval, Byzantine or 'Christian.'"[10] Yet these traditional labels fail to account for

---

[8] Maijastina Kahlos, *Debate and Dialogue: Christian and Pagan Cultures* c. 360–430 (Burlington, VT: Ashgate, 2007), p. 59. Kahlos notes Augustine's interesting use of Christian exceptionalism in his response to this claim.

[9] Marcel Simon, *Verus Israel: A Study of the Relations Between Christians and Jews in the Roman Empire (AD 135–425)*, tr. H. McKeating (Vallentine Mitchell & Co. Ltd.: 1948: 1996), pp. 224–233, 264–266; Jean Juster, *Les Juifs dans l'Empire romain. Leur condition juridique, économique et sociale.* 2 vols. (New York: Burt Franklin, 1914) I: 469–472; James Parkes, *The Conflict Between the Church and the Synagogue* (Jewish Publication Society: 1934: 1961), pp. 166–168, 187, 204–209, 235–236, 231, 244, 263; and Levine, *Ancient Synagogue*, pp. 68, 77, 115, 249, 258, 298, 308.

[10] Luke Lavan and William Bowden (ed.), *Theory and Practice in Late Antique Archaeology.* Late Antique Archaeology 1, (Boston, MA: Brill, 2003), p. vii.

the discontinuities observed by archaeologists of the period during which Christianization occurred. In this post-Diocletian period, the archaeology of religious sites reflects "long-term changes within Roman society" and a "recognizably distinct late antique situation."[11]

Not only does the archaeology of late antiquity reflect gradual social changes rather than abrupt decline, but, on a more microcosmic level, it reveals more incremental and subtle dynamics in the changing social fabric. These changes were not primarily motivated by religious impulses, as Anna Leone has demonstrated in her masterful analysis of the transformation of the religious landscape of late antique North Africa. Leone observes that "religion was not (apart from specific cases or events) a source of friction in Late Antique North Africa" whose results can be observed in the transformation of cityscapes.[12]

Among the processes of accommodation, deliberate destruction occurred relatively infrequently, despite numerous accounts of such violence left by ancient Christian historians.[13] Destruction that reconfigured the physical landscape itself was more often the result of natural disasters such as earthquakes and lightning fires or less spectacular human causes like neglect. Occasionally, property was forcibly seized and reappropriated, or even demolished, but these incidents are the exception rather than the norm. Sometimes these dispossessions occurred under legal auspices; more often, perpetrators were deemed to be in violation of Roman law and were duly punished.[14] Rather than perceiving the urban landscape as primarily

---

[11] Lavan and Bowden, *Late Antique Archaeology*, p. viii.

[12] Anna Leone, *The End of the Pagan City. Religion, Economy, and Urbanism in Late Antique North Africa* (New York: Oxford University Press, 2013), p. 235.

[13] Leone, *Pagan City*, pp. 237, 243; Stephen Emmel, Ulrich Gotter, and Johannes Hahn, "'From Temple to Church': Analysing a Late Antique Phenomenon of Transformation," *From Temple to Church. Destruction and Renewal of Local Cultic Topography in Late Antiquity*, ed. Johannes Hahn, Stephen Emmel, and Ulrich Gotter (Boston, MA: Brill, 2008), pp. 1–21. See also Aude Busine, "From Stones to Myth: Temple Destruction and Civic Identity in the Late Antique Roman East," *Journal of Late Antiquity* 6.2 (2013): 325–346; Troels Myrup Kristensen, *Making and Breaking the Gods: Christian Responses to Pagan Sculpture in Late Antiquity* (Aarhus: Aarhus University Press, 2013); Jitse Dijkstra, "The Fate of the Temples in Late Antique Egypt," in *The Archaeology of Late Antique "Paganism,"* ed. Luke Lavan and Michael Mulryan, pp. 389–436 (Leiden: Brill, 2011); and Richard Bayliss, *Provincial Cilicia and the Archaeology of Temple Conversion*, BAR International Series 1281 (Oxford: Archaeopress, 2004), p. 18.

[14] David Riggs has noted: "When one sets aside empire-wide generalizations about the conversion of the Roman world and allows the African narrative of rural Christianization to unfold according to the dictates of local evidence alone, a picture emerges in which the vitality of traditional worship and the tolerance of religious pluralism are much more conspicuous than sectarian violence and coercion and in which methods of persuasion, such as the propagation of Christian apologetic, appear to have played a more critical role in the

religious, city centers were conceptualized as predominantly "secular," that is, the province of a general public, where civic buildings reflected the collective memory of ruling elites.[15] To wit, Leone observes a fourth-century shift from the locus of temples to bath complexes as sites for producing elite memory.[16] She concludes that North African towns and cities were architecturally reconfigured and behaviors were adapted in order to accommodate new social and economic patterns of daily life.

These spatial changes occurred incrementally, in stages. In the pre-Vandal period, for example, marble statues and architectural features "were initially dismantled and stored or reused because they retained symbolic … as well as artistic value."[17] Statues, as Laura Nasrallah has shown, symbolized Roman values from idealized human traits to divine attributes, from individual triumphs to collective memories, from marital accord to public concord, and from personal attachments to a person's civic duty, status, and power.[18] Although Nasrallah is quick to point out that these meanings were certainly not stable, the sheer plethora of meanings attunes the modern observer to their social significance.[19] Not only were statues stored and reused for their symbolic value, they were also reused for their aesthetic and pragmatic worth. The reuse of marble coincides with the decline of the marble trade in North Africa.[20] Such social and economic exigencies influenced building practices, which reflected a desire "to maintain the monumentality of their cities and the intention to carry on this [ancient Roman] tradition."[21] As new places served as productive loci for displaying narratives of a past shared by their patrons, the geometry of the ancient city was transformed.

---

eventual 'triumph of Christianity' than is usually assumed" (David Riggs, "Christianizing the Rural Communities of Roman North Africa: A Process of Coercion or Persuasion?," *Violence in Late Antiquity. Perceptions and Practices,* ed. H. A. Drake, with Emily Albu, Susanna Elm, Michael Maas, Claudia Rapp, and Michele Salzman (Burlington, VT: Ashgate Press, 2006): 297–308, p. 297).

[15] Leone, *Pagan City,* p. 236. Note Leone's use of the term secular in scare quotes, "intended as indicating all the aspects of the municipal life in North African communities, encompassing issues such as legislation, economy, and religious power. The 'secular city', as Markus proposes, progressively from the 4th to the 6th century saw the reduction of the neutral space, gradually taken over by the Christian presence" (p. 14, citing Robert Markus, *The End of Ancient Christianity* (New York: Cambridge University Press, 1990), p. 15.

[16] Leone, *Pagan City,* p. 22.

[17] Leone, *Pagan City,* pp. 230–231.

[18] Laura Nasrallah, *Christian Responses to Roman Art and Architecture: The Second-Century Church Amid the Spaces of Empire* (Cambridge University Press, 2010).

[19] Nasrallah, *Christian Responses,* p. 10.

[20] Leone, *Pagan City,* p. 239.

[21] Leone, *Pagan City,* p. 242.

The theoretical assumptions about space, place, and identification that underlie my investigation are the subject of Chapter 1. Chapter 2 demonstrates that a particular conception of space made spatial contestation possible. I show that this conception emerged gradually, beginning in the second century, and was not a Constantinian innovation as some scholars have claimed. In Chapters 3, 4, and 5 I use archaeological evidence to help understand how Christian writers in late Roman North Africa deployed a discursive strategy of spatial supersession to convey a triumphalist understanding of the material world that they inhabited. The order of these chapters reflects my chronological argument that this spatial rhetoric was first developed within the context of intra-Christian disputes, then was subsequently deployed against traditional Roman sites and finally against Jewish synagogues.[22] In this manner, religious places were useful for concretely representing the abstract contestation over power and group identifications. Imperial reactions to the litany of petitions and legislation employing this discourse demonstrate that this strategy met with varying degrees of success.

My approach is grounded in the dismantling of certain assumptions that undergird certain scholars' treatment of the topic. I do not assume that Christianity was "inculcated" in late Roman society, because such approaches assume that "Christianity" was a static "entity" comprised of a certain set of beliefs and practices, and that late Roman society can be somehow identified apart from those beliefs and practices.[23] I show that although such a perception is promoted in the ancient sources, it is not useful for modern analyses of late antique social changes. I also reject the notion that the views presented by ancient Christian polemicists and apologists represent the views of all Christians of the time. Although writing is a vehicle for acquiring and exerting cultural power, preservation distorts the historical record by allowing later power realities to constrain the literary production of previous periods.

Method

Written and material remains are the extant witnesses to ancient spatial relations. Historians have generally relied on written accounts for

---

[22] The sequence of this dynamic in legal codes has been noted by Paula Fredriksen, "Roman Christianity and the Post-Roman West: The Social Correlates of the *Contra Iudaeos* Tradition," in *Jews, Christians, and the Roman Empire. The Poetics of Power in Late Antiquity*, ed. Natalie B. Dohrmann and Annette Yoshiko Reed, pp. 249–265 (Philadelphia, PA: University of Pennsylvania Press, 2013), pp. 260–263.

[23] For a recent example, see Paul Veyne, *Quand notre monde est devenu chrétien* (Paris: Editions Albin Michel D.A., 2007).

reconstructing the Roman past, while material evidence remained the provenance of archaeologists. Elena Isayev has documented the more recent shift toward interdisciplinary and multidisciplinary projects that attempt to bring together these bodies of evidence and their specialists.[24] Awareness of how scholars produce knowledge about antiquity is fundamental for understanding how we gather and interpret evidence, and why reconsideration of earlier findings has recently emerged. In their book *The New Production of Knowledge: The Dynamics of Science and Research in Contemporary Societies*, Michael Gibbons and his colleagues distinguish earlier types of discipline- and evidence-segregated research ("Mode One") from research that emerged in the second half of the twentieth century, which is question-based, contextual, and collaborative ("Mode Two").[25] Isayev applies this distinction to research about antiquity. She notes that historians are still largely shaped by the literary turn of the 1970s, while archaeologists have moved beyond the new or processual archaeology of the 1970s to embrace "questions of *why* and *how*."[26]

Some years ago, Garth Fowden encouraged historians to take all archaeological evidence into account, not merely inscriptions.[27] The field has responded to Fowden's exhortation to a limited extent; many historians still rely primarily on linguistic material evidence. In the past decade, histories of the ancient world have been written by scholars trained not only in History, but also in Art History, Archaeology, Classics, and Religious Studies; some of these scholars have been trained in multiple disciplines.[28] Religious Studies, my own discipline, is itself an interdisciplinary field, drawing on all of the humanities and social sciences for its methods and scope of evidence. As humanities departments are eliminated in the current cultural and economic climate, specialists are finding themselves reassigned

---

[24] Elena Isayev, "Archaeology ≠ Object as History ≠ Text: Nudging the Special Relationship into the Post-Ironic," *World Archaeology* 38.4, Debates in "World Archaeology" (December 2006): 599–610.

[25] Michael Gibbons, Camille Limoges, Helga Nowotny, Simon Schwartzman, Peter Scott, and Martin Trow, *The New Production of Knowledge: The Dynamics of Science and Research in Contemporary Societies* (Thousand Oaks, CA: Sage Publications Inc., 1994), p. vii.

[26] Isayev, "Archaeology ≠ Object as History ≠ Text," p. 603. For one example of an archaeologist's historical analysis, see Ann Marie Yasin, *Saints and Church Spaces in the Late Antique Mediterranean: Architecture, Cult and Community* (New York: Cambridge University Press, 2009).

[27] Garth Fowden, "Review: Between Pagans and Christians," *The Journal of Roman Studies* 78 (1988): 173–182, p. 180.

[28] See, for example, Karen B. Stern, *Inscribing Devotion and Death: Archaeological Evidence for Jewish Populations of North Africa* (Boston, MA: E. J. Brill, 2008).

to other departments: art historians to classics departments, archaeologists to anthropology departments, classicists to history departments. While this may seem like disciplinary chaos to those traditionally trained in singular fields, this "fuzziness of disciplinary boundaries" has forced these specialists to converge and collaborate around their subject areas, whether in departments, area studies, research projects, or conferences.[29] Gibbons et al. point out that earlier scholarship ("Mode One") put scholars at the center of the inquiry: a scholar formulated the research question within the constraints of her own disciplinary knowledge, as determined by her academic training, in search of the definitive meta-narrative.[30] By contrast, "Mode Two" research is collaborative, transdisciplinary, and often motivated by current cultural concerns.[31] Isayev reminds us that the last of these, termed by its detractors as "fads," is perfectly appropriate to the study of the past, because we can never "escape" our "presentist perspective."[32]

Since the last quarter of the twentieth century, archaeologists of North Africa have been addressing interpretive issues that question the validity of earlier excavation reports and the conclusions historians drew from them.[33] Newly and re-excavated sites have been able to answer questions about usage and function that eluded previous historians.[34] Although there is considerable material evidence for North African churches, the current state of archaeological excavation does not permit more than a few identifications of dissident churches, contrary to the claims of earlier historians.[35] As discussed in Chapter 3, the identification of a church with an inscription as "Catholic" is likely to indicate spatial contestation. While most of the evidence for intra-Christian spatial contestation is literary, the archaeological record does permit some general observations about sites that reflect spatial contestation.

---

[29] Gibbons et al., *The New Production of Knowledge*, p. 93.

[30] Gibbons et al., *The New Production of Knowledge*, pp. 90–110.

[31] Gibbons et al., *The New Production of Knowledge*, pp. 90–110.

[32] Isayev, "Archaeology ≠ Object as History ≠ Text," p. 605.

[33] See Gareth Sears, *Late Roman African Urbanism. Continuity and Transformation in the City*, BAR International Series 1693 (Oxford: Archaeopress, 2007); and Anna Leone, *Changing Townscapes in North Africa From Late Antiquity to the Arab Conquest*, Studi storici sulla Tarda Antichità 28 (Bari, Italy: Edipuglia, 2007).

[34] See, for example, Susan Stevens, Angela V. Kalinowski, and Hans VanderLeest, *Bir Ftouha: A Pilgrimage Church Complex at Carthage*, Journal of Roman Archaeology Supplementary Series no. 59 (Portsmouth, RI: JRA, 2005).

[35] See Sears, *Late Roman African Urbanism*, p. 36, overturning claims made by W. H. C. Frend. Sears' criteria of "the positioning of the churches on the site plans of a city" leads to a "Donatist" identification at Thamugadi, while inscriptions permit identification of an Alamiliaria martyr church (discussed in Chapter 3).

A similar predicament arises for synagogue conflicts. Apart from cemeteries and isolated synagogue remains, very little archaeological evidence exists for Jewish presence in late antique North Africa.[36] As Karen Stern, author of the most thorough treatment of Roman North African Jews to date, has pointed out, "the archaeological record is messy and unruly."[37] Stern's reconsideration of the archaeological evidence gives a remarkably rich and varied picture of Jewish life and identification in Roman North Africa, "clearing the brush" for explorations of other facets of North African Jewish experience, such as religious conflict.[38] How Jews figured into Christian discourse about spatial conflict, and to what extent the archaeological record can enhance our understanding of such portrayals is addressed in Chapter 5.

Archaeological evidence for temples is more extensive than for synagogues, yet the evaluation of such finds is fraught with challenges of dating, identification, and interpretation. Most excavations were carried out by French and Italian scholars, clergy, and soldiers in the late 1800s and early 1900s.[39] Their interest in North African archaeology grew out of their own colonial agendas and religious biases. Excavators sought to connect early Roman and Christian presence in North Africa to their own colonialist claims – as the heirs to Western civilization – to the ancient land. As a result, their stratigraphy reflects careless excavation of Islamic and late antique layers. Preservation and reconstruction, based on aesthetic principles, tended to focus on imperial and Byzantine periods.[40] Finds were often erroneously dated to the imperial period.[41] The postcolonial backlash produced equally problematic results, as archaeologists ignored forts, museums curated and stored artifacts poorly, and government officials did not protect excavated sites from despoliation and destruction. As the archaeological record has begun to be corrected, challenges remain that inhibit exploration of towns and cities located in or around currently expanding occupation, with the exception of the rescue excavations, rural settlements, and more remote towns.

This study brings together archaeological and historical research and employs spatial and identity theory to understand how one body of evidence

---

[36] See Stern, *Inscribing Devotion*, pp. 1–31, for the problems of Jewish archaeological evidence in North Africa.

[37] Stern, *Inscribing Devotion*, p. 31.

[38] Stern, *Inscribing Devotion*, p. 32.

[39] Stern, *Inscribing Devotion*, p. 6.

[40] Andrew H. Merrills, "Introduction," *Vandals, Romans and Berbers: New Perspectives on Late Antique North Africa* (Burlington, VT: Ashgate Publishing, 2004), p. 8.

[41] David J. Mattingly and R. Bruce Hitchner, "Roman Africa: An Archaeological Review," *The Journal of Roman Studies* 85(1995): 165–213, pp. 191, 201.

relates to the other. This approach, relying on the work of cultural geographers and spatial theorists, aims to demonstrate how the physical environment was not merely the stage on which history was acted out, but played an important role in shaping the direction of that history.[42] It is a commonplace in the study of history that winners write its accounts. Of course our surviving literary evidence has been preserved by those who prevailed in the intra- and interreligious competitions of late antiquity. In North Africa, however, another problem surfaces that also affects the historical record. Certain groups privileged oral over written communication and transmission. This fact emerges in the course of the defining Church council at Carthage in 411, where Catholics manipulated their opponents' dearth of written documents to promote their own version of history to the presiding imperial officials.[43]

Despite these inherent challenges of written sources, historians are confronted with the additional problem that literary evidence produced by ancient writers rarely matches up with archaeological evidence of the period. More often, scholars cite an archaeological find from one geographic location and a text referring to another to build a picture of antiquity. Consider, for example, Yann Le Bohec's discussion of funerary decorations that depict angelic beings, "graphic anthropomorphism," in the late Roman Gammarth necropolis outside Carthage: "These anthropomorphic representations pose difficult problems. ... They followed the relatively liberal tradition of the Pharisees."[44] The more "liberal" view of the second Temple group known as the Pharisees prohibited representations

---

[42] Notably Henri Lefebvre, *The Production of Space*, tr. Donald Nicholson-Smith (Malden, MA: Blackwell Publishing, 1974: 1991); Yi-Fu Tuan, *Space and Place: The Perspective of Experience* (Minneapolis, MN: University of Minnesota Press, 1977: 2001), *Topophilia: A Study of Environmental Perception, Attitudes, and Values* (Englewood Cliffs, NJ: Prentice-Hall, 1974), and *Religion: From Place to Placelessness* (Chicago, IL: Columbia College Chicago Press, 2010); Denis Cosgrove, *Social Formation and Symbolic Landscape*, 2nd ed. (Madison, WI: University of Wisconsin Press, 1998) and *Geography and Vision: Seeing, Imagining and Representing the World,* International Library of Human Geography 12 (New York: I. B. Tauris, 2008); and Edward Soja, *Postmodern Geographies: The Reassertion of Space in Critical Social Theory*, 2nd ed. (Brooklyn, NY: Verso, 2011).

[43] *Gest. Coll. Carth.* 3.176–179 (SC 224); Aug. *Don.* 25.44, as cited by Anthony Dupont and Matthew Gaumer, "Understanding Augustine's Changing Justification for State-Sponsored Religious Coercion and Its Context Within Donatist North Africa (Coerción religiosa patrocinada por el Estado: su contexto en Norteáfrica donatista y el cambio de la actitud de Agustín hacia aquélla)," *Augustinus* 54.214–215 (2009): 345–371, p. 362.

[44] Y. Le Bohec, "Les sources archéologiques du Judaïsme africain sous l'Empire romain," in *Juifs et Judaïsme en Afrique du Nord dans l'Antiquité et le Haut Moyen-age: Actes du Colloque International du Centre de Recherché et d'Études Juives et Hébraiques et du Groupe de Recherches sur l'Afrique Antique, 26–27 Septembre, 1983*, ed. C. Iancu and J.-M. Lassere, pp. 13–47 (Montpellier: Université Paul Valéry, 1985), p. 23.

of only God himself but permitted any other anthropomorphic images.[45] The relevance of Pharisaic sources from Roman Palestine to the finds at Gammarth is questionable given the regionalism of artistic styles. In some instances, claims by earlier historiographers and hagiographers are not borne out by more recent archaeological evidence, as in the case of Lepcis Magna, discussed in Chapter 5. Such contradictions require new interpretations.

Newly discovered and reexamined archaeological evidence has led recent historians to revisit the meaning of textual sources.[46] These approaches sometimes find that earlier historians' reconstruction of ancient evidence was based on erroneous assumptions or failure to consider archaeological along with literary evidence. In this vein, Stern concludes: "When Jewish burial and funerary practices are reviewed more carefully within their North African contexts, they no longer appear as idiosyncratic, transparent, or exclusive as some previous scholars have asserted."[47] Consequently, ancient literature has been subjected to new reading strategies that allow competing and stifled perspectives to emerge.[48] This reevaluative approach is evident in Leone's analysis of temple destruction, discussed in Chapter 4. Archaeological evidence has been particularly helpful in this hermeneutical enterprise. Aside from being relatively new, the enterprise of marrying archaeology to history is necessarily fragmentary and, as we have seen, often in need of revision in light of subsequent discoveries. As correctives emerge, the picture of late antiquity is both more complex and sporadic as well as less disjunctive with the imperial period than previous historians have suggested. It is my hope that this study will contribute to this more nuanced understanding of late antiquity.

Historical Background: Christians in North Africa

There are no ancient accounts of the origins of North African Christianity. Since the speculation of Adolf Von Harnack, some scholars regard the region's first Christians to have emerged from the Jewish community of

---

[45] See the Genizah fragment of Jerusalem Talmud, *Avodah Zarah* 3:3, 42d:97: "In the days of Rabbi Johanan they permitted (or, began to make) images (ציורין) on the walls, and he did not stop them. In the days of Rabbi Abun they permitted (or, began to make) images on mosaics, and he did not stop them" (tr. Steven Fine, *Art and Judaism in the Greco-Roman World* (New York: Cambridge University Press, 2005), p. 98).

[46] Two superior examples are Stern, *Inscribing Devotion* and Leone, *Pagan City*.

[47] Stern, *Inscribing Devotion*, p. 300.

[48] Elizabeth Clark, *History, Theory, Text: Historians and the Linguistic Turn* (Cambridge, MA: Harvard University Press, 2004).

Carthage.[49] The first Christian literary evidence, the *Acts of the Scillitan Martyrs*, suggests the presence of communities by the second century only in Carthage and in Scilli, a marble quarry in northern Proconsular Numidia.[50] Judging by Christian names in literary accounts, Christianity began to appear in North Africa both in the Punic-speaking villages among those who were bilingual (Punic and Latin), as well as among the Roman, urban population. According to J. Patout Burns and Robin M. Jensen, authors of the most recent full treatment of North African Christianity, "it would be reasonable to conjecture that some Christians had reached Africa a good half-century or more before the report of the Scillitan martyrs."[51]

Additional second-century evidence of Christianity in North Africa comes from a speech delivered by the mid-second century Numidian lawyer Fronto, which purportedly included "malicious remarks (*convicium*)" against Christians.[52] The remarks can be reconstructed from a response written by the second-/early third-century Christian lawyer, Minucius Felix. Apparently Fronto had alleged that Christians engaged in nocturnal "incestuous banquets (*incesta convivia*)," where they identify each other by the use of "concealed signs and signals (*occultae notae et insignia*)," "worship the head of an ass (*caput asini ... venerari*)," and their initiates perform infant sacrifice and cannibalism.[53] Minucius Felix defended his coreligionists by denying these activities, but admits that Christians did "in fact readily distinguish ourselves, not as you imagine by some bodily mark, but by the sign (*signum*) of virtue and modesty."[54] Graeme Clarke conjectures

[49] Von Harnack, *The Mission and Expansion of Christianity in the First Three Centuries*, tr. James Moffat, vol. 2, 2nd ed. (London: Williams and Norgate, 1908), pp. 276–277; Alfred Delattre, *Gamart ou la nécropole juive de Carthage* (Lyons: Mougin Rusand, 1895), pp. 49–50; and Paul Monceaux, "Les colonies juives dans l'Afrique Romaine," *Revue des études juives* 44 (1904): 1–28.

[50] Serge Lancel, *Actes de la conférence de Carthage en 411*, SC nos. 194, 195, 224, 373 (Paris: Éditions du Cerf, 1972), vol. 4, p. 1456, discussed in J. Patout Burns and Robin M. Jensen, *Christianity in Roman North Africa*, in collaboration with Graeme W. Clarke, Susan T. Stevens, William Tabbernee, and Maureen A. Tilley (Grand Rapids, MI: Wm. B. Eerdmans Publishing Co., 2014), pp. 3–4.

[51] Burns and Jensen, *Christianity in Roman North Africa*, p. 4.

[52] Minucius Felix, *Octavius* 31.2 (ed. Kytzler). For discussion of Fronto, see E. J. Champlin, *Fronto and Antonine Rome* (Cambridge, MA: Harvard University Press, 1980), pp. 64–66. For the view that Fronto's speech was not exclusively targeting Christians in a work frequently referred to by modern scholars as *Contra Christianos*, see Michael P. J. Van Den Hout, *A Commentary on the Letters of M. Cornelius Fronto* (Leiden: E. J. Brill, 1999), pp. 573–577.

[53] Minucius Felix, *Octavius* 31.1, 9.1, 9.3, 9.5 (ed. Kytzler). For discussion of the dating controversy of the *Octavius*, see Van Den Hout, *Commentary on the Letters of M. Cornelius Fronto*, p. 573.

[54] Minucius Felix, *Octavius* 31.8 (ed. Kytzler): *Sic nos denique non notaculo corporis, ut putatis, sed innocentiae ac modestiae signo facile dinoscimus.* For the view that such allegations were a

that this *signum* might refer to the sign of the cross or Christian symbols like signet rings and other objects bearing images of anchors, doves, fish, or boats.[55] To be used as a sign that allowed users to distinguish between Christians and non-Christians, it is most likely that the *signum* was the tracing of the sign of the cross on one's forehead which, as the first extant North African Christian writer, Tertullian, noted, was performed in a variety of circumstances that would have presented themselves frequently over the course of a typical day.[56] As Rebillard notes, this sign was a "means by which Christians could reveal their membership to outsiders."[57] The views of Minucius Felix and Tertullian show that North African Christians sought to distinguish themselves at various times and places from their broader social context. This desire for difference is most evident in the case of martyrdom.

The *Acts of the Scillitan Martyrs* likely dates to a period later than the one it describes, namely July 17, 180.[58] The account takes the form of a transcript of a hearing in Carthage before the consul of Proconsularis of twelve Christians from Scilli. The dialogue presents the Christians as adamant in their devotion to Christ, an allegiance that precludes their participation in traditional Roman sacrifice to the genius of the emperor. Their loyalty is represented by the public declaration *Christianus sum* ("I am a Christian"), an identification that became the hallmark of Christian martyrs. Despite being granted thirty days to reconsider, the Christians affirm their commitment and are sentenced to execution by beheading. By refusing to participate in the broader culture's sacrificial customs, these Christians not only

---

standard Greco-Roman trope for attacking groups perceived as enemies of social order, see Bart Wagemakers, "Incest, Infanticide, and Cannibalism: Anti-Christian Imputations in the Roman Empire," *Greece & Rome* 57.2 (2010): 337–354.

[55] Clarke, *The Octavius of Marcus Minucius Felix*, ACW 39 (New York: Newman Press, 1974), pp. 214–215.

[56] Tert. *Cor.* 3.4, tr. Clarke, discussed in Éric Rebillard, *Christians and Their Many Identities in Late Antiquity, North Africa, 200–450 CE* (Ithaca, NY: Cornell University Press. Kindle Edition, 2012), Kindle locations 426–428 (CCL 1): *Ad omnem progressum atque promotum, ad omnem aditum et exitum, ad vestitum, ad calciatum, ad lavacra, ad mensas, ad lumina, ad cubilia, ad sedilia, quacumque nos conversatio exercet, frontem signaculo terimus* (At every forward step and movement, at every going in and out, when we put on our clothes and shoes, when we bathe, when we sit at the table, when we light the lamps, on couch, on seat, in all the ordinary actions of daily life, we trace upon the forehead the sign).

[57] Rebillard, *Christians and Their Many Identities*, Kindle locations 435–436.

[58] Dating of the *Acts* is divided between those who consider the account to be based on an actual proconsular transcript and those who view that genre as a literary conceit. For the former view, see Herbert A. Musurillo, *The Acts of the Christian Martyrs*, Early Christian Texts (Oxford: Clarendon Press, 1972), pp. xxii–xxiii; for the latter, see Antoon A.R. Bastiaensen and Gioachini Chiarini, *Atti e Passioni dei Martiri* (Milan: A. Mondadori, 1987), pp. 97–105.

distinguished themselves from their fellow Romans, they earned for themselves the distinction of the title "martyr" within the Church.

As Christianity continued to grow throughout North Africa, harassment,
although sporadic and capricious, continued to afflict the Christian community. Tertullian reports the existence of Christians in Numidia, Byzacena,
and Mauretania, and attests to three periods of persecution, each lasting for
several months.[59] These conflicts produced similar outcomes as those of the
Scillitan martyrs.

Over the course of the third century, Christianity spread deeper into the
Numidian countryside and to the coastal cities of Mauretania.[60] In the middle of this turbulent century, Carthaginian Christians struggled with sporadic persecutions. According to the bishop Cyprian, many apostasized by
making the required sacrifices to the traditional Roman gods.[61] Confessors,
those who had been imprisoned for refusing to cooperate with Roman
authorities and so-called martyrs, those who had been condemned and
awaited execution, vied with bishops for the authority to grant forgiveness
to and readmit to the communion of the faithful those who had betrayed
their religious identification.[62] The abatement of persecution temporarily
resolved the struggle: bishops would determine the appropriate penance
and subsequently welcome the contrite back into the fold.[63] A new conflict,
however, emerged out of this crucible of oppression. The rigorist position
against the lapsed, that they could not be readmitted into communion, coalesced in a group of bishops in Rome, and subsequently in Carthage, who
elected their own bishops: Fortunatus and Maximus, respectively.[64] These
came to be referred to by the more lenient bishops as "Novatian's party."[65]

[59] Tert. *Scap.* 3–4, *Adv. Jud.* 7, *Scap.* 3, 4.2–3, 4.8, 5.1–2, *Mart.* 1, 6.2, *Apol.* 1.1, 12.3–5, 21.28,
30.7, 35, 49.3, 50.3–13, *Nat.* 1.17.4, and *Cor.* 1.5. The scholarly consensus that these persecu-
tions were sporadic and resulted in a small death toll is first articulated in De Ste. Croix,
"Why Were the Early Christians Persecuted?" *Past and Present* 26 (1963): 6–38 and Timothy
Barnes, "Legislation against the Christians," *Journal of Roman Studies* 58.1–2(1968): 32–50.
Rebillard reiterates this discussion, adding more recent scholarly treatments of the subject
(*Christians and Their Many Identities*, Kindle locations 871–1025).

[60] Council of Cirta, 305, and CIL 8. 8631–8632, cited in Monceaux, *Histoire littéraire de l'Afrique
chrétienne: Depuis les origines jusqu'à l'invasion arabe* 3 (Brussels: Culture et Civilisation, 1905:
1966), pp. 5–6.

[61] Cypr. *Laps.* 8–9 (CSEL 3.1: 242–3). For a nuanced treatment of the complexity of
Christian identity during this period, see Rebillard, *Christians and Their Many Identities*,
Kindle locations 1114–1302. For a deft treatment of Cyprian's leadership during his episco-
pacy, see J. Patout Burns, *Cyprian the Bishop*, Routledge Early Church Monographs (New
York: Routledge Press, 2002).

[62] Cypr. *Ep.* 27.1–3 (CSEL 3.2: 540–542); 17.2 (CSEL 3.2: 522). See Burns, *Cyprian*, pp. 5–20.

[63] Cypr. *Ep.* 55.6 (CSEL 3.2: 627). See Burns, *Cyprian*, pp. 22–25.

[64] Burns, *Cyprian*, pp. 6–8, 27–28, 89–91.

[65] Cypr. *Ep.* 59.9 (CSEL 3.2: 676–677). See Burns, *Cyprian*, pp. 88–90.

In response to this schismatic breach of authority, the lenient "Catholics," as they referred to themselves, issued a tract on the unity of the Church.[66] The notion of "one Church, one Baptism" incited a further break between those who advocated the rebaptism of heretics wishing to return to the Catholic Church (Cyprian et al.), and those who opposed it (Stephen of Rome et al.). In 256, a council of seventy-one bishops from Numidia and Africa Proconsularis adopted Cyprian's view, that the baptism of schismatics was invalid to begin with.[67] As a general principle with regard to schism, Cyprian declared, "*salus extra ecclesiam non est* (there is no salvation outside the Church)."[68]

Persecution returned with the emperor Valerian in 257, who targeted Christian clergy and members of the senatorial and equestrian classes in an attempt to stem the tide of diverting resources away from civic funds and funneling them to the Church.[69] Cyprian was expelled from Carthage, but returned to face martyrdom the following year.[70] The relative calm that followed emperor Gallienus' rescript of 260, granting Christians the right to recover churches that had been confiscated during the persecution, allowed Christians to reestablish their physical presence in the landscape of North Africa.[71]

Historical Background: Jews in North Africa

Legends of pre-Roman migrations aside, archaeological evidence for Jewish settlement in Roman North Africa dates to the second century. Among these earliest settlers were exiles from the Libyan Jewish revolts of 115–117 along with merchants, estate-holders, and perhaps even slaves from Italy. These Jews originally spoke mostly Greek, though as they disperse even further west over the next centuries, they would acquire the western imperial language Latin and adopt Latin names. With the Byzantine reconquest of North Africa from the Vandals in 533–565, Greek became even more prevalent. Little is known about the Jewish populations of North African

[66] Cypr. *Unit. eccl.* (CSEL 3.1: 212–215). The treatise was ultimately revised in light of the rebaptism controversy. See Burns, *Cyprian*, pp. 60–62, 93–95, 159–165.

[67] Cypr. *Ep.* 73.1 (CSEL 3.2: 778–779). See Burns, *Cyprian*, p. 9.

[68] Cypr. *Ep.* 72/73.21 (CSEL 3.2).

[69] Cypr. *Ep.* 80.1 (CSEL 3.2: 839–840), Eusebius, *Hist.eccl.* 7.10.4. See Rebillard, *Christians and Their Many Identities*, Kindle locations 1303–1371.

[70] Burns, *Cyprian*, p. 10.

[71] Eusebius, *Hist. eccl.* 7.13.1, discussed in Chapter 2 at note 25; Lact. *Mort.* 5.1–6; Petrus Patricius, frag. 14, discussed in Barnes, *Early Christian Hagiography and Roman History*. Tria Corda 5 (Tübingen: Mohr Siebeck, 2010), pp. 97–105.

cities and towns aside from just more than one hundred inscriptions, one synagogue excavation, one catacomb, some small finds, a handful of Roman laws, and sporadic mention in non-Jewish literature.[72]

Historical Background: The "Donatist Schism"

Spatial contestation in late antique North Africa begins with an intra-Christian schism. Unlike elsewhere in the empire, the fault lines that splin-tered North African Christians had little to do with doctrine and more to do with ecclesiology and authority. To the extent that the origins of the so-called Donatist-Catholic split can be reconstructed from tendentious documents assembled in hindsight, the root of these divisions can be traced to the Diocletian persecution (303–305).[73] During the persecution, bishop Mensurius of Carthage was called to report to state authorities for hiding a deacon accused of publicly defaming the emperor.[74] Sometime thereafter, a political battle over episcopal succession ensued.[75]

The difficulty with using the extant sources to attempt anything like a definitive history of the schism, as Brent Shaw has expertly demonstrated, is that each faction in the conflict produced its own, exceedingly tenden-tious, version of events.[76] As a result, there is no scholarly consensus on

---

[72] Tabulation based on Le Bohec, "Incriptions juives et judaïsantes de la'Afrique romaine," *Antiquités africaines* 17 (1981): 165–207 and Stern, *Inscribing Devotion*.

[73] Orosius attributes Christian schisms of all types to the emperor Julian and omits any men-tion of Christian instigators (*Hist.* 7.29.18). There is little historical merit to this argument, which is rooted in his anti-pagan apologetic.

[74] Optatus, *de schism. Don.* 1.17.1. Some scholars date this event to after the persecution, in 311 (W. H. C. Frend and K. Clancy, "When Did the Donatist Schism Begin?," *The Journal of Theological Studies* 28 (1977): 104–109, p. 109). I follow the scholarly view that events precipitating the division unfolded over a longer period of time (306/7–313) rather than the "compressed chronology" (311–313). For the expanded chronology, see Brent D. Shaw, *Sacred Violence. African Christians and Sectarian Hatred in the Age of Augustine* (New York: Cambridge University Press, 2011), Appendix B; T. D. Barnes, "The Beginnings of Donatism," *JTS* n.s. 26 (1975): 13–22 (summarized in *Constantine and Eusebius*, pp. 54–61); Serge Lancel, "Les débuts du Donatisme: la date du 'Protocole de Cirta' et de l'élection épiscopale de Silvanus," *REAug* 25 (1979): 217–229; and Otto Seeck, *Geschichte des Untergangs der Antiken Welt* III Anhang (Stuttgart: J. B. Metzlersche, 1921), p. 509. For the compressed chronology see Harold A. Drake, *Constantine and the Bishops. The Politics of Intolerance* (Baltimore, MD: Johns Hopkins University Press, 2000), pp. 212–221; Louis Duchesne, *Histoire ancienne de l'Église* (Paris: Albert Fontemoing, 1908), pp. 101–108; Paul Monceaux, *Hist. litt.* 4, pp. 8–9; W. H. C. Frend, *The Donatist Church: A Movement of Protest in Roman North Africa* (Oxford University Press, 1985), pp. 15–21; and W. H. C. Frend and K. Clancy, "When Did The Donatist Schism Gegin?" *JTS* 28.1 (1977): 104–109.

[75] Eusebius, *Mart. Pal.* [S] 13.12–13, *Hist. eccl.* 8.14.1, Optatus, *de schism. Don.* 1.18, *Gest. Zeno.*

[76] The topic has been treated extensively by historians. See, for example, Frend, *Donatist Church*; Klaus M. Girardet, *Kaisergericht und Bischofsgericht. Studien zu den Anfängen des*

how to interpret these various accounts.[77] Each party even went to such lengths as to alter or even forge court documents of the time to serve later political purposes.[78] For their part, the Numidian dissidents recounted the schism's origins in a dramatic and tragic narrative of the Christian martyrs from Abitinia (near Carthage).[79] The account fingered the Catholics as *traditores*, and attributed the split to the martyrs' excommunication of "traitors" amidst an embargo by Carthage bishop Mensurius. The bishop, claims the *Passio*, stationed his own guards outside the jail in order to prevent Christians from bringing in supplies to the prisoners from Abitinia who had been arrested during the persecution.[80]

In contrast to the dissidents, the Catholic faction traced the roots of the schism to a meeting of bishops held in Cirta (Numidia) in 306 before the peace of emperor Maxentius.[81] Peace began to arrive in North Africa in 305/306 with the turnover of the provincial gubernatorial terms, although it was not officially recognized until Maxentius revoked the Diocletian edict in 306/307.[82] Optatus charges the Numidian bishops with confessing to having collaborated with the imperial edicts to turn over church property, particularly Scriptures, in a council held in Cirta toward the end of the persecution.[83] Although the events most likely took place during the peace, Optatus – our only source – reports that the bishops attended an ecumenical council at Carthage during the persecution to ordain a successor to their former bishop,

---

Donatistenstreites (313–315) und zum Prozess des Athanasius von Alexandrien (328–346), Antiquitas Reihe 1 Andreas Alföldi 21 (Bonn: Rudolf Habelt Verlag, 1975); and Timothy Barnes, *The New Empire of Diocletian and Constantine* (Cambridge, MA: Harvard University Press, 1982); Shaw, *Sacred Violence*.

[77] For a comprehensive discussion of the divergent views, see Shaw, *Sacred Violence*, pp. 812–819.

[78] Barnes, "Donatism," p. 16, and Shaw, *Sacred Violence*, pp. 83, 187–188, 259, 557, 816.

[79] *Passio sanctorum Dativi, Saturnini presbyteri et aliorum* (ed. Maier, *Dossier* 1, no. 4, pp. 59–92), more commonly known as "The Acts of the Abitinian Martyrs," dated by Shaw to 411 (*Sacred Violence*, p. 106) or by Dearn sometime thereafter ("Abitinian Martyrs," pp. 1–18).

[80] *Passio sanctorum Dativi, Saturnini presbyteri et aliorum* 20–1. Eusebius' summary of an edict issued by the emperor Licinius outlawing such humanitarian aid supports the *Passio*'s claim that this kind of hospitality was illegal (Eusebius *Hist. eccl.* 10.8.11. This attribution relies on the law's subsequent repeal in 324 (*Cod. theod.* 15.14.1), yet Licinius did not attain imperial authority until 308. For a thorough discussion see John Noël Dillon, *The Justice of Constantine: Law, Communication, and Control* (Ann Arbor, MI: University of Michigan Press, 2012), pp. 92–97.).

[81] Optatus, *de schism. Don.* 1.14.1. The date is per Shaw, *Sacred Violence*, pp. 816–817.

[82] Eusebius, *Mart. Pal.* [S] 13.12–13, *Hist. eccl.* 8.14.1, Optatus, *de schism. Don.* 1.18 and *Gest. Zeno.*; Lact. *Mort.* 19.1, discussed in Shaw, *Sacred Violence*, p. 815, Barnes, "Donatism," p. 18.

[83] Optatus, *de schism. Don.* 1.14.2, tr. Edwards (SC 412): *Hi episcopi interrogante Secundo Tigisitano se tradidisse confessi sunt* (These bishops, on interrogation by Secudus of Tigisis, confessed their collaboration). As Shaw demonstrates, the date must have been May 13, 306 (*Sacred Violence*, pp. 817–819).

Mensurius.[84] The *seniores* objected to the election of Mensurius' deacon, Caecilianus, and they appealed to the Numidian bishops for support.[85] In response, the Numidian bishops elected their own anti-bishop, Maiorinus.[86]

Due to the bias and confusion of ancient sources, scholars disagree over the chronology and proximate cause of the schism. Timothy Barnes maintains that capitulation during persecution (*traditio*) and political loyalties lay at the heart of the struggle over the episcopacy, which he dates to 307–308. Around the time emperor Maxentius revoked the Diocletian edict for North Africa (after he was elected emperor on October 28, 306), Mensurius was unable to resume his seat, and a political battle over episcopal succession ensued.[87] The congregation of Carthage "unanimously elected" the deacon Caecilianus to fill Mensurius' seat, and he was able to recover the church property that Mensurius had stored away for safekeeping.[88] Two disgruntled congregants accused Caecilianus of *traditio*, and an interim *interventor* assumed Caecilianus' place while the matter was investigated.[89] After the *interventor* was murdered in the basilica, a council of bishops met in Numidia to evaluate the charges against Caecilianus. Although the council concluded that the evidence against Caecilianus was unconvincing, they found the bishop who had presided over his ordination guilty of *traditio*, which invalidated the sacrament.[90] Refusing to re-ordain Caecilianus, the Numidian council elected an entirely new bishop, the lector Maiorinus. According to Barnes, the Carthaginians rejected Maiorinus and invited Caecilianus to resume his see.[91]

Shaw reconstructs events somewhat differently than Barnes. Like Barnes, he attributes the conflict to "politicking" between powerbrokers who invoked the powerful specter of betrayal and exploited church

---

[84] Optatus, *de schism. Don.* 1.15.1. Mensurius had been exiled and/or executed or died during the persecution and never reclaimed his seat thereafter (Shaw, *Sacred Violence*, pp. 814–815).

[85] Shaw, *Sacred Violence*, p. 819.

[86] Optatus, *de schism. Don.* 1.15.2–3.

[87] Timothy Barnes, *Constantine and Eusebius* (Cambridge, MA: Harvard University Press, 1981), pp. 55–56, based on Eusebius, *Mart. Pal.* [S] 13.12–13, *Hist. eccl.* 8.14.1, Optatus, *de schism. Don.* 1.18, *Gest. Zeno.* The precise date of Maxentius' investiture is debated: Barnes gives October 28 (*Constantine and Eusebius*, p. 30), while Shaw gives October 26 (*Sacred Violence*, p. 814).

[88] Barnes, *Constantine and Eusebius*, p. 56, relying on Optatus, *de schism. Don.* 1.18–20. Barnes has reinterpreted Optatus' report, which does not say that the bishop recovered the property itself, but that he received the brief regarding the gold and silver (*brevis auri et argenti*), which Shaw construes as *commonitorium* ("memorandum"; Shaw, *Sacred Violence*, p. 814).

[89] Barnes, *Constantine and Eusebius*, p. 56. Barnes relies on the testimony of Augustine, who reports information related to him by a dissident bishop Fortunius of Tuburisicum not found in Optatus' account (*Ep.* 44.4.8).

[90] Barnes, *Constantine and Eusebius*, p. 56, relying on Optatus, *de schism. Don.* 1.18–20.

[91] Barnes, *Constantine and Eusebius*, p. 56, relying on Optatus, *de schism. Don.* 1.18–20.

valuables as pawns.[92] Yet Shaw highlights the role of the church elders (*seniores*). According to Shaw, Mensurius had left the valuables (sacred vessels and scriptures) for safekeeping with the *seniores* before he left Carthage.[93] Mensurius' failure to return to Carthage occasioned the episcopal election, which Shaw dates to "immediately following the end of the persecution" (i.e. after October 26, 306).[94] Following the election of Caecilianus over and against his two otherwise unknown rivals, the *seniores* refused to return the hidden church possessions to the newly ordained bishop, and appealed to the bishops of Numidia for support.[95] Soon thereafter, in the year 307, this anti-Caecilianist faction elected the lector Maiorinus as bishop.[96]

Unlike Barnes and Shaw, Harold Drake follows the traditional, compressed chronology, and he proposes an alternative provocation: Caecilianus' contempt for the martyrs, whom North Africans heroized and venerated.[97] In his position as deacon under Mensurius during the persecution, Caecilianus had embargoed food deliveries to the imprisoned faithful (confessors) and had prohibited veneration of private martyr relics.[98] Drake

---

[92] Shaw, *Sacred Violence*, pp. 66–81, 110.

[93] Shaw, *Sacred Violence*, pp. 812–814, based on Optatus, *de schism. Don.* 1.17.2.

[94] Shaw, *Sacred Violence*, p. 815. Note the slight discrepancy between Shaw's dating of Maxentian peace and that of Barnes.

[95] Shaw, *Sacred Violence*, p. 815, based on Optatus, *de schism. Don.* 1.18. Optatus portrays a Spanish noblewoman named Lucilla as a leader of the anti-Caecilianus party, but the *Gest. Zeno.* identify her only as a wealthy donor giving charity to the poor. Optatus may rhetorically re-position Lucilla to discredit the Maiorinus faction (1.18.3). Shaw notes that she served as one of those "vile Eve figures" (p. 328). Caecilianus would later be the only recorded North African bishop to attend the Council of Nicea. He supported its doctrinal affirmations, which he supposedly brought back to Africa (as noted in the minutes of the 419 Council of Carthage, *Codex Apiarii causae* (CCL 149: 94): *Omne concilium dixit: exemplaria fidei et statuta nicaeni synodi quae ad nostrum concilium per beatae recordationis olim prodecessorem tuae sanctitatis qui interfuit caecilianum episcopum adlata sunt* ... (The entire council declared: the copies of the creed and the statutes of the Synod of Nicea which at that time were brought to our council by bishop Cæcilean, the predecessor of your holiness, who was present at it ...)).

[96] Shaw, *Sacred Violence*, p. 84.

[97] Drake, *Constantine and the Bishops*, p. 213, following the traditional chronology and accepting the historicity of the *Pass. Dat. Saturn.* (see the following note) along with Optatus' account.

[98] Drake, *Constantine and the Bishops*, p. 214. Although Drake gives no indication of the sources he uses for this reconstruction, the martyr-relic incident is found in Optatus, *de schism. Don.* 1.16, and the embargo, attributed to a decree of emperor Licinius, appears in Eusebius (*Hist. eccl.* 10.8.11) but is related fully – with reference to Caecilianus – in the *Pass. Dat. Saturn.* 20–21. On the historicity of this martyr narrative, see A. Dearn, "The Abitinian Martyrs and the Outbreak of the Donatist Schism," *The Journal of Ecclesiastical History* 55.1 (January 2004): 1–18: "Modern scholars who approach the story of the Abitinian martyrs as a source of authentic evidence for the outbreak of the schism are therefore misled ..." (p. 3).

presents Caecilianus' election, which he dates to 311, as "a hasty consecration that prevented bishops from neighboring Numidia (modern Algeria),
where Donatist sentiment was strongest, from exercising their traditional
rights to participate."[99] The Numidians struck back by electing their own
anti-bishop, Maiorinus.[100]

The sequence of events following the episcopal succession controversy
is only slightly less opaque to the modern interpreter. The rift appears to
have intensified after an imperial decree restored North African Christian

[99] Drake, *Constantine and the Bishops*, p. 214. Note that this late date follows the traditional
chronology.
[100] Each one of these historians, while acknowledging that the literary sources have their
own *tendenz* based on events occurring at the time of their editing, reaches a different conclusion by evaluating the historical reliability of the evidence differently. The
origins of the split were likely recast repeatedly over the ensuing century. The most
complete of these literary productions to have survived are: First, documents apparently
presented during the conflict in Constantina (formerly Cirta, Numidia) of 320 CE
between a deacon named Nundinarius and the bishop Silvanus. The document collection bears the name of the Numidian consul, Zenophilus, who adjudicated the case. No
doubt the accusation from both sides that episcopal succession had been tainted by the
pollution of handing over church property to imperial officials during the Tetrarchic
persecution struck at the heart of an issue that had divided the Church since Cyprian's
time: the efficacy of baptism performed by polluted bishops (*Act. pur. Fel.*; Cyprian,
ep. 70.1.3; Discussion of the rebaptism controversy can be found in Chapter 3, and
see Burns, *Cyprian*, pp. 9–10, 100–131). This collection is appended to a second flash-
point at the beginning of the last third of the century. A debate between the dissident
Primate of Africa, Parmenian, who wrote a five-volume diatribe accusing Catholics
of schism, and the Catholic bishop of Milevis, Optatus, who selectively collected earlier materials and wrote a seething response to Parmenian. Third, evidence submitted by bishop Aurelius and his Catholic colleagues, including Augustine, against their
dissident rivals at the episcopal council of 411 convened by the emperor Honorius
(*Gest. Coll. Carth.*). Around this time, Augustine's own account of the schism appears
scattered throughout his works. The chronology of events depends on the dating of,
among others, Mensurius' recall and the Maxentian peace, neither of which are obvious from the extant evidence. Although the sources for the origins of the schism are
unclear and contradictory, matters are even worse for the events that followed. As Shaw
acknowledges, both the expanded and compressed chronologies leave huge gaps, either
following the competing elections of the two bishops until Constantine's intervention, from 307–313, or following the persecution until the episcopal elections, from
306–311 (see Shaw, *Sacred Violence*, pp. 814–815, 819). The source problem confronting
modern scholars suggests that ancient authors either faced an unexplainable gap in
their evidence or constructed one to avoid the disclosure of evidence incriminating
to their causes. Historical reconstructions must decide how the political turmoil of
the period is most likely to have affected North African Christians, either internally or
externally. According to the compressed chronology, the deferral of episcopal elections
would have resulted from the havoc wreaked by the Diocletian persecution. According
to the expanded chronology, the delay in registering formal complaints with the state
or the state's slowness to respond would have resulted from political turmoil incited
by the revolt of the African prefect Lucius Domitius Alexander (308–310) and the

assets that had been seized during the Tetrarchic persecution, either in 311 or 312.[101] In particular, Constantine's first letter to the African procon-sul Anullinus in the winter of 312/313 ordered property to be allocated solely to the Catholic Church and not to schismatics.[102] Above and beyond divisive religious issues, the problem of disunity posed a threat to govern-ance.[103] Allocation of funds and property as well as exemptions from *munera* (public patronage) could not be executed according to imperial mandate without clarifying which bishop, Caecilianus or Maiorinus, represented the "Catholic Church." Determining who was who – Catholics and schis-matics – provoked a series of imperial letters, petitions to civil authori-ties, and ecclesiastical councils. Constantine's second letter relating to the schism, addressed to Caecilianus and dated to 312/313, recognized the bishop as head of the Catholic Church, allocated imperial funds for distri-bution among Catholic clergy, and authorized him to report schismatics to

subsequent imperial power struggle between Alexander's ally Constantine and Maxentius (Zosimus 2.12, 14.2–4, CIL 8.22183, discussed in Barnes, *Constantine and Eusebius*, p. 33. Also see the coins minted by Alexander in Carthage: RIC VI 68, 72, 73). Alexander's embargo of grain exports from North Africa caused famine and riots in Rome (David Potter, *Constantine the Emperor* (New York: Oxford University Press, 2013), pp. 143–144). The former position, of post-persecution disarray, is supported by evidence that Christian leaders (*principes*) were meeting in private homes before their basilicas were restored and by the confusion surrounding the retrieval of the sacred property stashed by Mensurius (Eusebius, *Hist. eccl.* 10.5.15–17 and Optatus *de schism. Don.* 1.14.1, dis-cussed in Chapter 3 at note 13). It is unlikely, however, that the Carthaginian Church would have allowed the episcopal seat to go unoccupied for such an extended period without at least an interim bishop. Supporting the latter view, of a Church conflict that had been roiling for some time, are Eusebius' reference to the "crime" (ἐπιτριβή) that provoked Constantine's intervention, which must have had time to have occurred before being reported (Eusebius *VC* 1.45.2), Constantine's letter to the North African Catholics encouraging forbearance instead of revenge for these "injuries" (*iniuriae*, a technical legal term; *Ep. Const. episc. Afric.*), and his letter to bishop Alexander of Alexandria and his presbyter Arius referring to the North African controversy as having occurred in the past (Athanasius Alexandrinus Werke, *Urkunden zur Geschichte des arianischen Streites*, ed. Hans-Georg Opitz (Berlin: de Gruyter, 1934–5) vol. 3 #1, p. 32, quoted by Eusebius, *VC* 2.66). The delay was likely compounded by the fact that this was the first internal Christian issue in North African history presented to civil authorities.

[101] Eusebius, *Hist. eccl.* 10.5.15–17. The debate over whether Maxentius or Constantine issued the edict is discussed in Chapter 3.

[102] Eusebius, *Hist. eccl.* 10.5.16 (SC 55): ... εἴ τινα ἐκ τούτων τῶν τῇ ἐκκλησίᾳ τῇ καθολικῇ τῶν Χριστιανῶν ... (...if these things belonged to the Catholic Church of Christians ...). Dating is from Barnes, *The New Empire of Diocletian and Constantine*, p. 240.

[103] Michael Gaddis, *"There is No Crime for Those Who Have Christ". Religious Violence in the Christian Roman Empire* (Berkeley, CA: University of California Press, 2005), pp. 26, 49–50. Raymond van Dam relates Constantine's commitment to unity to his desire for "harmony in the empire" (*The Roman Revolution of Constantine* (New York: Cambridge University Press, 2007), p. 273; see also pp. 266–269, 272, 281, 300).

local state officials.[104] In a letter preserved only by Augustine, the proconsul reported to Constantine that he had tasked Caecilianus and his associates with unifying the divided Church, but that the other party presented two documents opposing Caecilianus and claiming the title "Catholic" for themselves.[105] Anullinus forwarded these documents to the emperor, who responded by convening episcopal councils at Rome and Arles, in 313 and 314, which upheld the election of Caecilianus.[106] Constantine himself attended the Arles assembly.

Almost a half-century after the events, around the year 370, the Catholic bishop of Milevis (Numidia), Optatus, wrote a six-book version of his earlier work on the North African schism in response to a tractate written by the dissident bishop of Carthage, Parmenian. This lengthy defense of the Catholic side describes the subsequent appeal by the losers to Constantine for arbitration to resolve episcopal succession. It is unlikely, however, that the emperor would have considered this issue worthy of state intervention on its own. Constantine's reluctance to become involved in the Church's internal affairs is clear from his letter of late summer 314 to the Catholic bishops following the council of Arles:[107]

> I have discovered that they demand my own judgment! ... They demand my own judgment, while I myself wait for the judgment of Christ. Indeed, I declare that, just as the truth speaks for itself, one must obey the judgment of the priests [at Arles] as if God himself were sitting in judgment. For they are allowed to hear and judge only because they have been trained by the instruction of Christ.

Sometime over the next five months, Constantine acquiesced to the dissidents' demands that the bishop who had ordained Caecilianus, Felix of Abthugni, be investigated for collusion during the Diocletian persecution.

---

[104] Eusebius, *Hist. eccl.* 10.6.1–5.

[105] Aug. *Ep.* 88.2.

[106] Rome: Eusebius, *Hist. eccl.* 10.5.18–20 and Optatus, *de schism. Don.* 1.23–24 (see also Aug. *c. part. Donat. post ges.* 33.56, *Brev. Coll.* 3.12.24, 3.17.31, and *Ep.* 43.5.16); Arles: *Ep. Const. Aelaf.*, Eusebius, *Hist. eccl.* 10.5.21–24, *Conc. ep. Arel.*, and canons 14 and 20 from *Conc. Gall. a. 314*.

[107] *Ep. Const. episc. cath.* (CSEL 26: 209): *..meum iudicium eos conperi postulare! ... meum iudicium postulant, qui ipse iudicium Christi expecto. dico enim, ut se veritas habet, sacerdotum iudicium ita debet haberi, ac si ipse dominus residens iudicet. nihil enim licet his aliud sentire vel aliud iudicare, nisi quod Christi magisterio sunt edocti.* Some scholars consider this letter to be fabricated by Catholics in order to disguise the abject failure of the Arles council, as claimed by Augustine in his letter 88.3 (José Fernández Ubiña, "The Donatist Conflict as Seen by Constantine and the Bishops," in *The Role of the Bishop in Late Antiquity: Conflict and Compromise*, ed. Andrew Fear, José Fernández Urbiña, and Mar Marcos Sanchez, pp. 31–46 (New York: Bloomsbury T&T Clark, 2013), p. 37. I suspect the document has been doctored to project a more pious Constantine, but the essential facts remain.

The proceedings, if accurately and fully preserved by Optatus, reveal that this local hearing was something of a show trial aimed at publicly shaming the Donatist camp into conceding.[108] Claims of document forgery, false testimony, conspiracy, and greed pervade the transcript. The proconsul Aelianus even strung up one of the witnesses on the rack. Felix was exonerated, once again upholding the election of Caecilianus. This time, however, the verdict was decided by a civil court.

As Shaw has duly noted, it was during this second phase of the conflict that the process of labeling each side of the split began.[109] These names derived from the legal briefs that referred to each side by the "legal person or persona on whose behalf legal actions could proceed."[110] As noted by Eusebius, the petitions divided their complainants into "two factions (διχοστατοῦντα)."[111] One side was named for Maiorinus and, after 313, his successor Donatus.[112] The other side, the *pars Caeciliani* (party of Caecilianus), soon laid claim to the term "Catholics," a term used in both civil and ecclesiastical rhetoric for those Christians who embraced Nicene orthodoxy.[113] The correlation between Caecilianists and orthodoxy acquired imperial sanction in 313 when Constantine wrote a second letter to Anullinus recognizing Caecilianus as presider over "the catholic Church" within the province and exempting its clergy from "public duties."[114] These "Catholics" accused their opponents of "rebaptizing" and called them "Donatists." "Donatists" used the term "Catholic" for themselves, whom they regarded as "without spot or wrinkle."[115] The rhetorical strategy of

---

[108] *Act. pur. Fel.* See Fergus Millar, *The Emperor in the Roman World* (Ithaca, NY: Cornell University Press, 1977), pp. 584–590; Shaw, *Sacred Violence*, pp. 799–800.

[109] Shaw, *Sacred Violence*, p.62. See also Alexander Evers, "Catholics and Donatists in Roman North Africa," *Frontiers in the Roman World: Proceedings of the Ninth Workshop of the International Network Impact of Empire (Durham, April 16–19, 2009)*, ed. Olivier Heckster and Ted Kaizer (Leiden: Brill, 2011): 175–198, p. 186.

[110] Shaw, *Sacred Violence*, p. 63.

[111] Eusebius, *Hist. eccl.* 10.5.18.

[112] For the relationship between this Donatus and the "Donatus of Casae Nigrae" mentioned in the fragmentary minutes of the 411 Council of Carthage, see Barnes, "Donatism," pp. 16–17, who concludes that "the distinction was bogus."

[113] Shaw, *Sacred Violence*, pp. 4–5.

[114] Eusebius, *Hist. eccl.* 10.7.2 (SC 55): διόπερ ἐκείνους τοὺς εἴσω τῆς ἐπαρχίας τῆς σοι πεπιστευμένης ἐν τῇ καθολικῇ ἐκκλησίᾳ, ᾗ Καικιλιανὸς ἐφέστηκεν, τὴν ἐξ αὐτῶν ὑπηρεσίαν τῇ ἁγίᾳ ταύτῃ θρησκείᾳ παρέχοντας, οὕσπερ κληρικοὺς ἐπονομάζειν εἰώθασιν, ἀπὸ πάντων ἅπαξ ἁπλῶς τῶν λειτουργιῶν βούλομαι ἀλειτουργήτους διαφυλαχθῆναι ...

[115] Rebaptizing: Optatus, *de schism. Don.* 1.24.1, purporting to be the ruling from a 313 Council of bishops convened in Rome. This term was already used by Cyprian, as noted by Eusebius (Cyprian, *Ep.* 73.1, 2, 9, e.g.; Eusebius, *Hist. eccl.* 7.7.4–5); Donatists: Optatus, *de schism. Don.* 3.3.15 (SC 412): ... *iam non christiani vocarentur sed donatistae* (... now they

labeling contributed to a perception that the two parties represented distinct groups, as observed by Optatus even in the midst of the conflict.[116]

Constantine was drawn further into the controversy by appeals to the finality of his authority: "some of you ... perhaps coming here so that, if the matter were investigated here and brought to an end, a proper and truthful procedure would not be required ..."[117] While the warring bishops were detained, the emperor sent episcopal delegates to Carthage to quell dissent.[118] Riots erupted. In 316, Constantine resorted to force, ordering the seizure of dissident basilicas and exiling their bishops.[119] Despite more hearings, letters, and decrees, the split only degenerated into further recriminations and violence.

A dispute between a Cirta bishop and his deacon in 320 escalated into a case before the Numidian governor. The case dossier included documents from the Diocletian persecution, collected by Optatus in what has been identified as the *Gesta apud Zenophilum*. Although the extant version of this dossier has been heavily edited by a Catholic hand to construe the crimes as *traditio* and misappropriating charity funds, it is more likely that, once again, political disputes over episcopal authority and property rights in the wake of basilica confiscation constituted the basis of legal complaints. As Victor, a grammarian from Cirta (Constantina), testifies before the consul, "I have no knowledge of the origin of the conflict, since our city has always had one church."[120]

The intransigence of the dissidents won a temporary reprieve. In 321, Constantine reversed himself again, now recalling the exiled bishops and

---

are not called Christians but Donatists); Catholics: *Pass. Dat. Saturn.* 1, tr. Tilley: ... *ut Ecclesiam catholicam teneat, sanctamque communionem a profana discernat* ... (to hold fast to the Catholic Church, and distinguish the holy communion from the unholy). See also *s. Pass. Don. et Advoc.* 12.

[116] Optatus, *de schism. Don.* 1.2.1 (SC 412): *nec falsorum vatum nomen et actus incurrerent* (... nor would they be acquiring the names and gestures of false soothsayers ...); "Without spot or wrinkle (*sine macula et ruga*):" Petil. apud *Gest. Coll. Carth.* 3.75 and Parm. apud Aug. *Parm.* 3.2.10 quoting Eph 5.27. The challenge of what terminology contemporary scholars should use for the North African factions is complicated by the fact that both sides were Nicene. For the sake of familiarity and simplicity, this book employs the upper-case "Catholic" to designate the Caecilianists, bias notwithstanding. Lower-case "catholic" is reserved for the universal Church. An excellent discussion of the problem is found in BeDuhn, *Augustine's Manichaean Dilemma* 2, pp. ix–x.

[117] *Ep. Const. episc.: quosdam ex vestris ... per hoc venire forsitan, ut, si ibidem cognoscatur, non ut condecet et veritatis ratio expostulat, res finem accipiat ...*

[118] Optatus, *de schism. Don.* 1.26.

[119] Aug. *Ep.* 88.3 (CCL 31A): *... loca congregationum vestrarum fisco vindicarentur* (your meeting places were arrogated to the imperial coffers).

[120] *Gest. Zeno.: ... inde originem scire dissensionis plene non possum, quoniam semper civitas nostra unam ecclesiam habet ...*

reverting to persuasion in order to broker unity.[121] He remained steadfast, however, in his Catholic allegiance by limiting clerical immunity from public service, patronage, and the decurionate.[122] In 330, he encountered further difficulty over basilica rights. Constantine wrote to the bishops of Cirta condemning the dissident party's appropriation of a formerly Catholic basilica.[123] His solution, to build a second church, conceded defeat.[124]

Constantine's involvement in these early fourth-century factional disputes would set a new precedent for the relationship between Christian administration and the Roman administrative apparatus, with consequences for other religious groups. Conflicts over church property recurred throughout the century that followed, spilling over into traditional Roman temples and Jewish synagogues. Furthermore, because property disputes were grounds for the state's involvement, its decisions helped to reshape the sacred landscape of late antiquity as well as the rhetoric of religious polemic.

New Terminology

Throughout this book I use the terms "architectural dispossession" and "spatial supersession" to distinguish between physical and rhetorical strategies. "Architectural dispossession" describes the process of evicting one group from a site and allocating it to another group, whether by law or by physical force (or both). The structure that had previously stood on the site may be reused or destroyed. Architectural dispossession may occur with the imperial treasury acting as a mediator by seizing the property and bestowing it to a different owner. Alternatively, a group might attack a building and forcibly occupy it, using adverse possession to claim ownership (*usucapio*). This term is meant to refer to the concrete, physical process of displacement.

---

[121] Aug. *c. part. Donat. post ges.* 31.54, 33.56, *Ep. Const. episc. Afric.*, and Eusebius *Vit. Const.* 2.66.

[122] *Cod. theod.* 16.5.1, 16.2.7.

[123] *Ep. Const. Zeu.* tr. Shaw, *Sacred Violence*, p. 161: … *et hisdem remittendo quod idem sibi indebitum atque alienum usurpare contendunt* (… men who are struggling to get what they think is owed to them and to usurp something which is not theirs); *conperi haereticos sive schismaticos eam basilicam ecclesiae catholicae, quam in Constantina civitate iusseram fabricari, solita inprobitate invadendam putasse et frequenter tam a nobis quam a iudioibus nostris ex nostra iussione commonitos et reddere, quod suum non erat, noluisse* … (I have discovered that the heretics or schismatics have with their usual depravity arranged to invade that basilica of the Catholic church which I had ordered to be erected in the city of Constantina, and that they were unwilling to return what was not theirs, though repeatedly warned both by us and by our judges on our orders …). The author also refers to dissidents as "the devil's party (*diaboli pars*)."

[124] *Ep. Const. Zeu.*: … *in quo tamen loco sumptu fiscali basilicam erigi praecepi* … (… as for the place I enjoined a basilica to be erected at the expense of the imperial treasury …).

The phrase "spatial supersession," on the other hand, denotes a rhetorical strategy. The strategy entails interpreting a construction built on top of a ruin site that once belonged to a competing group as the first group's loss of power and the dominance of the second group. Spatial supersession conveyed supremacy. The technique of spatial supersession appears in North African literature such as the *Passio Sanctae Salsae*, discussed in Chapter 5, regarding the construction of a church on the site of a previous synagogue and temple: "in the place where twin blasphemies prevailed before, now the Church shall triumph ..."[125] The strategy is employed throughout the empire, as illustrated by a famous passage in the fourth-century Church historian Eusebius' posthumous panegyric to the emperor Constantine regarding his construction of the Church of the Holy Sepulcher.[126] The emperor is said to have ordered the destruction of the Temple of Aphrodite and the construction of a church on the site claimed to be that of the Holy Sepulcher, which itself had been superseded by the temple. Despite Eusebius' claims, this early example is not archaeologically verifiable, yet it serves as the Christian model for subsequent historiography and hagiography.[127] According to Eusebius, Constantine himself described the anticipated building as "superior to those in all other places."[128] In a speech delivered on the occasion of the church's dedication in 335, Eusebius had referred to the "house of prayer" as "a holy temple of a holy God."[129] Kenneth Holum has characterized this construction as "the

---

[125] *Passio Salsae* 3 (ed. Piredda): *ut in loco in quo gemina regnabant ante sacrilegia, nunc ... triumphet Ecclesia.*

[126] Eusebius, *Vit. Const.* 3.26.2, 7, 3.33.1, 3.40, tr. Cameron and Hall (GCS 7): τοῦτο μὲν οὖν τὸ σωτήριον ἄντρον ἄθεοί τινες καὶ δυσσεβεῖς ἀφανὲς ἐξ ἀνθρώπων ποιήσασθαι διανενόηντο, ἄφρονι λογισμῷ τὴν ἀλήθειαν ταύτῃ πῃ κρύψαι λογισάμενοι. ... ἅμα δὲ προστάγματι τὰ τῆς ἀπάτης μηχανήματα εἰς ἔδαφος ἄνωθεν ἀφ' ὑψηλοῦ κατερρίπτετο, ἐλύετό τε καὶ καθῃρεῖτο αὐτοῖς ξοάνοις καὶ δαίμοσι τὰ τῆς πλάνης οἰκοδομήματα. ... ἡ νέα κατεσκευάζετο Ἰερουσαλήμ, ἀντιπρόσωπος τῇ πάλαι βοωμένῃ, ἣ μετὰ τὴν κυριοκτόνον μιαιφονίαν ἐρημίας ἐπ' ἔσχατα περιτραπεῖσα δίκην ἔτισε δυσσεβῶν οἰκητόρων. ... Τόνδε μὲν οὖν τὸν νεὼν σωτηρίου ἀναστάσεως ἐναργὲς ἀνίστη μαρτύριον βασιλεύς (It was this very cave of the Savior that some godless and wicked people had planned to make invisible to mankind, thinking in stupidity that they could in this way hide the truth ... At a word of command those contrivances of fraud were demolished from top to bottom, and the houses of error were dismantled and destroyed along with their idols and demons. ... New Jerusalem was built at the very Testimony to the Savior, facing the famous Jerusalem of old. ... This then was the shrine which the emperor raised as a manifest testimony of the Savior's resurrection ...).

[127] Emmel, Gotter, and Hahn, "'From Temple to Church'," p. 12.

[128] Eusebius, *Vit. Const.* 3.31.1, tr. Cameron and Hall (GCS 7): ὡς οὐ μόνον βασιλικὴν τῶν ἁπανταχοῦ βελτίονα.

[129] Eusebius, *De Sepulchro Christi* 18.3, tr. Drake (GCS 7, as *Laud. Const.*): οἶκον εὐκτήριον ... νεών τε ἅγιον ἁγίου θεου ...

visible footprint of an invisible social process, a building that gave tangible, monumental form to new social realities."[130] Likewise, John Chrysostom used this strategy in the fourth century to portray the destruction of the temple of Apollo in a suburb of Antioch by the martyr Babylas, and Severus of Minorca, in his collaboration with Consentius, employed the technique in his fifth-century description of the demise of the island's synagogue and the use of its spolia for a new basilica construction.[131] A fifth-century papyrus depicts the destruction of Alexandria's Serapeum in 391 with Patriarch Theophilus perched triumphantly atop the temple (Figure 0.1).

Such triumphal stances were familiar to their viewers from Roman coins celebrating military victories, which depicted the vanquished enemy underfoot.[132] The idiom of physical superimposition commonly appeared on imperial coinage to portray an enemy's defeat. This image, of Victory with her foot on a vanquished enemy, can be seen in the Solidus of emperor Arcadius minted in Ravenna at the beginning of the fifth century (Figure 0.2). As a recognizable symbol of Roman supremacy, the gesture of superimposition provided late antique North African Christians with a precedent for conveying triumph. The social process of spatial supersession, to which Holum refers, was not simply mirrored by the building process but was systematically constructed over an extended period of time. The mechanisms whereby churches were built and interpreted as symbolizing the defeat of other religious groups were more complex and attenuated than the "blinking of an eye" Holum suggests. Those mechanisms are the subject of this book.[133]

Architectural dispossession is part of the process that geographers call "materialization," while spatial supersession belongs to "spatialization." Edward Soja has explained:[134]

[S]patiality is socially produced, and, like society itself, exists in both substantial forms (concrete spatialities) and as a set of relations between individuals and groups, an "embodiment" and medium of social life itself. As socially produced space, spatiality can be distinguished from the physical space of material nature and the mental space of cognition and

[130]   Kenneth Holum, "In the Blinking of an Eye: The Christianizing of Classical Cities in the Levant," in *Religion and Politics in the Ancient Near East*, Studies and Texts in Jewish History and Culture ed. Adele Berlin, pp. 131–150 (College Park, MD: University Press of Maryland, 1996), p. 143.

[131]   John Chrysostom *De s. Babyla* 1–21, 40–50; See the discussion in Shepardson, *Controlling Contested Places*, p. 73; *Ep. Sev.* 14: *victoria nostra*.

[132]   See, for example, the solidus minted by Arcadius in Ravenna during the first decade of the fifth century (Peter Brennan, Michael Turner, and Nicholas L. Wright, *Faces of Power: Imperial Portraiture on Roman Coins* (Sydney, Australia: Nicholson Museum, 2006), p. 71 (Nicholson Museum 2004. 2627 (Sear 20727 = RIC X 1286)); see also Theodosius I RIC IX 63 from Antioch.

[133]   I understand these mechanisms' production of conquest as roughly analogous to our own culture's use of the American flag, be it on Iwo Jima or the moon.

[134]   Edward W. Soja, "Reassertions: Towards a Spatialized Ontology," *Human Geography. An Essential Anthology*, ed. John Agnew, David N. Livingstone, and Alisdair Rogers (Malden,

Figure 0.1 Papyrus Goleniscev folio 6v, in Adolph Bauer and Josef Strzygowski, *Eine Alexandrinische Weltchronik. Text und Miniaturen eines griechischen Papyrus der Sammlung W. Golenišev* (Vienna: Buchhändler der kais Akademie der Wissenschaften, 1905), plate VI, verso.

Figure 0.2 Solidus of Arcadius, Ravenna mint, AD 402–408, Nicholson Museum, The University of Sydney, NM2004.2627 from Peter Brennan, Michael Turner, and Nicholas L. Wright, *Faces of Power. Imperial Portraiture on Roman Coins* (Sydney, Australia: The Nicholson Museum, 2007), p. 60, figure 119, reverse image reproduced by permission.

representation, each of which is used and incorporated into the social construction of spatiality but cannot be conceptualized as its equivalent. Within certain limits (which are frequently overlooked) physical and psychological processes and forms can be theorized independently with regard to their spatial dimensions and attributes.

Following Soja's distinction, this study treats physical phenomena separately from psychological ones, which I take to be at least partially retrievable through literary evidence.

New Directions

Until recently, studies of spatial conflict only addressed temple destruction and conversion, omitting the worship spaces of other religious groups.[135] Studies of religious conflict have only recently begun to address its spatial dimension.[136] In order to understand the religious dimension of this spatial

MA: Blackwell Publishing, 1996: 2003): 623–635, p. 625, originally published in *Postmodern Geographies* (Verso/New Left Books, 1989), pp. 118–131.

[135] F. W. Deichmann, "Frühchristliche Kirchen in antiken Heiligtümern," *Jahrbuch des Deutschen Archaiologichen Instituts* 54 (1939): 105–136; R. P. C. Hanson, "The Transformation of Pagan Temples into Churches in the Early Christian Centuries," *Journal of Semitic Studies* 23.2 (1987): 257–267; Frank R. Trombley, *Hellenic Religion and Christianization c. 370–529* (Boston, MA: E. J. Brill, 2001); Richard Bayliss, *Provincial Cilicia and the Archaeology of Temple Conversion*, BAR International Series 1281 (Oxford, England: Archaeopress, 2004); *From Temple to Church. Destruction and Renewal of Local Cultic Topography in Late Antiquity*, ed. Johannes Hahn, Stephen Emmel, and Ulrich Gotter (Boston, MA: Brill, 2008).

[136] For example: Shepardson, *Controlling Contested Places*; Dayna Kalleres, *City of Demons: Violence, Ritual, and Christian Power in Late Antiquity* (Berkeley, CA: University of California Press, 2015); Harry Maier, "Private Spaces as the Social Context of Arianism in Ambrose's Milan," *JTS* 45 (1994): 72–93 and "The Topography of Heresy and Dissent in Late-Fourth-Century Rome," *Historia: Zeitschrift für alte Geschichte* 44.2 (1995): 232–249; Franz Alto Bauer, "Urban Space and Ritual: Constantinople in Late Antiquity," *Acta ad Archaeologiam et Atrium Historiam Pertinentia* 15, n.s. 1 (2001): 27–61; Kim Bowes, *Private Worship, Public Values, and Religious Change in Late Antiquity* (New York: Cambridge University Press, 2008); Ton Derks, "The Transformation of Landscape and Religious Representations in Roman Gaul," *Archaeological Dialogues* 4.2 (1997): 126–147; Christopher Haas, *Alexandria in Late Antiquity: Topography and Social Conflict* (Baltimore, MD: Johns Hopkins University Press, 1997); John Curran, *Pagan City and Christian Capital: Rome in the Fourth Century* (New York: Oxford University Press, 2000), pp. 116–157; Nasrallah, *Christian Responses*; Eberhard Sauer, *The Archaeology of Religious Hatred in the Roman and Early Medieval World* (Stroud and Charleston: Tempus, 2003); Johannes Hahn, *Gewalt und religiöser Konflikt. Studien zu den Auseinandersetzungen zwischen Christen, Heiden und Juden im Osten des Römischen Reiches von Konstantin bis Theodosius II* (Berlin: Akademie Verlag, 2004); Gregor Kalas, *The Restoration of the Roman Forum in Late Antiquity: Transforming Public Space* (Austin, TX: University of Texas Press, 2015); and *From Temple to Church. Destruction and Renewal of Local Cultic Topography in Late Antiquity*, ed. Johannes Hahn, Stephen Emmel, and Ulrich Gotter (Boston, MA: Brill, 2008). For work that explores religious violence in

transformation in comparative context, this study includes various types of religious site, that is, places where groups gathered for worship.

Recent research has also demonstrated how the transformation of the late antique Roman landscape exhibits regional differences, as Leone has noted:[137]

> When looking at the process of transformation of temples into churches within the late Roman empire there is a substantial difference between the East and the West, with the phenomenon appearing more frequently in the former. The cause of this substantial dissimilarity probably lies in the form of the classical town, which in the West had a more clearly defined space for the pagan cult: the forum. The situation is different in the East, where sanctuaries are distributed within the urban layout.

Likewise, Sabine MacCormack has shown that although the Western empire generally displayed a different spatial sensibility about the sacred than the East, Palestine presents an entirely different case:[138]

> Christian holy places of the western Mediterranean were the outcome of an intricate convergence both of pagan and Christian topography and of pagan and Christian perceptions and rituals. In Palestine, by contrast, paganism played a much smaller role in the formation of a Christian awareness of the environment.

She attributes this distinction to the pre-Constantinian demographic context. While Roman Palestine was dotted with sites associated with Scripture and therefore significant to Jews, in the rest of the Mediterranean, "places were imbued with memories going back to a sacred antiquity or with the aura of some divine presence."[139] Regionalism, therefore, warrants a separate treatment of sacred places in North Africa, although the evidence does permit some generalized comparisons to elsewhere in the empire.[140]

Regionalism is especially important when considering the implementation of imperial policy.[141] Among a host of other complicated factors, the repetition of legislation can be explained by regional variations of particular

general, see Hahn, *Gewalt und religiöser Konflikt*, Gaddis, *Religious Violence*, and Shaw, *Sacred Violence*.

[137] Leone, *Pagan City*, p. 33.

[138] Sabine MacCormack, "*Loca Sancta*: The Organization of Sacred Topography in Late Antiquity," in *The Blessings of Pilgrimage*, ed. Robert Ousterhout, pp. 7–40 (Chicago, IL: University of Illinois Press, 1990), p. 20.

[139] MacCormack, "*Loca Sancta*," p. 10.

[140] Shepardson, *Controlling Contested Places*, pp. 204–240.

[141] Peter Brown, *Power and Persuasion in Late Antiquity: Towards a Christian Empire* (Madison, WI: University of Wisconsin Press, 1992), p. 9. Johannes Hahn's study of temple destructions illustrates such an approach (Hahn, *Gewalt und religiöser Konflikt*, p. 292).

circumstances, rather than ineffectiveness, as is commonly claimed.[142] In addition, time and distance contributed to varied enforcement of imperial edicts. Considerable time (and interpretation) might elapse between a law's promulgation and its enforcement. Distance, both geographically and politically, between the imperial residences and the proconsular seat in the African capital of Carthage, not to mention official stations in the even more remote North African provinces to the West, also affected the application of imperial law.[143] Although administrators and soldiers stationed throughout the provinces wielded official imperial power, local elites and tribal leaders continued to exercise considerable influence over residents of towns and villages.[144] These competing loci of authority sometimes clashed as was the case, for example, in the fourth-century wars of Firmus and Gildo and, perhaps, in the violence attributed to *circumcelliones* (lit. around the silos) that erupted periodically in the fourth and fifth centuries.[145]

Michael Gaddis has examined such internecine conflicts as part of his study of religious violence in the fourth century. He observed that while pre-Constantinian violence against Christians under emperors Decius, Valerian, and Diocletian was premised on the *pax deorum* (gratifying the gods so they would protect the empire), Constantine adapted this "discourse of legitimacy" to accommodate his newfound Christian cosmology.[146] The emperor justified his deployment of troops to settle intra-Christian disturbances as a kind of *pax Christi*. "Unity" was the driving political idea behind Constantine's reunification of the Diocletian tetrarchy, and it was subsequently applied to Christian factionalism.[147] Although the exact

---

[142] Jill Harries, *Law and Empire in Late Antiquity* (Cambridge: Cambridge University Press, 1999), pp. 82–88. Specific reasons for repetition include the heightened power of recent laws, the need for legal clarification, and response to a particular case requiring adjudication.

[143] Alan Cameron, *The Last Pagans of Rome* (New York: Oxford University Press, 2011), p. 72.

[144] Dossey, *Peasant and Empire in Christian North Africa* (Berkeley, CA: University of California Press, 2010). See also Shaw, *Sacred Violence*, pp. 38–39.

[145] The origins and identity of the circumcellions is still debated. See Brent Shaw, "Who Were the Circumcellions?," A. H. Merrills ed., *Vandals, Romans and Berbers: New Perspectives on Late Antique Africa* (London: Variorum, 2004): 227–258. Optatus is the first author to mention them in connection with dissidents Axido and Fasir, who attacked slave-owners and creditors (*de schism. Don.* 3.4). Chapter 3 includes more discussion of the circumcellions.

[146] Gaddis, *Religious Violence*, p. 20.

[147] *Ep. Const. Zeu.* (ed. Ziwsa, p. 216.2–3, tr. Edwards): *si enim iussionibus nostris obtemperare voluissent, ab omni malo liberarentur* (For if they would submit to our bidding, they would be freed from every evil), discussed in Drake, *Constantine and the Bishops*, p. 221 and Timothy Barnes, *Constantine. Dynasty, Religion, and Power in the Later Roman Empire* (Malden, MA: Wiley-Blackwell, 2011), p. 105 and *Constantine and Eusebius* (Cambridge, MA: Harvard University Press, 1981), pp. 60–61, although see Shaw's revision of the accepted chronology (*Sacred Violence*, pp. 812–819).

chronology of events cannot be definitively determined, it is in this context of intimidation that the emperor ordered the seizure of dissident basilicas.[148] Constantine ultimately found such coercive methods to be unsustainable; he eventually encouraged Catholics to take a more irenic approach in order to both avoid conflict and to marginalize their opponents as violent extremists.[149]

Beginning with this inner Christian schism, sacred sites continued to serve as a potent battle ground for displaying power and control.[150] According to Peter Brown:[151]

> The presence of … a schismatic conventicle on a faraway estate became, even for a relatively minor representative of the Roman order, an opportunity to show, in its destruction, paternal authority over others, rendered active and majestic by the service of the one God.

This "opportunity" emerged from the growing importance of such sites. These locales were not only perceived as supercharged with divinity and religious meaning, they were portrayed as politically significant by imperial legislation and Christian polemicists alike. Christian adaptation of and construction at these sites reflected their high regard for them and symbolized Christian values and ideals.

Conflicts over values and ideals, therefore, found sacred places to be productive locales for negotiating those differences as well as producing and policing group boundaries. As Thomas Sizgorich has noted:[152]

> [T]he history of late antique religious violence is replete with acts of violence undertaken to impose boundaries blurred by simple curiosity, commerce, shared sets of semiotic devices, or ancient cultural patterns in confrontation with new ways of reckoning identity, as well as other common aspects of human behavior.

Buildings were good tools for boundary-maintenance, since their physical structures made it possible to allow certain people in and keep others out. In North Africa, *architectural dispossession* and *spatial supersession* were the

---

[148] The text of the edict does not survive but is mentioned in Aug. *Ep.* 88.5 and *C. litt. Petil.* 2.205.

[149] *Ep. Const. episc. cath.*; Aug. *Ps. c. Don.* 31.54, 33.56 (CSEL 53: 154–56, 158–59), *Ep. Const. episc. Afric.*

[150] This dynamic has been explored by earlier scholarship on Antioch, Jerusalem, Milan, Constantinople, Alexandria, Gaul, and Rome. See references in note 136 of this chapter.

[151] Peter Brown, *Authority and the Sacred* (Cambridge University Press, 1995: 1997), p. 20.

[152] Sizgorich, *Violence and Belief in Late Antiquity: Militant Devotion in Christianity and Islam* (Philadelphia, PA: University of Pennsylvania Press, 2009), p. 257.

weapons first deployed by warring Christian factions against each other in this rather untidy process of negotiation. Subsequently, these methods were marshaled by Christians against non-Christians. The order of book chapters thus follows this chronology of violence. Chapter 2 explores the ways that Christians portrayed and perceived places used for religious worship. Chapter 3 demonstrates how that conception affected the competition for sites that erupted among Christians of rival sacramental and political theologies over the course of the fourth and early fifth centuries. How this spatial contestation spilled over to Christian–non-Christian relations is the subject of Chapters 4 and 5.

Although the transformation of the late antique North African landscape during this first century of Christianization was gradual, reflecting structural continuities as well as discontinuities, certain Christian writers emphasized the discontinuities and their meanings. In the case of traditional Roman sanctuaries and shrines, discussed in Chapter 4, some Christian authors decried any comparison of churches and martyria to pre-Christian temples and shrines; they insisted that architectural differences reflected differences in spatial conceptions, despite the fact that some churches had been adapted from temples with only slight structural modifications and that martyria used the same symbolic idioms as Roman mausolea.

Chapter 5 explores how this rhetoric of replacement, or spatial supersession, eventually shaped Christian narratives about synagogue appropriations. In North Africa the archaeological evidence is too scanty to permit discussion of architectural dispossession, yet literary evidence provides sufficient material to argue that the paradigm of spatial supersession had already become so successful for describing intra-Christian and Christian–pagan relations that it was applied to the Christian–Jewish relationship as well.[153]

The social transformation of Late Roman society into Medieval Christendom is often termed "Christianization." Previous scholarship attempted to explain this phenomenon by addressing the question, Why Christianity? In response, Christianization was understood as occurring in the realm of ideas: it was either rooted in Christian conversion – a "change of belief" – or the result of social and political forces.[154] Even when scholars like Ramsay Macmullen included practice in their analyses of the

---

[153] For a thorough and trenchant analysis of the state of current scholarship on Jewish North Africa, see Stern, *Inscribing Devotion*, pp. xi–xiv, 1–23.

[154] A. D. Nock, *Conversion: The Old and the New in Religion from Alexander the Great to Augustine of Hippo* (Oxford: Oxford University Press, 1933), p. 7; R. MacMullen, *Christianizing the Roman Empire. A.D. 100–400* (New Haven, CT: Yale University, 1984), 5; J. Matthews, *Western Aristocracies and Imperial Court, A.D. 364–425* (Oxford: Clarendon Press, 1975), pp. xi, 146–172;

phenomenon, they still regarded Christianization as "something that happened to pagans ... and to the Roman empire."[155] Colonialism studies have noted that such transformations are rarely that private, one-sided or monolithic. Was Christianization something that one group did to another, or was it a complex, multifaceted process that included, among other dynamics, the production of difference? Did Christianization only affect practitioners of traditional Roman religion, or did it also distinguish among various expressions of Christianity? More recent studies have abandoned some of these earlier assumptions and begun to ask, What is Christianization? These approaches tend to examine individual aspects of the transformation rather than attempt a sweeping explanation, studying legal developments, social status, economic shifts, violence, healing and other miraculous events, the advent of new ideas and rituals, changes in ethical and aesthetic sensibilities, linguistic developments, and the transformation of the physical landscape, to name just a few.

The French philosopher Henri Lefebvre has observed that a "superstructure foreign to the original space serves as a political means of introducing a social and economic structure in such a way that it may gain a foothold and indeed establish its 'base' in a particular locality."[156] Lefebvre's description aptly describes how architects and urban planners of the imperial period redesigned the provincial landscape following Roman conquest.[157] Classical

---

respectively. See also R. L. Fox, *Pagans and Christians* (New York: Knopf, 1986), pp. 623–624. A discussion of the shortfalls of these perspectives can be found in M. R. Salzman, *The Making of a Christian Aristocracy: Social and Religious Change in the Western Roman Empire* (Cambridge, MA: Harvard University Press, 2002), pp. ix–xiii. See the trenchant critique of such "modernist perspective[s]" by Kenneth Holum, "In the Blinking of an Eye: The Christianizing of Classical Cities in the Levant," in *Religion and Politics in the Ancient Near East*, Studies and Texts in Jewish History and Culture, ed. Adele Berlin, pp. 131–150 (College Park, MD: University Press of Maryland, 1996), pp. 131–133.

[155] MacMullen, *Christianizing the Roman Empire: A.D. 100–400*, p. 10. Peter Brown also combined both approaches, explaining that "a deeply rooted collective representation of the universe ... gave late antique persons the intellectual and imaginative tools with which to grapple with the ambiguous religious situation of their age" and used "ceremonials" to "mobiliz[e] the 'set of symbolic forms'" (Brown, *Authority and the Sacred: Aspects of the Christianisation of the Roman World* (New York: Cambridge University Press, 1995), p. 14).

[156] Lefebvre, *Production of Space*, p. 151. Although Lefebvre makes this observation in the context of his analysis of Spanish-American colonial towns, the colonial context applies equally well to Roman North Africa.

[157] I recognize that the dynamic is more reciprocal and diachronic than this quotation from Lefebvre suggests, and that new Roman forms often integrated indigenous forms (e.g. "Romano-Punic" in Lepcis Magna, both from a practical standpoint of reuse and as a colonializing strategy. These hybrid forms often gave way, in time, to "Roman Imperial" architecture, as summarized by David J. Mattingly and R. Bruce Hitchner: "A number

archaeologist Elizabeth Fentress notes that "Roman rule transformed a loosely bonded and heterogeneous landscape and its people into a remarkably uniform series of towns, whose urban furniture was as predictable as their social structures."[158] This colonial strategy of spatial acquisition, which Lefebvre identifies as "the production of a social space by political power" (152), was a useful tool adapted by various groups in their struggles for power over the course of the post-Diocletian century. This shifting control of ritual places vividly illustrates the fitful and contested nature of the process of Christianization, rather than the linear trajectory presented in Christian historiography.[159] As demonstrated by Shepardson regarding Antioch:[160]

> Examining Antioch through the lens of spatial politics will reveal that fourth-century leaders' manipulation of the city's landscape was one means by which they actively engaged in the tumultuous local and imperial contests over religious and political power. Their activities not only changed the topography of the city and its surrounding region, but also in the process furthered the "Christianization" of the Roman empire and redefined the shape of religious orthodoxy.

Shepardson exposes the opportunism and serendipity of the Christianization process resulting from the chaos of the statues riot of 387 and its aftermath.[161]

Although few sites bear definitive archaeological witness to the competition for control of ritual places, literary accounts provide rich detail of how rival communities used buildings as arenas for negotiating and promulgating their power and constructing their religious identifications, or at least of how their authors saw and attempted to convey their own architectural control as vehicles for demonstrating their power and signifying the defeat of their opponents.

---

of epigraphic and archaeological studies have highlighted a boom in urban construction in African towns from the late first through early third centuries. While adopting many 'Roman' monuments, those responsible for public building programmes did not hesitate to make modifications in their design and scale. ... Study of both honorific/triumphal arches and capitolia shows that the former to a greater extent than the latter were connected with the promotion of towns, suggesting that Romanization was manifested in architectural monuments signifying loyalty to the emperor" (David J. Mattingly and R. Bruce Hitchner, "Roman Africa: An Archaeological Review," *The Journal of Roman Studies* 85(1995): 165–213, p. 185).

[158] Elizabeth Fentress, "Romanizing the Berbers," *Past and Present* 190 (February 1996): 3–33, p. 31.

[159] van Dam, *Roman Revolution*, p. 255.

[160] Shepardson, *Controlling Contested Places*, p. 10.

[161] Shepardson, *Controlling Contested Places*, pp. 146–160.

Property seizure and destruction was a well-established phenomenon in the Roman empire, whether as an outburst of mob violence or as a strategy of Roman imperial policy.[162] Emperors destroyed property in the course of their foreign conquests and as a punishment in judicial verdicts against its own citizens.[163] When used against enemies in battle or targeted at individual citizens, this strategy was portrayed by literary elites as a justifiable exercise of imperial power necessary for gaining control or maintaining order.[164] When targeted against whole classes of Roman citizens, however, this strategy drew enough attention to warrant comment.

Shaw's analysis of the literature produced in the midst of this conflict demonstrates that when the property of an entire *group* of citizens came under attack, and *they* were dispossessed of their own buildings, they were incited to lodge formal complaints in imperial courts and to publicly declaim the injustices done to them in sermons and letters. Court petitions filed in 313–314, the 340s, and the 390s–400s ensured that "the courts were an ever-present third-party representing the arbitrating power of the state that continually affected the ways in which the two sides were represented: not as catervic gangs but rather as parties to a legal dispute."[165] Catholics petitioned the imperial court rather than using the local governor and administrative bureaucracy.[166]

The court's legislative response to these petitions often provoked the very violence it sought to avoid: "the issuing of enabling legislation, requiring enforcement on the one hand and encouraging betrayal on the other, excited violent behavior."[167] Some of these attacks were launched by ad hoc groups of citizens without imperial consent and thereby violated imperial

---

[162] Second-century mob violence resulted in an attack on a "basilica" in Kolyda, Lydia (Peter Herrmann and Hasan Malay, *New Documents From Lydia, Denkschriften der Österreichischen Akademie der Wissenschaften, philosophisch-historischen Klasse 340* (Vienna: Verlag der Österreichischen Akademie der Wissenschaften, 2007): 110–113 = ILydiaHM no. 84, discussed in Angelos Chaniotis, "The Conversion of the Temple of Aphrodite at Aphrodisias in Context," in *From Temple to Church*, pp. 243–274).

[163] See, for example, *Cod. theod.* 7.12.1, 9.16.1, 9.21.1, 9.29.2, 12.6.5.

[164] Gaddis, *Religious Violence*, pp. 7–10.

[165] Shaw, *Sacred Violence*, p. 63. For the years 312/313–314: Optatus, *de schism. Don.* 1.22.1–2, App. 3 (*Ep. Const. Aelaf.*), 7 (*Ep. Const. Cels.*), 9 (*Ep. Const. episc. Afric.*), 10 (*Ep. Const. Zeu.*), Aug. *Ep.* 88.2, *C. litt. Petil.* 1.4.7, 1.5.10, 1.8.13, Eusebius, *Hist. eccl.* 10.5.18–20, 10.6; 340s: *Concil. Serd.* 8, discussed in Shaw, pp. 194–196; 390s–400s: *Concil. Carth., Concil. Carth.* September 13, 401 = *Reg. Eccl. Carth. Excerpt.* 84 (CCL 149: 205), *Concil. Carth.*, June 16, 404 (CCL 149: 211), Aug. *Ep.* 108.18, discussed in Shaw, pp. 224–229, 142–145, 694–695.

[166] Johannes Hahn, "The Challenge of Religious Violence: Imperial Ideology and Policy in the Fourth Century," in *Contested Monarchy: Integrating the Roman Empire in the Fourth Century AD*, ed. Johannes Wienand, pp. 379–404 (New York: Oxford University Press, 2015), p. 390.

[167] Shaw, *Sacred Violence*, p. 695.

laws, such as the mob attacks in Madauros in the early 390s.[168] Complaints
against these illicit actions stood the highest chances of receiving state punishment, while those against attacks sanctioned or assisted by imperial officers were generally overlooked or minimized.[169] Yet there was a large grey
area, where victims petitioned imperial authorities to intervene, forcing
state officials to take sides in the power struggle. This was the case in 347
when the emperor sent his court officers Paul and Macarius to enforce his
edict of Christian unity.[170] On numerous occasions these conflicts elicited
wholesale legislation that used the strategy of spatial control to condemn
entire groups of Roman citizens.[171]

Place was, therefore, a visible arena in which those vying for power
could contest their control. It might come as no surprise for those
familiar with the conflicts of the post-Diocletian century to learn that
battles for spatial control in Roman North Africa were waged more vig-
orously *among* Christians of various sorts than *between* Christians and
non-Christians. Although Constantine sought to eradicate certain ritual
practices from holy places that offended Christian sensibilities, he did not
generally confiscate ritual buildings of non-Christians as he did those of
Christians.[172] He certainly did not sanction the destruction of temples.[173]

---

[168] Aug. *Ep.* 16.2, tr. Shaw, *Sacred Violence*, p. 237 (CSEL 34.1): *diis hominibusque odiosa nomina,
qui conscientia nefandorum facinorum specie gloriosiae mortis scelera sua sceleribus cumulantes dignum moribus factisque suis exitum maculati reppererunt* (They are men who, in the shared guilt
of their unspeakable and evil acts, and for the sake of achieving a glorious death, pile one
criminal act upon another and, so defiled, acquire a death worthy of their own characters
and deeds).

[169] For the former, see the letter of the dissident bishops to Constantine in Optatus, *de schism.
Don.* 1.22.1–2; For the latter, see the case of the 401 attack on the statue of Hercules by
zealous Christians that only incurred a reprimand (Aug. *Serm.* 24.6, discussed in Shaw,
Sacred Violence, p. 230).

[170] Since the text of the edict does not survive, we are reliant for its contents on the account
of Optatus (*Parm.* 3.3.6 – 3.4.1, discussed in Chapter 3). See the analysis by Shaw (*Sacred
Violence*, p. 164).

[171] *Cod. theod.* 16.5.4, 11, 12, 14.

[172] Emmel et al. "'From Temple to Church,'" pp. 2–4.

[173] Eusebius, *Vit. Const.* 2.60.2, tr. Cameron and Hall (GCS 7): ταῦτα εἶπον, ταῦτα
διεξῆλθον μακρότερον ἢ ὁ τῆς ἐμῆς ἐπιεικείας ἀπαιτεῖ σκοπός, ἐπειδὴ τὴν τῆς ἀληθείας
ἀποκρύψασθαι πίστιν οὐκ ἐβουλόμην, μάλισθ᾽ ὅτι τινὲς ὡς ἀκούω φασὶ τῶν ναῶν
περιῃρῆσθαι τὰ ἔθη καὶ τοῦ σκότους τὴν ἐξουσίαν. ὅπερ συνεβούλευσα ἂν πᾶσιν
ἀνθρώποις, εἰ μὴ τῆς μοχθηρᾶς πλάνης ἡ βίαιος ἐπανάστασις ἐπὶ βλάβῃ τῆς κοινῆς
σωτηρίας ἀμέτρως ταῖς ἐνίων ψυχαῖς ἐμπεπήγει (I have said these things and explained
them at greater length than the purpose of my clemency requires, because I did not wish
to conceal my belief in the truth; especially since [so I hear] some persons are saying that
the customs of the temples and the agency of darkness have been removed altogether. I
would indeed have recommended that to all mankind, were it not that the violent rebel-
liousness of injurious error is so obstinately fixed in the minds of some to the detriment of

It was not until 399 that emperors Arcadius and Honorius ordered the confiscation of idols from temples in Carthage ("deconsecration"), and even this law included the limitation "that the condition of the buildings shall remain unimpaired."[174] This law stands in marked contrast to Egypt and the East, where harsher legislation applied.[175] Despite imperial efforts, it seems that local attempts to execute the decree met with sufficient backlash to force local authorities to back down in order to keep the peace.[176]

Sporadic conflicts in the physical realm relied on interpreters to construct meaning for those who viewed and learned of these conflicts. The literary discourse of spatial supersession developed to explain the significance of a particular spatial transformation or ownership transfer for the identification of this or that group. Emperors as well as other elites created and marshaled new vocabulary to interpret spatial practice and inform spatial discourse. Structures that may have once been understood as the province of Christians in general were labeled by Christian emperors and elites as the domain of "Catholics" to distinguish places occupied by imperially sanctioned Christians from those of others.

The term "Catholics" referred to those who met in certain places in addition to those who subscribed to the purportedly "universally" acclaimed Christian rites and doctrines. Those who gathered in other places received other appellations that emphasized their otherness: "Donatist," "Novatianist," or "Maximianist," after leaders associated with each of these movements. Without this campaign to distinguish and marginalize sectarian groups through rhetoric and place, the view of the average North African as expressed by Augustine in a 414 CE sermon would likely have held sway: "'God's here and God's there, what's the difference? It's people quarreling who have made these divisions. God is to be worshiped everywhere.'"[177] Christian polemicists applied the term "pagan" to places once

---

the common weal). See the general discussion of Constantine's policies toward traditional Roman cults in Van Dam, *Roman Revolution*, pp. 27–34 and David Potter, *Constantine the Emperor* (New York: Oxford University Press, 2013), pp. 276–277, 281.

[174] *Cod. theod.* 16.10.18, tr. Clyde Pharr, *The Theodosian Code and Novels, and the Sirmondian Constitutions, The Corpus of Roman Law = Corpus Juris Romani I.* (Princeton, NJ: Princeton University Press, 1952): *ut aedificiorum quidem sit integer status.* See also Aug. *Serm.* 62.18 and see in particular the ban on pagan rites in *Cod. theod.* 16.10.17, but note the permission of feasts.

[175] *Cod. theod.* 16.10.10, 11, 16.

[176] See in particular the Hercules beard incident (Aug. *Serm.* 24) and the Sufetula incident (Aug. *Ep.* 50).

[177] Aug. *Serm.* 46.15, tr. Hill (pt. 3 vol. 2, p. 273) (CSEL 41): *et hac et hac deus est, quid interest? homines inter se litigantes hoc fecerunt. ubicumque colendus est deus.*

understood as the province of all Romans as a way to distinguish Christian from non-Christian space. Imperial laws decreed that these non-sanctioned groups be evicted and banned from congregating in public, and later private, places. Rhetoric conspired with spatial dominance to privilege certain religious groups and marginalize others.

I

FOUNDATIONAL ASSUMPTIONS

AMONG SETTLED PEOPLES, THE BUILT environment constitutes that part of the human physical experience which is shaped by
human notions of space, often referred to as "place."[1] French philosopher
Henri Lefebvre is often credited with this distinction between the undif-
ferentiated, meaning-less environment (space) and the differentiated, mean-
ing-full environment (place), yet it can be traced back to the existentialist
philosopher Martin Heidegger, whom Lefebvre occasionally cites:[2] "Place
is not located in a pre-given space, after the manner of physical technologi-
cal space. The latter unfolds itself only through the reigning of places of a
region."[3] Heidegger rejects the Kantian subject/object distinction, asserting that space is an aspect of the human experience rather than a feature
of the mind. This phenomenology is one of Lefebvre's jumping off points,
though he rejects Heidegger's narrow "obsession with absolute space" on
account of its ahistoricity.[4] In an attempt to combine the phenomenological with the historical, Lefebvre turns to the more current anthropological work of architectural theorist Amos Rapoport, who helped to create

---

[1] The distinction between the terms "space" and "place" has a checkered history. The words
are sometimes used interchangeably, or they are employed in opposite ways by different
authors to make the same distinction (Compare Jonathan Z. Smith, *To Take Place: Toward
Theory in Ritual* (Chicago, IL: University of Chicago Press, 1987) and Michel de Certeau,
The Practice of Everyday Life (Berkeley, CA: University of California Press, 1984)). Lefebvre
never uses the term "place," preferring to qualify the term "space" with adjectives to distinguish various meanings. Except when quoting and discussing Lefebvre's work, I follow
Smith's usage, employing the term "place" to refer to the human encounter with the physical environment.

[2] Henri Lefebvre, *The Production of Space*, tr. Donald Nicholson-Smith (Malden, MA:
Blackwell Publishing, 1974: 1991).

[3] Heidegger, "Die Kunst und der Raum," tr. Charles H. Seibert, "Martin Heidegger: Art and
Space," *Continental Philosophy Review* 6.1 (February 1973): 3–8, p. 6.

[4] Lefebvre, *The Production of Space*, p. 122.

the environment-behavior movement.[5] Therefore Lefebvre's spatial theory relies on what he calls "the long *history of space*":[6] different expressions of place reflect different social circumstances in different historical contexts.[7]

Though not sharing all of his conclusions, the current study embraces the phenomenological viewpoint that place is a social product. To Lefebvre, places not only serve as arenas for the performance of human activities, they represent social meanings to those who conceive, finance, build, observe, use, and discuss them. These social meanings reveal how these individuals related to the world in which they lived, and how they wanted that world and those relationships to be understood by others. Inhabitants of the Roman empire lived in a world which they viewed as abundant in meaning. Interpreters in all areas of life conveyed its meaning to their audiences. Historians interpreted events past and present. Haruspices interpreted animal entrails. Astrologers interpreted skyscapes. The North African writers whose works survive interpreted religious spaces for their audiences, and, although less retrievable to the modern inquisitor, their audiences experienced those spaces for themselves and no doubt constructed their own meanings of them. This study explores how the battle over places regarded as "sacred" or "holy" affects their production.

As Ann Marie Yasin and previous scholars have shown, the first three centuries of Christian spatiality were characterized by ambiguity. On the one hand, polemicists and apologists rejected the localization of holiness, particularly the housing of divinity as construed by pagan temple-goers.[8] Conversely, adherents perceived their gathering places as distinct from other places and, in some regard, special.[9] Some scholars claim that all of this changed dramatically in the fourth century, citing Constantine's

---

[5] Lefebvre cites Rapoport's *House Form and Culture* on p. 123. Amos Rapoport, "On the Cultural Responsiveness of Architecture," *Journal of Architectural Education* 41.1 (Autumn, 1987): 10–15.

[6] Lefebvre, *The Production of Space*, p. 116 (emphasis in original).

[7] Lefebvre complains that "anthropologists cannot hide the fact that the space and tendencies of modernity (i.e. of modern capitalism) will never be discovered either in Kenya or among French or any other peasants" (*The Production of Space*, p.123). He also objects that sociologists and historians of religion, such as Claude Lévi-Strauss, Emile Durkheim, and Mircea Eliade, had tended to ignore the history of space in their analyses of cross-cultural comparisons (Claude Lévi-Strauss, *The Savage Mind* (Chicago, IL: University of Chicago Press, 1962: 1966), Durkheim, *The Elementary Forms of Religious Life*, tr. K. E. Fields (New York: The Free Press, 1912: 1995) and Eliade, *The Sacred and the Profane* (Orlando, FL: Harcourt, Inc., 1957: 1987)).

[8] Ann Marie Yasin, *Saints and Church Spaces in the Late Antique Mediterranean: Architecture, Cult and Community* (New York: Cambridge University Press, 2009), p. 26.

[9] Yasin, *Saints and Church Spaces*, pp. 34–44.

reconfiguration of the Holy Land landscape as the "tipping point" in this transformation.[10] The Constantinian project of church-building ushered in a new era of "place-bound sacrality, or the 'invention' of an early Christian concept of sacred place."[11] As I demonstrate in Chapter 2, however, this perceptual shift unfolds gradually; as early as the third century, religious place is perceived not only as special, but as an appropriate stage for negotiating group identification. During the mid-third-century Decian persecution, Cyprian attests to the splintering of factions into separate worship places over the controversy surrounding communion for lapsed Christians and the reconciliation conflict that followed.[12] Controversies over reconciliation and rebaptism regarding what to do with Christians who had lapsed during persecution divided the Christian community into opposing camps, both ideologically and physically. Different practices, rooted in different beliefs, led those who opposed Cyprian's position to move into new worship places. This spatial differentiation allowed Cyprian to claim that his camp was the true Church, while his opponents were the schismatics or heretics: "we did not withdraw from them, but they from us" (paraphrasing 1 Jn. 2:19).[13] Because each faction identified its own worship place with its particular type of Christianity, a place in which other factions were unwelcome, the meaning of factional distinctions came to be associated with the place itself.

Despite some Christians' unambiguous division of their environment into demonic and non-demonic spaces, other North African writings reveal a more ambivalent perception of place. The second-/early-third-century Christian lawyer Minucius Felix presents the anti-Christian interlocutor in his apology as claiming that Christians "have no altars, no temples, and no recognizable images," while simultaneously condemning the growth of Christians' "shameful shrines (*sacraria*) of impious intercourse."[14] The strategy of spatial

---

[10] See, for example, Andrew Jacobs, *Remains of the Jews: The Holy Land and Christian Empire in Late Antiquity* (Stanford, CA: Stanford University Press, 2004), p. 2; Yasin, *Saints and Church Spaces*, pp. 34–44.

[11] Yasin, *Saints and Church Spaces*, p. 26.

[12] Cypr. *Unit. eccl.* 12 (CCL 3): *non enim nos ab illis, sed illi a nobis recesserunt* ... Cyprian has earlier quoted 1 John 2:19 as a prooftext to support his view of schismatics (*Unit. eccl.* 9). See the discussion in J. Patout Burns, *Cyprian the Bishop*. Routledge Early Church Monographs (New York: Routledge, 2002), pp. 4–6.

[13] Cypr. *Unit. eccl.* 12. See also *Adv. Jud.* 3.78 on heretics and schismatics, *Ep.* 59.7.3 on ecclesiastical discipline, 70.3.2 supporting rebaptism, as well as his response to Magnus (*Ep.* 69.1.2), discussed in Burns, *Cyprian*, pp. 115–118. This same logic informs Augustine's accusation against Januarius, dissident bishop of Casae Nigrae and primate of the Numidian province (*Ep.* 88.11).

[14] Minucius Felix, *Octavius* 10.2 (ed. Kytzler, p. 8): ... *nullas aras habent, templa nulla, nulla nota simulacra* ...; 9.2 (ed. Kytzler, p. 6): ... *per universum orbem sacraria ista taeterrima inpiae*

differentiation continued into the fifth century, and was not restricted to North Africa.[15] In a sermon delivered in the first decade of the century, Augustine warned his baptized audience to resist the temptations of the circus:[16]

> There are many who do not lead lives consistent with the baptism they received: look how many have today chosen to crowd into the circus rather than this basilica! ... I suspect that there are some of you here whose friends wanted to drag you off to the circus or to some trashy festival that is being kept. Perhaps these people brought their friends with them to church instead. But whether they brought their friends along, or whether they simply resisted those friends' attempts to lure them to the circus, they have been proved in the water of contradiction.

Augustine believes that those who live their baptism should go to church rather than the circus. The decision to avoid the circus requires being in one place rather than another, thereby activating the Christian facet of their identification rather than their civic one. Augustine recognizes that the members of his audience and those Christians who skipped church to attend the circus use place to perform their identifications. This example from Augustine together with those of Paul, Tertullian, Cyprian, and Minucius Felix demonstrate that the impulse for Catholic Christians to differentiate themselves from adherents of traditional Roman religion and other Christians, as well as the broader Roman populace, occasioned new Christian conceptions about the meaning of place. Violence and imperial law subsequently helped to solidify this conceptual framework into a more materialized expression of religious identification.[17]

---

coitionis adolescunt. See the discussion in Yasin, *Saints and Church Spaces*, pp. 17–34. While Yasin asserts that the holiness of early Christian gathering places derived from the activities that took place there, my discussion focuses on the process of spatial differentiation as revealing places' symbolic meaning.

[15] For Antioch see Shepardson, *Controlling Contested Places*, pp. 28, 95–98, 126–135, 180–182 and Blake Leyerle, *Theatrical Shows and Ascetic Lives. John Chrysostom's Attack on Spiritual Marriage* (Berkeley, CA: University of California Press, 2001), pp. 18–19.

[16] Aug. *Enarrat. Ps.* 80.2, 11, tr. Maria Boulding, *The Works of Saint Augustine* (3rd Release). Electronic Edition. *Expositions of the Psalms*, 73–98, vol. III/18, ed. John E. Rotelle, Past Masters (Charlottesville, VA: InteLex Corporation, 2001) (CCL 39): *sunt enim multi non digne viventes baptismo quod perceperunt: quam multi enim baptizati hodie circum implere, quam istam basilicam maluerunt. ... arbitror esse hic nonnullos quos amici sui volebant rapere ad circum, et ad nescio quas hodiernae festivitatis nugas; forte ipsi illos adduxerunt ad ecclesiam. sed sive ipsi illos adduxerunt, sive ab eis ad circum abduci non potuerunt, in aqua contradictionis probati sunt.*

[17] Thomas Sizgorich has analyzed the ways that narratives of violence, or "militant forms of piety ... became such crucial resources for communal self-fashioning" (Sizgorich, *Violence and Belief in Late Anquity: Militant Devotion in Christianity and Islam* (Philadelphia, PA: University of Pennsylvania Press, 2009), p. 4).

In its growing embrace of solidity, therefore, although Christianity underwent a radical transformation from a church that considered its permanence to reside in the afterlife and regarded the earthly realm as ephemeral to one that invested increasing energy, resources, and symbolic value in its physical manifestations, namely buildings and their objects, the transformation was not sudden but a long, drawn-out process.[18] In his study of religious antiquity, religion theorist Jonathan Z. Smith identified this shift as turning from a "utopian" to "a locative vision of the world."[19] The increased attention to place in modern scholarship has been more generally named the "spatial turn," a term which effectively describes the ancient transformation.[20]

This seemingly dramatic transformation appears less abrupt if we focus our attention on the ideas about place and how they relate to Christian identification, namely "spatialization," instead of on the archaeological record, "materialization." With the spatialization of Christian communal identification in view, we see that the process of using place to shape identifications began in the first century and then materialized progressively over the subsequent 300 years as ideas about identification changed.[21]

In their production of place, practitioners of traditional Roman religion already had a long history of localization. Consider Ammianus Marcellinus' description of the Serapeum in Alexandria, second only to Rome's crowning temple, the Capitolium:[22]

Furthermore there are temples in the city soaring with lofty roofs, among which stands out the Serapeum, for which, granted, there are no words

---

[18] Patricia Cox Miller has called this shift the "material turn," although she was mainly referring to "saintly human bodies in their various 'thingly' permutations" (Patricia Cox Miller, *The Corporeal Imagination. Signifying the Holy in Late Ancient Christianity* (Philadelphia, PA: University of Pennsylvania Press, 2009), pp. 3, 1).

[19] Smith, *Map is Not Territory* (University of Chicago Press in cooperation with E. J. Brill: 1978: 1993), p. 101.

[20] Edward W. Soja appears to have coined the term "spatial turn" in a rhymed tetrameter book review of *Reworking Modernity: Capitalisms and Symbolic Discontent* by Allan Pred and Michael John Watts (*Annals of the Association of American Geographers* 84.1 (March 1994): 168–169, p. 169).

[21] I agree with Miller that the material turn reached an unprecedented level with the "legalization of Christianity by co-emperors Constantine and Licinius in C.E. 313," but its roots can be found earlier (Miller, *The Corporeal Imagination*, p. 4, citing Susan Ashbrook Harvey, *Scenting Salvation: Ancient Christianity and the Olfactory Imagination*. The Transformation of the Classical Heritage 42 (Berkeley, CA: University of California Press, 2006), p. 122).

[22] Ammianus Marcellinus, *Res Gestae* 22.16.12: *His accedunt altis sufflata fastigiis templa. Inter quae eminet Serapeum, quod licet minuatur exilitate verborum, atriis tamen columnariis amplissimis et spirantibus signorum figmentis et reliqua operum multitudine ita est exornatum, ut post Capitolium, quo se venerabilis Roma in aeternum attollit, nihil orbis terrarum ambitiosius cernat.* See Boeft, Drijvers, Hengst, Teitler, *Philological and Historical Commentary on Ammianus*

to do it justice; nevertheless, it is adorned with spacious colonnaded halls, with nearly breathing statues, and many other creations, that after the Capitolium, by which the venerable city of Rome eternally distinguishes itself, the whole world beholds nothing more magnificent.

The idea of civic pride deriving from the majesty of a religious building, in Alexandria's case the Serapeum and in Rome's the Capitolium, was well established in the cultural vernacular of ancient Roman vocabulary.

Some scholars have observed that in contrast to traditional Roman religion, pre-Constantinian Christianity lacked "spatial focalization."[23] As I demonstrate in Chapter 2, this is not entirely true. Although early Christian apologists claimed that the Christian *God* was neither tied to nor contained in one particular place, Christian *people* were localized.[24] Even before Constantine funded the construction of Christian basilicas throughout the empire, North African Christian communities located their ritual practices in particular places, especially their veneration of martyrs. Christian leaders used place to map out identification from the beginning; Christians located themselves, rather than their God, in place. The apostle Paul used heavenly as well as earthly spatial frameworks to construe the difference between those saved in Christ and those condemned in the End Time judgment. He promised believers a dwelling in heaven when they died, and instructed believers to physically distance themselves from places of idolatry.[25] Tertullian mapped this latter aspect of spatialized identification onto the specific African landscape by distinguishing places in Carthage where pious Christians should and should not go.[26] Cyprian differentiated catholic from schismatic space. Both Tertullian and Cyprian identified particular locations as "Christian," such as certain tombs and sites of assembly. By positioning Christians in various places in their environment, writers produced a conception of space that differentiated Christians from their neighbors.

Similarly, late antique Jewish perceptions of sacred place were deeply tied to notions of religious identification and the sacred, as Steven Fine

Marcellinus XXII (Groningen: Egbert Forsten, 1995), p. 298 for the metaphorical use of *sufflata* and the uniqueness of Ammianus' spatial application.

[23] Michael Lipka, *Roman Gods. A Conceptual Approach* (Boston, MA: Brill, 2009), p. 188.

[24] I use the term "localized" and "localization" throughout the book to describe what J. Z. Smith calls "a locative vision of the world" (Smith, *Map is Not Territory*, p. 101).

[25] 2 Cor 5.1–2; 1 Cor 8.10.

[26] Tert. pace *Spect.* John Chrysostom similarly maps Christian orthodoxy onto the landscape of Antioch (C. Shepardson, "Controlling Contested Places: John Chrysostom's Adversus Iudaeos Homilies and the Spatial Politics of Religious Controversy," *JECS* 15.4 (Winter, 2007): 483–516 and *Controlling Contested Places*, pp. 3, 92, 96, 124.

has demonstrated.[27] After the destruction of the Jerusalem temple, concepts about localization, and iconography, gradually shifted to synagogues
and study houses, which Fine has termed "templization" and *imitatio templi*.[28] The prevalence of temple symbolism found in late antique synagogue
decoration, along with notions about the sanctity of the Torah as expressed
in inscriptions, demonstrate the increasing degree to which Jews perceived
synagogues as sacred and replete with meaning. The phenomenon of templization is evident in the synagogue of Hammam Lif, outside Carthage, where
a floor mosaic depicts ceremonial objects that would have been used in the
Jerusalem temple. As noted by Stern these symbols and their accompanying
inscription (discussed in Chapter 5) are among the only features that index
Jewish difference in the synagogue.[29] In all other regards, Hammam Lif is
similar to other North African religious places. Its mosaic style, epigraphic
conventions, devotional objects, and architectural form firmly situate this
synagogue within its late antique North African context.[30] Stern concludes:[31]

> North African Jews used their regional cultural vocabularies to construct
> sacred space dedicated to deity and to publicly record their generosity....
> Jews, just as pagans and Christians, used the devotional vocabularies of
> their immediate environment to index their similarity to, and particular
> differences from, their surrounding cultures. Diverse genres of devotional
> practice facilitated the expression of complex and varied cultural identities.

The Jews of Hammam Lif, therefore, expressed their identifications both
as North Africans and as Jews in various ways in their religious building,
which they called a "sacred synagogue."[32] Like their Christian and Roman
traditionalist neighbors, Jewish production of place simultaneously produced their identifications.

Throughout this book, I use the geographical and anthropological
notions of place identity and place meaning to further understand the
symbolism of sacred places. Over the last half-century, place meaning has
been analyzed in different ways. Historian of religion Mircea Eliade considered sites to be vessels of signification, what he called "cosmological

[27] Steven Fine, *This Holy Place. On the Sanctity of the Synagogue during the Greco-Roman Period*
(Notre Dame, IN: University of Notre Dame Press, 1997), pp. 96–127.
[28] Fine, *This Holy Place*, pp. 32 and 55.
[29] Karen B. Stern, *Inscribing Devotion and Death: Archaeological Evidence for Jewish Populations of
North Africa* (Boston, MA: Brill, 2008), p. 250. Additional distinctive features are found in
other inscriptions, such as the use of office titles and the donation of implements.
[30] Stern, *Inscribing Devotion*, pp. 247–253.
[31] Stern, *Inscribing Devotion*, pp. 252–253.
[32] See my discussion of the appellation *sancta sinagoga* later in Chapter 5.

symbolism."[33] Likewise, architecture theorist David Saile explored how "ritual processes ... transform[ed] ... inert physical and spatial fabric."[34] Architectural anthropologist Labelle Prussin similarly observed that "architecture is created – rather, unfolds – on a stage structured by ... ritual."[35] More related to the subject of this book, Prussin noted that in "places of worship ... the liturgy defines the organization of the enclosed space. ... [T]he historically or legally established, institutionalized system of actions physically dictates the arrangement of assigned spaces."[36] J. Z. Smith also demonstrated that space is situational or dependent for its meaning on what people do there, namely ritual.[37] Differentiation, a key factor in late antique identity construction, figures prominently in Smith's observations. Although Smith's prioritization of ritual is a useful model for some contexts, his analysis begins with already-intact space and does not adequately consider the processes involved in their production.[38]

Certain phenomenologists have overcome this place/action dichotomy by focusing on the body, or bodies, as existing in space.[39] French theorists Henri Lefebvre and Pierre Bourdieu investigated the communal dimension of how space and human action interact.[40] Lefebvre recognized the way that space is intertwined with all aspects of the social in the case of what he calls "religious ideology":[41]

> What is an ideology without a space to which it refers, a space which it describes, whose vocabulary and links it makes use of, and whose code

---

[33] Eliade, *The Sacred and the Profane*, p. 58.
[34] Saile, "The Ritual Establishment of Home," in *Home Environments*, ed. I. Altman and C. M. Werner, pp. 183–212 (New York: Plenum Press, 1983), p. 87.
[35] Prussin, "When Nomads Settle: Changing Technologies of Building and Transport and the Production of Architectural Form among the Gabra, the Rendille, and the Somalis," in *African Material Culture*, ed. Mary Jo Arnoldi, Christraud M. Geary, and Kris L. Hardin, pp. 73–102 (Bloomington and Indianapolis, IN: Indiana University Press, 1996), p. 75.
[36] Prussin, "When Nomads Settle," p. 80.
[37] Smith, "The Bare Facts of Ritual," *History of Religions* 20.½ (August – November 1980): 112–127; *To Take Place*, pp. 26–28. For the terms "substantive" and "situational," see Jeanne Halgren Kilde, *Sacred Power, Sacred Space. An Introduction to Christian Architecture and Worship* (New York: Oxford University Press, 2008), pp. 5, 7.
[38] Smith, *To Take Place* p. 109; R. L. Grimes, *Rite Out of Place: Ritual, Media, and the Arts* (New York: Oxford University Press, 2006), p. 108.
[39] See, for example, Maurice Merleau-Ponty, *The Phenomenology of Perception*, tr. Colin Smith (New York: Humanities Press, 1945: 1962), and Gaston Bachelard, *The Poetics of Space*, tr. Maria Jolas (Boston, MA: Beacon Press; Reprint edition, 1958: 1994).
[40] Lefebvre, *The Production of Space*, pp. 182–183, esp. editor's note 16.
[41] Lefebvre, *The Production of Space*, p. 44. For a discussion of the problematic designation "Judeo-Christian" and its creation as a tool of American politics, see the foundational work by Arthur Allen Cohen, *The Myth of the Judeo-Christian Tradition* (New York: Harper

it embodies? What would remain of a religious ideology – the Judeo-Christian one, say – if it were not based on places and their names: church, confessional, altar, sanctuary, tabernacle? What would remain of the Church if there were no churches? The Christian ideology, carrier of a recognizable if disregarded Judaism (God, the Father, etc.), has created the spaces which guarantee that it endures. More generally speaking, what we call ideology only achieves consistency by intervening in social space and in its production, and by thus taking on body therein. Ideology per se might well be said to consist primarily in a discourse upon social space.

Lefebvre thus suggests that the spatial-discursive feature of religion is not inherent in space itself; it is constructed, sometimes over a long period of time. When applied to the first four centuries of the Common Era, this process of construction reveals a significant transition in late antique conceptions of place. Furthermore Lefebvre observed that "spatial practice regulates life – it does not create it. Space has no power 'in itself.'"[42] For its power, space relies on its mental and social dimensions. In Lefebvre's analysis, "space" is both "perceived" and "conceived" as well as "lived."[43] I employ Lefebvre's typology of the human interaction with place in this book, using the terms "perceive," "conceive," and "lived" (or "experienced") to refer to the (1) mental, (2) social, and (3) physical dimensions of space, all of which help explain how ancient North Africans interacted with their built environment.

Similarly Bourdieu proposed that place meaning began with the "mental structures" that produced them.[44] Bourdieu argued that the built environment was "structured according to ... mythico-ritual oppositions."[45] *Habitus*, the system of dispositions (practices) performed at particular times and locations, do not impute meanings (particularly social structures) so much as they reveal and reproduce them: "inhabited space ... is the principal locus for the objectification of the generative schemes."[46] Bourdieu further described the role of space in creating and transmitting culture: "All the actions performed in a space ... are immediately qualified symbolically and function as so many structural exercises through which is built up practical mastery of

and Row, 1969). Lefebvre's use of the term "ideology" to refer to religion must be understood within the context of his Marxist views and should not be taken too literally.
[42] Lefebvre, *The Production of Space*, p. 358.
[43] Lefebvre, *The Production of Space*, p. 39.
[44] Bourdieu, *Outline of a Theory of Practice*, tr. Richard Nice, Cambridge Studies in Social and Cultural Anthropology 16 (Cambridge: Cambridge University Press, 1977: 1998), p. 91.
[45] Bourdieu, *Outline of a Theory of Practice*, p. 89.
[46] Bourdieu, *Outline of a Theory of Practice*, p. 89; see also pp. 90–92.

the fundamental schemes."[47] These "fundamental schemes" are the "mental structures," the shared perceptions, that comprise culture.

In addition to the conceptual aspect of space, Yi-Fu Tuan has explored the "states of minds, thoughts and feelings … the ways people attach meaning to and organize space and place."[48] Tuan embraces the full range of human experiences, from emotion to thought, as data.[49] He includes the human body's sensory experiences along with thoughts and feelings about space in his inventory of the human encounter with the external world. He notes that "space is a special kind of object. It is a concretion of value."[50] This "concretion," or concretization, of value is achieved through a "total" experience which involves "all the senses as well as … the active and reflexive mind."[51] Tuan demonstrates that "it is a characteristic of the symbol-making human species that its members can become passionately attached to places of enormous size … of which they can have only limited experience."[52] In his earlier work, Tuan employed the term "topophilia" to describe this peculiarly human capacity for place attachment, yet he felt that did not adequately describe the full range of human experience of space and place.[53]

Furthermore, Tuan highlights the role of "permanence" in creating place attachment:[54]

> Permanence is an important element in the idea of place. Things and objects endure and are dependable in ways that human beings, with their biological weaknesses and shifting moods, do not endure and are not dependable.

This perceived quality of durability informed the place attachment of late antique Romans, thus rendering building destruction, as opposed to repurposing, a last resort. Despite this quality of durability, place attachment and meaning is susceptible to change, depending on people's experiences in that place, particularly human encounters.[55] As we shall see in the case of Roman North Africa, human experience can either devalue or elevate

---

[47] Bourdieu, *Outline of a Theory of Practice*, p. 91.
[48] Yi-Fu Tuan, *Space and Place: The Perspective of Experience* (Minneapolis, MN: University of Minnesota Press, 1977: 2001), p. 5.
[49] Tuan, *Space and Place*, p. 8.
[50] Tuan, *Space and Place*, p. 10.
[51] Tuan, *Space and Place*, p. 16.
[52] Tuan, *Space and Place*, p. 18.
[53] Tuan, *Topophilia: A Study of Environmental Perception, Attitudes, and Values* (Englewood Cliffs, NJ: Prentice-Hall, 1974); See his self-critique in *Space and Place*, p. v.
[54] Tuan, *Space and Place*, p. 140.
[55] Tuan, *Space and Place*, p. 140. Tuan cites Augustine's association of his once-cherished home town Thagaste with the death of his childhood friend.

place attachment and meaning. Finally, Tuan keenly observes that human beings possess remarkable adaptability and resilience for relocating places of supreme value when events such as destruction or exile force them to abandon those places.[56] Because supreme value like "center" can be "a concept in mythic thought rather than a deeply felt value bound to unique events and locality ... it can be moved as human beings themselves move."[57] This capacity for relocation also plays a role in late antique North African negotiation of religious sites.

Ancient elite writers reveal some of these mental, affective, sensory, and social dimensions of place when they interpret spatial interaction symbolically. In their study of the transformation of late antique Roman temples into churches, Stephen Emmel, Ulrich Gotter, and Johannes Hahn have coined the useful term "perceptual-symbolic quality" to describe this symbolic aspect of spatial interpretation.[58] The power of spatial supremacy's "perceptual-symbolic quality" made it a useful rhetorical tool for Christian historians to construct a narrative of Christian triumphalism. Symbolizing resistance on the part of the vanquished as well as dominance for the victor, the motif of spatial supremacy became a stock rhetorical device in narratives about religious conflict, even when these narratives ignored or distorted facts on the ground.[59] Furthermore, Emmel, Gotter, and Hahn propose that inconsistencies between archaeological remains and literary evidence demonstrate ancient authors' intent to represent and interpret spatial phenomena in ways that serve their particular agendas.[60] This interpretation of evidentiary discrepancy is among the foundational assumptions of the current study.

The agendas of ancient authors included exerting difference and dominance. By contesting place attachments and place meanings, ancient authors

---

[56] Tuan, *Space and Place*, pp. 149–150.

[57] Tuan, *Space and Place*, p. 150.

[58] Stephen Emmel, Ulrich Gotter, and Johannes Hahn, "'From Temple to Church': Analysing a Late Antique Phenomenon of Transformation," in *From Temple to Church. Destruction and Renewal of Local Cultic Topography in Late Antiquity*, ed. Johannes Hahn, Stephen Emmel, and Ulrich Gotter (Boston, MA: Brill, 2008): 1–24, p. 3.

[59] See later Greek hagiography as discussed by Helen Saradi, "The Christianization of Pagan Temples in the Greek Hagiographical Texts," in *From Temple to Church*, ed. Johannes Hahn, Stephen Emmel, and Ulrich Gotter, pp. 113–134 (Boston, MA: Brill, 2008).

[60] This approach contradicts the methodology expressed by Gisella Cantino Wataghin, that such discrepancies are the product of modern scholarly misunderstanding of the evidence: "[A]rchaeological and written sources are given equal significance, although each must be considered on its own terms; discrepancies between them may mean that one or maybe both have not been correctly understood" ("Christian Topography in the Late Antique Town," in *Theory and Practice in Late Antique Archaeology*, Late Antique Archaeology 1, ed. Luke Lavan and William Bowden, pp. 224–256 (Boston, MA: Brill, 2003), p. 251).

laid the necessary groundwork for spatial conflict; in turn, spatial conflict reshaped place attachments and meanings. Geoscientist Steven Semkin and sociocultural anthropologist Elizabeth Brandt have recently demonstrated the role of place attachment in "individual and sociocultural identity."[61] Most useful for my analysis of spatial contestation, they note that "[w]hen different groups have different senses of place attached to the same places or areas, conflict may occur."[62] In other words, high value, in addition to a clash of place meanings, is a necessary condition for spatial contestation. Semkin and Brandt's observations aptly describe the late antique Mediterranean, where rival religious groups attached competing place meanings to contested sites.

In the Roman empire, as in other non-nomadic societies, buildings were positioned, constructed, and decorated according to culturally developed norms of aesthetics, economics, engineering, usage, and symbolism. Architectural treatises and comments suggest that these norms were not only understood but seriously challenged in late antiquity.[63] After all, buildings, unlike their citizen occupants or the parties to which their occupants claimed allegiance, were property, and their control could be managed by legal means as well as by violence and other less savory or even efficient methods. Buildings used for religious rites gave material or physical expression to conflicts whose issues were often intangible. The type of buildings that Christians used for their assemblies helped concretize the abstractions that divided one group from another. Regarding the Catholic–dissident conflict, Peter Brown has observed:[64]

> Every local church was presented as the only place in its locality where the Holy Ghost was to be found. We cannot understand the sharpness of the rivalry between the two churches unless we enter into the conviction

[61] S. Semken and E. Brandt, "Implications of Sense of Place and Place-based Education for Ecological Integrity and Cultural Sustainability in Contested Places," in *Cultural Studies and Environmentalism: The Confluence of Ecojustice, Place-based (Science) Education, and Indigenous Knowledge Systems*, ed. D. Tippins, M. Mueller, M. van Eijck, and J. Adams, pp. 287–302 (New York: Springer Press, 2010), p. 294. See also Susan Davis, *Parades and Power: Street Theater in Nineteenth Century Philadelphia* (Philadelphia, PA: Temple University Press, 1986), p. 13.

[62] Semken and Brandt, "Implications of Sense of Place," p. 294. The authors go on to delineate the strategies deployed in such conflicts: "Places may be contested by competing rhetorics, public campaigns, advertising, political power, legal action, or threat of this where appropriate laws exist, but can also escalate to sabotage, direct conflict, and even wars."

[63] See, for example, the famous story of Hadrian and the architect Apollodorus, as recounted by the Roman historian Cassius Dio. When the architect expressed disapproval of the emperor's design for the Temple of Venus and Roma, the emperor had him executed (*Roman History Epitome of Book 69.4*).

[64] Peter Brown, *Through the Eye of a Needle: Wealth, the Fall of Rome, and the Making of Christianity in the West, 350–550 AD* (Princeton, NJ: Princeton University Press, Kindle Edition, 2013), p. 332.

of the bishops and clergy of each of them that it was their church – and their church alone – in which God dwelt. The church of their rivals was an empty shell, devoid of the presence of God. … Their churches were fake churches, even more sinister than pagan temples had been. Pagan temples reeked with the smoke of incense and sacrifice. They were plainly alien. But dead churches, though they still pretended to be Christian, were as toxic as any temple.

Place conferred a dimension of materiality to the abstractions of group differences. This level of meaning derived from its function as the arena in which a group performed the collective identification its leaders sought to construct.[65] As arenas for developing a certain type of religious place identity, religious buildings provided ideal sites for contesting group identifications.

On a more practical level, buildings and roads channeled where people went, and for what purpose. As Ramsay Macmullen has demonstrated, Christian rites were performed in open places, like cemeteries, as well as behind closed doors, in buildings that needed to accommodate worshippers in enclosed places.[66] As clergy attempted to gain control over open places by building enclosed martyr shrines and stationing door-keepers at their entrances who permitted the performance of only episcopally sanctioned rituals, Christian placement was increasingly regulated.[67] In both capacities of conveying meaning and conveying bodies, place was a tool used to negotiate and navigate social arrangements.

Church-building was the means by which a Christian community could put itself on the map, reaping the benefits of the prestige and power exercised by its seated bishop. As Brown puts it, "each church was an argument in stone in favor of one church or the other."[68] Leslie Dossey has demonstrated how this construction surge revolutionized the landscape of rural North Africa: "It was the *cathedrae* on estates and in villages that transformed the geography of power in North Africa."[69] She points out that

---

[65] Ann Marie Yasin characterizes this function of churches as three-fold: communion, theophany, and collective memory, or "community, ritual, and commemoration" (*Saints and Church Spaces*, p. 44).

[66] Ramsay Macmullen, *The Second Church. Popular Christianity A.D. 200–400*. Writings from the Greco-Roman World Supplement (Atlanta, GA: Society of Biblical Literature, 2009), pp. 52–53.

[67] For a more thorough discussion of this process, see my doctoral dissertation, "Ritual Power in Society: Ritualizing Late Antique North African Martyr Cult Activities and Social Changes in Gender and Status" (Ph.D. diss., The University of Pennsylvania, 2002).

[68] Brown, *Through the Eye of a Needle*, p. 334.

[69] Dossey, *Peasant and Empire in Christian North Africa* (Berkeley, CA: University of California Press, 2010), p. 136.

those who built these rural basilicas and elected the bishops who served them were formerly disparate *plebes*; their joint efforts united them as new Christian communities.[70]

Some of these structures also provided their communities with additional sources of income from pilgrims seeking to be healed or gain spiritual inspiration, which added an economic layer of significance to their multiple meanings. Rural martyr shrines on estates like Victoriana, with relics of the Milanese martyrs Protasius and Gervasius, or Fussala, Caspalium, Sinita, and Audurus Fundus, with relics of St. Stephen, offered miraculous healing to their visitors.[71] Similar building strategies were employed in suburban and urban areas for martyr shrines, like those in Calama and Hippo dedicated to St. Stephen, that attracted travelers from as far as Asia Minor.[72] The wealthy presbyter, Leporius, built a hostel for pilgrims in Hippo that earned revenue for the Church.[73] Even smaller towns like Uzalis joined the building boom. These new buildings were the locus of economic as well as social functions like caring for the sick, the poor, and the dead, creating new relational networks, and adjudicating interpersonal disputes.[74]

The same could be said for traditional Roman temples and synagogues. Both provided a range of social services, like tending the sick, supporting

---

[70] Dossey, *Peasant and Empire*, p. 136, citing AE (1894), 138: Venusianenses initiaverunt, (M?)ucrionenses columnas V dederunt, Cuzab(e)tenses dederunt columnas VI, omnes apsida[m] straverunt, plus Cuzabete(n)ses ornaverunt, Rogatus presbiter et Emilius zacon [=diaconius] edificaverunt (The Venusianenses began it, the Mucrionenses donated five columns, the Cuzabetenses donated six columns, all paved the apse, the Cuzabetenses decorated it the most). See also discussion in Brown, *Through the Eye of a Needle*, pp. 333–337.

[71] Aug. *civ. Dei* 22.8, discussed by Yvette Duval, *Loca Sanctorum Africae: Le culte des martyrs en Afrique du IVe au VIIe siècle. Collection de L'école française de Rome 58*, vol. 2 (Rome: École française de Rome, 1982), pp. 625–626, 655; and Jessica Gadis, "Caving Into The Will Of The Masses?: Relics In Augustine's City Of God," *Scripps Senior Theses. Paper 694*. 2015. Accessed at http://scholarship.claremont.edu/scripps_theses/694, on August 31, 2015.

[72] Paulus and Palladia came from Cappadocia seeking healing at the shrine of St. Stephen ("Paulus 8," *PCA* 1: 844; "Palladia," *PCA* 1: 809–810; Aug. *civ. dei* 22.8, *Serm.* 320, and *Serm.* 322.2).

[73] Aug. *Serm.* 356.10 (*Saint Augustine: Opera Omnia – Corpus Augustinianum Gissense. Sermones*: Part 1, tr. Hill, *The Works of Saint Augustine* (3rd Release). Electronic Edition. *Sermons* (341–400) on Various Subjects. Vol. III/10 (Charlottesville, VA: InteLex Corporation, 2001) (C. Lambot, "Sancti Aurelii Augustini Sermones selecti duodeviginti," *Stromata Patristica et Mediaevalia* 1 (1950): 139): *coepit enim de pecunia quae data erat ecclesiae propter xenodochium, et cum coepisset aedificare, ut sunt religiosi desiderantes opera sua in caelo scribi, adiuverunt prout quisque voluit, et fabricavit* (He began it, you see, with the money which had been given to the Church for the hostel, and when he had started building, devout people who desire to have their works recorded in heaven gave their help to the extent each wished, and up the building went).

[74] Brown, *Through the Eye of a Needle* and Dossey, *Peasant and Empire*.

the poor, and feeding the community.[75] In his famous letter to Arsacius, high-priest of Galatia, the emperor Julian bemoaned the decline of such services among gentiles:[76]

> For it is disgraceful that, when no Jew has to beg and the ungodly Galileans support their own needy and ours, our people are seen to lack assistance from us. Teach those who adhere to the Hellenic religion to make their contribution to these responsibilities … Accustom the Hellenes to these acts of generosity, teaching them that these have been our practice from ancient times.

By serving multiple roles in the lives of their users, religious buildings accumulated layers of meanings that informed the identifications of those users. Because of their diversity and fluidity, these meanings may elude modern interpreters. Nonetheless, the evidence allows us to conclude that each activity performed in these sites expressed and shaped certain self-understandings of their participants. Because these places symbolized a whole web of beliefs, social networks, and social functions, they were ideal stages for contesting these very aspects of religious group identification.

---

[75] For temples, see, for example, the Aesklepieia at Timgad, Lambaesis, Thignica, Musti, Thuburbo Maius, and Carthage (Tert. *Idol.* 20.2). Ghislaine van der Ploeg notes that "Asclepius was the most commonly worshipped healing deity in Roman Africa with most extant inscriptions dating to the 2nd century AD, indicating the height of the cult at that time" ("Sacred Laws in the Cult of Asclepius," *Rosetta* 14 (2013): 71–87, p. 14). For synagogues, see Julian's letter 84, noted subsequently, and the dining rooms excavated at Ostia, Aphrodisias, Delos, Caesarea, and Jerusalem (discussed in Lee Levine, *The Ancient Synagogue: The First 1000 Years* (New Haven, CT: Yale University Press: 2000: 2005), p. 292), as well as the rabbinic texts referring to communal meals held there (Y. Mo'ed Qatan 2, 3, 81b; Y. Sanhed. 8, 2, 26a–b; *Ber. Rab.* 65.15, discussed in Levine, *Ancient Synagogue*, p. 393 and Fine, *Art and Judaism* p. 177, and Z. Safrai, "The Communal Functions of the Synagogue in the Land of Israel in the Rabbinic Period," in *Ancient Synagogues: Historical Analysis and Archaeological Discovery* 1, ed. D. Urman and P.V. M. Flesher, pp. 181–204 (Leiden: E. J. Brill, 1995), p. 197). The view that one of the rooms at Hammam Lif also served this function is speculative (Levine, *Ancient Synagogue*, p. 387).

[76] Julian, *Lettres* (ed. Bidez), no. 84 (tr. A. D. Lee, *Pagans and Christians in Late Antiquity: A Sourcebook* (New York: Routledge, 2000), p. 98): Αἰσχρὸν γὰρ εἰ τῶν μὲν Ἰουδαίων οὐδὲ εἷς μεταιτεῖ, τρέφουσι δὲ οἱ δυσσεβεῖς Γαλιλαῖοι πρὸς τοῖς ἑαυτῶν καὶ τοὺς ἡμετέρους, οἱ δὲ ἡμέτεροι τῆς παρ' ἡμῶν ἐπικουρίας ἐνδεεῖς φαίνοιντο. δίδασκε δὲ καὶ συνεισφέρειν τοὺς Ἑλληνιστὰς εἰς τὰς τοιαύτας λειτουργίας … καὶ τοὺς Ἑλληνικοὺς ταῖς τοιαύταις εὐποιίαις προσέθιζε, διδάσκων αὐτοὺς ὡς τοῦτο πάλαι ἦν ἡμέτερον ἔργον. See the discussions in Harold A. Drake, *Constantine and the Bishops. The Politics of Intolerance* (Baltimore, MD: Johns Hopkins University Press, 2000), pp. 341–343, Demetrios J. Constantelos, "The Hellenic Background and Nature of Patristic Philanthropy in the Early Byzantine Era," in *Wealth and Poverty in Early Church and Society*, ed. Susan R. Holman, pp. 187–208 (Grand Rapids, MI: Baker Academic, 2008) and Glen Bowersock, *Julian the Apostate* (Cambridge, MA: Harvard University Press, 1978), pp. 87–88.

Memory and Place

What made religious places particularly potent for expressing changes in religious identifications and the resulting conflict may be so commonplace, or naturalized, that we take the phenomenon for granted. Space is an agent of memory, as Maurice Halbwachs has shown.[77] As philosopher Dylan Trigg eloquently puts it, "Without the memory of places, memory itself would no longer have a role to play in our conscious lives."[78] In antiquity, space was employed as a mnemonic device in rhetorical education.[79] A speaker could commit to memory the order of his remarks by picturing their central themes as located in various rooms, a memorization technique commonly referred to today as the "memory palace."[80] Augustine alludes to this technique in his *Confessions*, where he describes his own recollections in architectural terms: "And so I come to the fields and vast palaces of memory. ... From that I turned inward to the depths of my memory, like so many vast rooms filled so wonderfully with things beyond number ..."[81]

The importance of place to the faculty of memory is explored by Roger Friedland and Richard D. Hecht in their introduction to the volume *Religion, Violence, Memory, and Place*. They propose a series of axioms about sacred sites.[82] Although not all of these axioms apply to antiquity, and some

---

[77] Halbwachs, *Les cadres sociaux de la mémoire* (Paris: F. Alcan, 1925), p. 134. I thank E. Castelli for introducing me to this work. To memory Halbwachs adds society and time. I reject his distinction between history and memory, which correlates to the German Enlightenment distinction between *Historie* (the objective science) and *Geschichte* (what is memorable).

[78] Trigg, *The Memory of Place: A Phenomenology of the Uncanny* (Athens, OH: Ohio University Press, 2012), p. 1.

[79] The so-called "architectural mnemonic" is described in Rhetorica *Ad Herennium*, an anonymous first century BCE textbook on rhetoric (Thomas W. Benson and Michael H. Prosser, *Readings in Classical Rhetoric* (New York: Routledge, 1969: 2008), p. 290).

[80] Cicero, *Fin.* 5.2, On Moral Ends, ed. Julia Annas, tr. Raphael Woolf, p. 118: *Equidem etiam curiam nostram ... solebam intuens Scipionem, Catonem, Laelium, nostrum vero in primis avum cogitare; tanta vis admonitionis inest in locis; ut non sine causa ex iis memoriae ducta sit disciplina* (Even when I look at our own Senate-house ... I often think of Scipio, Cato, Laelius, and above all, my grandfather. Such is the evocative power that locations possess. No wonder the training of memory is based on them). For a modern reference, see Benedict Carey, "Remembering, as an Extreme Sport," *The New York Times*, May 19, 2014.

[81] Aug. *Conf.* 10. 8.12, 10.40.65, ed. Michael P. Foley (Indianapolis, IN: Hackett Publishing, 1993: 2006), tr. F. J. Sheed, pp. 195, 225: *venio in campos et lata praetoria memoriae ... inde ingressus sum in recessus memoriae meae, multiplices amplitudines plenas miris modis copiarum innumerabilium, et consideravi...*

[82] Oren Baruch Stier and J. Shawn Landres, ed. *Religion, Violence, Memory, and Place* (Bloomington, IN: Indiana University Press, 2006).

of their tenets have already been discussed earlier, two that are both new and relevant to my analysis are:[83]

> Axiom 4: Power and memory must be located at the very beginning. Power and memory are not latecomers. In order to institutionalize a cosmology, it must be put in place. ...

> Axiom 10: Central places, holy places, sacred places, memory places are material and immaterial. Architectural forms of rock, wood, concrete ... are infused with memory ... Matter encases memory and memory shapes matter.

The emplacement of cosmologies, mental constructs of the universe, occurs through the accumulation of place meanings. Trigg makes a similar observation:[84]

> Being attached to a place means allowing memories to be held by that place. In turn, being held by a place means being able to return to that place through its role as a reserve of memories. Not only do places hold memories in a material sense – as the archive of our experiences – but those same places crystallize the experiences that occurred there.

Places become meaningful through their connection to memories. The power to be associated with a variety of meanings, meanings accrued by means of both the individual human capacity for remembering and the creation and perpetuation of collective memories (using a range of strategies), is what makes sacred places particularly effective targets. Because of its identifiability, its physicality, and its fixed position (locatability), a structure is easier to destroy than a memory.

The reciprocal relationship between place and memory helps to explain the salience of place in religious conflicts.[85] Places are connected to individual memories of his or her own experiences in those places, as well as to collective memories of experiences shared there and of others' experiences there. Collective place memories are created through stories told about a certain place, which can be related to a single person or to a large audience, orally or in writing. Storytelling, whether in liturgy, sermons, testimonies, or public readings, was a central feature of late antique North

---

[83] Friedland and Hecht, "The Powers of Place," in *Religion, Violence, Memory, and Place*, ed. Oren Stier and J. Shawn Landres, pp. 17–36 (Bloomington, IN: Indiana University Press), pp. 34–35.

[84] Trigg, *The Memory of Place*, p. 9.

[85] Specific place meanings are sometimes inaccessible to modern interpreters, since the chronological relationship between architectural remains and literature is often indeterminate and the circumstances by which place meanings developed are frequently not preserved. Nonetheless, the broader significance of places is sufficient for understanding contestation.

African religious gatherings. North Africa was one of the first regions to include public readings of martyr-narratives as a regular feature of saints' day commemorations.[86] Even inscriptions were read aloud.[87] Storytelling was also an important literary technique, as revealed in virtually every piece of writing preserved from antiquity.

Place memories were also created through other sensory stimuli: Visually, through wall frescoes, floor mosaics, carvings, furniture and architecture;[88] olfactorily, with ambient smells;[89] auditorily, through music and sound-effects;[90] gustatorily, through the eucharistic sacrament;[91] and kinesthetically through clapping, kissing, kneeling, prostrating, dancing, signing the cross, and, less frequently, immersion and Chrismation.[92] And then there were the various sights, smells, and sounds of the people who shared these sensations. All together the repeated experiences produced powerful place memories.

Commensurate with the power of place memories, the strategy for obliteration of such memories was architectural dispossession. The fifth-century Church historian Socrates Scholasticus recounts the intentional erasure of

---

[86] *Cod. Can. Eccles. Afric. Can.* 36d/46, also *Brev. Hipp. c. 36* (CCSL 149, p. 43): *Liceat etiam legi passiones martyrum, cum anniversarii dies eorum celebrantur* (It is also permitted for the passions of martyrs to be read when their anniversary days are celebrated).

[87] Aug. Serm. 319.7, tr. Hill, modified (PL 38: 1442): *Quid vobis plus dicam et multum loquar? Legite quatuor versus quos in cella scripsimus, legite, tenete, in corde habete. Propterea enim eos ibi scribere voluimus, ut qui vult legat, quando vult legat. Ut omnes teneant, ideo pauci sunt: ut omnes legant, ideo publice scripti sunt. Non opus est ut quaeratur codex: camera illa codex vester sit* (Why should I say any more to you, and talk at length? Read the four lines of the verse which I have written in the shrine; read them, hold onto them, have them by heart. The reason I wanted to have them written there, after all, was so that any who wanted could read them, read them whenever they wanted. So that all could remember them, that's why they are few; so that all could read them, that's why they are written in public. There's no need to go looking for a book; let that little room be your book).

[88] See, for example, the Tabarka funerary portrait in ILCV 2098 = ILTun 1690, and the sculpted column from Oued R'zel (about 20 miles northwest of Bagaï in Numidia) picturing Noah's ark and the dove (See Fig. 2.8).

[89] Cypr. *Ep.* 34.1.

[90] Aug. *Conf.* 9.7.15. For Augustine's own reflection on the correlation between sensory impressions and memory, see *Conf.* 10.30.41–35.57.

[91] Aug. *Enarrat. Ps.* 106.2, 134.5, 141.9, 2 *Enarrat. Ps.* 33.12, *Ep.* 54 (*Retract.* 1.1), and *Io. Ev. tr.* 11.5–6.

[92] Clapping: Aug. *Ep.* 36.12; kissing: pseudo-Aug. *Serm.* 227, s. Dolbeau 4 = 198.16, *Mor. Eccl. Cath.* 1.34.75, and Optatus, *de schism. Don.* 1.15–18; kneeling: Tert. *Paen.* 9, Arnobius, *Ad. nat.* 31, Aug. *Serm.* 90.9, *Io. Ev. tr.* 3.21, and 2 *Enarrat. Ps.* 33.14; prostrating: Tert. *Pud.* 13.6–7 and Cypr. *Laps.* 33; dancing: Aug. *Serm.* 311.5–6 and *Reg. Eccl. Carthag. Excerpta* (401) c. 60; signing the cross: Tert. *Ux.* 2.5.2, *Apol.* 21.2, and *Marc.* 3.22.5–6; immersion: *Faust.* 19.16; Chrismation: Aug. *Serm.* 160.5, 198.51, *Trin.* 15.6.46, Con. Carth. a. 390, 3, and Bru. Hipp. 34.

memory with the second-century construction of the temple of Aphrodite on the site of the holy sepulcher:[93]

> Although those who were well-disposed toward Christ venerated this tomb during the season of his suffering, those who spurned Christ covered the place with earth, built a shrine to Aphrodite, and put up her statue there, so that Christians seeing the statue would not conjure up a memory of the place.

As the passages from Augustine and Socrates reveal, place memory (and its erasure) was appreciated in late antique culture. The idea of preventing conjuration (lit. production, ποιέω) of a specific memory associated with a particular place was deeply rooted in Roman history, and was one of the strategies associated with the practice of what scholars have come to call *damnatio memoriae*.[94]

The obliteration of memory through monument destruction is well attested in the ancient world. As Roman historian Harriet Flower notes:[95]

> Memory sanctions are deliberately designed strategies that aim to change the picture of the past, whether through erasure or redefinition, or by means of both … [S]anctions looked ahead to a future that was never too far away in Rome, a future when a new generation would be learning the story of the (not necessarily so distant) past from the collective remembrance and monuments of the city.

The extent to which memory sanctions "looked ahead to a future" does not apply only to collective remembrance; the imperial decree of 405 addressed to the praetorian prefect of Italy and Africa, known as the "Edict

---

[93] Scholasticus, *hist. eccl.* 1.17.2 (SC 417, electronic version): Οἱ μὲν τὰ τοῦ Χριστοῦ φρονοῦντες μετὰ τὸν καιρὸν τοῦ πάθους ἐτίμων τὸ μνῆμα, οἱ δὲ φυγαδεύσαντες τὰ τοῦ Χριστοῦ <κατέκρυψαν> χώσαντες τὸν τόπον <καὶ> Ἀφροδίτης κατ᾽ αὐτοῦ ναὸν κατασκευάσαντες ἐπέστησαν ἄγαλμα, <ἵνα ἰδόντες οἱ Χριστιανοὶ τὸ ἄγαλμα> μὴ ποιήσωσι μνήμην τοῦ τόπου. Jennifer Clark. "'This Special Shell': The Church Building and the Embodiment of Memory," *Journal of Religious History* 31. 1 (2007): 59–77. Philip Sheldrake, *Spaces for the Sacred: Place, Memory, and Identity* (Baltimore, MD: Johns Hopkins University Press, 2001).

[94] On erasure, see Joan Branham, *Sacred Space Under Erasure: Gender, Sacrifice, and Architecture in Ancient Judaism and Early Christianity* (New York: Cambridge University Press, forthcoming), Harriet I. Flower, *The Art of Forgetting: Disgrace and Oblivion in Roman Political Culture* (Chapel Hill, NC: University of North Carolina Press, 2006), and Jack L. Davis, "Memory Groups and the State: Erasing the Past and Inscribing the Present in the Landscapes of the Mediterranean and the Near East," in *Negotiating the Past in the Past: Identity, Memory, and Landscape in Archaeological Research*, ed. Norman Yoffee, pp. 227–256 (Tucson, AZ: University of Arizona Press, 2007).

[95] Flower, *The Art of Forgetting*, pp. 2, 6.

of Unity," sanctioned the memories of individual heretics: "No one shall dredge up the memory of Manichaeans or Donatists who, we have come to learn, have not renounced their lunacy."[96] How did one "dredge up (*revocare*)" or evoke a memory?

The field of cognitive science sheds light on the process of retrieving memories.[97] Memories must first be encoded and stored before they are retrieved. In simple terms, two types of information, episodic and semantic, are encoded and then stored in various areas of the brain.[98] Recent evidence shows that affect assists with encoding and storage; experiences that are accompanied by strong emotions are better remembered than those with weak emotional associations.[99] Memories can be retrieved using sensory and verbal cues.[100] In the context of antiquity, memories of "heretics" such as those identified in the Edict of Unity could be recalled through story-telling (e.g. reading their biographies, martyr-acts and miracle accounts, hearing sermons on them, or engaging in discussion about them), reading their own writings (e.g. letters or treatises), seeing and/ or reading and writing their names in graffiti, epitaphs, and monuments, invoking their names in ritual contexts (e.g. prayer, incantations, or hymns), and experiencing physical sensations that were in some way associated with them (e.g. anointing, touching, smelling or kissing their tombs, viewing their portraits, smelling fragrances of incense, perfumes, or flowers, or seeing rays or reflections of light). Recalling the memories of these forebears was a multisensory, affective, and conceptual experience.

---

[96] *Cod. theod.* 16.5.38, ed. Mommsen: *nemo manichaeum, nemo donatistam, qui praecipue, ut comperimus, furere non desistunt, in memoriam revocet.*

[97] M. W. Matlin, *Cognition* (Hoboken, NJ: John Wiley & Sons, 2005).

[98] Augustine privileges the visual in his analysis of memory (Aug. *civ. Dei* 10.16.26–24.35 and discussion in Brian Stock, *Augustine's Inner Dialogue: The Philosophical Soliloquy in Late Antiquity* (New York: Cambridge University Press, 2010), pp. 211–223). Cognitive science affirms that mental imagery plays a significant role in storing and retrieving memories (David Rubin, *Memory in Oral Traditions: The Cognitive Psychology of Epic, Ballads, and Counting-out Rhymes* (New York: Oxford University Press, 1995), pp. 39–64). Interestingly, experiments show that the mind stores physical information about objects by splitting it into two discrete components: appearance (left hemisphere) and location (right hemisphere); Rubin, *Memory in Oral Traditions*, p. 57, and Jay Friedenberg and Gordon Silverman, *Cognitive Science: An Introduction to the Study of Mind* (Thousand Oaks, CA: Sage Publications, 2012), p. 176.

[99] Friedenberg and Silverman, *Cognitive Science*, pp. 304–305.

[100] Friedenberg and Silverman, *Cognitive Science*, pp. 204–206. Aug. *Serm.* 280.1 and *civ. Dei* 16.38.2; Seneca writes that just a few words (*uno aut altero verbo*) could jog someone's memory, and Augustine notes that such prompting could help someone identify that a particular idea was not the memory without actually retrieving the memory itself (Sen. *Ben.* 5.25.6, Aug. *Sol.* 2.34).

Not only did late antique Romans regard memory as an internal, abstract feature of the mind; they also believed it existed as an externalized construct. The legislation against heretics of 407 makes this clear, drawing by analogy on crimes of *maiestas*: "Certainly if it is permitted to indict the memory of the dead for crimes of high treason, in this case [the memory] is deservedly obliged to be tried."[101] Not only did a person's memory survive his death, it also could stand trial. This externalized conception of memory is concretized in the second meaning of *memoria*, "memorial."[102] The function of memorials was to assist viewers in retrieving memories of the deceased. As Augustine argues, the Latin and Greek words for "monument" (*monumentum, memorium,* μνῆμα and μνημεῖον) relate to verbs for remind, remember, and instruct:[103]

> But then the only reason why those graves of the dead which are made prominent are called "memorials" or "monuments" is because their capacity to remind evokes the memory of the dead, so those whom death has taken from the eyes of the living might not also be taken from the heart by amnesia. For the term "memorial" most clearly indicates this, and "monument" is so named because it brings to mind, that is reminds. Because of this the Greeks call *mnhmeon* that which we term "memorial" or "monument," because in their language the memory itself, by which we remember, is called *mnhmh*. Therefore, when the intellect is recalling where the body of a dear one is buried, and a place named for a venerable martyr comes to mind, its devotion commends the beloved soul to that martyr for protection through recollection and supplication.

---

[101] *Cod. theod.* 16.5.40.5 (ed. Mommsen): *Nam si in criminibus maiestatis licet memoriam accusare defuncti, non inmerito et hic debet subire iudicium.* See the discussion by Richard Alexander Bauman, "The 'Leges iudiciorum publicorum' and their Interpretation in the Republic, Principate and Later Empire," *ANRW* 2.13 (1980): 103–233.

[102] Paula Rose, *A Commentary on Augustine's De cura pro mortuis gerenda: Rhetoric in Practice,* Amsterdam Studies in Classical Philology 20 (Boston, MA: Brill, 2013), p. 198, citing Alfred Ernout and Antoine Meillet, *Dictionnaire étymologique de la langue latine: Histoire des mots* (Paris: Klincksieck, 1959), p. 395.

[103] Aug. *cura mort.* 4.6 (CSEL 41): *sed non ob aliud vel memoriae vel monumenta dicuntur ea quae insignite fiunt sepulcra mortuorum, nisi quia eos, qui viventium oculis morte subtracti sunt, ne oblivione etiam cordibus subtrahantur, in memoriam revocant et admonendo faciunt cogitari. nam et memoriae nomen id apertissime ostendit et monumentum eo quod moneat mentem, id est admoneat, nuncupatur. propter quod et graeci* μνημεῖον *vocant, quod nos memoriam seu monumentum appellamus, quoniam lingua eorum memoria ipsa, qua meminimus,* μνήμη *dicitur. cum itaque recolit animus, ubi sepultum sit carissimi corpus, et occurrit locus nomine martyris venerabilis, eidem martyri animam dilectam commendat recordantis et precantis affectus.* Rose notes that this is not a scientific but, rather, a rhetorical etymology designed to support Augustine's view of *ad sanctos* burial (Rose, *Commentary on Augustine's De cura pro mortuis gerenda,* p. 195). Rose points out an alternative etymology of *memoria* (Varro, *De ling. lat.* 6.49).

Augustine's analysis of memory-retrieval entails visual prompting, verbal and spatial association, and emotion, all of which have been identified by cognitive scientists as playing significant roles in memory-processing. The correlative processes for memory-obliteration would involve the destruction or deprivation of these essential elements.

While memory sanctions and perpetuation looked forward, they also related the present to the past. As Flower observes, "sanctions represent society's political hindsight."[104] In the case of individuals, such punishments were considered "worse than death" because they obliterated a person's posthumous commemoration and ancestral associations.[105] Roman commemorative monuments and buildings reified the imagined memory emperors and other elites wanted to convey to their fellow citizens and bequeath to the cultural stockpile of Roman civilization. The usefulness and significance of these places, which escalated over the course of the fourth century, made them subject to spatial conflict, whether physical or imaginal. In the case of late antique North Africa, we find the same strategies of memory sanctions deployed against religious groups and their heroes (saints and martyrs) in ecclesiastical literature, civil legislation, and monuments. Groups whose members were rhetorically (re)defined as apostates (*apostatae*), schismatics (*schismatici*), heretics (*haeretici*), opponents (*adversarii*), and enemies (*inimici*) encountered spatial violence that attempted to sever the link between their memories and their gathering places.

Spatial Violence or Vandalism?

Although there is an extensive bibliography on religiously motivated violence, very few of these theoretical studies deal specifically with spatial violence.[106] In fact, many discussions of religious violence consider spatial contestation to be only one among many facets of the conflict.[107]

My analysis of spatial relations is rooted in the assumption that spatial conflict over religious sites is symbolic, as the term "place meanings" suggests. Intentional defacement or destruction of property used for religious

---

[104] Flower, *The Art of Forgetting*, p. 8.

[105] Flower, *The Art of Forgetting*, p. 9.

[106] A comprehensive bibliography by Charles K. Bellinger can be found at "Religion and Violence: A Bibliography," *Wabash Center for Teaching and Learning in Theology and Religion* www.wabashcenter.wabash.edu/resources/article2.aspx?id=10516. Exceptions are noted in the Introduction.

[107] For example, see Wendy Mayer, "Religious Conflict: Definitions, Problems and Theoretical Approaches," in *Religious Conflict from Early Christianity to the Rise of Islam*, ed. David Luckensmeyer, Wendy Mayer, and Bronwen Neil, pp. 1–20 (Berlin: De Gruyter, 2013), p. 3.

rites is thereby distinguished from vandalism, despite the fact that until 409 CE, with the promulgation of Sirmondian constitution 14, Roman law made no such distinction.[108] Both spatial violence and vandalism entail intentional property destruction or damage. They differ, however, in how their targets are chosen. While vandalism's target may be chosen arbitrarily or at random, providing a convenient or proximate outlet for anger or aggression, targets of spatial violence are deliberately chosen because of their functional and symbolic values. The recognition of this distinction in imperial legislation of 409 reveals a shift in late antique Roman understanding of spatial violence, somewhat akin to the creation of the modern category "hate crime."

Scholars theorizing on the topic of religious violence in general, most notably Mark Juergensmeyer, have proposed distinguishing "symbolic violence" from "real violence."[109] Juergensmeyer defines acts of symbolic violence as "intended to illustrate or refer to something beyond their immediate target: a grander consequence, for instance, or a struggle more awesome than meets the eye."[110] While some of the late antique North African attacks on religious buildings were motivated by the functional goal of seizing control over them, other attacks were meant to show disdain and disapproval of their place meanings. Even when the aim was practical, Christian writers and leaders interpreted these attacks as having larger significance, as portending divine favor or retribution. This particular interpretation of historical events has been referred to as "providentialism."[111] The providentialist view of spatial contestation developed by fourth- and fifth-century North African writers like Optatus of Milevus and Augustine of Hippo

---

[108] The implications of this watershed are considered in Chapter 4.
[109] Mark Juergensmeyer, *Terror in the Mind of God: The Global Rise of Religious Violence* (Berkeley, CA: University of California Press, 2000: 2003), pp. 125–127, 188–191, 217–218.
[110] Juergensmeyer, *Terror in the Mind of God*, p. 125.
[111] Gavin Kelly, "Ammianus and the Great Tsunami," *The Journal of Roman Studies* 94 (2004): 141–167, p. 142; F. Jacques and B. Bousquet, "Le raz de marée du 21 JUILLET 365," *MEFRA* 96 (1984): 423–461; M. Henry, "Le témoignage de Libanius et les phénomènes sismiques de IVe siècle de notre ère. Essai d'interprétation," *Phoenix* 39 (1985): 36–61; G. J. Baudy, "Die Wiederkehr des Typhon. Katastrophen-Topoi in nachjulianischer Rhetorik und Annalistik: zu literarischen Reflexen des 21 Juli 365 n.C.," *JAC* 35 (1992): 47–82; M. Mazza, "Cataclismi e calamità naturali: la documentazione letteraria," *Kôkalos* 36–37, *Studi pubblicati dall'Istituto di Storia Antica di Palermo* 1990–91 (1994): 307–330; Lepelley, "Le presage du nouveau disastre de Cannes: la signification du raz de marée du 21 juillet 365 dans l'imaginaire d'Ammien Marcellin," *Kôkalos* 36–37 (1994): 359–374; G. Waldherr, "Die Geburt der 'kosmischen Katastrophe.' Das seismische Grofereignis am 21. Juli 365 n. Chr.," *Orbis Terrarum* 3 (1997): 169–201; F. Paschoud, "Justice et providence chez Ammien Marcellin," *Hestiasis. Studi di tarda antichità offerti a Salvatore Calderone* 1 (Messina, IT: Sicania 1986), pp. 139–161, cited in Kelly.

illustrates that these property conflicts were, according to Juergensmeyer's definition, symbolic.

These writers' cosmic interpretation of spatial contestation begins with the internecine conflict between dissidents and so-called "Catholics." Chapter 3 explores how the particular variety of intra-Christian conflict between groups of competing Christians occasioned a new spatial discourse of identification and power. Chapters 4 and 5 describe how infrequent temple and synagogue violence, which came later to North Africa than to the eastern parts of the empire, marshaled this discourse and contributed to its growth.[112] The connection between all three of these groups is evident in the triad heretics-pagans-Jews, portrayed by Catholic Christians as a sometimes united column of opposition.[113] Legislation that grouped them together reveals a growing Catholic perception that these groups presented the final obstacles to (orthodox) Christian dominance.[114] The literature of the era portrays Catholic opposition as physicalized in attacks, or counterattacks, on the sacred places of these three groups. From the examples discussed in this book I argue that places became important arenas for negotiating power and for constructing ideological boundaries between various competing groups in late antique North Africa.

In contrast to Juergensmeyer, comparative literature professor Joel Black argues that religious violence – regardless of its type – is always, at its core, symbolic:[115]

Issues of representation – specifically related to questions of realism and symbolism – lie at the heart of much religious violence … Inasmuch as

---

[112] The delayed advent of temple violence is likely related to the fact that aristocratic conversion to Christianity occurred relatively late in the region, in the last quarter of the fourth century (M. Salzman, *The Making of a Christian Aristocracy: Social and Religious Change in the Western Roman Empire* (Cambridge, MA: Harvard University Press, 2002), p. 93). To the extent that the meager evidence can be thought to demonstrate a lag in synagogue attacks is likely due to the comparatively low level of hostility between Jews and Christians (Paula Fredriksen, *Augustine and the Jews* (New Haven, CT: Yale University Press, 2010), pp. 274–276).

[113] Aug. *Serm.*62.12.18.

[114] See, for example, *Cod. theod.* 16.5.46.

[115] Joel Black, "'Obliterating an Idol of the Modern Age': The New Iconoclasm from the Twin Buddhas to the Twin Towers," in *Belief and Bloodshed: Religion and Violence across Time and Tradition*, ed. James K. Wellman, Jr., pp. 179–196 (Rowman & Littlefield, 2007), p. 181. Those familiar with Foucault's use of the term "symbolic violence" will note that Black proposes a completely different definition. Foucault uses the term to refer to the way that dominant discourse embeds and masks the patterns of thinking and acting used by the powerful to instill and maintain compliance from the powerless (Michel Foucault, *The History of Sexuality* vol. 1, tr. Robert Hurley (New York: Pantheon, 1978), p. 95).

religious terrorism is a matter of rituals and symbols, it's impossible to ignore the topic of iconoclasm – the defacement or destruction of arti-facts belonging to a rival religious tradition.

In his analysis of the 9/11 attacks, Black suggests that the iconic value of the World Trade Center Twin Towers invited acts of symbolic violence, and that the human casualties of their victims were merely collateral damage.[116] It is precisely because these physical objects represented so many abstract notions about culture, identification, and power – their place identity – that they served as effective targets for religious violence.

North African attacks on religious buildings and Christian writers' depic-tion of such events suggests that Black's observation is equally helpful for understanding violence in antiquity as in the modern world. Internecine Christian spatial conflicts included symbolic religious artifacts, like altars and eucharistic loaves, while Christian–pagan conflicts included symbolic objects like cult statues.[117] Tertullian, based on Rev. 6:9–11, and subsequent North African writers associated altars (*altar, altare, mensa, aedes, altarium, ara*) with sacrificial death, of both Christ and the martyrs, thereby symbolizing the point of access to the mediated divine.[118] Church altars were platonic

---

[116] Joel Black, "'Obliterating an Idol of the Modern Age,'" p. 180.

[117] Optatus, *de schism. Don.* 2.19.1–2, tr. Brent Shaw, *Sacred Violence. African Christians and Sectarian Hatred in the Age of Augustine* (New York: Cambridge University Press, 2011), pp. 156–157 (SC 412): *Iusserunt eucharistiam canibus fundi … Ampullam quoque chrismatis per fenestram ut frangerent iactaverunt, et cum casum adiuvaret abiectio …* (They ordered the eucha-rist to be cast out for dogs to eat. … And they also threw the phial that was used for giving the chrism out of the window so that it would break); Aug. *Serm.* 24.6 (*Saint Augustine: Opera Omnia – Corpus Augustinianum Gissense. Sermones: Part* 1, tr. Hill, modified, *The Works of Saint Augustine* (3rd Release). Electronic Edition. *Sermons* (20–50) *on the Old Testament.* Vol. III/2 (Charlottesville, VA: InteLex Corporation, 2001) (CCL 41: 332): *Puto ignomini-osius fuisse Herculi barbam radi, quam caput praecidi. … Deus fortitudinis solet dici Hercules. Tota virtus eius in barba* (I think it was a much greater humiliation for Hercules to have his beard shaved off than to have his head cut off. … Hercules is usually called the god of strength. His whole virility was in his beard), discussed in Shaw, *Sacred Violence,* pp. 230–231. *de schismate Donatistarum* is the form of the title listed in most editions of Optatus' work, yet Mandouze preferred *Contra Parmenianum Donatistam* ("Optatus," *PCA* 1: 795–797). Monceaux noted that neither title was preserved in ancient manuscripts; the Codex Remensis has *ad Parmenianum schismaticorum auctorem.* See Monceaux, *Histoire littéraire de l'Afrique Chrétienne depuis les origines jusqu'a l'invasion arabe,* 7 vols. (Brussels: Impression Anastaltique. Culture et Civilisation, 1901–1923: 1966) vol. 5, p. 248. Optatus composed a seven-volume edition later around 384 (Frend, "Donatus," p. 617).

[118] Tertullian, *An.* 55.4 and *Scorp.* 12 (25). *Or.* 19.4; Cyprian *Ep.* 63.17.1; Optatus, *de schism. Don* 2.9–10, 3.4.6, 5.3; Aug. *Serm.* 313.5; the dissident *Sermo. Passio Donat. et Advocat.* 13.2 (Jean-Louis Maier, *Le Dossier du Donatisme* (Berlin: Akademie-Verlag, 1987) 1.201–211). The literalness with which this concept was interpreted is reflected in the custom of positioning altars over or nearby martyr tombs or relics (J. Patout Burns and Robin

copies of the heavenly one.[119] Partitions and canopies marked the privileged status of the altar.[120] Altars also symbolized the "people of God."[121] Cyprian specifically associated altar, priesthood, and bishop with Christian unity, thereby linking sectarian altars with schism.[122] The eucharistic bread and drink represented the body and blood of Christ and the communion of its parts, the Church.[123]

Beyond the symbolic value of the various objects within churches that were repeatedly targeted for dispossession, desecration, and destruction, the buildings themselves were symbolic. As Shaw observes:[124]

> Each basilica represented not only the community of the living, but also the community of the dead, including the martyrs and saints. In part, the possessory invasions of basilicas were made in order to gain control over burial grounds and for a double reason. The ownership of the burial places reasserted one's own claim to the past, but it also prevented access to proper burials for the other side.

Temples and synagogues were similarly symbolic, representing not only the past and present communities of their users, but also users' entire religious systems of belief and practice. In the words of Augustine, reflecting

M. Jensen, *Christianity in Roman North Africa*, in collaboration with Graeme W. Clarke, Susan T. Stevens, William Tabbernee, and Maureen A. Tilley (Grand Rapids, MI: Wm. B. Eerdmans Publishing Co., 2014), p. 113).

[119] In addition to the previous Tertullian citations, see Aug. *Serm. Dolb.* 26 (198*).53–54, 57 and the useful discussion in Burns and Jensen, *Christianity in Roman North Africa*, p. 283.

[120] Burns and Jensen, *Christianity in Roman North Africa*, pp. 97, 101.

[121] Tertullian, *Cor.* 9.8 (CCL 2): *Atquin si figurae nostrae fuerunt – nos enim sumus et templa dei et altaria et luminaria et vasa – hoc quoque figurate portendebant, homines dei coronari non oportere* (If indeed they were types of us [1 Cor 10:6] – for we are temples of God, and altars, and lights, and vessels – then they are also prefiguring that it would be unbecoming for the people of God to be crowned).

[122] Cyprian, *Ep.* 43.5.2, tr. Graeme W. Clarke, *The Letters of St. Cyprian of Carthage,* Vol. 2. ACW 43 (New York: Newman Press, 1984) (CCL 3B): *Deus unus est et Christus unus et una ecclesia et cathedra una … Aliud altare constitui aut sacerdotium novum fieri praeter unum altare et unum sacerdotium non potest* (God is one and Christ is one. There is one Church and one chair … It is not possible that another altar can be set up …). See also *Ep.* 66.8.3 and comments by J. Patout Burns, *Cyprian the Bishop.* Routledge Early Church Monographs (New York: Routledge, 2002), p. 86. Dissident Christians also associated sectarian (i.e. Catholic) altars with schism (*Passio ss. Dativi Presb. et Aliorum* 22.2

[123] The drink could be wine, water, milk, or curdy whey. Tertullian, *Marc.* 1.19, 4.40, *Pass. Perp.* 4.9–10, Cypr. *Ep.* 63.13.1–5, 63.14; 69.5.2; Aug. *Ev. Io.* 26.18, *Pecc. merit.* 1.31.60; *Psal.* 30.2.1.4; 142.3; *Serm.* 294.10.10. See discussion in Burns and Jensen, *Christianity in Roman North Africa*, pp. 276–282. Also see Tertullian's discussion of the symbolism of the cross (*ad Nat.* 12.1 (CCL 1): *Crucis qualitas signum est de ligno* … (The nature of the cross is a symbol made of wood)).

[124] Shaw, *Sacred Violence*, p. 694.

on the decommissioning of temples, "the powers of this world, which were at one time persecuting the people of the Christians in defense of their idols, have been defeated and subdued."[125] Appealing to the symbolism of sacred places, Augustine's providentialist interpretation of Theodosian legislation helps to construct Christian self-understanding in opposition to traditional Roman religion. Late antique North African spatial contestation, therefore, supports Black's conviction that all types of religious violence are symbolic. The symbolic nature of sacred places and of the violence done to them is a key component in constructing the meanings of these acts.

One of the ways that the symbolic valence of religious places is expressed is through language. These places are described in literature and inscriptions as "holy (*sanctus*)" and "sacred (*sacer*)." As such sites were increasingly perceived as imbued with holiness, as they were infused with more and more layers of meaning, their symbolic value multiplied. They became what Bourdieu called "indeterminate and overdetermined symbols,"[126] or what we might call "super-symbols," objects that can be observed and interpreted as well as collectively experienced. The perception of such places as "super-symbols" helps explain why North African Christians targeted these particular places as sites in which to negotiate religious group relations throughout the fourth and early fifth centuries.

The super-symbolic nature of buildings is comprised of two types of symbolism.[127] First, the site must be considered cosmically symbolic to the people who visit or use it. The terms used to indicate this perception are holy (*sanctus, hagios, kodeš*) and sacred (*sacer, hieros, kodeš*). Cosmic symbolism is constructed both horizontally (socially), among humans, and vertically (theologically), between humans and the divine. Horizontally, the place functions diachronically: it might be a place where someone considered a member of their group experienced a noteworthy religious action in the past (martyrdom, revelation, or healing, for example), or it could be a building randomly designated by the group as its ritual arena. If the site has no connection with a past religious event, then symbols are often installed to create that connection (images, inscriptions, relics, or ritual objects, for

---

[125] Aug. *Ep.* 232. 3, tr. Teske (CCL 57): ... *huius saeculi potestates, quae aliquando pro simulacris populum christianum persequebantur, victas et domitas* ... For a similar sentiment expressed toward synagogue destruction, see *Passio Salsae 3* discussed in Chapter 5.

[126] Pierre Bourdieu, *The Logic of Practice*, tr. Richard Nice (Stanford, CA: Stanford University Press, 1980: 1990), p. 88.

[127] These criteria are specific to celestial religions like those under consideration. Chthonic, pantheistic, or nontheistic religions would have different criteria.

example). Vertically, the place is understood as a portal to the divine, or, in the words of Brown, "the joining of heaven and earth."[128] In other words, the place may be conceived as where divinity (and/or supernatural entities) dwells, appears or has appeared, or is most directly accessible (acting like a cosmic worm hole connecting the location of the adherents and that of the divine).[129] This vertical conception relies on the spatialization of divinity, where the divine is understood as existing in or occupying a particular realm or place. The bidirectionality of a building's cosmic symbolism helps explain why Christian writers interpreted spatial contestation as significant in both the social and theological realms.

Second, those who attack the site must be aware of its religious significance to the group associated with it and, at some level, be familiar with the architectural symbol system from which it derives religious meaning. Even if attackers do not ascribe the same meaning to the site as their opponents, their recognition of the site's value to their victims demonstrates the attackers' familiarity with the *way* meaning is derived. This second component is necessary if an attack itself is to convey meaning to both attackers and those whose site they attack. This meaning may not be exactly the same, but it must overlap to some degree in order for the attacks to be symbolic. The examples from North Africa discussed in this book reveal a deepening of the symbolism of sacred places over time.

Identity versus Identification

Identity is an elusive and debated concept. Except when the term is inextricable from scholarly usage, for example in the phrase "place identity," I employ the term "identification." Sociologists, psychologists, and anthropologists all define the phenomenon differently. For the purposes of this study, I follow the more fluid and multiform understanding of identification proposed by social constructionists.[130] In this view, an individual may self-identify as a member of multiple groups – both at each stage of life and

---

[128] Peter Brown, *The Cult of the Saints* (Chicago, IL: University of Chicago Press, 1981), p. 1.

[129] Lindsay Jones, *The Hermeneutics of Sacred Architecture: Experience, Interpretation, Comparison, Vol. 1: Monumental Occasions. Reflections on the Eventfulness of Religious Architecture* and *Vol. 2: Hermeneutical Calisthenics: A Morphology of Ritual-Architectural Priorities* (Cambridge, MA: Harvard University Press, 2000).

[130] *The Politics of Multiculturalism in the New Europe: Racism, Identity and Community*, ed. Tariq Modood and Pnina Werbner (New York: Zed Books, 1997), pp. 10–12; see also Fredrik Barth, *Ethnic Groups and Boundaries: The Social Organization of Cultural Difference* (Boston, MA: Little, Brown, 1969); and Zoe Bray, *Living Boundaries: Frontiers and Identity in the Basque Country* (Brussels: Presses INTERUNIVERSITAIRES EUROPÉENNES, Peter Lang, 2004), pp. 223–229.

over the course of his or her lifetime – and expresses this range of identifications through language, dress, activities, and location. Identity, in this sense, is understood as a social process of self-identification and identification performed and observed by individuals in a variety of contexts rather than as a fixed or essentialist aspect of human self-perception.

Thus, while the term "identity" may imply a certain stasis and singularity, "identification" better captures the multiplicity and intersection of an individual's dynamic complex of identifications which s/he understands as self-defining, and which s/he (re)presents to others through an elaborate series of observable behaviors. Sociologist Erving Goffman defines this identity-performance as:[131]

> [T]he way in which the individual in ordinary work situation presents himself and his activity to others, the ways in which he guides and controls the impression they form of him, and the kinds of things he may and may not do while sustaining his performance before them.

No less in antiquity than today, people identify with multiple groups simultaneously as well as diachronically. I use the terms collective identification, group identification, and social identification to refer to the shared perception that a group of individuals have of themselves as belonging to, or part of, a single entity along with the defining characteristics of the group and its members as well as the behaviors the group performs. This common perception may be shaped by external views that others have of these individuals, but this study is mainly concerned with internal perspectives rather than external ones. External perceptions will be discussed when relevant.

This fluid understanding of identity is usefully employed by Éric Rebillard in his work on late antique North African Christians. Following the work of sociologist Peter Burke, Rebillard notes: "an individual may hold multiple identities within a single group and within intersecting groups. … Multiple identities in intersecting groups occur when different groups, in which an individual has different identities, overlap."[132] One of these identities is noticeable solely when it is activated. Rebillard argues that Christians were only visible when they were "expressing Christian membership."[133] He concludes that "Christianness was given salience only intermittently in everyday experience [and] groupness based on

---

[131] Erving Goffman, *The Presentation of Self in Everyday Life* (Edinburgh: University of Edinburgh Social Sciences Research Centre, 1956), prologue.

[132] Rebillard, *Christians and Their Many Identities*, Kindle locations 119, 121–122, citing Burke, "Relationships between Multiple Identities," in *Advances in Identity Theory and Research*, ed. Peter J. Burke, Timothy J. Owens, Richard Serpe, and Peggy A. Thoits, pp. 195–214 (New York: Kluwer Academic/Plenum Publishers, 2003), p. 201.

[133] Rebillard, *Christians and Their Many Identities*, Kindle locations 295–296.

Christianness also occurred only intermittently."[134] Not only did ritual arenas provide the main venues for precisely those "intermittent" activations of Christianness, spatial conflict presented strategic opportunities to express and produce "groupness based on Christianness."

The strategic use of spatial boundaries for creating group boundaries, or groupness such as Christianness, relies on a relational understanding of social boundaries. Isabella Sandwell identifies various strategies for boundary construction in her exploration of religious identity in Antioch. She notes that "religious identities … result from boundaries that are constructed by human actors, who choose to identify themselves with some people and differentiate themselves from others."[135] Because these boundaries are relational, we see "identity constructed from the marking out differences from others."[136] As Judith Lieu and Daniel Boyarin have previously shown, Christian writers accomplished this through contrast with "Judaism" and "paganism."[137] The fourth century inaugurated a period of "mass-marketing" of Christian identities.[138] Sandwell claims that "basilica-style churches" made this expansion possible.[139] Yet the production of these churches – who built them, for whom, and how – shaped Christianness in and of itself. Similarly, the contestation over these sites, alongside the rhetorical construction of boundaries, played a significant role in marking out difference and what Sandwell calls "strategic use of religious allegiance."[140]

Unlike disputes over material goods or natural resources, conflict rooted in social identification, what sociologists call "identity-based conflict," is more intractable.[141] International relations scholar Ronald Fisher has noted:[142]

[H]istorical factors in multicommunal societies often lead to structural inequalities and differential access to political power, which become

---

[134] Rebillard, *Christians and Their Many Identities*, Kindle locations 2165–2166.
[135] Sandwell, *Religious Identity in Late Antiquity* (New York: Cambridge University Press, 2011), p. 4. The degree to which such boundaries are naturalized reflects the depth of their acceptance or integration in a particular social and historical context.
[136] Sandwell, *Religious Identity*, p. 5.
[137] Lieu, *Christian Identity in the Jewish and Graeco-Roman World* (New York: Oxford University Press, 2004), and Boyarin, *Border Lines. The Partition of Judaeo-Christianity* (Philadelphia, PA: University of Pennsylvania Press, 2004).
[138] Sandwell, *Religious Identity*, p. 5.
[139] Sandwell, *Religious Identity*, p. 5.
[140] Sandwell, *Religious Identity*, p. 91.
[141] Ronald Fisher, "Cyprus: The Failure of Mediation and the Escalation of an Identity-Based Conflict to an Adversarial Impasse," *Journal of Peace Research* 38.3 (2001): 307–326, p. 307. See also Jay Rothman, *Resolving Identity-based Conflict in Nations, Organizations, and Communities* (San Francisco, CA: Jossey-Bass, Kindle Edition, 1997).
[142] Fisher, "Cyprus," p. 308.

expressed in the domination of one group over another with resulting discrimination, victimization, and the socialization of communal hatreds.

This analysis aptly describes Roman North Africa of late antiquity. Imperial support for one group, self-described "Catholic" Christians, provided adherents access to government officials and their military resources. Catholic Christians used this access to power to marginalize the indigenous form of North African Christianity, which resisted attempts at Catholicization, commonly referred to as "Donatists."[143] Conflict resolution expert Jay Rothman observes that using conventional methods to solve such intangible conflicts merely exacerbates the situation by widening the rift between competing social groups and reinforcing their ethnic, cultural, or religious polarization.[144] In the case of North Africa, opposing parties resorted to the Roman court system to resolve conflicts that were couched in terms of property disputes. Because powerful forces – imperial officials, armed groups, and religious leaders – continued to frame the conflict in adversarial terms, parties became entrenched in group identity-forming antagonism.[145]

Navigating between plural simultaneous identifications was a regular feature of late antique daily life. Certain plural identifications incited harsh responses from bishops, who admonished their congregants to choose between them. On one occasion Augustine berated his audience for three hours about their participation in "pagan" New Year celebrations; being Christian and "pagan" were, for Augustine, mutually exclusive group identifications.[146] That day, Augustine kept his congregation in his basilica and off the streets long enough to prevent their participation in the New Year's Day festivities. He either instituted a New Year fast or prolonged the Sunday fast prior to eucharist so that they would be unable to feast along with the rest of the populace.[147] Along with ritual,

---

[143] For the use of "dissident" as a preferable term for "Donatist," see Shaw, *Sacred Violence*, pp. 5–6. I use the term "Donatist" advisedly in full agreement with the caution issued by Shaw, "African Christianity: Disputes, Definitions, and 'Donatists,'" in *Orthodoxy and Heresy in Religious Movements: Discipline and Dissent*, ed. Malcolm R. Greenshields and Thomas A. Robinson, pp. 5–34 (Lampeter, Wales: Edwin Mellen Press, 1992), reprinted in *Rulers, Nomads, and Christians in Roman North Africa*, Collected Studies Series 497 (Brookfield, VT: Variorum, 1995).

[144] Rothman, *Resolving Identity-based Conflict*, Kindle location 228.

[145] Rothman, *Resolving Identity-based Conflict*, chapter 2.

[146] Aug. *Serm.* Dolbeau 4 = 198.

[147] Aug. *Serm.* Dolbeau 4 = 198.1, 6, tr. Hill, modified (F. Dolbeau, *Augustin d'Hippone. Vingt-six sermons au peuple d'Afrique*, Collection des Études Augustiniennes, Série Antiquité 147 (Paris: Institut d'Études Augustiniennes, 1996), pp. 366 and 371: *sollemnitas gentium quae fit hodierno die; hoc tempore ieiunare* ...

Augustine used the place of his basilica to inculcate in his congregants the sense that "Christian" and "pagan" were mutually exclusive identifications. Conflict is an effective tool in producing group identification. In her study of a mixed-race student group, sociologist Jennifer Jones has written:[148]

> Group identity formation is a negotiated process involving strategies to achieve a sense of belonging and cohesion … [B]y using experiences of social conflict to construct shared experiences, the members of this mixed-race organization developed collective identity.

As late antique groups coalesced around various political and religious issues, they used multiple strategies to create a shared sense of "belonging and cohesion." Chief among these strategies were spatial conflict and discourse. Furthermore, as Jones observes, "collective identity is formed by producing new meaning from an existing knowledge set of political, social, economic, and cultural experiences shared by multiple persons."[149] In the course of the spatial conflicts of the fourth and fifth centuries, places regarded as sacred came to assume new meaning woven together from North Africans' shared experiences of their physical landscape and rituals. By gathering together as a group in their own places, with their own rites, distinct groups reinforced their developing social identifications. Physical boundaries erected in places helped to construct social or ideological boundaries between groups seeking to separate. In addition to their religious definitions, spatial differentiation mutually reinforced these distinctive identifications in ways that were not the case for adherents of traditional Roman religion.[150] Devotees of various deities did not identify exclusively as Isiacs or Mithraists, for example, and this polyform identification was reflected not only in their accessing multiple shrines but in the pluralism of the iconography displayed therein.

Buildings "concretized" or "physicalized" and sometimes explicitly symbolized self-perceptions and categorical abstractions about identification. In their essay on the relationship of identification to place, anthropologists Akhil Gupta and James Ferguson draw attention to the human enterprise of "place-making."[151] By de-naturalizing the phenomenon, they help

---

[148] Jennifer A. Jones, "Who are We? Producing Group Identity through Everyday Practices of Conflict and Discourse," *Sociological Perspectives* 54. 2 (2011): 139–162, p. 139.

[149] Jones, "Who are We?" p. 140.

[150] I thank Ross S. Kraemer for this valuable insight.

[151] Akhil Gupta and James Ferguson, "Beyond 'Culture': Space, Identity, and the Politics of Difference," in *Culture, Power, Place: Explorations in Critical Anthropology,* ed. Akhil Gupta and James Ferguson, pp. 33–51 (Durham, NC: Duke University Press, 1997).

illuminate how people use place to localize community and construct identification. They point out that "changing schemes of categorization and discourses of difference" actually constitute, not merely influence, constantly forming individual subjects.[152] This observation leads them to conclude that:[153]

> Keeping in mind that notions of locality or community refer both to a demarcated physical space and to clusters of interaction, we can see that the identity of a place emerges by the intersection of its specific involvement in a system of hierarchically organized spaces with its cultural construction as a community or locality.

The reconstruction by North African religious leaders of the meaning of the late antique landscape for their communities is what Gupta and Ferguson call "reterritorialization."[154] The examples of reterritorialization explored throughout this book show how ancient writers mobilized oppositional images of place to create religious difference. This spatialization of religious difference is occasionally "performed" as violent spatial interactions between competing religious groups. "Us vs. them" is thus isomorphically mapped onto "here vs. there."[155] This is not to say that all individuals who identified with the "we" group embraced this perception, but, rather, that the discourse deployed by image-makers sought to create such a map in order to produce a spatially differentiated, collective religious identification.

The interwoven observations about memory and place, spatial violence, and group identifications discussed in this chapter reveal my foundational assumptions for scrutinizing ancient evidence. The aim of this attempt to be explicit and self-conscious about the various strands of thought that have shaped the current study is to explain and expose its interdisciplinary methodology. As readers will undoubtedly observe, this approach leads to multilayered interpretations whose final tapestry, it is hoped, will enrich their understanding of the ancient world and of the ongoing phenomenon of spatial contestation throughout history.

---

[152] Gupta and Ferguson, "Culture, Power, Place: Ethnography at the End of an Era," *Culture, Power, Place*: 1–32, p. 12.

[153] Gupta and Ferguson, "Beyond 'Culture,'" p. 36.

[154] Gupta and Ferguson, "Beyond 'Culture,'" pp. 36–37. Although the authors use the concept to develop the postmodern, postcolonial notion of "deterritorialization," the fundamental characterization of the process can be usefully applied to late antiquity.

[155] Gupta and Ferguson, "Beyond 'Culture,'" p. 42.

2

CHRISTIAN PERCEPTIONS
OF COMMUNAL PLACES

A Welshman was shipwrecked at sea and marooned on a desert island. When
a passing vessel picked him up five years later the crew were amazed to find
his little island covered in fine buildings that he had built himself. With pride
the Welsh Robinson Crusoe took the captain round the island and pointed
out to him his house, his workshop, electricity generator and two chapels.
"But what do you need the second chapel for?" asked the captain. "Oh, that's
the one I don't go to," he replied.[1]

THE ABSURDITY OF SPATIALIZING THE schismatic tendency of
a decentralized Scottish Presbyterianism despite the absence of actual
human community makes this joke funny. Besides its humor, the joke
betrays the truth that human building is a social product; architecture both
physicalizes and symbolizes social relations. The two chapels in this joke
materialize Church divisions which have become so deeply embedded in
the Welshman's psyche that he cannot express his religious identification
without reference to the symbolic "other."

Although this joke was told in the twentieth century, the reality it reflects
was as true then as in the earliest centuries of Christianity explored in this
chapter. I trace the development of North African perception about places
where Christians gathered for religious activities from the third through
fifth centuries. The evidence surveyed suggests that conceptions of religious sites consistently deploy a strategy of differentiation. Distinguishing
Christian from non-Christian places mapped certain group identifications
onto the North African landscape. Understanding this particular map or
conception of landscape is foundational to an analysis of spatial contestation

---

[1] Christie Davies, *Welsh Jokes* (Cardiff, Wales: John Jones Cardiff Ltd, 1978), p. 25. The same
joke is told about Jews (see Adam Kirsch, "House Divided: The History of the Synagogue
in America, a New Book Shows, Is One of Rifts, Splits, Factions and the Ever-Evolving
Tension between Tradition and Modernity," *The New York Jewish Week*, May 24, 2011).

because it helped to create those very place meanings and attachments which were disputed in the fourth and fifth centuries. This chapter traces the evolution of North African spatialization of Christian identifications in its social and rhetorical context of differentiation.

Perceptions of Space

Broadly speaking, the late antique Roman landscape was, in the words of Robert Markus, "full of holy places."[2] Yet early Christian apologists and polemicists went to great lengths to differentiate "pagan" holy places from Christian sites. Their arguments confirm Markus' observation that "no place was [considered] inherently sacred."[3] Most Christian writers represented this plethora of places as idolatrous and thereby harmful to their audiences, while practitioners of traditional Roman religion described the sites as "sacred (*sacrum*)" or "holy (*sanctus*)."[4] As a result, the adjectives "sacred" and "holy" (or any of its synonyms) are not found in the earliest Christian descriptions of their own places of assembly.[5]

Christians throughout the Mediterranean considered a variety of places to be collectively meaningful. Ann Marie Yasin has recently pointed out that this significance derived from a variety of sources: the people who met there, those who were buried there, the rituals that were performed there, the objects used in those rituals, or historical events that had once happened, or thought to have happened, there.[6] Since the phenomenological work of Harold Turner, other theorists have used the terms *domus ecclesiae* and *domus dei* to distinguish between competing perceptions of sacred place, namely whether a place was perceived as housing a community or occupied by its divinity.[7] Standard architecture handbooks

---

[2] Robert Markus, *The End of Ancient Christianity* (New York: Cambridge University Press, 1990), p. 141.

[3] Markus, *End of Ancient Christianity*, p. 140, citing Aug. *Serm.* 337.2; Tert. *Cor.* 9.2; Minucius Felix, *Oct.* 32.1–3; and the later Cesarius of Arles *SERM.* 229.2.

[4] See especially Tert. *Idol.* 2 and *Spect.* 4–15 for a presentation of idolatrous space as ubiquitous and dangerous. For a full discussion of this pattern, see Ann Marie Yasin, *Saints and Church Spaces in the Late Antique Mediterranean: Architecture, Cult and Community* (New York: Cambridge University Press, 2009), pp. 14–45.

[5] I suspect that the position reflected in extant sources is that of apologists and polemicists, and that any sources which might have offered a positive Christian perception of non-Christian holy places have not survived. Hints of this more positive assessment can be gleaned from reading against the grain.

[6] Yasin, *Saints and Church Spaces*, pp. 14–20.

[7] Turner, *From Temple to Meeting House: The Phenomenology and Theology of Places of Worship* (New York: Mouton Publishers, 1979), pp. 157–177. This dichotomy strikes me as an artificial

tend to follow the distinction made by some ancient writers between the
Christian sense of holy place as ritual arena, *domus ecclesiae*, and the notion
of traditional Roman temples as "houses of God (*domus dei*)." This analysis,
focused on form rather than perception, divides Christian church-building
into eras before and after Constantine (often termed *ante-* and *post pacem*),
when Christians were thought to have adopted Roman spatial sensibility.[8] Alternatively, Christine Mohrmann tentatively suggested a half century ago that the concretization of *ecclesia* occurred earlier in Latin than
in Greek.[9] The appellation *domus dei*, in both physical and metaphysical
senses, appears in Christian sources from the third through the fifth century. Literary sources of the third century and building dedications from
the fourth and fifth centuries indicate that *domus dei* enjoyed a long history in Roman North Africa.[10] This evidence also suggests that the two

distinction born from a theology of differentiation (no less so now than in Antiquity), similar to the views promulgated in the apologetic arguments of Arnobius. I would suggest that,
given the Christian theological notion of the community as the body of Christ already
evident in the metaphoric language of the apostle Paul, these two supposedly distinct para-
digms would inexorably converge. It was only Christian antagonism toward non-Christian
ideas of holiness (both pagan and early Jewish) that postponed this inevitability.

[8] Richard Krautheimer, *Early Christian and Byzantine Architecture* (New Haven, CT: Yale
University Press, 1965), pp. 42–43. Michael White uses the term *domus ecclesiae* for the
second stage of emerging Christian architecture, building on a history of architectural
terminology critiqued by Kristina Sessa, "*Domus Ecclesiae:* Rethinking a Category of Ante-
Pacem Christian Space," *Journal of Theological Studies*, New Series 60.1 (April 2009): 90–108.
White emphasizes discontinuity between the pre-Constantinian *domus ecclesiae* and the
expanded *aula ecclesiae*, on the one hand, and post-Constantinian basilicas on the other,
allowing for the latter to exist simultaneously (L. Michael White, *The Social Origins of
Christian Architecture: Building God's House in the Roman World*, vol. 1 (Valley Forge, PA:
Trinity Press International, 1996), pp. 14–20). For an example of the traditional Roman
usage *domicilium deorum*, see Cicero, *Har. res.* 28. The fourth-century polemic by Firmicus
Maternus of Sicily, *The Error of Pagan Religions*, ties Jeremiah's prophecy regarding the
destruction of the *domus deorum* (Bar 6:54) to the imperial destruction of statues in his own
day (*Err. prof. rel.* 28.5–6).

[9] Christine Mohrmann, "Les Dénominations de l'église en tant qu'edifice en grec et en
latine au cours des premiers siècles chrétiens," *Revue des Sciences Religieuses* 36 (1962): 155–
174, p. 161.

[10] AE 1904: 6 (= CIL 8.17414, based on reconstruction of D D), AE 1935: 119 (on a
stone door in a basilica in Ksar el Kelb (Vegesela, Numidia), identified by P. Cayrel
as Donatist based on an adjacent inscription "Deo laudes h[ic] omnes dica-
mus" and a memoria for the martyr Marculus), BCTH-1894-87, BCTH-1972B-
137 = AE 1937: 155, CIL 8: 18713, CIL 8: 8275, CIL 8: 10642, CIL 8: 16720, CIL 8:
17758. Frend identifies two of these *domus dei* inscriptions as Donatist (Frend,
"The *Memoriae Apostolorum* in Roman North Africa," *The Journal of Roman Studies*
30.1 (1940): 32–49, p. 43). CIL 8.2220 (p 948) = CIL 8.17614 = ILCV 1830 (em) =
ILCV +01929 = ILCV +02492 = AfrRom-07-02-750 from Ain Ghorab in Numidia
is dated to the second half of the fifth century by Duval (but by Tabernee to 495,
based on Lucas' reconstruction), tr. William Tabernee, *Montanist Inscriptions and*

Christian place meanings, *domus dei* and *domus ecclesiae*, emerged concur-
rently.[11] By analyzing the sources using the Lefebvrian lens of conceived-
perceived-lived space, we can see that North African writers, among others,
first employed the term *ecclesia* in both the concrete and the metaphoric
senses prior to the age of Constantine, and described the places where they
gathered as *domus dei* beginning in the third century.[12] This emphasis on

---

Testimonia: Epigraphic Sources, Patristic Monograph Series of the North American
Patristic Society 16 (Washington, DC: Catholic University of America Press, 1996),
p. 539, modified: H(i)c domus d(e)i nos[tri Chr(ist)i] h(ic) (h)a<b=V>itatio sp(iritu)
s s(an)c(t)i p[aracleti(?)] / h(i)c memoria beati mart<y=I>ris dei consulti [E]mer[iti] /
h(i)c exaudietur omnis q(u)i invocat nomen d(omi)ni d(e)i omnipot[entis] / cur
homo miraris d(e)o iu<v=B>ante meliora vide<b=V>is a(nno) [p(rovinciae)]
...]XL[...] (Here (is) the dwelling place of Christ our God, here the habita-
tion of the Holy Spirit, the Paraclete. Here (is) the memorial of the blessed martyr Emeritus, God's advocate. Here everyone who invokes the name of the Lord
god almighty will be heard. Why, person, do you marvel? With the help of God
you will see (even) greater (marvels). In the provincial year ... 40). See also AE
1909: 118 = ILCV 1842 from Ain Ghorab in Numidia, dedicating a dais (tribunal):
Ad hanc do/mum dei tr/ibunal basi/licae domi/nae Castae / sanctae ac / venerand(a)e /
martiri(!) / Sabinianus / una cum con/iuge et fili(i)s / votum per/fecit (To this house
of god, a tribunal of the basilica for a Lady Casta, holy and revered martyr. Sabianus
together with his wife and children fulfilled his vow). CIL 8.17714 = ILCV +01830,
dated by Frend to the fourth–fifth centuries, from Khenchela / Mascula in Numidia is
highly speculative: Hic e[st dom]/us [dei hic] / memo[riae] / apostol[or(um) et] / beati
Emeri/ti gloriosi / consulti (Here is the house of god. Here is a memorial of the apostles
and blessed Emeritus, glorious advocate). Although a synagogue dedication at Hammam
Lif (Naro, Tunisia) was once thought to contain *Domus dei*, Karen Stern's reconstruction
suggests otherwise. Instead of Asterius filius Rus/tici arc(h)osinagogi / margaritari(i)
d(omus) dei par/tem portici tesselavit (AE 1996: 1713 = CIL 08, 12457b = CIL 08,
12457b add. p. 2450 = ILCV 4940b = AE 1998: 1536), Stern reads: Asterius filius Rus/tici
arcosinagogi / margarita riddei par/tem portici tesselavit "Asterius, son of Rusticus the
synagogue leader (*archosinagogus*), and Margarita, daughter/wife of Riddeus, tessellated
part of the portico" (Stern, *Inscribing Devotion*, pp. 226–228).

[11] The Greek equivalent of *domus ecclesiae* is found in Eusebius (*Hist. eccl.* 7.30.19 (SC 41): ...
ἐκκλησίας οἴκου ...).

[12] Although Christine Mohrmann made this observation in her catalogue of Christian
terms for "church," the point is overlooked by subsequent scholars ("Les Dénominations
de l'église, p. 163). For example, Robert A. Markus dates the association of Christian
places with holiness to the post-Constantinian era ("How on Earth Could Places
Become Holy? Origins of the Christian Idea of Holy Places," *Journal of Early Christian
Studies* 2.3 (Fall 1994): 257–271. As White notes, Tertullian is not the earliest reference
to "an identifiable Christian edifice, [which] comes from the Syriac *Edessene Chronicle*"
(White, *Building God's House*, p. 118). The use of the Greek term to designate a building appears later (Origen, *Or.* 31.7), discussed in Valeriy A. Alikin, *The Earliest History
of the Christian Gathering: Origin, Development and Content of the Christian Gathering
in the First to Third Centuries* (Leiden: Brill, 2010), p. 56. Pre-Constantinian examples
from other regions include Alexandria (Clement, *Strom.* 7.5 (29.3–4), *Paed.* 3.11
(79.3, 80.1)), Arbela (modern Erbil, Iraq; *Chron. Arb.* 3 [CSCO 467–8]), Edessa (modern

the materiality of space also allows us to see how Christians deployed space to patrol ideological boundaries. Additionally, the increasing usefulness of space for constructing and perpetuating Christian identification further contributed to the place attachment, or high regard, Christians harbored toward their spaces.

Waxing apologetically, Tertullian constructs place meaning by contrasting Christian *domus dei* with idol workshops:[13]

> On this account the zeal of faith will deliver its laments, crying out, "Does a Christian come from idols into the assembly, from the workshops of the adversary into the house of God; does he lift up to God the Father hands that are the mothers of idols, to worship with those very hands which in the forum are worshipped in opposition to God; does he lay on the body of the Lord those very hands that provide bodies for demons?"

Tertullian's characterization of the Christian meeting space as a "house of God" disconnects it from any and all activity associated with idolatry. According to Tertullian, Christians must eschew any contact with idols (here their manufacture) in order for their Christian worship to be acceptable. The theoretical "Christian" he berates may harbor the more permissive notion that mere contact with idols does not affect his own worship. He or she moves seamlessly between the idol factory and the "house of God." The use of locality to contrast idolatry with proper worship reflects an emergent spatial sensibility that the place where Christians gathered for prayer in some way or another "housed" their God, or was in some way holy.[14] This place meaning relies not only on distinctions but on alignments as well. Tertullian's contrast of "workshops of the adversary" with "house of God" attempts to drive a wedge between Christian and idolatrous sites while simultaneously acknowledging a certain parallelism in spatial

---

Urfa, Turkey; *Chron. Edess.* 1, although this may be a later interpolation), some of which are discussed by White. The phrase describing the Edessene church is interesting because it uses the word *hayklah*, meaning temple, church, or nave (CSCO 1.1: 2.4): *bhykl' d'dt' dkrstyn'* ("the nave of the church of the Christians," tr. Brock, "Syriac Historical Writing: A Survey of the Main Sources," *Journal of the Iraq Academy, Syriac Corporation* 5 (1979–1980): 1–30, p. 3).

[13] Tert. *Idol.* 7.1, tr. White, *Social Origins* v. 2 p. 54, modified (CCL 2): *Ad hanc partem zelus fidei perorabit ingemens: Christianum ab idolis in ecclesiam venire, de adversaria officina in domum dei venire, attollere ad deum patrem manus matres idolorum, his manibus adorare, quae foris adversus deum adorantur, eas manus admovere corpori domini, quae daemoniis corpora conferunt?*

[14] While Yasin broadly upholds the scholarly consensus (*Saints and Church Spaces*, p. 36), she concedes that "it is possible to say that, by association at least, the sites in which Christians gathered were seen from the beginning as a kind of holy space" (p. 37).

perception of the two locations. The term *domus dei* further suggests an understanding of Christian place as God's dwelling-place and not merely as the gathering place of the community. The rhetorical contrast between divine and idolatrous place differentiates one from the other, which Tertullian explicitly states further on in this treatise: "we keep ourselves separate from idolatry."[15] The broader context of this passage, Tertullian's assault on the cardinal sin of idolatry, discloses a hierarchical valuation encoded in this differentiation: only the place of Christian assembly is worthy of his esteem.

Scuffles between Christians and practitioners of traditional Roman religion at these sites drive the wedge even further. In his *Apology*, Tertullian bemoans raids on Christians in their places of worship: "Every day we are besieged; every day we are betrayed; most are caught at our own meetings and assemblies."[16] Tertullian notes that cemeteries also provided a stage for attacks. He reports an episode in the year 202 when Carthaginians violated Christian tombs while shouting, "No grounds for them (*areae non sint*)."[17] Tertullian's account of cemetery desecration indicates that outsiders could identify Christian graves even though, according to Éric Rebillard, the tombs themselves were not physically distinguishable from others and Christians did not have separate cemeteries.[18] Rebillard convincingly argues that "individual Christians were probably known as such to their neighbors and acquaintances, and that, in case of tensions, their burial plots could be violated."[19]

While Tertullian's portrayal of Christian assembly places and burial sites may have emerged initially as a polemical stance in order to distinguish Christian from traditional Roman religious places and to discourage Christians from entering places associated with idols and idolatry, it reveals his perception that these locations were both special and differentiated from other places in the North African landscape. Furthermore, his contrast

---

[15] Tert. *Idol.* 15 (CCL 2): *ab idololatria separamus. ...*

[16] Tert. *Apol.* 7.4 (CCL 1): *Cottidie obsidemur, cottidie prodimur, in ipsis etiam plurimum coetibus et congregationibus nostris opprimimur.* See discussion in Rebillard, *Christians and Their Many Identities, 200–450 CE.*

[17] Rebillard, *Christians and Their Many Identities*, Kindle location 392.

[18] Rebillard, "Les areae carthaginoises (Tert. *Scap.* 3, 1): Cimetières communautaires ou enclos funéraires de chrétiens?" *Mélanges de l'École française de Rome, Antiquité* 108.1 (1996): 175–189; *The Care of the Dead in Late Antiquity*, tr. Elizabeth Trapnell Rawlings and Jeanine Routier-Pucci (Ithaca, NY: Cornell University Press, 2003: 2009), pp. 7–12; and *Christians and Their Many Identities*, Kindle location 401.

[19] Rebillard, "Les areae carthaginoises," 175–189; Rebillard, *Care of the Dead*, pp. 7–12; and Rebillard, *Christians and Their Many Identities*, Kindle location 401. See also Tert. *apol.* 37.2.

between idolatrous and Christian places relies on their physicality. Tertullian uses the physical locality that allows the human body to move from one place to the other and to stay in one or the other to pose them as opposites and thereby construct an ideological boundary between the two.

Tertullian is also the first to associate the term *ecclesia* with a physical building: "we drive [egregious sexual offenders] away not only from the threshold [of the assembly] but actually from the roofed areas of the whole building of the church."[20] Tertullian employs the architectural terms "threshold" (*limine*) and "roof" (*tecto*), parts of "the whole building of the church," to refer to physical features of the building. Moreover, he suggests that Carthaginian Christians ejected sinners whose offenses were considered unforgiveable "unnatural acts (*monstra*)" from the church entrance and from under the eaves. This practice demonstrates that as early as the end of the second century, some Christians made use of their buildings' physical boundaries to exclude those who did not meet the Church's standards, whether because of their association with idols or their sexual offenses.[21] In addition to the ritual of communion itself, permanent excommunication, or exclusion, used church walls to produce and reproduce the boundary between those who could participate in the ritual and those who could not.[22] Physical enclosure simultaneously included and excluded: only those on the inside were able to assert their Christian-ness, creating shared memories and reinforcing group affiliation. Boundary-patrol was both a material and figurative aspect of Christian identification.

Tertullian's observations demonstrate that this materiality was a feature of both internal and external identification of Christian groups. Outsiders continued to target Christian sites throughout the next two centuries. Sometime around the time of the Valerian persecution (257–260), imperial officials confiscated places where Christians assembled and even banned communal gatherings at *coemeteria*.[23] These sanctions are corroborated by

[20] Tert. *Pud.* 4.5, modified from White, *Social Origins* vol. 2, p. 61 (CCL 2): *non modo limine verum omni ecclesiae tecto submovemus*. This observation was made as early as 1909 by Stuart A. Donaldson (*Church Life and Thought in North Africa AD 200* (New York: Cambridge University Press, 1909), p. 18).

[21] Scholars disagree on the meaning of *monstrum*, suggesting bestiality or incest (J. N. Adams, *The Latin Sexual Vocabulary* (Baltimore, MD: Johns Hopkins Press, 1982), p. 34; and William P. Le Saint, *Treatises on Penance: On Penitence and On Purity*, ACW 28 (New York: Paulist Press, 1959), p. 245).

[22] This practice is attested in the gospel of John's ἀποσυνάγωγος (Jn 9:22, 9:34, 12:42, 16:2). For a more detailed description of the process of excommunication, see Tert. *apol.* 39 and *pud.* 5, 13.10–12, 14.16–17, 15.3, 9–11, 18.2, 8, 12–18.

[23] Eusebius, *Hist. eccl.* 7.11.10, tr. H. J. Lawlor and J. E. L. Oulton, *Eusebius: The Ecclesiastical History II*. Loeb Classical Library Series 265 (Cambridge, MA: Harvard University Press,

the martyrdom account of Cyprian, who was executed during the Valerian persecution: "The emperors have also given orders that no meetings are to be held anywhere, nor shall they enter the burial areas."[24] The rescript of emperor Gallienus in 260, which ended the persecution, mentions the return of "places of worship" and "the lands of the so-called *koimeterioi.*"[25] Policing Christian boundaries was not only an internal matter; imperial officials also joined the effort.[26]

The binary spatial dynamic of pro/con-in/out intensified over the course of the next two centuries. During the Decian (249–250) persecution, which required inhabitants of the empire to participate in traditional Roman sacrifices, controversies erupted among Christian leaders over how to handle readmission into the Church of the lapsed or those who had merely obtained faked records of their having done so.[27] The conflict produced competing bishops in Rome, the rigorist Novatian and his rival Cornelius, who adhered to the more lenient position of reconciliation.[28] African bishops were summoned to resolve the controversy, which only exacerbated the division in both locales. In 251, lapsed bishops ordained Fortunatus bishop of Carthage and formed their own episcopal college with colleagues in Numidia.[29] Fortunatus and his faction sought

---

1965) (SC 41, electronic version): οὐδαμῶς δὲ ἐξέσται οὔτε ὑμῖν οὔτε ἄλλοις τισὶν ἢ συνόδους ποιεῖσθαι ἢ εἰς τὰ καλούμενα κοιμητήρια εἰσιέναι (And it shall in no way be permitted either to you or to any others either to hold assemblies or to enter the cemeteries, as they are called), quoted in Rebillard, *Care of the Dead*, p. 6.

[24] *Acta Proconsulari sancti Cypriani* 1.7, tr. Musurillo (PL 3): *Praeceperunt etiam, ne in aliquibus locis conciliabula fiant, nec coemeteria ingrediantur,* discussed in White, *Social Origins* vol. 2, p. 77, note 25.

[25] Eusebius, *Hist. eccl.* 7.13.1 (SC 41): τοι τόποι τῶν θρησκευσίμων ... τὰ τῶν καλουμένων κοιμητηρίων. Although the vocabulary may belong to Eusebius, the meaning is clear. On the significance of this rescript for toleration of Christianity, see Fergus Millar, *The Emperor in the Roman World 31 BC – AD 337* (London: Duckworth, 1977), p. 572, T. D. Barnes, *Early Christian Hagiography and Roman History,* Tria Corda 5 (Tübingen: Mohr Siebeck, 2010), pp. 97–103, and Graeme W. Clarke, "Third-Century Christianity," in *The Cambridge Ancient History, Vol 12: The Crisis of Empire, A.D. 193–337,* ed. Alan K. Bowman, Peter Garnsey, and Averil Cameron, pp. 589–671 (Cambridge, England: Cambridge University Press, 2005), pp. 645–646.

[26] I do not mean to imply that imperial officials were not Christian, merely that when they were executing anti-Christian imperial orders they may not have been expressing their Christian-ness. I also consider the possibility that, even before Constantine chose sides in sectarian conflicts, officials may have used anti-Christian orders to oppress particular groups of Christians.

[27] J. B. Rives, "The Decree of Decius and the Religion of Empire," *The Journal of Roman Studies* 89 (1999): 135–154.

[28] J. Patout Burns, *Cyprian the Bishop.* Routledge Early Church Monographs (New York: Routledge, 2002), pp. 88–89.

[29] Burns, *Cyprian,* p. 89.

recognition from Cornelius, but the Roman clergy refused to oust Cyprian from his see.

The use of church buildings to patrol these ideological group boundaries is evidenced by two letters written during the height of the schism. The first, written in 250 from the Roman clergy to Cyprian, disapproves of the laxists' practice of reconciling those lapsed who had obtained letters from imprisoned confessors (anticipating martyrdom).[30] These certificates promised the lapsed that, once martyred, the confessor would intercede on his or her behalf to obtain divine forgiveness, thereby circumventing the process of penance. The Romans' letter endorses Cyprian's position that readmission be delayed until persecution abated, at which time a council of the faithful should convene to decide the matter; in the meantime, the faithful should pray for the lapsed to patiently await the time when they could recognize their sin, submit to penance, and be welcomed back into communion.[31] The authors describe this liminal state in relation to the physical placement of the lapsed outside the church building: "By all means let them knock on the doors, but certainly let them not destroy them; let them approach the threshold of the church as suppliants, but certainly not jump over it."[32]

A second letter from Cyprian written to Bishop Cornelius of Rome in the year 252 uses *ecclesia* the same way. Clergy whom Cyprian regards as "false" along with those who had received communion from them "do not dare to come to or enter upon the threshold of the church."[33] In case they were prepared to repent, Cyprian reminds Cornelius, "the church here is not closed to anyone."[34] His use of the words *limen* (threshold) and *cludo* (closed) along with *ecclesia* is particularly concrete.

Cyprian's description includes the section of the church reserved for clergy, which he describes as "sacred" (*sacer*) and "venerated" (*venerandus*).[35]

---

[30] Novatian apud Cypr. *Ep.* 30.3–4.

[31] Novatian apud Cypr. *Ep.* 30.5–6. The authors present this as a way to stave off an outbreak of violence (*inquies*).

[32] Novatian apud Cypr. *Ep.* 30.6 (CCL 4): *Pulsent sane fores, sed non utique confringant. Adeant ad limen ecclesiae, sed non utique transiliant.*

[33] Cypr. *Ep.* 59.16.2, tr. White, *Social Origins* vol. 2, p. 74, slightly modified (dated to 252; CCL 3C): ... *nec audent venire aut ad ecclesiae limen accedere....* Cyprian's use elsewhere of *ecclesia* (with *sancta*) is either ambiguous or refers to an assembly (e.g. Cypr. *Unit. eccl.* 6, *Ep.* 70.1.2, 71.2.3).

[34] Cypr. *Ep.* 59.16.3, tr. White, *Social Origins* vol. 2, p. 74, slightly modified (dated to 252; CCL 3C): ... *Nec ecclesia istic cuiquam cluditur ....*

[35] Cypr. *Ep.* 59.18.1, tr. White, *Social Origins* vol. 2, p. 75 (CCL 3C): *in cleri nostri sacrum venerandum que congestum* ([T]he sacred and venerated gathering area of our clergy). This is the only occurrence of *sacer* in Cyprian's extant writings. Over a century ago,

Both adjectives associate the *congestus* (chancel) with divinity. For Cyprian, the sanctity of the chancel may have derived from the holiness of the rituals and the objects used there in the course of the liturgy, most notably the Scriptures.[36] North African Christians commonly referred to the Scriptures as "consecrated" (*deifici*) and "holy" (*sancti*).[37] Such ritual objects were regarded as holy, as evidenced by their role in the fourth-century Christian schism, where handing them over constituted the egregious sin of *traditio*. It is possible that through a kind of transitive property of holiness, the divine nature of the Scriptures conveyed sanctity to the places in which they were read.[38]

The connection between worship space and the attribute of holiness is later attested archaeologically in an inscription from Castellum Tingitanum (Chlef/Orléansville), Mauretania Caesariensis (Algeria).[39] The pavement's dating is problematic, since the building dedication claims a foundation date of 324 while the inscription itself dates to the fifth century, when renovations added a second apse in order to house the remains of bishop Reparatus.[40] The edifice, dedicated to a certain Marinus "servant of God," was likely endowed by emperor Constantine.[41] The dedication describes

E. W. atson interpreted *congestus* as a physical location or object: "the dais on which were the altar and seats for the clergy" (*Style and Language in the Writings of Saint Cyprian*, Studia Biblica et Ecclesiastica 4 (Oxford: Clarendon Press, 1896), p. 303). This view is repeated by Graeme W. Clarke (*The Letters of St. Cyprian of Carthage* 3, ACW 46 (New York: Newman Press, 1984), p. 263). White also notes that the use of *congestus* to designate this area is the "first known reference to give such an area a technical term" (76). Most interestingly, given the relationship of church architecture to synagogue development, the earliest epigraphic attestations of *locus sanctus* or its Greek equivalent, *hagios topos*, are from synagogue fragments in Stobi, Macedonia (IJO 1, Macc1, dated to late second/early third century) and Alexandria, Egypt (CIJ 2.1437 = Horbury/Noy JIRE 17, dated from the first century BCE to the third century CE).

[36] Yasin argues for pre-Constantinian sanctity on the basis of activity alone (*Saints and Church Spaces*, p. 44).

[37] *Le dossier du Donatisme*, ed. Jean Louis Maier, Texte und Untersuchungen zur Geschichte der altchristlichen Literatur 134 (Berlin: Akademie-Verlag, 1987), vol. 1, p. 50, citing Thesaurus Linguae Latinae 5 I, 403–404. See, for example, *Passio sancti Felicis episcopi* 1, tr. Musurillo, slightly emended (PL 8: 679B): ... *et propositum est per colonias et civitates principibus et magistratibus, suo cuique loco, ut libros deificos extorquerent de manibus episcoporum et presbyterorum* ... (The order was given to the rulers and magistrates throughout the cities and colonies that each in his locality should wrest the consecrated books from the hands of the bishops and presbyters) and Cypr. *Ep.* 72/3.25 *ad Jubaianum* (= *de Haereticis baptizandis*): ... *scriptura sancta declarat* ... (Holy Scripture states).

[38] For an anthropological analysis of this "transitive" phenomenon in a negative way, or "contagion," see Mary Douglas, *Purity and Danger: An Analysis of Concepts of Pollution and Taboo* (New York: Routledge & Kegan Paul, 1966: 2003), pp. 1–35.

[39] F. Prévost, "Notice Sur Orléansville," *Revue Archéologique* 4.2 (1848): 653–669, p. 664 and plate 78.

[40] Jean-Pierre Caillet, "Le dossier de la basilique chrétienne de Chlef [anciennement El Asnam, ou Orléansville]," *Karthago* 21 (1986–87): 135–161.

[41] Gregory T. Armstrong, "Constantine's Churches," *Gesta* 6 (January, 1967): 1–9, p. 6.

the building as a *basilica*.[42] Another floor mosaic in the westernmost bay of the basilica's northern aisle, adjacent to both the nave and the narthex at the time (before a second apse was added), describes the *ecclesia* as *sancta*.[43] Letters of the words "SANCTA ECLESIA" are embedded in an elaborate pattern at the center of a labyrinth (Figure 2.1).[44] In her study of Roman labyrinth mosaics, Rebecca Molholt has noted:[45]

> [L]abyrinth mosaics are representations of spatial experience that unify art and architecture … Maurice Merleau-Ponty's emphasis on the "lived perspective of the visible world in relation to our living body" provides an important model here, since he describes perception as "our kinaesthetic, prescientific lived-bodily presence to the world."

Unlike most of the other North African labyrinths, nearly half of which appear in public baths, this mosaic is too small to be entered with the whole

---

[42] CIL 8.9708 = ILCVı 1821, transcribed by Léon Renier, *Inscriptions romaines de l'Algérie* (Paris: Imprimerie Impériale, 1855), #3700: Pro(vinciae) / CCLXXX et V XII Kal(endas) / Dec(embres) eius basilicae / fundamenta posita / sunt et fa[…]m / pro(vinciae) CCLXX[… in] / mente habeas […] / servum dei[… in] / deo vivas (In the provincial year 285, on the 12th day (prior to the) kalends of December [= Nov. 20, 324 CE], the foundations of this basilica were laid and … the 2[90th] provincial year … May you keep in mind … the servant of God. … May you live in God). For discussion see G. Vidal, *Un témoin d'une date célèbre: la basilique d'Orléansville* (Algiers: Fontana, 1936), N. Duval, "Les Églises à deux absides d'Algérie: analyse critique," *Corsi di cultura sull'Arte Bizantina e Ravennate* 17 (1970): 121–127, Caillet, "Le dossier de la basilique chrétienne de Chlef," 135–161, Yasin, *Saints*, pp. 140–143, and J. Patout Burns and Robin M. Jensen, *Christianity in Roman North Africa*, in collaboration with Graeme W. Clarke, Susan T. Stevens, William Tabbernee, and Maureen A. Tilley (Grand Rapids, MI: Wm. B. Eerdmans Publishing Co., 2014), pp. 133–134. As Yasin observes, "the inscription explicitly aimed to preserve the memory of the church's historic foundation through direct appeal to the viewers" (p. 142).

[43] Its similarity to other third- and fourth-century square labyrinth mosaics suggests that it may have been part of the original pavement. Compare the mosaics from Hadrumetum (Sousse, Tunisia), dating to 200–250, Salzburg, Austria, now Vienna Art Museum, dating 275–300, Belalis Maior (Hr. el Faouar, Tunisia), dating ca. 300, and Thuburbo Maius (Hr. Kasbat, Tunisia), dating to the late third/early fourth century. Rebecca Molholt has observed that "Large-scale labyrinth mosaics were especially popular in the baths of Roman North Africa, where the demands of their traversal and their peripatetic viewing prompted broader, metaphoric meanings to come into play" ("Roman Labyrinth Mosaics and the Experience of Motion," *The Art Bulletin* 93.3 (2011): 287–303, p. 287). Molholt notes that while the majority of Roman labyrinth mosaics are found in domestic contexts (nine in North African villas), seven are found in North African baths (p. 287). Some of these directly allude to the myth of Theseus and the Minotaur, depicted at the center of the mosaic in the baths at Belalis Maior, Tunisia.

[44] CIL 8.9710 = ILCVı 1580 = AE 1914: 49. The position of the mosaic in the left aisle facing north, four meters from the dedicatory inscription, at the opposite end of the nave from the original apse, suggests that it was for use in contemplation rather than in the course of the liturgy.

[45] Molholt, "Roman Labyrinth Mosaics," p. 288.

Figure 2.1 Mosaic in the Basilica of Reparatus. Drawing by Charles Saunier, from F. Prévost, "Notice Sur Orléansville," *Revue Archéologique* 4.2 (1847–1848): 653–669, plate 78, enhanced by author. Reprinted by permission.

body. Rather, it was intended for visual use.[46] The eye could trace a path that the mind knew would find its way to the center, perhaps linger on the word puzzle at the center to decipher the unusual arrangement of letters, and then back out again. Instead of the Roman ritual of bathing, however, this labyrinth appeals to the experience of the viewer in the Christian ritual of communion. The "holy Church" word puzzle replaces the standard central motif of Theseus slaying the Minotaur. In the prologues to his commentaries on the prophets, Jerome quotes Vergil's references to the myth, suggesting that Christ guides his faithful through the maze of life.[47] In the

---

[46] Molholt, "Roman Labyrinth Mosaics," p. 290.
[47] Jerome, *Comm. Ezech.* prologue 14, after quoting Vergil's allusion to the myth (Aen. 5.588–591) "A letter from Jerome (410–414)," tr. Joan Ferrante, accessed at http://epistolae.ccn-mtl.columbia.edu/letter/274.html, accessed on July 24, 2015 (CCL 75): *ita et ego, sanctarum scripturarum ingressus oceanum et mysteriorum dei ut sic loquar labyrinthum – de quo scriptum est: posuit tenebras latibulum suum et: nubes in circuitu eius –, perfectam quidem scientiam veritatis mihi vindicare non audeo, sed nosse cupientibus aliqua doctrinae indicia praebuisse: non meis viribus sed christi misericordia, qui, errantibus nobis, ... ipse dolos tecti ambages que resolvit, caeca regens*

original mosaic, now in the Sacred Heart Cathedral of Algiers, a wavy red thread can be seen finding its way out from the center of the maze, perhaps representing Jerome's "thread of Christ," showing viewers the way to the holy Church and on to eternal life. If this mosaic dates to the first quarter of the fourth century, just decades after the Diocletian persecution, the route to the holy Church would have been fraught with danger, much like the path of Theseus.[48]

Although it could be argued that the word *ecclesia* here may denote the Christian community, its inscription within the physical confines of this particular assembly's meeting place literally unites the two meanings. As discussed earlier, Tertullian and Cyprian used *ecclesia* in both senses. Already

spiritu sancto vestigia (So I, having entered on the ocean of holy scriptures and mysteries of God shall speak like the labyrinth about which it is written: "he put his refuge in darkness" and "clouds are all around him" [Ps 96:2]. I do not dare to claim perfect knowledge of truth for myself but I know I have offered some disclosures to those desiring doctrine not by my strength but by the mercy of Christ who, to us wandering, "helped resolve the wiles and mazes, guiding the blind footsteps" [Aen. 6.29–30] with the holy Spirit), and Jerome, *Comm. Zach.* prolog. 2 (CCL 76A, modified): *abyssus abyssum invocat, in voce cataractarum dei; et gyrans gyrando vadit spiritus, et in circulos suos revertitur. labyrinthios patimur errores, et christi caeca* regimus *filo vestigia* ("Deep calls to deep with the sound of god's floodgates" [Ps 41.8] and "the spirit rushes around and around and is reversed in its circle" [Eccl. 1:6], we are afflicted by the labyrinth of our straying, and "our blind footsteps" are "guided by the thread" of Christ [reworking Aen. 6.30]). See also Tertullian, *Marc.* 3.18.4 (CCL 1): *Ioseph, et ipse christum figuraturus ... quod persecutionem a fratribus passus est ob dei gratiam, sicut et christus a iudaeis carnaliter <fratribus,> cum benedicitur a patre etiam in haec verba: tauri decor eius, cornua unicornis cornua eius, in eis nationes ventilabit pariter ad summum usque terrae, non utique rhinoceros destinabatur unicornis nec minotaurus bicornis, sed christus in illo significabatur, taurus ob utramque dispositionem, aliis ferus ut iudex, aliis mansuetus ut salvator, cuius cornua essent crucis extima. Nam et in antemna, quae crucis pars est, extremitates cornua vocantur, unicornis autem mediae stipitis palus. Hac denique virtute crucis et hoc more cornutus universas gentes et nunc ventilat per fidem, auferens a terra in caelum, et tunc per iudicium ventilabit, deiciens de caelo in terram* (Joseph was also a type for Christ ... that he suffered persecution from his brothers on account of the grace of God, just as Christ did from the Jews, his brothers after the flesh; but when he is blessed by his father with these words: "His majesty is that of a bull, his horns are the horns of a unicorn; with them he will drive the nations to the ends of the earth (Deut 33:17)," certainly he is not destined to be a one-horned rhinoceros nor a two-horned Minotaur, but Christ was prefigured in him, a bull with regard to both of his natures: for some as fierce as a judge, for others as mild as a savior whose horns were the extremities of the cross. For the ends of the transverse, which is a part of a cross, are called horns (cf. Virgil, *Aen.* 3.549), while the "unicorn" refers to the uppermost protrusion of the middle stake).

[48] It is this interpretation that leads Maria Teresa Bua to conclude that the church is Donatist (*I giuochi alfabetici delle tavole Iliache. Memorie dell'Accademia dei Lincei* Ser. 8, 16.1 (Rome: Accademia Nazionale dei Lincei, 1971), p. 27). See also the analysis of Piotr Rypson, "'Homo Quadratus in Labyrintho.' The Cubus or Labyrinth Poem," in *European Iconography East and West: Selected Papers of the Szeged International Conference*, June 9–12, 1993, ed. György E. Szónyi, pp. 6–21 (Leiden: E. J. Brill, 1996), pp. 11–12.

by the third century, Cyprian considered that part of the building where the clergy performed the sacred liturgy to be sacred and venerated. This fourth (or fifth) century mosaic reveals that some Christians were prepared to inscribe that perception of holiness into the floor of the building itself, reminding those who entered that this was no ordinary place.

Besides the word *ecclesia*, the term most familiar to students of Christian architecture is *basilica*. *Basilica* is first applied to Christian buildings in fourth-century inscriptions and literature. It has been argued that the term was initially selected by Christians because of its religious "neutrality"; Margherita Carucci has therefore proposed avoiding the word altogether and using the translation "audience-chamber," which conveys the broader place meaning envisioned in antiquity.[49] Although the translation is cumbersome, it is useful for conveying the degree to which *basilica* was, at least initially, a religiously nonvalent term. It is only over time, as the term was repeatedly invoked in Christian contexts, that it acquired a religious place meaning. The earliest extant North African example of *basilica* used in an archaeological context is a suburban cemetery church inscription in Altava, Mauretania Caesariensis (Ouled Mimoun, Algeria) dated to the year 309. The inscription dedicates a *mensa* (altar-table), describing its location as a "basilica of the Lord" as well as a *memoria*.[50]

---

[49] Neutrality: William J. Diebold, *Word and Image: An Introduction to Early Medieval Art* (Boulder, CO: Westview Press, 1999), p. 60 (who argues that the form was not borrowed from Roman precedents), Inge Nielsen, "basilica," in Brill's New Pauly (online version: http://referenceworks.brillonline.com/browse/brill-s-new-pauly, accessed June 12, 2015), and Mohrmann, "Les Dénominations de l'église," p. 169. Audience-chamber: Margherita Carucci, *The Romano-African Domus: Studies in Space, Decoration, and Function*, BAR International Series 1731 (Oxford: Archaeopress, 2007), p. 8. Jewish literature of the period also uses the term *basilica* in its generic Roman architectural sense (for example, *Tosefta Sukkah* 4.6, describing the great synagogue of Alexandria).

[50] AE 1969/70: 737c: Me[n]sa Ianuari mar[t]uris. P[i]e, zeses … [Confe]ssione sancti et bas{s} ilica dominica / [et] memoria bb(eatorum) vv(irorum) L(uci) Honorati L() P() Ta[n]/ [n]oni Victoris <di=Z>(aconi) et Tannoni Ru[fini]/ani L() P() fecit L(ucius) Tannonius Roga[tus] / [3]s IIII ab Honorato a(nno) p(rovinciae) CCLXX = 309 CE (An altar-table of martyr Januarius. Drink! May you live! … An acknowledgement of the holy one and a basilica of the Lord and a memorial of the blessed men Lucius Honoratus LP, Tannonius Victor deacon at Tannonius Rufinus LP. Lucius Tannonius Rogatus made it. … fourth son of Honorus, in the provincial year 270); J. Marcillet-Jaubert, *Les Inscriptions d'Altava* (Aix-en-Provence: Éditions Ophrys, 1968) 32–35 (= no. 19). For discussion see White, *Social Origins* vol. 2, p. 241 and Yvette Duval, *Loca Sanctorum Africae: Le culte des martyrs en Afrique du IVe au VIIe siècle*. Collection de L'école française de Rome 58, vol. 1, pp. 412–417 and vol. 2, p. 584 (Rome: École Française de Rome, 1982). Note that the term *basilica* requires modification with the adjective *dominica* to clarify its status as a Christian church. Duval points out that the term *basilica* eventually disappears in connection with martyria when relic depositions replace actual tombs or cenotaphs (*Loca Sanctorum* vol. 2, p. 584).

Even if Christians accepted the term *basilica* because of its "secularity," it was soon embroiled in the same sectarian squabbles as the buildings them- selves.[51] Minutes of the 315 hearing of Abthugni bishop Felix quote the non-Christian duovir Alfius Caecilianus as saying: "at Zama and at Furnos I saw audience-chambers being destroyed [under Diocletian]."[52] During the same persecution, bishop Mensurius of Carthage was accused of allow- ing Roman officials to confiscate certain books from the *basilica Novarum*.[53] During the course of an imperial investigation of the Christian schism of 320 CE, a testifying witness identified the church of the dissident bishop Silvanus in Cirta (Constantine) as a *basilica*.[54] As noted earlier, the floor ded- ication from Castellum Tingitanum identifies the building as a *basilica*.[55]

A few decades later, Optatus describes the *basilicae* of dissident Christians as redundant.[56] Optatus' Catholic perspective, viewing those he calls "Donatists" as schismatics, leads him to portray dissident structures as unnecessary duplications. This staunchly partisan perspective misrepresents the situation throughout most of North Africa, where more than 170 sees claimed both dissident and Catholic bishops in the year 411, even after imperial sanction.[57] Optatus' comments reveal his disdain and disregard for dissident churches. His characterization of them as redundant is likely to reflect the situation on the ground, as archaeologist Gareth Sears points out: "many basilicas were unnecessary probably because of the duplicating effect of having both Catholics and dissidents in a city."[58] The dissidents,

---

[51] Mohrmann, "Les Dénominations de l'église," p. 170.

[52] *Act. pur. Fel.* 4, tr. *Paganism and Christianity, 100–425 C.E.: A Sourcebook*, ed. Ramsay MacMullen and Eugene Lane (Minneapolis, MN: Augsburg Fortress, 1992), p. 242 (CSEL 26: 199): *Alfius Caecilianus dixit: … vidi iam exempla et Zama et Furnis dirui basilicas …* See discussion in the next chapter as well as Barnes, *Constantine and Eusebius*, p. 58.

[53] Aug. *Brev. Coll.* 3.13.25 (CSEL 53): *qui tamen non scripserat se sanctos codices tradidisse, sed potius ne a persecutoribus invenirentur abstulisse atque servasse, dimisisse autem in basilica novarum quae- cumque reproba scripta haereticorum* (He had not handed over the books written by the saints but rather it was spurious writings of the heretics, which he had deposited in the basilica Novarum, that were discovered, confiscated, and held by the persecutors).

[54] *Gest. Zeno.* 15, discussed by Mohrmann, p. 171.

[55] CIL 8.9708 = ICLV 1821, in an ornate mosaic medallion: Pro(vinciae) | CCLXXX et V. XII kal. | Dec. eius basilicae | fundamenta posita | sunt et fa[stigiu]m | a(nno) pro(vinciae) CCLXX[X....] in | mente habeas [Marinum?] | servum dei, [et] in | deo vivas! (In the provincial year 285, in the calends of December, the foundations of this basilica and the pediment were laid. In the provincial year 2[8?]. May you have in mind Marinus, a servant of God, and may you live in God!)

[56] Optatus, *de schism. Don.* 3.1.2 (SC): *basilicas fecerunt non necessarias.* See also 4.6.7 (*colligitis*, assemblies).

[57] Dossey, *Peasant and Empire*, p. 261n1.

[58] Sears, *Late Roman African Urbanism*, p. 97.

portrayed as sectarian break-aways, had created what Optatus considered to be unnecessary places because, to his way of thinking, their occupants should simply rejoin the fold and worship in the "main" (i.e. Catholic) basilicas.

As far as we know, no easily recognizable features distinguished Catholic from dissident basilicas. This ambiguity not only challenges identifications by modern archaeologists, but apparently was perceived in antiquity as well. In his anti-Manichaen treatise written around 396, Augustine suggests that classifying buildings as either "Catholic" or "Donatist" relied on their users' interpretation:[59]

> Finally, the name "Catholic" holds me in the Catholic Church. It was not without reason that this Church (*ecclesia*) alone, among so many heresies, acquired this name so that, though all heretics want to be called Catholic, no heretic would dare to point out his own basilica (*basilica*) or house (*domus*) to some stranger who asked where the Catholic [Church] was assembled.

This identification process provided an opportunity to use place in the strategy of producing difference between the two groups. This passage also reveals that the nomenclature for religious buildings varied. While here Augustine refers to the dissidents' gathering place with the words *basilica* and *domus*, elsewhere he suggests that *ecclesia* was interchangeable with *basilica*, denoting both the place of worship and the Christians who assembled there: "Just as, then, we call the church the *basilica* that contains the people, who are properly called the *ecclesia*, so that by the term *ecclesia*, that is, the people who are contained, we signify the place that contains them ..."[60]

The term *domus* without the genitive *dei* associates another place meaning of Christian worship space with the Roman family and its dwelling. This association likely emerged from early gatherings in private homes, as indicated by a dissident martyrdom account of the Abitinian martyrs under Diocletian: "I am the guardian in whose house (*domus*) the congregation was assembled ... In my house (*domus*) we conducted the Lord's Supper."[61] In a similar fashion,

[59] Aug. *Fund.* 4, tr. Roland Teske, slightly modified, The Works of Saint Augustine (3rd Release), Electronic edition, The Manichean Debate, vol. I/19 (Charlottesville, VA: InteLex Corporation, 2001) (CSEL 25): *tenet postremo ipsum catholicae nomen, quod non sine causa inter tam multas haereses sic ista ecclesia sola obtinuit, ut cum omnes haeretici se catholicos dici velint, quaerenti tamen alicui peregrino, ubi ad catholicam conveniatur, nullus haereticorum vel basilicam suam vel domum audeat ostendere.*

[60] Aug. *Ep.* 190.19 (CSEL 57): *sicut ergo appellamus ecclesiam basilicam, qua continetur populus, qui vere appellatur ecclesia, ut nomine ecclesiae, id est populi, qui continetur, significemus locum, qui continet ...*, dated to 418.

[61] *Acta Saturnini presbyteri, Felicis, Dativi, Ampelii et al.* 8–9, tr. White, *Social Origins* vol. 2, p. 89 (PL 8: 694D–95C, cited by White as 690): *Ego sum auctor, inquit, in cujus domo collecta facta fuit. ... in domo mea, inquit, egimus dominicum.*

a recently identified Donatist sermon of the fifth century describes the *eccle-sia* as a tabernacle, a "dwelling-place of Christ."[62] The homilest compares Abraham's relocation from Ur to Canaan, where he built "an altar to the Lord" (Gen 12:1–8), to the way Christians make their home in the Church:[63]

> In like manner, when a Christian arrives in this country, which is the Church, he pitches a tent, finds a home, and erects a dwelling. We say that the tent is the Church, the dwelling-place we call "Christ our Lord."

While some Christians gathered in private homes, even nonresidential worship space continued to evoke a sense of belonging, protection, and group identification.[64]

Besides the well-attested designations *ecclesia, basilica,* and *domus,* North African literature uses other names for Christian worship spaces. Perhaps because of its association in Latin literature with Roman religious activity, Cyprian uses the word *conventicula* to refer to the ritual arenas of those he regards as heretics.[65] In the wake of the Decian persecution (249–251 CE), the bishop notes the physical separation between opposing factions in the controversy over rebaptism: "[A]fterwards when heresies and schisms were generated while establishing for themselves different meeting places (*conventicula*), they abandoned the source and origin of truth."[66]

---

[62] Anon. *H. Esc.* 59.3 ("*De principiis de Christiani nominis,*" in François J. Leroy, "Les 22 inédits de la catéchèse donatiste de Vienne. Une édition provisoire," *Recherches Augustiniennes et Patristiques* 31 (1999): 149–234).

[63] Anon. *H. Esc.* 59.3 (ed. Leroy): *Similiter, christianus in hanc terram, id es ecclesiam, veniens tab-ernaculum figit, domicilium invenit, habitationem instituit. Tabernaculum ecclesiam dicimus, habitacu-lum Christum dominum nuncupamus …*

[64] Private homes: See *Cod. theod.* 16.6.4.1, tr. Pharr (ed. Mommsen): *Si vero his nesciis per con-ductorem procuratoremve eorum in domo agitatum huiusmodi facinus comprobatur …* (If, however, without the knowledge of the owners, such a crime is proved to have been committed in their home …).

[65] Tacitus, *Annales* 14.15.2, tr. Church and Brodribb (ed. Heubner): *quin et feminae inlustres deformia meditari; exstructa que apud nemus, quod navali stagno circumposuit Augustus, conventicula et cauponae et posita veno inritamenta luxui* (Noble ladies too actually played disgusting parts, and in the grove, with which Augustus had surrounded the lake for the naval fight, there were erected places for meeting and refreshment, and every incentive to excess was offered for sale) and Apuleius, *Metamorphoses* 10.19 (ed. Zimmerman): *Fuit in illo* conventiculo *matrona quaedam pollens et opulens* [emph. mine] (Among that assembly was a rich and powerful noblewoman); Cypr. *Unit. eccl.* 12 (CCL 3) cited and translated in Chapter 1. See also *Ep.* 59.14.1, tr. Clarke (CCL 3): *… foris sibi extra ecclesiam et contra ecclesiam constituisse* conventiculum *perditae factionis, quo male sibi consciorum et deum rogare ac satisfacere nolentium* caterva *conflueret …* [emph. mine] (It was not enough for them to have set up for themselves outside and beyond the Church and in opposition to the Church a conventicle for their lawless faction, to which there might throng the guilt-ridden mob of those who refused to entreat God's mercy and make Him reparation).

[66] Cypr. *Unit. eccl.* 12 (CCL 3): *… cum haeresis et schismata postmodum nata sint dum* conven-ticula *sibi diversa constituunt,* veritatis *caput adque originem reliquerunt* [emph. mine].

The bishop expresses the emerging sectarian identification of his community and that of his opponents in spatial terms that distinguish his gathering place from theirs. Spatial practice, therefore, embodied the concept of "no salvation outside the Church," both in the sectarian sense Cyprian originally intended and in the broader religious context to which it was later applied.[67] Although *conventiculum* (meeting-place) is a relatively neutral term for the places of opposing bishops, Cyprian also uses the word *latebra* (lair), which explicitly conveys secrecy, slyness, and illegitimacy.[68] Cyprian lobs this negatively valent word at his opponents in order to construe them as schismatic instigators; *they* are the ones who separated from the core, not him. Despite the fact that there was often no overtly discernible architectural distinction between opposing groups' structures, Christian rhetoric construed spatial separation as theological deviance.

Notwithstanding its disparaging association in Cyprian, the late third century Numidian rhetorician Arnobius of Sicca uses the same term *conventicula* to describe his own place of worship, without any negative connotations.[69] Although third-century Sicca was not comparable to Carthage as a cultural center, Sicca was a well-established, important Roman *colonia* with a vigorous Christian community.

A fragment of the third-century Neoplatonist Porphyry suggests that Arnobius was responding to the philosopher's defense of pagan piety and attack on Christian worship places:[70]

---

[67] Cypr. *Ep.* 73.21.2, tr. Clarke, biblical references added (CCL 3B): *Quod si haeretico nec baptisma publicae confessionis et sanguinis proficere ad salutem potest, quia salus extra ecclesiam non est, quanto magis ei nihil proderit, si in latebra et in latronum spelunca adulterae aquae contagio tinctus non tantum peccata antiqua non exposuerit, sed adhuc potius* nova *et maiora* cumulaverit? (If, then, not even the baptism of blood and of public confession will profit the heretic for salvation – for there is no salvation outside the Church – how much more must this be so if in some lair, in some "den of thieves" (Jer 7.11; Mk 11.17 and parallels), a man is bathed in polluted and spurious water, and so far from putting off his old sins, he loads himself with yet more fresh and graver ones).

[68] Cypr. *Ep.* 73.21.2.

[69] Arnobius, *Ad. Nat.* 4.36 (152; PL 5: 1076A): *Nam nostra quidem scripta cur ignibus meruerunt dari? cur immaniter conventicula dirui? in quibus summus oratur Deus ...* (Why did our writings deserve to be consigned to flames? Why did our meeting places [deserve] to be savagely demolished? In which the highest God is supplicated ...). For later uses of *conventiculum* to refer to a church, see Lact. *Instit.* 5.11.10: *Aliqui ad occidendum praecipites exstiterunt; sicut unus in Phrygia, qui universum populum cum ipso pariter conventiculo concremavit* (Some stood quick to kill, as someone in Phrygia who burnt an entire crowd together with their church). See "ecclesia," Thesaurus Linguae Latinae 5.2.1: 32–39; "conventiculum," Thesaurus Linguae Latinae 4:844–845. The examples cited for the latter from Ammianus Marcellinus 15.5.31 and 27.3.13 are not definitive.

[70] Porphyry, *Ad. Christ.*, frag. 76, ed. A. Harnack, *Porphyrius: "Gegen die Christen"* (Berlin: Verlag der Königlich-Preußische Akademie der Wissenschaften, 1916), tr. White, *Social Origins*

But the Christians, imitating the construction of temples, erect great buildings in which they meet to pray, though there is nothing to prevent them from doing this in their own homes since, of course, their Lord hears them everywhere.

In addition to remarking how Christians imitate pagans by building churches, Porphyry implies that they undertake such building projects in violation of their own theological principles. In his refutation, Arnobius denies any resemblance between Christian places of assembly (*conventicula*) and those of pagans (*aedes, templa, delubra, fana, sacella*). In so doing, he either completely ignores or is unaware of the adoption of certain spatial concepts associated with Roman temples by earlier writers Tertullian and Cyprian. He points out that while Christians assembled to "pray to God," non-Christians built temples to house their no-gods.[71] Arnobius puts these "pagan" claims against Christians in the mouth of an anonymous interlocutor who, among a whole litany of complaints, accuses Christians of failing to construct "consecrated habitations" (*aedes sacra*) for worship. Arnobius counters this accusation by asserting that real gods don't need "houses."[72] He unequivocally rejects the notion that Christian worship places house the divine, that they could in any way be what Tertullian had called a *domus dei*. With the exception of the Scriptures and divine power, Arnobius reserves the term "sacra" for pagan paraphernalia. This view diverges from Cyprian's notion of the *congestum* as *sacra*.[73]

vol.1, p. 104: ἀλλὰ καὶ οἱ Χριστιανοὶ μιμούμενοι τὰς κατασκευὰς τῶν ναῶν μεγίστους οἴκους οἰκοδομοῦσιν, εἰς οὓς συνιόντες εὔχονται, καίτοι μηδενὸς κωλύοντος ἐν ταῖς οἰκίαις τοῦτο πράττειν, τοῦ κυρίου δηλονότι πανταχόθεν ἀκούοντος. The fragment is preserved in an early fourth-century Christian apology by Macarius Magnes of Magnesia.

[71] Arnobius, *Ad. Nat.* 4.36 (152), quoted in Monceaux 3.11: *conventicula ... in quibus summus oratur ... Deus.*

[72] Arnobius, *Ad. Nat.* 6.1 (PL 5:1162b): *In hac enim consuescitis parte crimen nobis maximum impietatis affingere; quod neque aedes sacras venerationis ad officia construamus.* See also *Ad. Nat.* 6.3 (PL 5:1164b, 1168–1169A): *Numquid enim delubris aut templorum eum constructionibus honoramus? ... Ita non prima et maxima contumelia est, habitationibus deos habere districtos, tuguriola his dare, conclavia et cellulas fabricari, et eis existimari necessarias res esse, quae hominibus, felibus, quae sunt formiculis, et lacertis, quae fugacibus, pavidis, atque exiguis muribus?* (For do we give honor with shrines or by building temples? ... Is it not, then, the prime and greatest insult to have harassed the gods in habitations, to give them little huts, to build [them] chambers and cells, and to think that the things that are considered necessary for them are the same as for men, cats, ants, and lizards, and even for scampering, fearful, little mice?).

[73] Arnobius, *Ad. Nat.* 1.28, 51, 2.5; 1.24, 28, 43, 2.42, 67, 70, 73, 76, 3.3, 15, 23, 4.16, 31, 35, 5.1, 2, 5, 7, 15, 17, 18, 19, 21, 22, 23, 24, 26, 29, 39, 42, 6.1, 5, 13, 15, 17, 21, 7.3, 6, 9, 11, 12, 13, 14, 17, 18, 19, 20, 23, 24, 25, 26, 31, 33, 37, 38. 3.2 is an exceptional reference to Christian sacred customs (*communia sacra*), but it is put in the mouth of the pagan interlocutor.

Arnobius' hostility is in part a reaction to the spatial rhetoric and representation of his environment. A late third-/early fourth-century inscription from Sicca praises a colonial curator for restoring a statue of Venus which thieves had stolen.[74] Responding to events like this, Arnobius argues that gods are unable to protect their temples.[75] He adduces further evidence to buttress his claim of the gods' impotence: various ritual objects had been damaged by natural disasters or human malfeasance. Throughout his discussion, Arnobius never admits that Christians owned similar objects that had been confiscated in the course of the Diocletian persecution.[76] Nor does he acknowledge any similarities between Christian and Roman traditionalist notions of place.

It is worth pausing to recall that, according to Jerome, Arnobius wrote this treatise to the bishop of Sicca to demonstrate the sincerity of his Christian affirmation so that he would be accepted into the Church.[77] Arnobius' own introductory remarks suggest he is refuting Roman attacks against Christians.[78] The two claims are not at odds but, rather, are likely to be the case when we consider that prior to his identifying as Christian,

---

[74] CIL 8.15881, tr. Ulrich Gehn, "Last Statues of Antiquity," accessed at http://laststatues. classics.ox.ac.uk/database/discussion.php?id=2828, on July 12, 2016, quoted in Michael Bland Simmons, *Arnobius of Sicca. Religious Conflict and Competition in the Age of Diocletian* (New York: Oxford University Press, 1995), p. 104: Mirae bonitatis adque in/tegritatis viro Valerio Romano, / v(iro) c(larissimo), curatori reip(ublicae) col(oniae) Siccensi/um et Veneris ob restauratum / deae Simulacrum quod iam dudum / a latronibus fuerat interrupta / templi munitione sublatum / statuam Venerii ad propagandam / saeclis omnibus memoriam / patrono fido amore posuerunt (To a man of extraordinary goodness and integrity, Valerius Romanus, of clarissimus rank, curator of the city (res publica) of the most splendid colony of the Siccenses and of Venus. On account of the restoration of the statue of the goddess which was taken by bandits who had broken the walls of the temple. The faithful followers of Venus, to spread his memory through all centuries, set up (this) statue to their patron with devoted love); "Valerius Romanus 13," PLRE I: 770.

[75] Arnobius, *Ad. Nat* 6.20–3.

[76] A list of gold, silver, and bronze objects is enumerated in the administrative records of Munatius Felix, colonial curator in Cirta (*Act. Mun. Fel.* in *Gest. Zeno.* 3–4 (CSEL 26: 186–188), translated in White, *Social Origins* vol. 2, pp. 105–110.

[77] Arnobius was known for his anti-Christian attacks (Jerome, *Chron.* 326–327 CE, tr. Roger Pearse et al., "The Chronicle of St. Jerome," accessed at www.tertullian.org/fathers/jerome_chronicle_00_eintro.htm, 2005 on May 20, 2012) (Corpus Berolinense 47): *arnobius rhetor in africa clarus habetur. qui cum siccae ad declamandum iuvenes erudiret et adhuc ethnicus ad credulitatem somniis compelleretur neque ab episcopo impetraret fidem, quam semper inpugnaverat, elucubravit adversum pristinam religionem luculentissimos libros et tandem velut quibusdam obsidibus pietatis foedus impetravit* (In Africa, Arnobius the rhetor is considered important, who when he was in Sicca teaching the youths to declaim, and, being still a pagan, was compelled by dreams to believe, although he had not obtained from the bishop by asking the faith that he had always attacked, he composed the most splendid books against the former religion, and finally, as if with these as offerings, he requested and obtained the covenant of faith).

[78] Arnobius, *Ad. Nat.* 1.1.

Arnobius had himself used Roman works to attack Christians. The writer's association with Neoplatonists like Porphyry explains the bishop's hesitation to baptize him.[79] Based on the evidence of third- and fourth-century authors, Porphyry's writings were well known among Christian literati.[80] Due to the circumstances in which *Against the Nations* was composed, Arnobius' remonstrations are adamant and belligerent. Arnobius wrote between 302 and305 CE having witnessed two formative series of historical events: First, in the period 284–306 CE, twenty-one temple constructions and renovations were undertaken in Africa Proconsularis; and second, in three years of Christian persecution under Diocletian (303–305), African Christians suffered numerous executions and property confiscation.[81] The combination of Roman temple expansion and Christian basilica destruction undoubtedly contributed to Arnobius' ambivalence, if not outright hostility, toward religious structures.[82]

Arnobius' crowning argument against traditional Roman temples is that they "cover bones and ashes and [merely] serve as tombs of corpses."[83] He proceeds to list nine Roman temples which contain tombs of mythic individuals.[84] He tops his list with a mischievous pun, that the Roman capitolium acquired its name from the head of a man named Aulus/Olus laid in its foundation (hence caput + olium, "the head of Olus"), citing the authority of no less than four ancient authors.[85] The entire argument is rather strained given the status and function of cemetery sites for North African Christians, and demonstrates the extent of Arnobius' animosity toward Roman religious spaces.[86]

---

[79] Simmons, *Arnobius*, p. 9. Porphyry of Tyre's anti-Christian writings were likely epitomized under the title *Against the Christians* around 1000 CE (Robert M. Berchman, *Porphyry. Against the Christians* (Leiden: Koninklijke Brill NV, 2005), p. 5). Modern critical editions compile fragments attributed to Porphyry in Christian works.

[80] Berchman, *Porphyry*, p. 4.

[81] Simmons, *Arnobius*, pp. 121, 93.

[82] This view is repeated by Arnobius' student Lactantius, who wrote that Christians should pray to god at home rather than in temples (Lact. *Instit.* 6.25.3).

[83] Arnobius, *Ad. Nat.* 6.6 (CSEL 4): *Quid quod multa ex his templa, quae tholis sunt aureis et sublimibus elata fastigiis, auctorum conscriptionibus conprobatur contegere cineres atque ossa et functo-rum esse corporum sepulturas [esse]?* Timothy Barnes points out that this polemic was adopted by pagans and thrown back at Christians in the fourth century (*Ammianus Marcellinus and the Representation of Historical Reality*, Cornell Studies in Classical Philology 56 (Ithaca, NY: Cornell University Press, 1998), p. 85).

[84] Arnobius, *Ad. Nat.* 6.6.

[85] Arnobius, *Ad. Nat.* 6.7 (CSEL 4): *... ex Oli capite Capitolium quam ex nomine Iovio nuncupare* (naming it after the head of Olus, "Capitolium," rather than the name Jupiter).

[86] Gerard Bartelink notes that *sepulchrum* is a tool of religious invective, and that its Greek equivalent (τάφος) is found earlier in Clement of Alexandria (*Prot.* 3.44.4, 4.49.3, and

Arnobius' attack on buildings that housed corpses notwithstanding, cemeteries served as sites for veneration of the dead throughout the
ancient Mediterranean. For Christians, burial sites offered one of the earliest opportunities to publicly and physically delineate boundaries of community and identification. As discussed earlier in this chapter, Tertullian
reports that those *coemeteria* owned by Christians were desecrated by mobs
of Carthaginians.[87] Archaeological excavations reveal that already by the
time of Tertullian, these cemetery sections (*area*) were enclosed by walls.[88]
Coemeteria were not merely cemeteries, but included monumental tombs
built over inhumations, often of martyrs.[89] Along with their ordinary dead,
Christians put up monuments to mark the spots either where martyrs were
killed or where they were subsequently buried. Tertullian, author of the
famous saying about the blood of martyrs being seed of the Church, also
remarked that the souls of the martyrs lay beneath the altar (citing Rev. 6.9
regarding the fifth seal).[90] Some of these monuments were merely commemorative, some were epitaphs, some were mausoleums, and others were
tables for funerary banquets (which at some point in time came to include
the eucharist). In this regard, Christians adapted Roman funerary practices
to meet their own communal needs.[91] Christian congregations celebrated
the eucharist in commemoration of the dead on their anniversaries, as
attested by Tertullian and Cyprian.[92] The earliest archaeological evidence

10.91.1; Bartelink, "Repression von Häretikern und anderen religiösen Gruppierungen im
    späteren Altertum, in der Sprache widerspiegelt," in *Violence in Ancient Christianity: Victims
    and Perpetrators,* ed. Albert C. Geljon and Riemer Roukema, pp. 185–197, Supplements to
    Vigiliae Christianae 125 (Boston, MA: Brill, 2014), p. 192. Clement and Arnobius list the
    same temples from the same ancient sources, but only Arnobius includes the Capitolium, a
    recurring target of his attacks (1.34, 6.16, 6.23, 7.40).
[87] Tert. *An.* 5.17, *Scap.* 3.1, and *Apol.* 37.2, quoted in Rebillard, *Care of the Dead,* pp. 4, 8,
    10. A fourth-century *coemeteria* dedication plaque from Caesarea Mauretania (Cherchel) is
    thought to be based on an earlier inscription (CIL 8.9505/20958, discussed in Duval, *Loca
    Sanctorum* I, pp. 380–383).
[88] Rebillard, *Care of the Dead,* p. 9.
[89] Rebillard, *Care of the Dead,* pp. 5–6.
[90] Tert. *An.* 9.
[91] Victor Saxer, *Morts martyrs reliques en Afrique chrétienne aux premiers siècles. Les témoignages de
    Tertullien, Cyprien, et Augustin à la lumière de l'archéologie africaine* (Paris: Beauchesne, 1980),
    pp. 228–229. See also the Donatist martyr acts *Passio martyrum Isaac et Maximiani* 13 and
    Passio benedicti martyris Marculi 15.
[92] Hippolyte Delehaye, *Les origines du culte des martyrs* (Brussels, Belgium: Bureaux de la
    société des Bollandistes, 1912), p. 49, citing Tert. *Cor.* 3.3 and Cypr. *Ep.* 12.1.1–2. At some
    point certain Christians adopted the custom of feeding the eucharist to the deceased
    posthumously, which was subsequently prohibited by conciliar declaration (*Breviarium
    Hipponense* 4a, dated to 397 (CCL 149): *Ut corporibus defunctis eucharistia non detu* ... (The
    eucharist is not to be administered to the bodies of the deceased.))

for these mortuary practices, however, is a collection of inscriptions that mention *convivia* or *simposia* in connection with martyr commemorations, dating to the second half of the fourth century.

The most common word used in the inscriptions that dedicate these monuments is *memoria*.[93] Because these loci served as burial sites as well as ritual arenas, it is natural that their monuments used the term *memoria*; the word had a well-established history in the vocabulary of Latin epitaphs.[94] Ordinary epitaphs generally used the word *memoria* in the dative case to designate that the monument or mausoleum had been erected for or in memory of the deceased.[95] In this capacity they functioned as visual prompts for constructing and retrieving important memories. Beginning in the late third century, however, epitaphs use *memoria* in the nominative with *hic* (or *haec*) to refer to the accompanying monument itself and its location on that very spot: "Here is a memorial."[96] This grammatical shift

---

[93] Ennabli notes that *memoria* is sometimes found in epitaphs of nonmartyrs to designate a tomb (ICKarth 196, 383). See also the epitaph (CIL 8.20300) of the priest Securus (PCA I: 382) from 363 CE, identified as a *memorie* [= *memoriae*] *depositionis*: M[e]mori(a)e depos/ itionis presb<y=I>t/eri Securi posita / a fratres Fatale / et Flora vi<x=CS>it an/nos LVI an(n)o p(rovinciae) CCC/XXIIII depositio B/assi fratris VII Id/us Octobres. This epitaph displays all the terminology of a relic deposition, yet in the case of a nonmartyr it would seem to only signify a secondary burial.

[94] Dating is based on the *terminus ad quem* of the dissolution in 251 of the federation of the four colonies, and the *terminus a quo* of the use of the formula *memoriae*: The term is only found from the end of the second century onward (H.-G. Pflaum, "Remarques sur l'onomastique de Cirta," in *Limes-Studien, Vortäge 3*, Third International Congress of Roman Frontier Studies 1957, Rheinfelden, Aargau; Basel (Basel: Schriften Des Institutes für Ur- und Frühgeschichte der Schweiz, 1959): 96–133), cited in Mounir Bouchenaki, "A propos de la confederation cirtéenne (à partir d'une nouvelle inscription)," in *Hundertfünfzig-Jahr-Feier Deutsches Archäologisches Institut Rom* (Mainz: P. von Zabern, 1982), p. 174.) One example of the use of the term *memoria* in a non-Christian Roman epitaph is found in a mausoleum inscription from Sigus (Bou Hadjar) near Cirta (Constantina) in the Province of Numidia dating to the first half of the third century (AE 1982: 954): Chioni / memoriae / P(ubli) Exoppi / P(ubli) fil(ii) Quir(ina) / Nivalis / quaest(oris) aed(ilis) IIIvir(i) / quinq(uennalis) omnibusq(ue) / honoribus IIII coloniar(um) funct(i) / v(ixit) a(nnos) LXXV / Chioni / Exoppia / Saturnina patri incomparabili (Chionius. To the memory of Publius Exoppius Nivalis Publius son of Publius of the Quirina tribe, Chionius. By Exoppia Saturnina for her unequalled father). See M. Bouchenaki, "A pro- pos de la confederation cirtéenne," pp. 174–178 for a discussion of the inscription's signifi- cance for Roman administration in North Africa.

[95] See also Stern, *Inscribing Devotion*, p. 160, for its use in Jewish epitaphs.

[96] For example, AE 1997: 1722 from Uchi Maius (Rihana) from Africa Proconsularis (Tunisia), dated to 271–400: Haec memoria q(uondam) M(?)[---] / Nicasiae scolasti[cae quae] / vixit annis XX men[sibus ---] / [---]hist[---]t[---] (Here (is) a memorial of formerly M--- Nicasia the rhetorician who lived 20 years...). See discussion in Antonio Ibba, "L'epitafio inedito di Nicasia scolastica rinvenuto a Rihana," in *Uchi Maius 1: Scavi e ricerche epigrafiche in Tunisia*, ed. Attilio Mastino and Mustapha Khanoussi, pp. 327–336 (Sassari, Italy: EDES, 1997).

suggests that the object dedicated to the memory of the deceased itself became identified as the *memoria*.

Literature reflects a similar externalized conception and concretization of a person's memory. The third-century North African writer Lactantius disparagingly compares veneration of the divinized dead with images (*imagines*) to public veneration of their *memoria* (*memoria defunctorum colunt*).[97] Augustine uses the same phrase to describe veneration of the martyrs at their memorials (*honoranda memoria defunctorum*), while admonishing his audience to restrain their reverence from becoming divinization.[98]

A Christian inscription from Tixter (Ras el Oued / Thamallula) in Mauretania Caesariensis (Algeria) refers to the *mensa* (table) on which it is inscribed as a *memoria sancta*. The identification of such *memoriae* as sacred suggests that their dedicants perceived these objects and the places they marked as special and associated with divinity.[99] The memorial, dating to 359, identifies the site as a deposit of relics of the Holy Cross "from the Promised Land where Christ was born" (Figure 2.2).[100] The *memoria sancta* inscription is also embellished with a christogram at its center (Figure 2.3). Earlier depictions of the chi-rho monogram that appear on military equipment and on coins depicting the *labarum* use the sign in a

---

[97] Lactantius, *Inst.* 1.15.4 and 4.28.13–14.

[98] Aug. *conf.* 6.2.2; see also *cura mort.* 4.6. See also *cura mort.* 1.1.

[99] Other *memoriae* dedicate chapels (*cellae*; See, for example AE 1965: 150 dated 361 from Sitifis in Mauretania Caesariensis (Z'Dim, Algeria)): C(aius) Iul(ius) Castus grado sacerdotali legis / sacrae secundus C(ai) Iul(i) Honorati filius / iam LVIIII annos agens hoc sibi in animam / deliberavit ut incolumis et in rebus huma/nis agens hanc suae memoriae sedem / perpetuam constituere a(nno) p(rovinciae) CCCXXI cel/lam martyrum vocavit Luciani et Luciliae dep(ositus) / VI K(alendas) Sep(tembres).

[100] CIL 8:20600 = ILCV 2068 = AE 1890: 114 = AE 2000: 119: memori/a sa(n)cta // de ter(r)a promis(si)onis ube[sic] natus est C(h)ristus / apostoli Petri et Pauli nomi-/ na m[a]rturu(m) Datiani Dona-/ [t]ian[i] Cipriani Nemesani / Citini et Victo- / [ri]a[i]s an(n)o provi- / n[ciae t]recenti viges(imo) / posuit Bene- / natus et Pequaria / Victorinus / Miggin / et Dabula [e]t / de ligno crucis / septimu(s) id- / us Sept(e)m(b)r(es) (A holy memorial from the Land of Promise where Christ was born. To the apostles Peter and Paul. The names of the martyrs Datianus, Donatianus, Cyprian, Nemesanus, Citinus, and Victoria. Ben(en)atus and Pequaria put it up in the provincial year 320 (= 359 CE). Victorinus, Miggin, and Dabula, [an]d from the wood of the cross. The 7th of the ides of Sept ... (= Sept. 7)). Duval offers contradictory interpretations of this inscription. On the one hand "the formula *memoria sacta* designates the monument itself, in this case the table, and not the relics: the word is in the singular, and the verb of the dedication *posuit*, followed by the names of the faithful, refers not to a relic deposit but to the dedication of the mensa. The epithet *sacta* (for *sancta*) refers to the relics and to the names of the saints that follow: but the classic formula for these tables, *memoria sanctorum*, is not used here undoubtedly due to the presence of the relics of Christ, to avoid placing the Lord on the same plane as the saints and the apostles" (Duval, *Loca Sanctorum* I, p. 334). However, she translates the text as "saint memorial."

Figure 2.2 *Mensa* (martyr table). Third quarter of the fourth century CE. Kherbet Oum el Ahdam, Algeria. Limestone. Musée du Louvre, Paris, France, Ma 3023 (MNC 1287). Photo: Hervé Lewandowski © RMN-Grand Palais / Art Resource, NY. Reproduced with permission.

relatively minor position to convey power and victory, thereby protecting its users.[101] In 353, however, the usurper of emperor Constans, Magnentius issued coins with a full-sized chi-rho on the reverse flanked by an alpha and omega (Figure 2.4).[102] Unlike earlier imperial productions, Magnentius'

[101] P. Bruun, "Early Christian Symbolism on Coins and Inscriptions," *Congresso Internazionale di Archeologia Cristiana* 6 (1962): 528–534; Don Pasquale Colella, "Les abbreviations ℧ et ℟ (XR)," *Revue Biblique* 80 (1973): 547–558; and Robin M. Jensen, *Understanding Early Christian Art* (New York: Routledge, 2000), pp. 148–149.

[102] Sear comments: "Following the evacuation of Italy in 352, Magnentius issued a new denomination of double value, replacing the centenionalis of the previous 10 years. This new coin of increased weight had little or no silver content and is evidence of the

Figure 2.3 Enlargement of center of Figure 2.2.

christogram was flanked by an alpha and omega and provided the sole motif on the coin's reverse. By the time that the Tixter monument was erected, the christogram not only symbolized power, it conveyed Christian-ness as well.[103]

Although the roles that early Christian *memoriae* served in the production of place meaning and collective memory might have been similar to those of the nine temples disparaged by Arnobius, there is no evidence that the Christian *memoriae* physically resembled those of temples. The architecture of the earliest Christian cemetery buildings, however, like the Chapel of St. Salsa in Tipasa, did imitate other house-tombs rather than temple-tombs or temples (Figure 2.5).[104] Both Arnobius and Porphyry agreed

financial trouble faced by Magnentius toward the end of his reign" (*Roman Coins and Their Values* (Los Angeles, CA: Numismatic Fine Arts, 1988 (4th edition)).

[103] André Grabar, *Christian Iconography. A Study of Its Origins.* Princeton, NJ: Princeton University Press, p. 39; Jensen, *Understanding Early Christian Art*, pp. 148–149.

[104] Gareth Sears, *Late Roman African Urbanism. Continuity and Transformation in the City*, BAR International Series 1693 (Oxford: Archaeopress, 2007), p. 104, who follows N. Duval in dating it to the early fourth century. Damous el-Karita and the *Basilica Maiorum* in Carthage were originally dated to the same period, yet Duval has revised the date to the fifth century at the earliest (Noël Duval, "Études d'architecture chrétienne nord-africaine. Les monuments chrétiens de Carthage. Études critiques," *Mélanges de*

Figure 2.4 Double Centenionalis of Usurper Magnentius. Image provided by David R. Sear, Ancient Coin Certification Service. Reproduced with permission.

that Christian buildings were architecturally indistinguishable in-and-of-themselves from those of other Romans; it is this very similarity which invited controversy over their symbolic meaning in the first place. Because it was not the architecture that distinguished such buildings from those of other Romans, difference had to be created by the people who built them and gathered there, by inscriptions which conveyed their perceptual-symbolic quality, and by the rituals that were performed there.[105] To that end, the east lintel of the Chapel of St. Salsa displayed a Christianizing votive inscription (Figure 2.6).[106] Based on Yvette Duval's reconstruction, this inscription proclaimed the chapel's connection to "Christ," unequivo-cally conveying its provenance to all viewers: "Promises for God's gifts. Here ... Salsa ... rests in the name of Christ." The inscription publicized to passersby that the Salsa buried in this tomb was and should be perceived as Christian.[107]

l'Ecole française de Rome. Antiquité 84.2 (1972): 1071–1172, pp. 1113 and 1119). The structure is somewhat similar, however, to Mithraea, although it was not even partially subterranean.
[105] For discussion of how Christians differentiated their funerary customs, see Rebillard, Care of the Dead, pp. 125–126.
[106] N. Duval, with J. P. Caillet, P. Chevalier, and A. Lorquin, Basiliques chrétiennes d'Afrique du nord, vol. 2. Illustrations (Paris: Institut d'Études Augustiniennes, 1992), p. 42, from Grandidier's drawing. CIL 8.20915 = ILCV 1946, as revised by Duval, Loca Sanctorum I, p. 363: De (donis) Dei promissa [...]ic qu[ies] / cit in nomine Cris[ti ...]tra[...] / Salsa [...
[107] Henri Gregoire and others have suggested that the Salsa who was buried there would not have identified herself as such but that Christians subsequently invented a Christian martyr from her epitaph (Gregoire, "Sainte Salsa, roman épigraphique," Byzantion 12

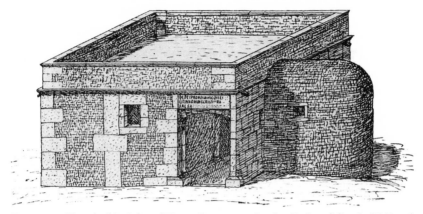

Figure 2.5 Chapel of St. Salsa of Tipasa. Reconstruction by O. Grandidier, in N. Duval, with J. P. Caillet, P. Chevalier, and A. Lorquin, *Basiliques chrétiennes d'Afrique du nord*, vol. 2. *Illustrations* (Paris: Institut d'Études Augustiniennes, 1992), p. 42. Reproduced with permission.

Tombs further shaped and expressed Christian identification by providing an enclosed ritual arena.[108] The construction of monuments over the tombs of martyrs in cemeteries imbued these gathering places with a sense of supernatural power that derived from the "holy ones" (*sancti*) buried there.[109] Tertullian connects martyrs to altars in a comment on *Revelation* 6.9, just as the first-century grammarian Zeno of Myndus (Caria, Asia Minor) quoted by Arnobius claimed that the prophet Telmessus was buried in his eponymous city underneath the altar of the Apollo temple.[110] Until the Last Judgment, Tertullian writes, "in the meantime, the souls of the gentle martyrs repose under the altar."[111] Monuments erected in honor of martyrs were initially portrayed as "for the memory of the holy ones" (*memoriae sanctorum*), as attested by numerous inscriptions.[112]

(1937): 212–234; David Woods, "An Unnoticed Official: The *Praepositus Saltus*," *The Classical Quarterly* 44.1 (1994): 245–251, p. 249).

[108] Despite her general Constantinian dating for the sacralization of place, Yasin does admit the earlier propensity of North Africa "toward connecting altars and relics ... than other [areas]" (*Saints and Church Spaces*, p. 153).

[109] The term *martyr* is coupled with the adjective *sanctus* as early as Tertullian (*Fug.* 5) and *Pass. Perp.* 1.6.

[110] Arnobius, *Ad. nat.* 6.6 (CSEL 4): *Sub Apollinis arula, quae Telmessi apud oppidum visitur, Telmessum esse conditum vatem non scriptis constantibus indicatur?* (Isn't it revealed by well-known writings that the prophet Telmessus is buried under the little altar of Apollo, which can be seen in the city of Telmessus?).

[111] Tert. *Scorp.* 12.9 (CCL 2): *Sed et interim sub altari martyrum animae placidum quiescunt ...*

[112] Africa Proconsularis: AE 1946: 56, AE 1982: 928b, AE 1992: 1772, CIL 8.10515, CIL 8.14040, CIL 8.17382, IFCCarth 3.299, ILTun 63, Numidia: AE 1904: 129, AE 1935: 94,

Figure 2.6 Epitaph of St. Salsa of Tipasa. Drawing by O. Grandidier in N. Duval, with J. P. Caillet, P. Chevalier, and A. Lorquin, *Basiliques chrétiennes d'Afrique du nord*, vol. 2. *Illustrations* (Paris: Institut d'Études Augustiniennes, 1992), p. 42. Reproduced with permission.

Later in the fourth century, however, large cemetery basilicas were constructed over important tombs.[113] As shrines for the martyrs (*loca sanctorum*) were expanded to accommodate worship in the fourth century, and houses of worship increasingly housed the holy through the *depositio* of relics (mid-fourth–fifth century),[114] these sites themselves were described as *loca sancta*.[115] "A church housing the remains of a saint," Yasin notes, was understood as "a special kind of space which focused Christian memory and invited prayer."[116]

As if the holiness of the holy ones contained in these sites transferred to the buildings themselves, martyr shrines were perceived as exerting miraculous power, including the capacity to tweak a person's conscience. At the dawn of the fifth century, Augustine was stumped by a controversy between two of his clergy. One, a novitiate seeking ordination, had demanded the resignation of the other, a presbyter accused of "corrupting his chastity" (*pudicitiam contaminare*).[117] The dispute divided the Hippo congregation, and

AE 1998: 1584, CIL 8.10665, CIL 8.17608, CIL 8.18656, CIL 8.19414, CIL 8.27958, CIL 8.27991, Mauretania Caesariensis: AE 1936: 109, CIL 8.21570 (dated 422).

[113] The evolution of cemetery churches is well-demonstrated in Dominique Raynal's chronological analysis of basilica II of Upenna (Henchir Fraga/ Chigarnia) in Byzacena (*Archéologie et histoire de l'Église d'Afrique: Uppenna II* (Toulouse, France: Presses Universitaires du Mirail, 2005)). The identification of this basilica as Donatist is questionable (Duval, *Loca Sanctorum* I, p. 66).

[114] Markus, *End of Ancient Christianity*, pp. 149–150.

[115] This phrase, "holy places" (*loci sancti*) or "holy areas" (*loca sancta*) appears, for example, in Ambrose's eulogy of Theodosius, referring to Holy Land sites (*loca sancta*; *Ob. Theo.* 43) and in a letter from Constantine to Macarius and the rest of the bishops in Palestine as recorded by Eusebius in Greek concerning the shrine of Mamre in particular and shrines generally (οἱ ἅγιοι τόποι; *Vit. Const.* 3.52.1).

[116] Yasin, *Saints and Church Spaces*, p. 221.

[117] Aug. *Ep.* 78.2. Note that *pudicitia* means restricting sexuality within marriage, not celibacy.

Augustine was forced to intervene. Although he suspected that the priest was innocent, he was tentative in his judgment. In his letter to the Church, the clergy, and elders of Hippo, he recommended that the two opponents should travel to the shrine of the martyr Felix in Cimitile, the necropolis of Nola (Italy), "a holy place (*locus sanctus*) where the awesome acts of God might more readily disclose the bad conscience of anyone and might compel him to confession because of punishment or fear."[118] At this point in his career, Augustine recognized the influence of Felix in Nola, even though he was unwilling to acknowledge that the African martyr shrines possessed the same power.[119]

Some Christians understood this sacred power as fixed in particular locations. Augustine suggests that the power that the dead, which were buried in specific church buildings, exerted over their descendants who congregated there deterred dissident Christians from abandoning their ancestral churches and joining Catholics in their basilicas:[120]

> We have found some, though, who are sluggish and reluctant to move, and who say ... "My dead father is there, my mother is buried there." ... Your parents were Christians of the party of Donatus; perhaps their parents too were Christians; their grandparents or great-grandparents were certainly pagans. So those who first became Christians, did they freeze up against the truth when they carried out their pagan parents for burial? Did they bow to the authority of their dead parents, and not rather prefer the living Christ to their dead parents?

It was not only dissidents, however, who revered the buildings in which their sacred dead reposed. By the beginning of the fifth century, Catholics began to merge the holiness of basilicas with that of martyria.

Although the "unity party" had initially disparaged the dissident Christian practice of burying their special dead within church walls, they came to embrace the concept that the sanctity of certain corpses lent holiness to the

---

[118] Aug. *Ep.* 78.3, tr. Teske, The Works of Saint Augustine (4th Release). Electronic Edition. Letters 1–99, Vol. II/1 (Charlottesville, VA: InteLex Corporation, 2014) (CSEL 34.2): ... *ad locum sanctum se pergituros, ubi terribiliora opera dei non sanam cuiusque conscientiam multo facilius aperirent et ad confessionem vel poena vel timore compellerent.*

[119] Aug. *Ep.* 78.3, tr. Teske (CSEL 34.2): *et tamen nusquam hic scimus talia fieri* (we know that such things do not happen anywhere here).

[120] Aug. *Serm.* 359.8, tr. Hill (pt.3 vol. 10, p. 205), preached in 411 (PL 39: 1596): *invenimus autem homines aliquando pigros dicentes ... "pater meus ibi est mortuus, mater mea ibi sepulta." ... parentes tui christiani fuerunt in parte donati: parentes eorum forte et ipsi christiani, avi aut proavi certe pagani. qui ergo primi facti sunt christiani, cum extulissent parentes suos paganos, numquid contra veritatem frigidi fuerunt? numquid auctoritatem mortuorum parentum secuti sunt, et non potius mortuis parentibus vivum christum praetulerunt?*

places where they were interred. According to Optatus, sometime after 388 CE, "... they had begun to bury the dead inside some local basilicas. ..."[121] The church to which Optatus likely referred was located on an estate, Vegesela (Numidia), where the remains of the martyred dissident bishop Marculus were buried along with nine other sets of remains, likely those of his fellow bishops.[122] The minutes of the Council of Carthage held in 411 CE reveal that the Vegesela basilica was later seized by Catholics, giving the Catholic bishop Privatianus cause to claim exclusive jurisdiction over the locale.[123]

As martyr chapels and shrines were expanded and appropriated, Catholics expressed the same regard for their martyr-churches as dissident Christians. In a sermon probably delivered in 405 CE in the Mappalian basilica of Carthage located about 250 meters north of the city limits, Augustine explains how God "consecrated" the place (locus) with Cyprian's "holy" body.[124] Usually reserved by North African Christian writers for

---

[121] Optatus, de schism. Don. 3.4.7, tr. Shaw, Bringing in the Sheaves. Economy and Metaphor in the Roman World, Robson Classical Lectures (Buffalo, NY: University of Toronto Press, 2013), p. 269 (SC 413: 42): Ex quorum numero cum aliqui in basilicis sepeliri coepissent. The imperial edict of 381 (Cod. theod. 9.17.6) only referred to burials ad sanctos.

[122] Duval, Loca Sanctorum II, p. 705. Duval took the reference in Gesta coll. carth 1.187 to the martyr's blood as referring to a tomb in Nova Petra, where Marculus was martyred, yet sanguis could have been used to refer to blood shed at the martyrdom site (and considered sacred) even after the rest of the remains had been buried at Vegesela. For a thorough discussion of the events surrounding the martyrdom, see Shaw, Sacred Violence, pp. 178–185.

[123] Gesta coll. Carth. 1.133 (SC 195: 756): Et accedente Donato Cillitano episcopo, idem dixit: 'Diaconos illic habeo, vicina plebs agit, diocesis mea est.' Privatianus episcopus ecclesiae Catholicae dixit: 'Ubi conveniunt?' Donatus episcopus dixit: 'Et loca et memorias martyrum tamen prohibuisti. Candidum non habui presbyterum inde?' See discussion in Shaw, Sacred Violence, p. 575.

[124] Augustine Serm. 312.6, dated by Hill to 405 CE (p. 85n17; PL 38: 1422): illi laus, illi gloria, domino deo nostro, regi saeculorum, creatori et recreatori hominum, qui suo tali antistite huius civitatis ecclesiam ditavit, et tam sancto corpore huius loci amplitudinem consecravit (To him be praise, to him be glory, to the Lord our God, to the king of the ages (1 Tim 1.17), to the creator and recreator of mankind, who enriched the Church of this city with this wonderful bishop of his [Cyprian], and consecrated this spacious site with so holy a body). For further references see Aug. conf. 5.8.15, Serm. 305A, 308A, 311, 313, 313C, 313F, 330, en. Ps. 32.2.1, 85, quoted in Liliane Ennabli, Carthage. Une métropole chrétienne du IVe à la fin du VIIe siècle, Études d'Antiquités africaines (Paris: CNRS Editions, 1997), p. 21, and Serm. 359B.5 (= Dolbeau 2, Mainz 5). The late fifth-/early sixth-century historian Procopius of Caesarea confirms Augustine's location of the basilica near the harbor (Procopius, de Bell. Vand. (Book III) 1.21.18, ed. Wirth: παρὰ τὴν τῆς θαλάσσης ἠιόνα). Although this cemetery church has been identified with the church of St. Monica on the basis of fifth-century literary descriptions, there are no inscriptions that corroborate Augustine's perception of the building as sacred (Ennabli, Carthage, pp. 129–131, discussed in Leone, Changing Townscapes, pp. 110 and 177). The most elaborate description is from Gregory of Tours, Liber in gloria martyrum I.93.

sacraments and saints, *consecro* is expressly associated by Augustine with the place.[125] Earlier uses of the term are confined to civic or Roman traditionalist dedications.[126] Augustine's usage of *consecro* is noteworthy on two accounts: First, it demonstrates a willingness to use the same terminology in describing Christian places as that used for public civic structures, formerly including traditional Roman temples – a rhetorical strategy expressly rejected earlier by Arnobius; and second, it reveals a perception that the Mappalian cemetery church which housed Cyprian's tomb was in-and-of-itself sacred.[127] A year later, Augustine refers to certain Christian sites where drunkenness abounds, perhaps martyr shrines, as "holy places" (*loci sancti*).[128] This marks a substantial turn-about for Augustine, who, we recall, had previously sent two of his clergy to the shrine of St. Felix in Nola, Italy in order to have God adjudicate their dispute over sexual impropriety because he did not consider any place in Africa powerful enough. Indeed, some years later Augustine would describe the Mappalian church as a "holy place ... where the body lies of such a holy martyr."[129]

Despite Augustine's early reluctance to admit the degree of power manifest in African martyr shrines, his treatise on the *Care of the Dead*, written twenty years after his letter regarding Boniface, reveals a marked shift in his views.[130] The change of heart is triggered by the arrival of the relics of the protomartyr Stephen in Africa around the year 423, and the circulation of miracle reports by the bishop Euodius who had built a shrine in Uzalis to

---

[125] Based on an electronic search of *Library of Latin Texts* (Brepolis). This Augustine reference is not included in the *Thesaurus Linguae Latinae* entries cited later in this chapter.

[126] See, for example, Tert. *Idol.* 10 and CIL 8.8426, 9257, and 9293 (*Thesaurus Linguae Latinae* Vol. 4, "consecratio" and "consecro," pp. 378–384).

[127] See also Aug. *Serm.* 325.2, tr. Hill (PL 38: 1449): *in hoc sancto loco* ... "in this holy place" – referring to the shrine of the twenty martyrs rather than the "main basilica" (*maiore basilica*) of Hippo which awaited further rituals. Anton Zwinggi dates this sermon to 408 CE (Hill, p. 169n1).

[128] Aug. *In Iohannis euangelium tractatus* 10.9 (CCL 36); *Serm.* Dolbeau 198.16 (= Mainz 62: 379), dated to 404 CE, and *cura mort.* 4.6 (CSEL 41).

[129] Aug. *Serm.* 311.5, tr. Hill, who dates the sermon to 417 CE (p. 85n17; PL 38: 1415): *istum tam sanctum locum, ubi iacet tam sancti martyris corpus* ... Augustine evokes the distant memory of rowdy behavior in the church, supporting Hill's proposed reversal of the traditional dates ascribed to sermons 311 and 312.

[130] Dennis Trout suggested that the powerful influence of his friendship with martyr impresario Paulinus was decisive in Augustine's shift (*Paulinus of Nola. Life, Letters, and Poems* (Los Angeles, CA: University of California Press, 1999), pp. 237–238). Markus, on the other hand, claims that this shift marked a stage in Augustine's "personal evolution," which included an acknowledgment of miracles and increased disillusionment with natural law (*Ancient Christianity*, p. 149). Yasin does not fully accept the evolutionary view (*Saints and Church Spaces*, pp. 216–222).

house them.[131] The proliferation of martyr shrines had turned Augustine's "spatial world" into what Robert Markus calls "a network of holy places."[132] In the year 424, Augustine oversaw the construction of a *martyrium* adjacent to the basilica in Hippo with the relics of St. Stephen.[133] The project was funded by Eraclius, the deacon whom Augustine appointed to succeed him, although it was undertaken at Augustine's own initiative. In a sermon on the clergy, the bishop mentioned Eraclius' largess. In the course of his panegyric, he addresses the concern of Eraclius' wealthy family that Augustine was using his ecclesiastical influence to try to steal the boy's patrimony.[134]

Augustine's anxiety about the donation demonstrates that the relationship between bishop and patron entailed a delicate balance of power.[135] Christian philanthropy created an alternative structure to established Roman patronage. Yet the concentric social circles that structured Roman patronage, family (*domus*), tribe (*gens*), class (*ordo*), and civic body (*civitates* or *res publicae*), overlapped with the new social network of the Church, creating an environment of competition.[136] Eraclius' donation publicly affirmed his ties to his fellow clergy and other Christians rather than to his aristocratic family and the townspeople of Hippo, a pattern repeated in building dedications throughout North Africa.[137]

[131] In the miracle section (22.8) of the *Civitate dei*, Augustine writes that the Hippo shrine has existed for "not quite two years (*nondum … biennium*)." Augustine admits that both the Uzalis and Calama shrines predated the one at Hippo (*civ. dei* 22.8, tr. Babcock (CCSL 48: 823): *Calamae vero, ubi et ipsa memoria prius esse coepit et crebrius dantur, incomparabili multitudine superant. Uzali etiam, quae colonia Uticae vicina est, multa praeclara per eundem martyrem facta cognovimus; cuius ibi memoria longe prius quam apud nos ab episcopo Euodio constituta est* (And at Calama, where the shrine was inaugurated earlier and reports were drawn up more often, the number is incomparably greater. At Uzalis, too, which is a colony near Utica, I know of many outstanding miracles done by the same martyr. His shrine there was established by bishop Evodius, long before ours at Hippo.))

[132] Markus, *End of Ancient Christianity*, p. 142. Markus contends that this transformation took centuries, with the growth of martyria constituting only the first stage (pp. 142–151). Stage two is "the multiplication of urban churches," and stage three is "the integration of the two in the spreading custom of 'translating' relics into urban churches" (p. 147). Yet in the case of North Africa, the transformation can be discerned much earlier in certain Christians' changing perception of their physical landscape.

[133] This date follows Brown (Brown, *Augustine of Hippo: A Biography. New with an epilogue* (London: Faber, 2000), table E).

[134] Aug. *Serm.* 356.7. Eraclius' family apparently felt that his beneficence did not follow the proper procedure of patronage, since it was construed as initiated by the clergy rather than by the donor and his family.

[135] In this particular instance, tension may have resulted from the perception that the building of the shrine was more Augustine's idea than that of the donor family.

[136] As noted by Brown, *Through the Eye of a Needle*, p. 74.

[137] Compare the temple-building in the third century by "the inhabitants of large estates and *pagi*" (Dossey, *Peasant and Empire*, p. 110).

Although we do not possess the family's account of the events, it is possible that they perceived this project as executed inappropriately because nonaristocratic clergy had usurped the role usually played by aristocratic peers. The family clearly viewed the expenditure as illegitimate in some way, or else they would not have accused Augustine of larceny. Those who had sufficient funds, whether clerical or lay, could afford to buy their own relics and build their own shrines, even on their own private estates. They could subvert the network of social relationships to assert their aristocratic status. The *martyrium* of Hippo was built by Augustine with the funds of his deacon adjacent to his rapidly expanding ecclesiastical complex. In this new system of euergetism, donations funded buildings used by the Church – baptisteries, basilicas, chapels, monasteries (i.e. ecclesiastical housing), and cemeteries. These contributions were administered by bishops rather than by municipal authorities and appointees, as was the case with public works.

With their dedicatory inscriptions, these benefactions reminded viewers of the relationships and influence that were cultivated among those who identified themselves as Christian. By publicizing and accommodating particular groups of Christians, structures provided concrete, visible vehicles for both advertising and noticing varieties of Christian-ness and the communities of those who expressed them. These structures were not only monuments to the holy ones whose remains they honored, but also to the particular social networks of those who patronized them.

Churches as Seats of Episcopal Authority

Optatus is the first North African to mention that a church contained an actual bishop's seat, or *cathedra episcopatus*.[138] Contemporary art historians often take for granted that the episcopal *cathedra* (Greek *thronos*) was both an idea as well as a piece of furniture.[139] The *cathedra* was an architectural feature adapted from civil basilicas, where it symbolized the seat of authority; in the ecclesiastical context, it served as the primary representation of a bishop's jurisdiction, which Optatus makes clear in his reply to Parmenian:[140]

---

[138] Earlier references in Cyprian are abstract rather than concrete. Jerome uses the term conceptually as well (*Ep.* 117.1).

[139] The subordinationist Paul of Samosata had claimed this privilege for himself as bishop of Antioch in the mid-third century, for which he was excommunicated (Eusebius, *Hist. eccl.* 7.30.9 (SC 41): βῆμα μὲν καὶ θρόνον ὑψηλὸν ἑαυτῷ κατασκευ). These seats were often portable (see, for example, the Archbishops' throne from Ravenna (Deborah Mauskopf Deliyannis, *Ravenna in Late Antiquity* (New York: Cambridge University Press, 2010), fig. 72, p. 215).

[140] Optatus, *de schism. Don.* 2.2.1, tr. Edwards (SC 412): *Ergo quia probavimus eam esse ecclesiam catholicam quae sit in toto terrarum orbe diffusa, eius iam commemoranda sunt ornamenta*

Since, therefore, we have proved that the catholic church is the one that is spread throughout the whole compass of the earth, we must describe its trappings and we must see where are the five gifts, which according to you are six. The first of these is the seat, to which unless the bishop occupies it, the second gift cannot be joined ..."

In addition, Optatus claims that the setting up of the historic altar used by previous bishops Cyprian, Carpophorius, and Lucian symbolized Caecilianus' authority and continuity.[141] The altar functions synecdochically for all of Christian ritual, as indicated in many Church canons where the setting up of an alternative altar is regarded as a sectarian or heretical gesture.[142]

The associations of church furniture with episcopal succession, ecclesiastical authority, and divine power linked these meanings to the buildings in which they were positioned. It is hardly surprising that conflicts over succession, authority, and power should consider structures to be valuable targets in negotiating those disputes. The perceptual-symbolic value of the sites made them vulnerable to attack.

Places as Bodies

North African churches did not merely house dead bodies, they were viewed as bodies themselves. As early as the turn of the common era according to Roman architect Vitruvius, buildings were understood as deriving their architectural structure from that of the human body: "[I]n the human

---

et videndum ubi sint quinque dotes quas tu sex esse dixisti, inter quas cathedra est prima, ubi nisi sederit episcopus, coniungi altera dos non potest ... The other four (or five) gifts are angelus (presiding bishop), Spirit, baptismal font, and seal (Optatus would add the altar, mentioned in 1.19). For another mention of the bishop's seat as a physical object, see 1.17. For the identification of the signs, see P. Marcelli, "La simbologia delle doti della Chiesi in Ottato di Milevi," Studi e materiali di storia delle religione 14 (1990): 219–244. These gifts might roughly correlate to what developed into the visible markers of a bishop's rank: Throne, headgear, pallium, shoes, and ring (Allan Doig, Liturgy and Architecture from the Early Church to the Middle Ages (Burlington, VT: Ashgate, 2008), p. 38).

[141] Optatus, de schism. Don. 1.17.

[142] See, for example, canon 8 from the 390 Council of Carthage (Concil. Carth. 390, Canon 8 (CCL 149: 16)): Felix episcopus selemselitanus dixit: nec illud praetermittendum est, ut si quis forsitam presbyter ab episcopo suo correptus [aut excommunicatus], tumore vel superbia inflatus putaverit separatim deo sacrificia offerenda vel aliud erigendum altare, contra ecclesiasticam fidem disciplinam que crediderit agendum, non exeat impunitus (Felix, bishop of Selemsela, stated: nor should it be omitted that if any presbyter reprimanded [or excommunicated] by his bishop, whether swollen with tumid arrogance to consider separately offering sacrifices to God or setting up one altar against another, who is believed to have acted against the discipline of ecclesiastical truth, shall not escape punishment).

body there is a kind of symmetrical harmony between forearm, foot, palm, finger, and other small parts; and so it is with perfect buildings."[143] Religious buildings were particularly human-like: "Without symmetry and proportion there can be no principles in the design of any temple; that is, if there is no precise relation between its members, as in the case of those of a well shaped man."[144] As Christians came to view their churches in much the same way as Romans viewed temples, their personification of them grew.

Like other early Christian writers, Tertullian and Cyprian referred to the Church as "mother."[145] While these references use the metaphor in reference to the corporate Christian entity, a few passages use *mater* when discussing ritual places.[146] Speaking of baptism, Tertullian writes:[147]

> [W]hen you ascend from that most sacred font of your new birth, and spread your hands for the first time in the presence (*apud*) of your mother (*matrem*), together with your brethren ...

While the usage clearly distinguishes the structure from the mother herself, the juxtaposition of *apud* and *matrem* suggests a close relationship between the place and the metaphor. This connection is illustrated by the shape of many North African baptisteries, like that at the fourth century Chapel of Jucundus in Sbeitla, Tunisia.[148] Burns and Jensen note that "The design of the older, fourth-century Chapel of Jucundus ... may have been meant to evoke a woman's vulva and birth canal, underscoring the idea that the Church is mother and her font is the womb of newborn Christians."[149]

---

[143] Vitruvius, *Arch.* 1.2.4, tr. M. H. Morgan, *Vitruvius: The Ten Books on Architecture* (Cambridge, MA: Harvard University Press, 1914), p. 14.

[144] Vitruvius, *Arch.* 3.1.1, tr. Morgan, p. 72.

[145] Robin M. Jensen, "*Mater Ecclesia* and *Fons Aeterna*," in *A Feminist Companion to Patristic Literature*, ed. Amy-Jill Levine and Maria Mayo Robbins, pp. 137–153 (New York: T & T Clark, 2008). Paul invokes the metaphor for the heavenly Jerusalem, quoting Isaiah 54:1 (Gal 4:26–27).

[146] Tert. *Mart.* 1, *Mon.* 7; Cypr. *Laps.* 2, *Ep.* 10.1.1.

[147] Tert. *Bapt.* 20.5 (SC 35: 75): ... *cum de illo sanctissimo lavacro novi natalis ascenditis et primas manus apud matrem cum fratribus aperitis* ... See R.-F. Refoulé's comments on p. 16, note 2, citing the work of J. C. Plumpe, *Mater Ecclesia* (Washington, DC: Catholic University of America Press, 1943), pp. 45–62. See also Robin M. Jensen, *Baptismal Imagery in Early Christianity: Ritual, Visual, and Theological Dimensions* (Grand Rapids, MI: Baker Academic, 2012), pp. 57, 144, and Burns and Jensen, *Christianity in Roman North Africa*, p. 170. For the contrary view that this expression does not refer to a place, see the recent dissertation of Bradley M. Peper, "The Development of *mater ecclesia* in North African Ecclesiology," PhD. diss., Vanderbilt University, 2011 (ProQuest Digital Dissertations), p. 53.

[148] Jensen, "*Mater Ecclesia*," p. 153.

[149] Burns and Jensen, *Christianity in Roman North Africa*, p. 110.

Figure 2.7 Tomb mosaic from Tabarka, Tunisia, fifth century. Musée National du Bardo, Tunis, Tunisia. © Gilles Mermet / Art Resource, NY. Reproduced with permission.

By the second quarter of the fifth century, this architectural metaphor of the Church would be represented visually. A martyrial chapel mosaic from Tabarka depicts the "ecclesia mater" as a building (Figure 2.7).[150] This mosaic illustrates that the abstract image of the Church as mother had acquired a tangible dimension.[151] The building of Christian assembly became identified with the Church "body" that gathered there. The basilica's function and its symbolism had converged.

Ultimately, bodies, like buildings, were not permanent. Augustine puts this similarity to work in a sermon on resurrection delivered in the winter of 411. He compares the ephemeral nature of the events of Christ's ministry, death, and resurrection as precursors to the Church, and its promise of eternal life to the building of the basilica in which he is preaching:[152]

> An architect uses scaffolding and machinery that is going to be removed, in order to build a house that is going to remain. I mean in this building

[150] Dating follows the most recent assessment of Joan M. Downs, "The Christian Tomb Mosaics from Tabarka: Status and Identity in a North African Roman Town," Ph.D. diss., University of Michigan, 2007 (ProQuest Dissertations), p. 73.

[151] Similarly, John Chrysostom identifies his own church building as a refuge from the marketplace and a consoling mother (μήτηρ ... παραμυθήσεταί; De statuis 4.1/59, discussed in Wendy Mayer and Pauline Allen, The Churches of Syrian Antioch (300–638 CE) (Walpole, MA: Peeters, 2012), pp. 101–102 and Shepardson, Controlling Contested Places, p. 159).

[152] Aug. Serm. 362.7–8, tr. Edmund Hill, The Works of Saint Augustine (3rd Release). Electronic Edition. Sermons, (341–400) on Various Subjects, vol. III/10, ed. John E. Rotelle, Past Masters (Charlottesville, VA: InteLex Corporation, 2001) (PL 39: 1615): architectus aedificat per machinas transituras domum mansuram. nam in isto tam magno et amplo, quod videmus, aedificio, cum instrueretur, machinae fuerunt, quae hic modo non sunt; quia quod per eas aedificabatur, iam

so vast and spacious, which we can see, while it was being put up there were all sorts of scaffolding and machinery here which are not here now; because what was being built with them now stands here completed. ...

Would your graces please observe a wonderful building? These earthly buildings, of course, press down on the ground with their weight, and all the weight in this immense structure is bearing down on the ground by the force of gravity – and unless it is held up, it will sink to lower and lower depths, where its weight is dragging it. So because it is being built on earth, a foundation is first laid in the ground so that on this foundation the builder may put up his edifice without any further worries. That's why he places the most stable and solid mass right at the bottom, something that will be suitable to support what is placed on top of it; and the more massive the building, the more massive the foundation prepared for it. But it is in the ground, in the earth, as I said, because what is being built on top of it is also, of course, being located on the ground, on earth.

Augustine cannot push the simile too far: resurrection is only sort of like a building. So he has to stretch the analogy to include the heavenly built Jerusalem: "That Jerusalem of ours, though, still in exile, is being built in heaven. That's why Christ, its foundation, preceded it into heaven."[153] Christ, the foundation of resurrection, is ultimately to be found in heaven rather than on earth. Only the heavenly edifice, which are eternal, compare to the resurrection.

In the midst of his discussion, Augustine recognizes the paradox of needing an earthly basilica for spiritual activities, nevertheless:[154]

[W]e urged you to receive spiritual blessings and contribute carnal ones. Buildings erected in this present age are necessary to house the bodies either of the living or of the dead, but only in this passing era. After God's judgment, shall we be raising these structures up to heaven? No, but in

---

perfectum stat. ... attendat caritas vestra aedificium mirabile. aedificia quippe ista terrena pondere suo terram premunt, totusque nutus ponderum in ista structura magnitudine ad terram nititur, et nisi contineatur, ad inferiora contendit, quo pondus adducit. quia ergo in terra aedificatur, in terra fundamentum praemittitur; ut supra fundamentum securus instruat qui aedificat. ergo ponit in imo firmissimas moles, ut idonee possint portare desuper quod imponitur, et pro magnitudine aedificii magnitudo fundamenti praeparatur: in terra tamen, ut dixi, quia et illud quod aedificatur supra, utique in terra collocatur.

[153] Aug. *Serm.* 362.8, tr. Hill, Electronic edition (PL 39: 1615): *Ierusalem illa nostra peregrina in caelo aedificatur. ideo praecessit fundamentum Christus in caelum.*

[154] Aug. *Enarrat. Ps.* 80.4, tr. Maria Boulding, *The Works of Saint Augustine* (3rd Release). Electronic Edition. *Expositions of the Psalms*, 73–98, Vol. III/18, ed. John E. Rotelle, Past Masters (Charlottesville, VA: InteLex Corporation, 2001) (CCL 39): *hoc est quod vos et ad illam mensam beati martyris exhortati sumus, ut accipientes spiritalia, daretis carnalia. haec enim quae exstruuntur ad tempus, ad recipienda corpora vel vivorum vel mortuorum necessaria sunt, sed*

the present age we cannot do without them if we are to achieve what will win us heaven. If you are avid to receive spiritual blessings, then, be assiduous about material contributions.

Augustine is clear about the relationship between resurrection, the theme of his sermon, and capital funding: Christians must continue donating to their building projects if they want to enjoy salvation. This place meaning associates buildings and, in particular, their donors with salvation. This otherworldly linkage increases the value of religious sites beyond the earthly plane to the realm of the transcendent and supernatural. The donations that support places that house Christian bodies ensure bodily afterlife for the donors.

Place Meanings and Ritual Behaviors

Ritual behaviors that involve architectural elements of Christian buildings reveal how practitioners perceived the structures with which they came into contact. The series of ritual actions we will examine confirms what other literary and archaeological evidence demonstrates, namely, that Christians came to regard their ritual places and their accoutrements as increasingly sacred, holy, and powerful. The first activity, church-purification, dates to the mid-fourth century.

In his refutation of the dissident bishop of Carthage, Parmenian, Optatus ridicules the dissidents for having purified houses of worship upon seizing them from Catholics during the reign of emperor Julian. The dissidents apparently sprinkled and scrubbed the walls with salt water, melted down or sold the ritual vessels, washed the vestments (*pallas*), and scraped, sold, or destroyed the altars.[155] Optatus interprets the action of scrubbing the church as an attempt to rid it of pollution, to purify it. The notion of pollution was neither sectarian nor solely the province of traditional Roman religion. A 356 law of the emperor Constantius forbids reusing building materials from tombs because of pollution.[156] While this type of pollution

---

tempore praetereunti. numquid post iudicium dei istas fabricas in caelum levabimus? sine his tamen hoc tempore agere quae ad possidendum caelum pertinent non poterimus. si ergo avidi estis in spiritalibus accipiendis, devoti estote in carnalibus erogandis.

[155] Casaubon emends *pallas* to *pallia*, but either can mean curtains, coverings, or vestments. Optatus, *de schism. Don.* 6.1, 2, 5, 6. The act of ritual purification with water can be found in *ActsPet* 19.

[156] *Cod. theod.* 9.17.4, tr. Pharr (ed. Mommsen): *Qui aedificia manium violant, domus ut ita dixerim defunctorum, geminum videntur facinus perpetrare, nam et sepultos spoliant destruendo et vivos polluunt fabricando* (Those persons who violate the habitations of the shades, the home,

derives from association with death, the dissident Christians' sense of pollution derives from sin.[157] Catholics and dissidents disagreed on this very point, as demonstrated by Augustine's discussion of rebaptism:[158]

> For if those who did not have true baptism were received in this condition coming from the heretics with communion, whether of the kind administered by those before Cyprian or by Cyprian himself, and their sins were upon them, it is necessary to acknowledge one of two things: either that the Church was destroyed by the defiled communion of such folks, or that anyone abiding in unity is not hurt even by the infamous sins of others.

Although Augustine uses the verb *maculo* rather than Optatus' *polluo*, both verbs convey pollution or defilement.[159] While Augustine's discussion shows that the dissident Christians perceived such pollution to be contagious, such attitudes were not novel. As early as the mid-third century, Cyprian had admonished his congregants to avoid "becoming polluted by contact with the guilty (schismatics)."[160]

---

so to speak, of the dead, appear to perpetrate a twofold crime. For they both despoil the buried dead by the destruction of the tombs, and they contaminate the living by the use of this material in building).

[157] See Maureen Tilley's discussion of this idea (*The Bible in Christian North Africa. The Donatist World* (Minneapolis, MN: Augsburg Fortress, 1997), pp. 165–166).

[158] Aug. *Bapt.* 5.1 (CSEL 51: 262): *si enim vere baptismum non habebant, qui venientes ab haereticis ita suscipiebantur, et super eos erant peccata eorum, cum communicatum est talibus sive ab eis qui erant ante cyprianum sive ab ipso cypriano, necesse est ut unum dicatur ex duobus, aut perisse iam tunc ecclesiam talium communione maculatam aut non obesse cuiquam in unitate permanenti aliena etiam nota peccata.*

[159] Optatus, *de schism. Don.* 6.6.4, tr. Edwards (SC 413): *Nam et fovendorum corporum causa eadem nos et vos lavacra pariter abluerunt et ante vos frequenter nostrorum loti sunt multi. Si post nos purificanda putatis omnia, lavate et aquam si potestis! Aut si vestigia, ut supra diximus, nostra vobis videntur esse polluta, sufficeret terra. Ut quid et parietes lavare voluistis in quibus humana non possunt poni vestigia? Parietes non calcare sed tantum videre potuimus! Si et quod tangit aspectus lauandum esse censetis, cur cetera dimisistis illota? Videmus tectum, videmus et caelum, haec a vobis lavari non possunt! Illa lavando promeriti estis Deum, ista non lavando inexpiabile videmini incurrisse peccatum!* (Tell us what there was there that you could wash. If we Catholics have trodden our footprints into the neighbourhood and the street, why do you not clean everything? For it is equally true of our people and yours that they washed themselves with the same intention of looking after the body, and many of ours washed frequently before you. If you think that everything should be purified in our wake, wash the water also, if you can. Or if our footprints, as I said above, seem to you to be polluted, let the earth be enough; why have you chosen also to wash walls, on which human footprints cannot be placed? We cannot tread on walls, but only look at them. If you judge that what strikes the eyes must be washed, why have you left the rest unwashed? We look at the roof, we look at the sky; these cannot be washed by you. By washing the former you have pleased God, by failing to wash the others you appear to have committed an inexpiable sin).

[160] Cypr. *Ep.* 67.9.2 (CCL 3C): … *nocentium contactibus polluuntur.* …

Optatus inquires how the walls of a church could have become impure if they had not come into physical contact with Catholic persons themselves and wonders, rather sarcastically, whether it is merely the gaze of Catholics that rendered them impure. Unfortunately, we no longer possess Parmenian's original tract to represent actual dissident Christian intentions, but we can infer from Optatus' description that they regarded the building itself subject to impurity, by whatever means. This perception and the actions it evinced may have been shaped by biblical treatment of architectural leprosy, which is referred to as a *macula* (Vulgate Lev 14.44). The dissident Christians' actions suggest that once the basilica had been scrubbed down and all impure elements removed, it was perceived as purified and fit for occupancy. This process of purification seems to convey an awareness of the potential sanctity of the building itself in addition to the sanctity of its ritual objects. Although Optatus reports no ceremony of re-consecration upon the dissident Christians' occupation of the basilica, the act of purification performed the same ritual function and may be seen as analogous to the dissident Christians' baptismal theology of re-baptism.[161]

Another behavior involving architectural elements is the veneration (*adoratio*) of tombs, pictures, and pillars. In 348 CE, the Catholic Council of Carthage condemned dissident veneration of what Catholics considered to be false martyrs at their tombs.[162] In 388, Augustine condemned the veneration of tombs and pictures, which may refer to the kissing of either

---

[161] No doubt the inhumation of new martyrs in cemetery basilicas and old martyr's relics in new basilicas transferred some aspects of funerary ceremony that served as consecration rituals. See ACTA CYPRIANI, 5.6, tr. Musurillo, ACTS OF THE CHRISTIAN MARTYRS, p. 175: *per noctem autem corpus eius inde sublatum est; ad cereos et scolaces in areas Macrobii Candidiani procuratoris (quae sunt uia Mappaliensi iuxta piscinas) eum uoto et triumpho magno deductum est et illic conditum* (At nightfall, however, it [his body] was removed from there, and, accompanied by a cortege holding tapers and torches, was conducted with prayers in great triumph to the cemetery of Macrobius Candidianus the procurator, which lies on the Mappalian Way near the fishponds, and was there buried).

[162] Conc. Carthag. A. 345–348, c. 2 (CCL 149): *Martyrum dignitatem nemo profanus infamet, neque passiva corpora quae sepulturae tantum propter misericordiam ecclesiasticam commendari mandatum est redigant, ut aut insania praecipitatos aut alia ratione peccati discretos, non ratione vel tempore competenti, quo martyria celebrantur, martyrum nomen appellent, aut si quis in iniuriam martyrum claritati eorum adiungat insanos; placeat eos, si laici sunt, ad paenitentiam redigi, si autem sunt clerici, post commonitionem et post cognitionem honore privari* (Let no ignoramus dishonor the dignity of the martyrs, nor shall anyone confer such dignity on bodies unless it has been mandated that they be commended for burial by ecclesiastical authority; so that either crazy cliff-jumpers or those who are killed by committing another type of sin, whether intentionally or fortuitously, should not be called or worshipped as martyrs; or if anyone offends the martyrs by associating the insane ones with the real martyrs' glory, let it please them, if they are lay, to seek penance, and if they are clergy, already ordained and assigned to a post, let them be deprived of their office).

painted walls or the carved doors of shrines and churches, or perhaps even to murals or mosaics in private homes.[163] In a New Year's Day sermon of 404 CE, Augustine rebuked his audience for venerating (adorare) "the columns in the church," of which they were accused by neighboring elite pagans who dismissed similar practices among their own faithful as gestures of the imperiti (ignoramuses).[164] The veneration of columns likely entailed a kiss, either by mouth directly or by touching one's hand to the mouth and then to the column.[165] This ritual action of venerating columns may relate to the adoration of pictures, given that Christian sacred narratives were often depicted on both. For example, a sculpted chancel arch pillar from a dissident church in Oued R'zel (about twenty miles northwest of Bagaï in Numidia) pictured Noah's ark and the dove (Figure 2.8). Augustine's venerators of columns (adoratores columnarum) used the kiss, a gesture of affection and reverence, for this type of architectural ornament.[166]

---

[163] Aug. Mor. eccl. 1.34.75 (CSEL 90): Novi multos esse sepulcrorum et picturarum adoratores (I am aware that many are venerating tombs and pictures.) Paulinus referred to his technique of painting the walls of shrines in order to distract visitors from engaging in drinking bouts, which he described as "adorned with pictures and columns" (Paulinus, carm. 28.14 (CSEL 30): pictura laquearibus atque columnis; See also carm. 27.542–544). He claimed that he wrote epigrams to narrate pictures in newly built churches (Paulinus, Ep. 32.17 (CSEL 29). Paulinus composed a poem for his estate basilica that described Jesus as a lamb, crowned for his martyrdom, separating a group of goats from a flock of lambs, which the Jesus-lamb welcomed into heaven. Prudentius claimed that the wall of the shrine of Hippolytus depicted the martyr's death. In perist. 11.125, Prudentius described the location of these paintings as super tumulum (above the tomb). For biblical scenes carved on a church door, see the Roman Basilica Santa Sabina (J.-M. Spieser, "The Iconographic Programme of the Doors of Santa Sabina," tr. Featherstone, in Urban and Religious Spaces in Late Antiquity and Early Byzantium (Burlington, VT: Variorum, 2001), p. 2). For a discussion on the problems of archaeological corroboration of such paintings, see A.-M. Palmer, Prudentius on the Martyrs, Oxford Classical Monographs (New York: Oxford University Press, 1989), pp. 273–275.

[164] Aug. Serm. Dolbeau 4 = 198.10, tr. Hill (dated by Dolbeau: F. Dolbeau, Augustin d'Hippone. Vingt-six sermons au peuple d'Afrique, Collection des Études Augustiniennes, Série Antiquité 147 (Paris: Institut d'Études Augustiniennes, 1996), p. 374): Imperiti pagani faciunt hoc, ut idolum tamquam idolum adorent, quomodo faciunt et vestri qui adorant columnas in ecclesia (Uneducated pagans do this, so that they venerate the idol as an idol, just as your people also do, those who venerate the columns in the church). See also Aug. Serm. Dolbeau 4 = 198.16, tr. Hill, modified: … quoniam nobis dicunt: "Habetis et vos adoratores columnarum et aliquando etiam picturarum." Atque utinam non haberemus, et praestet dominus ut non habeamus! (They say to us, "You people also have your venerators of columns (adoratores columnarum), and sometimes even of pictures." And would to God that we didn't have them, and may the Lord grant that we don't go on having them!).

[165] Brown, "Imperiti," pp. 368–369.

[166] Brown, Society and the Holy, p. 260. Perhaps the dividing line assumed between the Eastern understanding of icons and the Western concept of images is not as solid as scholars have presumed.

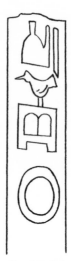

Figure 2.8 Line drawing by author of sculpted chancel pillar from dissident church in Oued R'zel, Algeria, based on photograph in André Berthier, *Les vestiges du Christianisme antique dans la Numidie centrale* (Algiers: Imprimerie polyglotte africaine, Maison-Carrée, 1943), Plate 24, number 46.

Ritual practices such as washing and kissing employ gestures that convey reverence and affection. Such habitual actions reveal and create place attachment and a sense of awe and appreciation toward the buildings these actions entailed. These place meanings are congruent with those found in the rhetorical evidence discussed earlier in this chapter, which regarded these sites as distinctive, special, and infused with divine power.

Summary

The views of space presented in this chapter are neither homogeneous nor polarized. Although the apologetic and polemical rhetoric of differentiation aimed to produce a distinctive Christian-ness among former Roman traditionalists by forming a wedge between these two ways of identifying (among a host of others) and representing them as binary opposites, Christian place meanings can be plotted along a broad spectrum of attitudes toward religious sites. On the one hand, the rhetoric of differentiation influenced how some Christians, like Arnobius, understood, or at least portrayed, their buildings.[167] In their view, Christian buildings simply *could*

---

[167] It is worth noting the distinction between how Arnobius actually perceived place from the way he portrayed it to his audience, despite the inaccessibility of the former.

not share place meanings with pagan buildings, because Christians were the opposite of pagans. On the other hand, some of these meanings overlapped with other place meanings.

Whether the earliest places of Christian assembly were architecturally distinctive (and therefore recognizable to archaeologists) is not an objective assessment. As much today as in antiquity, similarity, or difference, was in the eyes of the beholder. According to the argument between Arnobius and Porphyry, sacred places were perceived differently by different observers, depending on where they stood. Arnobius was attempting to describe his understanding of Christian place from the inside, while Porphyry was looking only from the outside. At some point, different optical perspectives notwithstanding, Christian places were externally identifiable as such to non-Christians as well as to Christians themselves. Once Christian places were distinguishable to those who did not participate in the rituals that took place there, they became susceptible to contestation, as the Valerian interdict against Christian *coemeteria* assembly attests.

Although previous historians have dated Christian perceptions of spatial holiness to the Constantinian era, pre-Constantinian North African conceptions of Christian place included sacrality, even if only in relation to discrete elements of the place. Yasin has persuasively argued that this spatial perception was not a Christian innovation but was adapted from Greco-Roman notions of worship places.[168] Our examination of literary evidence along with inscriptions and ritual practices illustrates an increasing perception of Christian sites and buildings as holy, sacred, and powerful over the course of the third and fourth centuries. Tertullian's use of *domus dei* with material imagery along with the emergence of Christian cemetery areas reflects an early sensibility of the physicality of Christian place that is distinct from non-Christian, or idolatrous, place. Cyprian singled out the church's *congestum*, where the clergy sit, as sacred. In his polemical rejection of Porphyry's comparison of Christian construction projects to traditional Roman temples, Arnobius resisted this materialization of the sacred. At the same time, Christian cemetery shrines and memorials were expanding, at first indistinguishable from Roman house-tombs then becoming increasingly prominent and monumentalized. Christians labeled their places with inscriptions and symbols to distinguish them from other types of place and to designate them as uniquely Christian.

---

[168] Yasin, *Saints and Church Spaces*, pp. 16–26. My regional focus shows that Yasin's Constantinian dating of the *locus sanctus* perception was not universal.

With expanding growth came an increased understanding of these structures as charged with cosmic meaning. Rituals reflected this increased symbolic significance, as worshippers felt the need to purify places of pollution
or demonstratively revere their power. This increasing valuation of sites of
assembly shows that they functioned as super-symbols, overdetermined
with meaning ascribed to them by their interpreters. The conception of
these places as hosting both congregation and divinity rendered them vulnerable – as lived environments – to power struggles between groups negotiating their own identifications, as the next chapter will explore.

3

INTERNECINE CHRISTIAN
CONTESTATION

Nullas infestas hominibus bestias, ut sunt sibi ferales plerique Christianorum
No wild beasts are as hostile to humans as the majority of Christians are fatal
to one another.

– Ammianus Marcellinus, *Res Gestae 22.5.4*

INTERNAL CHRISTIAN ATTITUDES TOWARD THEIR SITES OF worship, as discussed in Chapter 2, reflect a certain degree of ambivalence. Whether they housed the divine as well as the community, whether or not they provided access to the supernatural powers of saints, whether or not they shared common features with traditional Roman temples, and whether their architectural components should be objects of veneration rituals like washing and kissing were all subjects of disagreement. Although place meanings varied, the mere fact of place attachment is more universally attested. These places were important to those who built and used them. The state seizure of Church buildings contributed to their significance externally, within the context of third-century power struggles and imperial attempts at consolidation.[1]

Spatial Contestation

As we shall see in this chapter, numerous literary accounts portray violence or coercion as a popular tool for gaining spatial control. Seizure and destruction of property that was considered religiously significant, however, was not new to the ancient world. It was common practice among conquerors

[1] This argument is a subset of the broader thesis, expounded by James Rives, that the state's involvement in verifying and documenting religious activity in the mid-third century dramatically transformed cult–state relations (James B. Rives, "The Decree of Decius and the Religion of the Empire," *The Journal of Roman Studies* 89 (1999): 135–154.

at least as far back as ancient Mesopotamia and was used routinely by the Roman empire as part of their colonial conquest and reconstruction program.[2] Violence between ethnic or religious groups sometimes converged on devotional structures, whether first-century synagogues in Alexandria (Egypt), a second-century Cyrene temple (Egypt), or third-century shrines in a Roman military camp in Gholaia at the Limes Tripolitanis (Bu Njem, Libya).[3] In the last case, the indigenous African population selectively attacked Roman religious sites left by the departed army in order to symbolically express their freedom from military occupation.[4]

Imperial seizure and destruction of Christian property during the Valerian and Diocletian persecutions had served as a form of punishment and sanction. Recall that Eusebius mentions seizure of *coemeteria* during the third-century repression of Valerian.[5] The Church historian also reports the destruction of basilicas under Diocletian:[6]

> It was the nineteenth year of the reign of Diocletian (303), and the month Dystrus, or March, as the Romans would call it, in which, as the festival of the Savior's Passion [Easter] was coming on, an imperial letter was

---

[2] Christopher Walker and Michael Dick, *The Induction of the Cult Image in Ancient Mesopotamia* (Sastamala, Finland: Vammalan Kirkjapaino Oy, 2001), p. 7. For North Africa in particular, see Elizabeth Fentress, "Romanizing the Berbers," *Past and Present* 190 (February 1996): 3–34.

[3] Alexandria: Philo, *In Flaccum* 48; Cyrene: CJZC 17–19, 21, 22, the last of which specifically mentions a temple, discussed in Miriam Pucci Ben Zeev, *Diaspora Judaism in Turmoil, 116/117 CE: Ancient Sources and Modern Insights* (Leuven: Peeters, 2005), p. 6; Gholaia: This assessment is based on stratigraphic analysis (Béatrice Caseau, "Sacred Landscapes," in *Interpreting Late Antiquity. Essays on the Post-classical World*, ed. G. W. Bowersock, Peter Brown, and Oleg Grabar, pp. 21–59 (Cambridge, MA: Harvard University Press, 1999), p. 21: "They [the locals] carefully desecrated the religious spaces inside the [abandoned] Roman camp and destroyed the cult statues. This gesture was meant to prove the weakness of the Roman gods, already demonstrated by the retreat of the army. It was also a gesture of fear. By destroying the cult statues of Victory and Fortune, these people were making sure that the goddesses would not have any means of harming them.").

[4] Anna Leone, *The End of the Pagan City. Religion, Economy, and Urbanism in Late Antique North Africa* (Oxford: Oxford University Press, 2013), p. 31. Although imperial edicts of persecution targeted Manichaean property (*patrimonia*) as early as 296, accounts of Manichaean persecution focus on human violence (*Mosaicarum et Romanarum Legum Collatio* 15.3 quoting *Cod. Greg.* 7 *de maleficis et Manichaeis*, addressed to the African proconsul). Rives notes the significance of the rubric of this law (likely added by its late third-century compiler, Gregorius) that expands the category of "religious deviance" beyond magic ("Magic, Religion, and Law. The Case of the *Lex Cornelia de sicariis et veneficiis*," in *Religion and Law in Classical and Christian Rome*, ed. Clifford Ando and Jörg Rüpke, pp. 47–67 (Stuttgart: Franz Steiner Verlag, 2006): pp. 66–67).

[5] Eusebius, *Hist. eccl.* 7.13.1 discussed earlier, Chapter 2, note 25.

[6] Eusebius, *Hist. eccl.* 8.2.4, tr. Lawlor and Oulton (SC 55, electronic version): ἔτος τοῦτο ἦν ἐννεακαιδέκατον τῆς Διοκλητιανοῦ βασιλείας, Δύστρος μήν, λέγοιτο δ' ἂν οὗτος Μάρτιος κατὰ Ῥωμαίους, ἐν ᾧ τῆς τοῦ σωτηρίου πάθους ἑορτῆς ἐπελαυνούσης ἥπλωτο πανταχόσε

everywhere promulgated, ordering the razing of churches (*ekklesia*) to the ground and the destruction by fire of the Scriptures, and proclaiming that those who held high positions would lose all civil rights, while those in households, if they persisted in their profession of Christianity, would be deprived of their liberty.

The centrality of Christian basilicas in the Diocletian persecution emerges again later in a North African martyrdom account now dated to after 411.[7] The narrative goes so far as to assert that the principal goal of the crackdown was "to destroy the basilicas of the lord (*basilicas dominicas subverteret*)."[8] By the fifth century, these basilicas had become symbols of sectarian identification. In its summation, the martyrdom account contrasts dissidents and Catholics in spatial terms: "the church of the martyrs" (*ecclesia martyrum*) vs. "the conventicle of traitors" (*conventiculum traditorum*).[9] Quoting Paul's second letter to the Corinthians (6.16), the author states that the former is a "temple of the living God" (*templum Dei vivi*) while the latter is a "temple of idols" (*templum simulacris*).[10] The early fifth-century dissident Christian author of this martyrdom account interprets the anti-Christian violence of a century earlier as a battle over space akin to the conflict of his own time.

The association of sectarian identification with the Diocletian persecution results from the ways the origins of the so-called Donatist schism were remembered, as noted in this book's Introduction.[11] As with the mid-third-century persecutions, Christians were divided on the issue of how to respond to the persecution; in this particular instance, whether Christians should comply with the demand of Roman authorities to hand over sacred objects and texts or to offer sacrifices in the imperial cult. Numidians, most especially, seemed to rally around a strict approach to Christian obedience and condemned those who acquiesced to imperial mandate as *traditores* (traitors). These Christians, like bishop Felix of Thibiuca and his four companions, chose martyrdom over betrayal.

βασιλικὰ γράμματα, τὰς μὲν ἐκκλησίας εἰς ἔδαφος φέρειν, τὰς δὲ γραφὰς ἀφανεῖς πυρὶ γενέσθαι προστάττοντα, καὶ τοὺς μὲν τιμῆς ἐπειλημμένους ἀτίμους, τοὺς δ' ἐν οἰκετίαις, εἰ ἐπιμένοιεν τῇ τοῦ Χριστιανισμοῦ προθέσει, ἐλευθερίας στερεῖσθαι προαγορεύοντα. Orosius corroborates the burning and destruction of basilicas (*Hist.* 7.25.13).

7 Alan Dearn, "The Abitinian Martyrs and the Outbreak of the Donatist Schism," *Journal of Ecclesiastical History* 55.1 (January 2004): 1–18.

8 *The Acts of the Abitinian Martyrs* 2, tr. Tilley, *Donatist Martyr Stories: The Church in Conflict in Roman North Africa*, Translated Texts for Historians 24 (London: Liverpool University Press, 1996), p. 28 (PL 8: 690B).

9 *The Acts of the Abitinian Martyrs* 22, tr. Tilley, *Donatist Martyr Stories*, p. 47 (PL 8: 701D).

10 *The Acts of the Abitinian Martyrs* 22, tr. Tilley, *Donatist Martyr Stories*, p. 47 (PL 8: 702A).

11 See especially T. D. Barnes, "The Beginnings of Donatism," *JTS* n.s. 26 (1975): 13–22.

The Roman magistrate in charge of carrying out the Tetrarchic edict recounts that he witnessed the destruction of two North African basilicas, at Zama and at Furnos (Tunisia), even before receiving the imperial order himself.[12] The assembly of bishops in Cirta that ordained the bishop Silvanus in 306 CE met in the home of Urban Carisus because the basilicas had not yet been restored after the destruction.[13] The Christians for whom these places bore significance viewed imperial demolition as a swift, brutal, and violent business.

The North African writer Lactantius vividly recounts the raid and destruction of the great church of Nicomedia (Asia Minor) in the year 303 by the eastern caesar Galerius that inaugurated the persecution of Christians. At the time, Nicomedia was the eastern capital of the empire in the province of Bithynia, and Lactantius' home:[14]

> [S]uddenly while it was hardly light the prefect with commanders, tribunes, and officers of the treasury came to the church. When its doors had been pulled away it was searched for an image of the god. When the scriptures were found they were burned. It [the building] was opened to all for desecration; it was looted, tossed, and trampled. ... [T]he praetorian guard came arranged in battle array with axes and other tools. They

[12] *Act. pur. Fel.* 4, tr. *Paganism and Christianity, 100–425 C.E.: A Sourcebook*, ed. Ramsay MacMullen and Eugene Lane (Minneapolis, MN: Augsburg Fortress, 1992), p. 242 (CSEL 26: 199): *Alfius Caecilianus dixit: Zama ieram propter lineas comparandas cum Saturnino, et cum veniremus illo, mittunt ad me in praetorio ipsi christiani, ut dicerent: sacrum praeceptum ad te pervenit? ego dixi: non, sed vidi iam exempla et Zama et Furnis dirui basilicas et uri scripturas vidi. itaque proferte, si quas scripturas habetis, ut iussioni sacrae pareatur* (Alfius Caecilianus said, "I had gone to Zama with Saturninus to buy some linen, and when we got back, the Christians themselves sent to me in the praetorium, to say 'Did the sacred [imperial] order reach you?' I said 'No, but I have already seen copies; both at Zama and at Furnos I saw basilicas being destroyed and scriptures burned. Therefore produce any Scriptures you have, so that you may obey the sacred [imperial] command.'"). See discussion in Timothy Barnes, *Constantine and Eusebius* (Cambridge, MA: Harvard University Press, 1981), p. 58.

[13] Optatus, *de schism. Don.* 1.14.1, tr. Edwards (SC 412): *Hi et ceteri, quos principes tuos fuisse paulo post docebimus, post persecutionem apud Cirtam civitatem, quia basilicae necdum fuerant restitutae, in domum Urbani Carisi consederunt die III Iduum Maiarum ...* (These and others, whom we shall prove a little further on to have been your leaders, assembled after the persecution in the city of Cirta, since the churches had not yet been restored, at the house of Urbanus Carisius on March 13 ...). On the dating, see Brent Shaw, *Sacred Violence. African Christians and Sectarian Hatred in the Age of Augustine* (New York: Cambridge University Press, 2011), pp. 816–817.

[14] Lact. *Mort.* 12.2, 5, tr. White, *Social Origins*, vol. 2, p. 100, modified slightly (CSEL 27): *... repente adhuc dubia luce ad ecclesiam praefectus cum ducibus et tribunis et rationalibus venit, et revulsis foribus simulacrum dei quaeritur, scripturae repertae incenduntur, datur omnibus praeda, rapitur, trepidatur, discurritur. ... Veniebant igitur praetoriani acie structa cum securibus et aliis ferramentis et immissi undique fanum illud editissimum paucis horis solo adaequarunt.*

attacked everywhere, and in a few hours they levelled to the ground that very lofty sanctuary.

Lactantius points out that scriptures were burned in place of cult statues to convey the symbolic significance of the action: this attack was designed to strike at the heart of Christian worship. The looting (*rapere*) suggests bellicose appropriation of property, reinforced by the description of the soldiers arranged in battle-array (*acie structa*).

Eusebius also describes the Diocletian attack on churches and its aftermath in violent and vengeful terms in his panegyric to Constantine delivered on the thirtieth anniversary of the emperor's reign in 336:[15]

> For those who had but lately been driven by madness of soul to war against God, raving like dogs yet powerless against God Himself, had vented their spleen on inanimate buildings. They tore down the oratories from top to bottom, digging up their very foundations, and so created the impression of a city captured by its enemies. ... On the heels of those who beleaguered the houses of prayer followed the wages of their sin, and straightway they became rootless and homeless, lost to hearth and lost to sight.

Like Lactantius, Eusebius employs war imagery, yet he also conveys lack of control with the phrases "driven by madness (*aponoia*)," "raving like dogs (*hōrmēmenoi kunōn*)," and "vented their spleen (*luttōntes*)." By construing the exile of those who attacked Christian "houses of prayer" as divine punishment for their crimes, he promotes a providentialist explanation of events. In the fifth century, the Iberian priest Orosius, who considered Augustine his teacher, would cast retributions such as these as the biblical ten plagues visited on the Egyptians.[16] In another speech delivered at the dedication of the Church of the Holy Sepulcher, Eusebius suggests that this turnabout in fortune was predicted and achieved by Jesus when he foretold the destruction of the Jewish temple.[17] For Eusebius, these were no ordinary

---

15 Eusebius, *Laud. Const.* 9.13, 19, tr. H. A. Drake, *In Praise of Constantine: A Historical Study and New Translation of Eusebius' Tricennial Orations* (University of California Press, 1976) (GCS 7): οἱ μὲν γὰρ ψυχῆς ἀπονοίᾳ πρὸ μικροῦ θεομαχεῖν ὡρμημένοι κυνῶν δίκην λυττῶντες κατὰ τῶν ἀψύχων οἰκοδομημάτων, ὅτι μὴ κατ' αὐτοῦ θεοῦ δυνατὸν ἦν αὐτοῖς, τοὺς θυμοὺς ἠφίεσαν, εἶτ' ἐξ ὕψους εἰς ἔδαφος καταρρίπτοντες ἐξ αὐτῶν τε βάθρων ἀνασκάπτοντες τὰ προσευκτήρια ἑαλωκυίας ὑπὸ πολεμίων πόλεως παρεῖχον θέαν. ... διὸ τοῖς μὲν τοὺς εὐκτηρίους οἴκους πολιορκήσασι παρὰ πόδας εἵπετο τἀπίχειρα τῆς δυσσεβείας, ἄρριζοί τε καὶ ἄοικοι ἀνέστιοί τε καὶ ἀφανεῖς καθίσταντο παραχρῆμα.

16 Orosius, *Hist.* 7.27.1–13.

17 Eusebius, *De Sepulchro Christi* 17.8, tr. Drake, *In Praise of Constantine* (GCS 7, in *Laud. Const.*): ἢ τίς οὕτω ταχὺς ἔκδικος τῶν εἰς αὐτὸν τετολμημένων ἀποδέδεικται, ὡς ἅμα τῇ

events merely progressing through the course of human history; they were displays of the divine will that the Church would ultimately triumph over the enemies of God. Both Lactantius and Eusebius construe the Tetrarchic persecution and its resolution in religiously symbolic terms.

The use of architectural dispossession as a symbol of victory was firmly rooted in both biblical and Roman convention.[18] King Jehu's destruction of a Baal shrine together with its priests is recounted in 2 Kings 10:27: "Then they demolished the pillar of Baal, and destroyed the temple of Baal, and made it a latrine to this day." The symbolism of converting an active temple into a toilet is striking. What was formerly esteemed by its worshippers as a place of sanctity has been relegated to a place for human waste. Roman literature, too, employs the rhetorical symbolism of temple destruction to signify triumph. The first-century Jewish historian Josephus writes that, in 19 CE, the emperor Tiberius "razed the temple of Isis and ordered her cult statue to be thrown into the Tiber river."[19] According to Josephus the demolition was provoked by the infamous scandal in which an Isiac priest constructed an elaborate ruse in the temple to enable a Roman noblewoman to be seduced by the lovesick aristocrat who lusted after her.[20] Likewise,

κατ' αὐτοῦ δυσσεβείᾳ τὸ πᾶν Ἰουδαίων ἔθνος ἀοράτῳ δυνάμει μετελθεῖν, ἄρδην τε τὸν βασιλικὸν αὐτῶν τόπον ἐκ βάθρων ἀρθῆναι, αὐτό τε τὸ ἱερὸν ἅμα τοῖς ἐν αὐτῷ σεμνοῖς εἰς ἔδαφος κατενεχθῆναι; τίς δὲ προρρήσεις αὐτῶν τε τούτων πέρι τῶν ἀσεβῶν ἀνδρῶν ἀμφί τε τῆς πρὸς αὐτοῦ καθ' ὅλης τῆς οἰκουμένης ὑποστάσης ἐκκλησίας καταλλήλους τοῖς πράγμασιν ἀποφθεγξάμενος, πιστὰς ἔδειξε ταύτας τοῖς ἔργοις, ὡς ὁ ἡμέτερος σωτήρ; περὶ μὲν τοῦ τῶν ἀσεβῶν ἱεροῦ φήσας "ἀφίεται ὑμῖν ὁ οἶκος ὑμῶν ἔρημος" (Who has ever wrought such swift vengeance for the crimes committed against Him? Or was not the entire race of Jews scattered by an invisible power simultaneously with their impiety against Him, and was not their royal seat completely lifted off its foundations, and the temple itself, together with the sacred objects in it, brought down to the ground? Who, like Our Savior, having uttered clear predictions concerning both these impious men themselves and the establishment by Him of a universal church, made good these pledges with deeds? For He said about the temple of the impious ones, "Your house is left unto you desolate ..." (Mt 23.38)).

[18] For the Christian exegetical tradition that construes the Jewish temple destruction and exile as punishment for their attitude toward Christ, see, for example, Minucius Felix, *Octavius* 33.2 and Eusebius, *Hist. eccl.* 3.5.4–7. Christian providentialism is already present in the New Testament (Hebrews 2:14–15, e.g.).

[19] Josephus, *Ant.* 18.3.4 (79) (ed. Niese): ... τόν τε ναὸν καθεῖλεν καὶ τὸ ἄγαλμα τῆς Ἴσιδος εἰς τὸν Θύβριν ποταμὸν ἐκέλευσεν ἐμβαλεῖν.

[20] Although the tale is generally thought to have been embellished or fabricated by Josephus, the emperor's sanction against Egyptian cults is corroborated by Roman historians (Suetonius, *Tib.* 36.1; Tacitus *Ann.* 2.85). For a reconsideration of the tale's historicity in light of depictions of Anubis in archaeological remains of temples, see David Klotz, "The Lecherous Pseudo-Anubis of Josephus and the 'Tomb of 1897' at Akhmim," in *Et in Ægypto et ad Ægyptum Recueil d'études dédiées à Jean-Claude Grenier*, Équipe. Égypte Nilotique et Méditerranéenne 5140, Archéologie des Sociétés Méditerranéennes, ed. Annie Gasse,

Appian writes in his description of the Roman defeat of Carthage that after the Punic commander Hasdrubal secretly surrendered, the Romans "then burned the temple [of Aesculapius] and they were burned alive in it."[21] Appian weaves a dramatic narrative in which Hasdrubal's wife throws herself and their two children into the flames, but not before she reproaches him for surrendering, branding him a "traitor against homeland and temples."[22]

Uniting both biblical and Classical rhetorical traditions, the discourse of architectural dispossession took hold to such an extent that the motif became a stock rhetorical device in Christian narratives about conversion, conflict, and victory.[23] Although Constantine restored buildings throughout the empire and contributed huge sums to his program of Christian architectural expansion, *architectural dispossession* and *spatial supersession* continued to serve as weapons in sectarian controversies.

The emperor Constantine's emphasis on religious unity induced him to single out dissident Christians as the stumbling block to his goal of "harmonious and brotherly observance" in his letter to the North African bishops discussed in this book's Introduction.[24] This attempt to appear more irenic is reflected in the emperor's rhetoric exhorting the Catholic bishops to "mercy" (*misericordia*), "forbearance" (*patientia*), and "serenity" (*quieta*).[25] These words ostensibly reject violence as a viable solution to the conflict.

Frédéric Servajean, and Christophe Thiers, pp. 383–396 (CNRS – Université Paul Valéry – Montpellier III), Montpellier, 2012). On this tale generally see Helga Botermann, "Die Maßnahmen gegen die stadtrömischen Juden im Jahre 19 n. Chr.," *Historia* 52.4 (2005): 410–435, pp. 423–425; Robert Turcan, *The Cults of the Roman Empire*, tr. Antonia Neville (New York: Oxford University Press, 1996), pp. 88–89; Sharon Kelly Heyob, *The Cult of Isis among Women in the Graeco-Roman World*, Etudes préliminaires aux religions orientales dans l'Empire romain 51 (Leiden: E. J. Brill, 1975), pp. 117–119; and Michel Malaise, *Les conditions de pénétration et de diffusion des cultes égyptiens en Italie*, Etudes préliminaires aux religions orientales dans l'Empire romain 22 (Leiden: E. J. Brill, 1972), pp. 88, 391. For the use of Roman noblewomen in constructing *apologia* and male anxiety about female roles as religious experts as revealed in Josephus' narrative, see Shelly Matthews, *First Converts: Rich Pagan Women and the Rhetoric of Mission in Early Judaism and Christianity* (Stanford, CA: Stanford University Press, 2002), pp. 12–13, 20, 24–27, 97–98.

[21] Appian, *Hist. rom.* 8.19 (131) (ed. Mendelssohn): ... τὸν δὲ νεὼν ἐνέπρησάν τε καὶ κατεκαύθησαν.

[22] Appian, *Hist. rom.* 8.19 (131) (ed. Mendelssohn): ... πατρίδος τε καὶ ἱερῶν ... προδότην γενόμενον ...

[23] As evident in later Greek hagiography in addition to the Latin material discussed subsequently (Helen Saradi, "The Christianization of Pagan Temples," *From Temple to Church*, ed. Johannes Hahn, Stephen Emmel, and Ulrich Gotter (Boston, MA: Brill, 2008), pp. 113–134).

[24] *Ep. Const. Aelaf.*, tr. Edwards (CSEL 26): ... *concordi observantiae fraternitate* ...

[25] *Ep. Const. episc. Afric.* Eusebius alludes to the correspondence in *Vit. Const.* 1.45.1 (GCS 7): τούτων δ' οἱ μὲν ἀπηλλάττοντο καταιδούμενοι τὰς παραινέσεις (Some of them respected

As appeals to "unity" increasingly became the centerpiece of imperial legal discourse, the concept was invoked to distinguish legitimate from illegitimate uses of power. The concept of unity also masked the coercion used by the state-endorsed Catholics against their dissident opponents to force them to abandon their separate congregations and capitulate to the Catholics. Dissident basilicas became a flash point in this violent conflict.

The decision of the Roman emperor to become embroiled in the controversy, as Harold Drake has duly noted, "inaugurated the whole trail of events which brought Constantine and the bishops together in Constantinople a quarter century later."[26] Once the emperor was involved, there was no turning back; he had become the arbiter of Christian sectarian disputes. Petitions filed by dissidents and their opponents were forwarded by the African proconsul to Constantine.[27] The emperor appointed two successive councils to hear the case at Rome and Arles, both of which supported Caecilianus' episcopacy while allowing the principle of seniority to determine the succession of episcopal sees, regardless of party affiliation.[28]

In the midst of this controversy over episcopal succession, the emperor restored Christian property. Some scholars attribute this act of restitution to Maxentius, who began a similar policy in Rome in 311.[29] Most, following Eusebius, credit Constantine, which puts the date in the following year, 312/313, in response to African petitions.[30] Constantine wrote a letter

his rebukes and desisted ...). See François Decret, *Early Christianity in North Africa*, tr. Edward Smither (Eugene, OR: Cascade Books, 1996: 2009), p. 105.

[26] Drake, *Constantine*, p. 213.

[27] Aug. *Ep.* 88.2.

[28] *Ep. Const. Aelaf.* in Maier, *Le dossier du donatisme* 1, pp. 153–171. See J. Patout Burns and Robin M. Jensen, *Christianity in Roman North Africa*, in collaboration with Graeme W. Clarke, Susan T. Stevens, William Tabbernee, and Maureen A. Tilley (Grand Rapids, MI: Wm. B. Eerdmans Publishing Co., 2014), p. 48.

[29] Aug. *Brev. Coll.* 3.18.34 (CCL 149A): ... *litteris Maxentii imperatoris et litteris praefecti praetorio ad prefectum urbi, ut ea reciperent quae tempore persecutionis ablata memoratus imperator christianis iusserat reddi* (A letter from emperor Maxentius and a letter from the praetorian prefect to the city prefect, saying that we had received the items taken from the churches during the persecution and that the same emperor made restitution to Christians), *and Parm.* 13.17 (CSEL 53): ... *ut reciperent loca quae fuerant a Christianis tempore persecutionis ablata* (Shaw, *Sacred Violence*, p. 819; Drake, *Constantine and the Bishops*, p. 172; Bernard Green, *Christianity in Ancient Rome: The First Three Centuries* (New York: Bloomsbury T&T Clark, 2010), pp. 218–220; Simon Corcoran, *The Empire of the Tetrarchs: Imperial Pronouncements and Government, AD 284–324* (New York: Oxford University Press, 1996: 2000), p. 145, n. 97; B. Kriegbaum, "Die Religionspolitik des Kaisers Maxentius," *Archivium Historiae Pontificiae* 30 (1992): 7–54, pp. 44–49).

[30] Eusebius, *Hist. ecl.* 10.5.15–17, 6.1–4, and 7.1–2 (Barnes, "Donatism," p. 21, *Constantine and Eusebius*, p. 39, and *Constantine*, p. 100; Charles Odahl, *Constantine and the Christian Empire* (New York: Routledge, 2004), p. 114).

to Caecilianus informing him that his supporters, clergy of "the legitimate and most holy universal Church," would be receiving imperial funds.[31]
Recognizing the Caecilianists as aligned with the universal Church, or
"Catholics," politically marginalized the supporters of Maiorinus within
the empire as a whole. By specifically naming "Catholics" as beneficiar-
ies of restitution, the state took sides in the conflict over religious space.[32]
This partiality was further expressed in a subsequent letter to the proconsul of Africa.[33] When dissident Christians appealed the verdict, Constantine
convened a second commission of bishops in Arles. The council affirmed
Caecilianus over Maiorinus' successor, Donatus. In response, Constantine
ordered the seizure of all dissident basilicas.[34] Eusebius reports that
Constantine also ordered that ownership of martyr shrines and cemeteries be transferred from private individuals to the Catholic Church, which
would have expropriated dissident Christian shrines as well.[35]

---

[31] Eusebius, *Hist. eccl.* 10.6.1, tr. Lawlor and Oulton (SC 55): Κωνσταντῖνος Αὔγουστος
Καικιλιανῷ ἐπισκόπῳ Χαρταγένης. ἐπειδήπερ ἤρεσεν κατὰ πάσας ἐπαρχίας, τάς τε
Ἀφρικὰς καὶ τὰς Νουμιδίας καὶ τὰς Μαυριτανίας, ῥητοῖς τισι τῶν ὑπηρετῶν τῆς ἐνθέσμου
καὶ ἁγιωτάτης καθολικῆς θρησκείας εἰς ἀναλώματα ἐπιχορηγηθῆναι τι, ἔδωκα γράμματα
πρὸς Οὖρσον τὸν διασημότατον καθολικὸν τῆς Ἀφρικῆς καὶ ἐδήλωσα αὐτῷ ὅπως
τρισχιλίους φόλλεις τῇ σῇ στερρότητι ἀπαριθμῆσαι φροντίσῃ (Constantine Augustus to
Caecilianus, bishop of Carthage. Forasmuch as it has been our pleasure in all provinces,
namely the African, the Numidian and the Mauritanian, that somewhat be contributed
for expenses to certain specified ministers of the lawful and most holy Catholic religion,
I have dispatched a letter to Ursus, the most distinguished finance minister of Africa, and
have notified to him that he be careful to pay over to your Firmness three thousand folles).
[32] Eusebius, *Hist. eccl.* 10.5.16, 6.1, 6.4, and 7.2.
[33] Eusebius, *Hist. eccl.* 10.7.2 (SC 55): διόπερ ἐκείνους τοὺς εἴσω τῆς ἐπαρχίας τῆς σοι
πεπιστευμένης ἐν τῇ καθολικῇ ἐκκλησίᾳ, ᾗ Καικιλιανὸς ἐφέστηκεν, τὴν ἐξ αὐτῶν ὑπηρεσίαν
τῇ ἁγίᾳ ταύτῃ θρησκείᾳ παρέχοντας, οὕσπερ κληρικοὺς ἐπονομάζειν εἰώθασιν, ἀπὸ
πάντων ἅπαξ ἁπλῶς τῶν λειτουργιῶν βούλομαι ἀλειτουργήτους διαφυλαχθῆναι ...
[34] This "decree" is only mentioned in Augustine *Ep.* 105.9 and 88.3 and *C. litt. Petil.* 2.92 (205),
(PL 43: 326): *Constantinus vobis basilicas jussit auferri* (Constantine ordered that the basilicas
be taken from you). It is not preserved in any of the legal compendia. See also Eusebius,
Hist. eccl. 10.6.1–5. For discussion, see Decret, *Early Christianity in North Africa*, pp. 104–105.
[35] Eusebius, *Vit. Const.* 2.40, tr. Cameron and Hall (GCS 7): Καὶ μὴν καὶ τοὺς τόπους
αὐτούς, οἳ τοῖς σώμασι τῶν μαρτύρων τετίμηνται καὶ τῆς ἀναχωρήσεως τῆς ἐνδόξου
ὑπομνήματα καθεστᾶσιν, τίς ἂν ἀμφιβάλοι μὴ οὐχὶ ταῖς ἐκκλησίαις προσήκειν, ἢ οὐχὶ
καὶ προστάξειεν ἄν; ἡνίκα μήτε δῶρον ἄμεινον μήτε κάματος χαριέστερος καὶ πολλὴν
ἔχων τὴν ὠφέλειαν ἕτερος ἂν γένοιτο, ἢ τοῦ θείου προτρέποντος νεύματος τὴν περὶ
τῶν τοιούτων ποιεῖσθαι σπουδήν, καὶ ἃ μετὰ πονηρῶν ἐξῃρέθη προφάσεων τῶν ἀδίκων
καὶ μοχθηροτάτων ἀνδρῶν, ἀποκατασταθέντα δικαίως ταῖς εὐαγέσιν αὖθις ἐκκλησίαις
ἀποσωθῆναι (Furthermore the places themselves which are honored by the bodies of the
martyrs and stand as monuments to their glorious decease, who could doubt that they
belong to the churches, or would not so decree? Since no gift could be better nor other
labor more agreeable and rich in advantage, than at the instigation of the divine will to

The seizure of basilicas was sometimes a bloody encounter, whether by dissidents or state-backed Catholics. Constantine acknowledges as much regarding the basilica of Cirta/Constantina in his letter to the Caecilianist bishops of Numidia.[36] The basilica had been constructed earlier with imperial funds, but dissidents took control of the buildings with "gangs and violence."[37] Although we possess no details of how dissidents appropriated the building, the fact that Catholic bishops appealed to imperial authority for intervention as they had done in disputes over episcopal succession reveals that they felt the takeover was unlawful. In this case, the emperor's conciliatory response was to donate a public building for temporary Catholic use and build them a new basilica rather than to evict the dissidents by force.[38]

This decision comports with the imperial tactical shift regarding dissidents from coercion to persuasion in 320.[39] Constantine advised North African Catholic bishops:[40]

take active steps about such things, and that what was on evil pretexts of lawless and foul men taken away, should be rightfully restored to the holy churches and conserved).

[36] Ep. Const. Zeu., tr. Edwards (CSEL 26): Accepta igitur epistola sapientiae et gravitatis vestrae, conperi haereticos sive schismaticos eam basilicam ecclesiae catholicae quam in Constantina civitate iusseram fabricari, solita inprobitate invadendam putasse et frequenter tam a nobis quam a iudicibus nostris ex nostra iussione commonitos et reddere quod suum non erat, noluisse ... (Having therefore received the letter from your wise and eminent persons, I have learnt that the heretics or schismatics have, with their wonted shamelessness, thought fit to invade the basilica of that church which I had ordered to be built in the city of Constantina, and that – though frequently admonished, not only by our judges on our orders but by ourselves, to give back that which was not theirs – they refused ...). Edwards doubts Optatus was the compiler of this document, taking Optatus' statement that "we have appended to the last part of this book a complete record of these matters as a full confirmation" to refer to the other appended documents (p. xxvi, citing Optatus, de schism. Don. 1.14.2, tr. Edwards, p. 14 (SC 412): Harum namque plenitudinem rerum in novissima parte istorum libellorum ad implendam fidem adiunximus). Eusebius alludes to this letter in Vit. Const. 1.45.2, tr. Cameron and Hall (GCS 7): ... τοὺς ἐπὶ τῆς Ἄφρων χώρας διαστασιάζοντας εἰς τοσοῦτον συνέβαινεν ἐπιτριβῆς (... it came about that those in Africa reached such a pitch of dissension that crimes were committed ...).

[37] Ep. Const. Zeu., tr. Shaw, Sacred Violence, p. 161 (CSEL 26, corrected by Maier): ... inter turbas atque contentus sui similes incitarent atque ita aliquid exsisteret quod sedari vi oporteret (With the use of gangs and violence they incite people like themselves. In this way, something is arising that will have to be repressed with force).

[38] We only have Optatus' version of the story.

[39] Michael Gaddis, "There is No Crime for Those Who Have Christ". Religious Violence in the Christian Roman Empire (Berkeley, CA: University of California Press, 2005), pp. 57, 64, citing the Acts of the Conference of Carthage 3.548–551 (SC 195 = PL 11: 1257, ##549–552): 549. Ubi recitatur epistola Constantini ad vicarium Verinum destinata, qua libertatem agendi tribuit Donatistis. 550. Prosecutio Catholicorum quae dicit pro se magis epistolam facere Constantini, quia non de Caeciliano aliquid judicatum est, sed furori ipsi permissi sunt. 551. Interlocutio Catholicorum dicta confirmans. 552. Ubi Donatistae petunt ut judex de permissa sibi a Constantino arbitrii libertate pronuntiet.

[40] Ep. Const. univ. episc. Afric., tr. Edwards (CSEL 26): nihil ex reciproco reponatur iniuriae (cf. Rom 12.17); vindictam enim, quam deo servare debemus (cf. Rom 12.19), insipientis est manibus

Let nothing be done to reciprocate an injury, for it is a fool who would usurp the vengeance which we ought to reserve to God, particularly when our faith ought to be confident that whatever suffering result from the madness of people of this kind will have value in God's eyes by the grace of martyrdom.

Rather than using force to evict the dissidents, Constantine gave the Caecilianists funds to build a new basilica.[41]

This kind of imperial favoritism ignited upheaval, and Constantine could send a militia to control the violence and enforce the transfer of property. Sometime between 317 and 320, the Roman army forced a dissenting congregation (probably in Carthage) to admit Catholics.[42] The congregation apparently opened its doors without much resistance, as a dissident sermon preached decades later recalls that no bodily harm resulted. What is remembered is only how Catholics degraded the basilica in the course of the seizure, turning it "into a tavern … [and profaning it] by impure deeds."[43] The theme of basilica desecration evoked not only the deep sense of betrayal dissidents felt toward Catholics, but also the biblical images of impurity associated with idolatry and opponents of God (Zech 13:12; Ezek 36:25).[44]

The confiscation at Sicilibba, 45 km outside Carthage (Bordj Alaouine, Tunisia), in 317 was a more violent affair. The dissident congregation and its bishop resisted by barricading themselves inside the basilica, forcing the commanding Roman official (*comes*), general (*dux*), and commander (*tribunus*) to intervene. Conflict ensued, resulting in multiple fatalities.[45] The dissident basilica later memorialized this violence with "inscriptions; memory preserves the name of the persecution as Caecilianist until the end of time,"

---

usurpare, maxime cum debeat fides nostra confidere, quicquid ab huiusmodi hominum furore patietur, martyrii gratia apud deum esse valiturum.

[41] *Ep. Const. Zeu.*, tr. Edwards (CSEL 26: 216): *In quo tamen loco sumptu fiscali basilicam erigi praecepi* … (However, as to the place in which I commanded a basilica to be built with fiscal revenue).

[42] *Passio Sancti Donati* 2, tr. Tilley, *Donatist Martyr Stories: The Church in Conflict in Roman North Africa*, Translated Texts for Historians 24 (London: Liverpool University Press, 1996), p. 53. Contrary to Tilley's claim, the sermon discusses events at three different sites: Carthage, Sicilibba, and Advocata, analyzed by Shaw, *Sacred Violence*, pp. 187–193. For a discussion of why the site attribution Avioccala (instead of Advocata) made by Tilley and others is unlikely, see Shaw, *Sacred Violence*, p. 193 n. 106.

[43] *Passio Sancti Donati* 4, tr. Tilley, *Donatist Martyr Stories*, p. 55, modified (BHL 2303b: 259): *Basilica in popinam, ne turpius dicam, conversa est. Qui dolor videre in domo Dei tantum piaculum, locum illum castis precibus et votis assuetum, incestis operibus, et spuriis vocibus profanari!*

[44] Maureen Tilley, *The Bible in Christian North Africa. The Donatist World* (Minneapolis, MN: Augsburg Fortress, 1997), pp. 94, 160.

[45] *Passio Sancti Donati* 7–8.

and instituted an annual commemoration on the anniversary of the martyrs' deaths.[46] The same dissident sermon that recalled the Carthaginian basilica seizure later recounted the Sicilibba attack by imperial soldiers.[47] The homilest describes the military action in graphic terms:[48]

> Homes are encircled with battalions … bands of soldiers serving the Furies of the *traditores*. They were brought together to perform a crime … the exaction of blood according to some contract … [T]he people of God … flew undaunted to the house of prayer with a desire to suffer … [T]his cohort of soldiers marshaled by latter-day Pharisees sets forth from their camps to the death of Christians. Against innocent hands stretched out to the Lord [in prayer], their right hands are armed with cudgels … Finally, bloodshed marked the end of this hatred. Now the soldiers endorsed the contract and the covenant of crime in no other way than by the seal of blood … each age group and sex was killed, cut down in the midst of the basilica … water [of baptism] might be joined to blood.

The state-sanctioned killing of victims who had sought protection in the sanctuary, the very place legally recognized as an inviolable refuge, inspires outrage. This "murder in the cathedral" violated all social and civic norms; it was a "crime *(facinus)*." The preacher notes that the bodies of those killed, now regarded as martyrs, had been buried in the basilica. He dramatically points to the commemorative inscriptions as bearing witness to the tragedy for posterity.

As if mass murder in the cathedral was not a bad enough crime to pin on the Catholic bishop, the speaker goes on to describe "an *even greater*

---

[46] *Passio Sancti Donati* 8, tr. and quotation from Tilley, *Donatist Martyr Stories*, p. 57 (BHL 2303b: 261): *illic ex titulationibus nominum persecutionis etiam Caecilianensis usque in finem memoria praerogetur …*

[47] Tilley, following Jean-Paul Brisson and Frend, dates it to "not long after the events narrated" (*Donatist Martyr Stories*, p. 52), but dating of Donatist documents has recently been revised to later (Timothy Barnes, *Early Christian Hagiography and Roman History*. Tria Corda 5 (Tübingen: Mohr Siebeck, 2010), p. 153). The mention of inscriptions and memory suggests that some time had elapsed since the events transpired.

[48] *Passio Sancti Donati* 3, 6, 8, 11, tr. Tilley, *Donatist Martyr Stories*, slightly modified, pp. 55–58 (ed. Maier): *circumdantur vexillationibus domus … militum manus traditorum furiis minstrantes, quae ad perpetrandum tanti facinoris (opus memoratorum mercede) conductae sunt … exactionem locate sanguinis … populous dei … ad orationis domum voto passionis animosius convolavit … cohors militum progreditur ad christanorum necem a pharisaeis neotericis procurata. Manus contra innocuas ad dominum extensas armantur fustibus dexterae … Denique huius odii simper exitus effusione sanguinis signatus est sicut et nunc pactum conventionemque sceleris non aliter quam consignatione sanguinis transegerunt cum omnis aetas et sexus … caesa in media basilica necaretur … qua sanguini iungeretur.*

madness ... the killer thought he could *seize* the same basilica, as if she should surrender herself to his love for the place."[49] The basilica is conceived of as a body, as we saw in the previous chapter. In this case, it is a female body, making it susceptible to violation. The sexual overtones of this imagery, with its personification of the basilica as the object of Caecilianus' desire, make clear why the homilist describes seizing the basilica as "even greater" than human carnage.[50] The basilica's purity, the very future of the sacraments, was at stake. This sexualized rhetoric of the raped virginal church resonates with earlier North African portrayals of heresy as sexual deviance: "Whoever breaks off from the Church and bonds with an adulteress separates himself from the promises of the Church."[51] In the century that had elapsed from the age of Cyprian to that of the dissident preacher, the purity of the Church had expanded from the community who constituted the Church body to include the actual building in which the community assembled. The later fourth-century dissident homilist personifies the Sicilibba basilica, ascribing to it qualities associated with the (female) body. In keeping with biblical notions of (female) purity, the purity of the basilica purity is determined by what (or who) goes in and comes out of it. As we saw earlier in Optatus' description of dissidents washing the walls of basilicas seized from Catholics, pollution and purity were understood as transferable from individuals to buildings. In the case of the Sicilibba basilica, the pollution caused by the Catholic invasion of sacred space was purified by the burial of human bodies, the martyrs' remains, within the body of the basilica.

The sectarian dispute continued apace. In 320 the governor of Numidia, Domitius Zenophilus, investigated a dispute between a deacon and his bishop.[52] The extant transcript of those hearings suggests that the deacon Nundiarius, disappointed that he did not achieve the desired outcome from the Numidian bishops, had taken his case to the civil court despite the bishops' ardent protests.[53] In the course of the proceedings, evidence

---

[49] *Passio Sancti Donati* 10, tr. Tilley, *Donatist Martyr Stories*, slightly modified (emphasis added), p. 58 (BHL 2303b: 263): *Adhuc autem quod dementiae maioris fuit ... eandem basilicam possidendam homicida putavit, quasi amore loci subcumberet.*

[50] Shaw briefly notes this rhetorical device (*Sacred Violence*, pp. 192–193). The feminized corporealization of the basilica also occurs in Lactantius' description of the Nicomedian basilica attack (Lact. *Mort.* 12.5).

[51] Cypr. *Unit. eccl.* 6 (CCL 3): *Quisque ab ecclesia segregatus adulterae iungitur, a promissis ecclesiae separatur ...* See Shaw for usage of this imagery by Optatus and Augustine (*Sacred Violence*, pp. 326–332).

[52] *Gest. Zeno.*

[53] *Gest. Zeno.* 2.

was submitted documenting the betrayal of church property by Numidian bishops during the Diocletian persecution.[54] As Shaw notes:[55]

> Whereas Roman courts and civil judges might have been adverse to having their courts used to resolve theological or ecclesiastical issues, disputes over property ownership were something that they were well equipped to handle and which they were probably willing to entertain as valid legal actions.

Knowing that the courts were likely to hear complaints about spatial contestation led the parties to the African internecine controversy to focus on property disputes. With attention fixed on basilicas, shrines, and other ritual arenas, the political currency of these properties increased. Confiscation of religious spaces, formerly the province of the state during times of persecution, figured prominently in the conflict.

Constantine was not entirely convinced of the tactic's success, however. His letter to the African Church of 321 CE acknowledges the failure of these measures and proposes a new approach, toleration. Appealing to "the mercy of Almighty God," Constantine suspended anti-Donatist legislation.[56] This cessation of imperial hostilities was only a short-term solution. When the economic and political issues that festered in North Africa once again erupted in rebellion during the reign of emperor Constans (r. 337–350), the third and youngest son of Constantine, Christians once again battled over sacred sites.

The rebellion was led by Axido and Fasir. Shaw remarks that "from their names alone, it is surmised, surely correctly, that these men emerged from local African social ranks that were not fully integrated with the Romano-Latin culture of the towns."[57] The revolt leaders also invoked religious authority to support their cause.[58] Optatus notes that they were called *duces sanctorum* (generals of the saints) by their followers, who included those he calls "circumcellions."[59] The only other contemporaneous use of *dux sanctorum* is in a dissident sermon, among a host of epithets describing Christ, including "judge of the world, deliverer of all seeking his refuge … rearer of the innocent, slayer of vice … friend of the faithful, repayer of the

---

[54] *Gest. Zeno.* 3–5.
[55] Shaw, *Sacred Violence*, pp. 118–119.
[56] *Ep. Const. episc. Afric.*, tr. Edwards (CSEL 26: 213): … *omnipotentis dei misericordia.* …
[57] Shaw, *Sacred Violence*, p. 169. For the same conclusion, see Bruno Pottier, "Les circoncellions. Un mouvement ascétique itinérant dans l'Afrique du Nord des IVe et Ve siècles," *Antiquités africaines* 44.1 (2008): 43–107, p. 50.
[58] Pottier, "Les circoncellions," p. 46.
[59] Optatus, *de schism. Don.* 3.4.3, 4

pious ... remover of humiliation, savior of the defeated ... aid to those who perform good works."[60] Each of these descriptions could equally apply to the relief that Axido and Fasir aimed to bring those who suffered under the economic tyranny of debt repayment and bonded labor.[61] Rebel leaders and their followers could draw on a long history of Christian solidarity with the poor to support their cause.[62] In particular, the invocation in the daily prayer, "forgive us our debts as we forgive our debtors," was construed literally by some, as Valerio Neri has pointed out.[63] Augustine corrects his listeners' interpretation of the phrase: "each is not urged to repay a debt of money to debtors, but to forgive another who may have sinned against us."[64]

Among the instigators of these debt riots, Optatus includes those whom he calls "agonistic circumcellions."[65] Shaw and Dossey have convincingly argued that Optatus' presentation of the circumcellions as the guerrilla arm of the dissident Church is a rhetorical fabrication.[66] In fact, the polemicist's

---

[60] Ps.-Aug. *In Natali Domini* XIII (D. A. B. Caillau, *Sancti Aurelii Augustini, Hipponensis episcopi, Sermones inediti*, p. 33), (PLS 2: 931–34): *Ipse enim hodie manifestatus est Archangelorum magister, Angelorum instructor, arbiter sæculorum, liberator omnium ad se confugientium ... nutritor innocentiae, vitiorum interfector, superstes sæculorum, amicus fidelium, remunerator piorum, amator convertentium, ablator sordium, salvator vulnerum, ostensor vitae, adjutor in bono opere laborantium, dux sanctorum ...* (In fact, this very one [Jesus Christ] was revealed as the master of archangels, the teacher of angels, the judge of the world, deliverer of all seeking his refuge ... rearer of the innocent, slayer of vice, stander over the ages, friend of the faithful, repayer of the pious, lover of converts, remover of humiliation, savior of the defeated, revealer of life, aid to those who perform good works (cf. John 10:33), general of the saints ...). See Leslie Dossey, *Peasant and Empire in Christian North Africa* (Berkeley, CA: University of California Press, 2010), p. 178.

[61] A detailed analysis of the issue can be found in Dossey, *Peasant and Empire*, pp. 176–180.

[62] See Peter Brown, *Through the Eye of a Needle: Wealth, the Fall of Rome, and the Making of Christianity in the West, 350–550 AD* (Princeton University Press: Kindle Edition, 2013), p. 82.

[63] Neri, "Ancora sui circumcelliones (alla luce di studi recenti)," *Mediterraneo Antico* 12.1–2 (2009): 185–198.

[64] Aug. *Serm. Dom. in monte* 2.8.28 (CCL 35): *non hic ergo quisque urgetur pecuniam dimittere debitoribus, sed quaecumque in eum alius peccaverit.*

[65] Optatus, *de schism. Don.* 3.4.1.

[66] Scholars have sought motivations for circumcellion violence along a spectrum ranging from the religious to the secular, or economic. Since Shaw provides a thorough survey of this literature, I will not rehearse the arguments here (Shaw, *Sacred Violence*, Appendix F.) The attempt by some scholars to segregate religious from economic and political motivations for rebel actions disregards the degree to which religious actors, practices, and ideas are embedded in their social contexts (Emile Durkheim, *Les formes élémentaires de la vie religieuse* (Paris: Les Presses universitaires de France, 1912: 1968)). Although Shaw has repeatedly argued that "there is little evidence for any serious connections between these forms of violence – that is, religious conflicts and peasant uprisings," Dossey suggests that there is some religious dimension to the circumcellion and agonistici involvement in North African revolts (Shaw, *Sacred Violence*, p. 778; Dossey, *Peasant and Empire*,

attempt to link the circumcellions exclusively to the "Donatists" is contradicted by the dissident reaction to the violence.[67] It was the dissident bishops who appealed to the *comes* Taurinus to suppress hostilities, which the public official did with a bloody, public massacre in the rural marketplace serving the villages of Octavensis and Subbullensis.[68] Dissidents put up *mensae* (altar tables) to memorialize the dead as martyrs.[69] Their bishop, however, could tolerate only so much veneration of those associated with such uprisings. When a dissident priest tried to inter the bodies of the dead "in basilicas," his bishop overruled him.[70]

The valorization of the slain as martyrs by creating a ritual site and attempting to bury them in extant basilicas reveals just how embroiled religious and political categories could become in the late antique context. The use of space to express this convergence added another layer of place meaning to Christian sites such as these, as we can see in other events that followed the uprising. By 343, numerous petitions had been filed in the courts over the Catholic–dissident conflict.[71] Each side pleaded for the state to intervene. Constans issued a decree of unity, and sent two of his court officials, Paul and Macarius, to North Africa to handle the matter.[72] In 347,

---

pp. 173–185). Rebels targeted their victims, creditors (*creditores*), and slave owners (*domini*), in rural marketplaces, which, as Dossey has observed, "were often located next to temples and scheduled to coincide with pagan festivals" (Optatus, *de schism. Don.* 3.4.4–5; Dossey, *Peasant and Empire*, p. 176).

[67] Shaw, "State Intervention and Holy Violence: Timgad/Paleostrovsk/Waco," *Journal of the American Academy of Religion* 77.4 (December 2009): 853–894, p. 883.

[68] Optatus, *de schism. Don.* 3.4.5–7.

[69] Optatus, *de schism. Don.* 3.4.6.

[70] Optatus, *de schism. Don.* 3.4.7 (SC 413): ... *in basilicis sepeliri coepissent* ...

[71] *Concil. Serd.* 8 dated to 343 (H. Hess, *The Early Development of Canon Law and the Council of Serdica* (Oxford: Oxford University Press, 2002), pp. 216–217): *Inportunitas, nimia frequentia, iniustae petitiones, fecerunt nos non tantam habere nec gratiam nec fiduciam, dum quidam non cessant ad comitatum ire episcopi (et maxime Afri qui, sicuti cognovimus, sanctissimi fratris et coepiscopi nostri Grati salutaria consilia spernunt adque contemnunt), ut unus homo ad comitatum multas et diversas ecclesiae non profuturas perferat causas, nec, ut fieri solet aut oportet, ut pauperibus ac viduis aut pupillis subveniatur; sed et dignitates saeculares et administrationes quibusdam postulant. Haec itaque pravitas olim murmurationem non sine scandalo excitat* (The insolence of overly frequent unjust petitions curries neither favor nor trust as long as certain bishops incessantly go to court (and especially the Africans who, as we have learnt, scorn and disparage the wholesome advice of our most holy brother and fellow bishop Gratus). For example, one man would bring to court many different cases, not for the benefit of the Church, nor, as is customary and appropriate, to aid the poor, widows or orphans, but he requests both civic honors and services for certain people. Therefore this depravity elicits scandalous grumbling). See the discussion in Shaw, *Sacred Violence*, pp. 163–164 and T. Barnes, *Athanasius and Constantius. Theology and Politics in the Constantinian Empire* (Boston, MA: Harvard University Press, 2001), pp. 71–81.

[72] *Passio Marculi*, 3.9–11; *Passio Isaac et Maximiani* 4.18; *Concilium Carthaginiense* a. 348; Optatus, *de schism. Don.* 3.1.1–4, 3.3.2, 3.4.1.

the imperial commissioners attempted to unify a fractured Church with equitable distributions of alms for the poor and furnishing for local church buildings to both sides.[73] The dissident bishop Donatus refused to accept the imperial disbursements and beseeched his clergy to do the same.[74]

As the state officials traveled to the town of Bagaï in Numidia (Baghai, Algeria), dissident Christians circulated a report claiming that Macarius had set up imperial images on church altars in Carthage during the liturgy of the eucharist.[75] Responding to reports of mounting armed opposition, the imperial officials garnered the support of *comes* Silvester and his troops.[76] Donatus had marshaled *agonistici* (crusaders) to protect not only his churches, but the storehouses of grain which abutted them.[77] Rather than

---

[73] Optatus, *de schism. Don.* 3.3.6, 3.4.1, tr. Edwards, modified (SC 413): *Miserat enim ornamenta domibus Dei, miserat pauperibus eleemosynam, nihil Donato. ... Veniebant Paulus et Macarius qui pauperes ubique dispungerent et ad unitatem singulos hortarentur;* (For he had sent furnishings to the houses of God, he had sent alms to the poor, but nothing to Donatus. ... Paul and Macarius were coming to ameliorate the poor everywhere and exhort each [church] to unity). See also *Concilia Africae* (ed. Maier), introduction: *... qui imperavit religiosissimo Constanti imperatori ut votum gereret unitatis et mitteret ministros operis sancti famulos dei Paulum et Macarium* (He [God] charged the very religious emperor Constans with realizing the desire of unity and dispatching as ministers of these holy tasks the servants of God, Paul and Macarius).

[74] Optatus, *de schism. Don.* 3.3.7, tr. Edwards, slightly modified (SC 413): *Et cum illi qui missi fuerant dicerent se ire per provincias singulas et volentibus accipere se daturos, ille dixit ubique se litteras praemisisse ne id quod adlatum fuerat pauperibus alicubi dispensaretur* (And when they who had been sent told him that they were going through several of the provinces and would give to those who wanted to accept them, he said that he had already sent letters everywhere to prevent what had been brought from being distributed anywhere to the poor).

[75] Gaddis, *Religious Violence*, p. 82, citing Optatus, who accuses the Donatists of concocting the whole story as a false rumor, *de schism. Don.* 3.12.2–3, tr. Edwards, modified (SC 413): *Dicebatur enim illo tempore venturos esse Paulum et Macarium qui interessent sacrificio ut, cum altaria solemniter aptarentur, proferrent illi imaginem quam primo in altare ponerent, et sic sacrificium offerretur. Hoc cum acciperent aures, percussi sunt et animi et uniuscuiusque lingua in haec verba commota est, ut omnis qui haec audierat diceret: Qui inde gustat de sacro gustat* (For it was said that at that time that Paul and Macarius would come to attend the [eucharistic] sacrifice, so that, while the altars were being solemnly prepared, they might bring out an image, which they would first put on the altar and thus the sacrifice would be offered. When this reached the people's ears, they were stricken in spirit, and everyone's tongue was agitated in response to these words, so that all who had heard them exclaimed, "The one who tastes of this tastes of a pagan rite!"). Frend's claim that "they attended Gratus' services, and apparently intervened openly to sway public opinion in his favor" does not seem to be supported by the citation given (Frend, *Donatist Church*, p. 178; Optatus, *de schism. Don.* 7.6). Gaddis suggests that the account is plausible because such images would convey Macarius' authority to act on behalf of the emperor (*Religious Violence*, p. 106).

[76] Optatus, *de schism. Don.* 3.4.8.

[77] Brown, *Through the Eye of a Needle*, p. 333, citing A. Leone, "Clero, proprietà, cristianizzazione delle campagne nel Nord Africa tardoantica: Status quaestionis," *Antiquité tardive* 14 (2006): 95–104, pp. 103–104.

accepting the imperial handouts, the Bagaï clergy preempted state officials and began handing out distributions of their own from their basilicas.[78] Under siege, the dissidents and circumcellion "Holy Fighters" withdrew into the basilica.[79]

Although there is considerable scholarly disagreement about the identification of the circumcellions, in this instance the agonistici functioned as guards.[80] The fighting culminated in a massacre of dissidents in the basilica, as described by Optatus:[81]

> They had there an innumerable mob of those they had summoned, and it is agreed that sufficient supplies of grain had been prepared; they made, as it were, public barns out of the basilica, awaiting the arrival of those on whom they would be able to vent their madness; and they would have done whatever their insanity had dictated but for the resistance of the armed military force ... even their captains were powerless to restrain the enraged soldiers.

To punish the perceived instigators of the conflict, imperial authorities seized dissident basilicas, exiled their bishops, and handed over the basilicas to Catholics.[82]

Dossey sees the Bagaï standoff as the refusal of dissident bishops to accept charity tainted by the socioeconomic injustices of its donors.[83] Patronage

---

[78] Optatus, *de schism. Don.* 3.4.

[79] Optatus, *de schism. Don.* 3.4.10.

[80] For a thorough treatment of the topic, see Shaw, "Bad Boys: Circumcellions and Fictive Violence," In *Violence in Late Antiquity. Perceptions and Practices*, ed. H. A. Drake, with Emily Albu, Susanna Elm, Michael Maas, Claudia Rapp, and Michele Salzman, pp. 179–196 (Burlington, VT: Ashgate Press, 2006).

[81] Optatus, *de schism. Don.* 3.4.10, tr. Edwards, modified (SC 413): *Habebant illic vocatorum infinitam turbam et annonam competentem constat fuisse praeparatam. De basilica quasi publica fecerant horrea, expectantes ut venirent in quos furorem suum exercere potuissent et facerent quicquid illis dementia sua dictasset, nisi praesentia armati militis obstitisset.*

[82] Augustine refers to these seizures in his response to the Gaudentius incident in Thamugadi (discussed subsequently): *Gaud.* 1.6.7 (CSEL 53: 204): *profiteris sane, innocens homo, aliis quidem verbis, cum ecclesia te ac tuos interituros. cum enim dicis in ecclesia, quid aliud vis intellegi nisi cum ecclesia, quandoquidem id agere ignibus praeparas? haec est innocentia partis donati, ut hoc faciatis adiunctis mortibus vestris, quod etiam apud carthaginem in invidiam nostram de basilicis, quae vestrae fuerunt, sicut potuistis et cum quibus potuistis, fecisse asseveramini sine mortibus vestris* (In other words, you undoubtedly declare, innocent man, that you and yours "will perish with the church." For when you say "in the church," you do suggest nothing other than "with the church," since it is through fire that you are ready to do what you say. Such is the innocence of the Donatist party, that you would do this at the cost of your own life to make us out as hateful, just as you did in Carthage with the basilicas which were yours, since you had the power and could have acted in earnest without causing your deaths). See Shaw, *Sacred Violence*, p. 733.

[83] Dossey, *Peasant and Empire*, pp. 180–185.

was not charity, because it came with strings attached; it was "a form of tyranny."[84] Following Dossey, Brown also analyzes this event in economic and political terms, seeing imperial intervention as an attempt "to introduce a Constantinian style of church government into the province."[85] The attempt failed. Donatus' resistance, Brown argues, was rooted in a particular view of Christian economics, that "only the bishop could distribute wealth within the churches, in a closed circuit of holy giving that began with the offerings of the faithful within the church to their bishop and that continued through the outward flow of wealth in the churches from the holy hands of the bishop."[86] To Donatus, imperial funds tainted the purity of charity and broke the circle of holiness. Church buildings were sites where Christian contributions were collected and allocated; the state had no business interfering.

As the emissary Macarius traveled further into the dissident heartland of southern Numidia, he was again received with outright violence. A further confrontation between imperial officials and dissident clerics resulted in the beating and death of bishop Marculus, who plummeted to his death from the cliff fortress in the town of Nova Petra in November of that same year, 347.[87] The Donatist account of his death records that his parishioners gathered his remains and gave them a proper burial.[88]

The shrines of dissident martyrs such as Marculus must have generated enough veneration to elicit a response from the Catholic bishops who assembled at the Council of Carthage. In 348 they declared a ban on the rampant expansion of martyria:[89]

Let no common person dishonor the dignity of the martyrs, nor shall anyone confer such dignity on bodies unless ecclesiastical authority has ordered that they be commended for burial; so that either crazy cliff-jumpers or those who are killed by committing another type of sin, whether intentionally or accidentally, should not be called martyrs

---

[84] Dossey, *Peasant and Empire*, p. 184.
[85] Brown, *Through the Eye of a Needle*, p. 333.
[86] Brown, *Through the Eye of a Needle*, p. 333.
[87] *Passio Marculi* 6.
[88] *Passio Marculi* 15.
[89] Conc. Carthag. A.345–348, c. 2 (CSL 149: 4): *Martyrum dignitatem nemo profanus infamet, neque passiva corpora quae sepulturae tantum propter misericordiam ecclesiasticam commendari mandatum est redigant, ut aut insania praecipitatos aut alia ratione peccati discretos, non ratione vel tempore competenti, quo martyria celebrantur, martyrum nomen appellent, aut si quis in iniuriam martyrum claritatem eorum adiungat insanos; placeat eos, si laici sunt, ad paenitentiam redigi, si autem sunt clerici, post commonitionem et post cognitionem honore privari*, discussed briefly in Shaw, *Sacred Violence*, p. 770, n. 140.

wherever martyr shrines are thronged; or if anyone insults the martyrs by attaching the martyrs' glory to the crazies, they are welcome, if they are lay, to seek penance, and if they are clergy (already ordained and assigned to a post), to be deprived of their office.

The Catholic bishops who promulgated this canon sought to delegitimize recently acclaimed dissident martyrs and their shrines by instituting ecclesiastical sanctions for those who venerated them. These clergy also employed the rhetorical strategy of denying the title of martyr to dissidents who died in sectarian conflicts: "those … should not be called martyrs." Rather, they dub them the derogatory epithet "crazies." The term "cliff-jumpers" alludes to the death of Marculus; it would eventually become a derisive term of art in later Catholic references to dissident victims of sectarian conflict revered as martyrs.[90]

The desire to valorize the dead with basilica burials and a venerable title reveals how basilicas became associated with power and sanctity. As the *mensae* and interments suggest, basilicas also served as venues for expressing communal identification and cosmology. The Christians who built shrines to their martyrs were connected to each other through the places where they gathered for memorialization and worship. They shared the symbolic meanings and memories of these sites through their rituals of commemoration. In the examples of Octavensis and Subbullensis, these self-perceptions were contested and negotiated through the basilicas themselves. The canon of 348 shows that shrines, too, were drafted into the service of contesting affiliation and authority. As the incident at Bagaï reveals, basilicas were also part of the economy, particularly in towns and villages, where they functioned as a clearing house for collecting and distributing resources. This place meaning contributed to the vulnerability of these sites for staging conflicts, most especially those conflicts rooted in socioeconomic and political tensions.

Within decades of the dissident martyrdoms at Nova Petra in Numidia, the bones of "Lord Marculus," as the dedicatory inscription labels him, were interred in a monumental basilica in Vegesela (Ksar El Kelb, Algeria [Numidia]) and memorialized.[91] Catholics could not abide this dissident architectural and

---

[90] Aug. *Serm.* 313E.2, tr. Shaw, *Sacred Violence*, p. 748 (PLS 2: 616): *Haeretici autem et Donatistae, qui se ad Cyprianum falso iactant pertinere, si episcopatum eius attenderent, non se separarent; si martyrium, non se praecipitarent* (The heretics, though, and the Donatists, who falsely boast that Cyprian belongs to them, ought to pay attention to the way that he went to his martyrdom. If they did so, they wouldn't throw themselves off cliffs.

[91] See Jean-Louis Maier, *Le dossier du donatisme*, Bd. 1: *Des origines à la mort de Constance II* (303–361) (Berlin: Akademie-Verlag, 1987), pp. 275–291 and Duval, *Loca Sanctorum* I, pp. 158–160. Also discussed in Shaw, *Sacred Violence*, pp. 183–185. Although the identity of

political triumph. By 411, when an attempt at reconciliation brought bishops from the two factions together in Carthage, Catholics had seized the basilica and prevented dissidents from venerating their martyr.[92] Judging from the excavated remains, however, these Catholic confiscators did not attempt to desecrate or destroy the memorial of the martyr itself (Figure 3.1). Furthermore, the martyrial dedicatory inscription was found intact (Figure 3.2). In this instance, unlike the other examples we have surveyed, violence did not seem to repeat itself. Perhaps all that was needed to obscure the inscription from view was a well-placed piece of portable furniture.

Because shrines and basilicas like these spatialized the martyrs themselves, they concretized the abstract opposition between true and false religion, particularly when the distinction between the two groups was a matter of ecclesiology, namely, who constituted the true Church. According to dissidents, Catholics were *traditores*, betrayers, because the sin of handing over sacred vessels and scriptures to the Roman authorities during the Great persecution rendered their sacraments, and hence their entire Church, invalid. Dissidents regarded themselves as the only pure Christians, while Catholics considered theirs to be the true, universal Church. As the conflict over basilicas and shrines demonstrates, buildings provided leaders on each side with concrete means to separate insiders from outsiders, to literally enforce the ideological boundaries, which were so abstract, perhaps too abstract, for their Christian audiences. This seemed particularly true in North Africa, where basilicas, like martyria, memorialized the very special dead, who themselves had sacrificed their lives rather than abandon their own understanding of what it meant to be Christian.

Although the use of imperial force to intervene in interreligious conflicts was rare, it made such an impression on the culture of North Africa that it shaped how Christians portrayed conflict. Although it may not be possible to assess the extent to which imperial pro-Catholic policies beginning in 317 were enforced, such policies do reveal an imperial attempt to represent Roman power as aligned with Catholic Christians over and against schismatics and heretics. Imperial appeal to the authority of bishops for repeated

---

the excavated basilica as Donatist is not secure, this is likely due to its subsequent Catholic takeover, as attested by the acerbic exchange recorded in the Council at Carthage minutes (see following note).

[92] *Gesta coll. Carth.* 1.133 (SC 195: 756): *Et accedente Donato Cillitano episcopo, idem dixit: 'Diaconos illic habeo, vicina plebs agit, diocesis mea est.' Privatianus episcopus ecclesiae Catholicae dixit: 'Ubi conveniunt?' Donatus episcopus dixit:* **'Et loca et memorias martyrum tamen prohibuisti.** *Candidum non habui presbyterum inde?' Privatianus, episcopus ecclesiae catholicae, dixit: "et ubi agebat?,"* discussed in Shaw, *Sacred Violence,* p. 575.

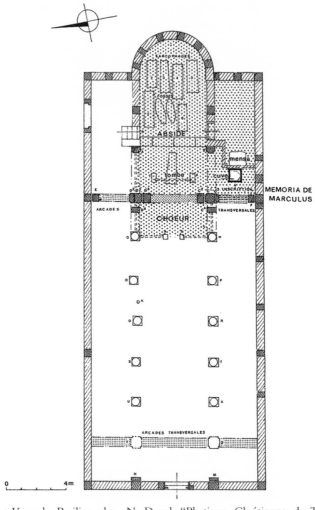

Figure 3.1 Vegesela Basilica plan. N. Duval, "Plastique Chrétienne de Tunisie et d'Algérie," *Bulletin archéologique du Comité des travaux historiques et scientifiques*. New Series 8 (1972), fig. 49. BnF. Reproduced with permission.

legislation against various religious groups perpetuated the view that Christian authority of a particular variety was backed by military power. The potential threat of imperial military power hovered over every conflict, most particularly between Catholics and their so-called Donatist opponents. Although the lines between orthodoxy and heresy sometimes shifted, the doctrinal controversies that divided the empire at large only affected divisions between dissident Christians and Catholics in North Africa to

Figure 3.2 Lord Marculus Memoria. 115 cm x 48 cm. Photo from P. Cayrel, "Une basilique donatiste de Numidie," *Mélanges d'archéologie et d'histoire* 51 (1934), fig. 6. Reproduced with permission.

the extent that Donatists were accused of being Arian supporters.[93] In this southwesternmost region of the empire, as opposed to locales such as Milan and Antioch, differences were more ecclesiological than doctrinal.[94]

Although Catholics enjoyed imperial support under Constantine, they exchanged privileged status with dissidents until the Theodosian period. With dissidents bishops exiled from their churches and prevented from exercising episcopal leadership in Carthage, attempts to bring reconciliation in the name of Church unity ensued. These efforts did not succeed; conflict continued to mark the relationship between leaders of these two Christian groups.

[93] Jerome, *Vir. ill.* 93, Epiphanius, *Pan.* 59.13, and Theodoret, *Compendium Haereticarum Fabularum* 4.6, a charge which Augustine went to great lengths to repudiate (Aug. *Ep.* 185.1.1). Donatists supported the semi-Arians at Philippopolis, whereas Catholics supported Hosius at Serdica (Frend, *Donatist Church*, p. 170). Nicene and Homoion lines of conflict plagued the East and Egypt but did not seem to affect North African sectarianism, as Shaw comments: "… within Africa these aberrant Christianities were relatively unimportant" (*Sacred Violence*, p. 313).

[94] For doctrinal conflicts between Homoian (Arian) and Nicene Christians in Milan, see Daniel Williams, "Ambrose, Emperors, and Homoians in Milan: The First Conflict over a Basilica," in *Arianism after Arius: Essays on the Development of the Fourth-Century Trinitarian Conflicts*, ed. Michel Barnes and Daniel Williams, pp. 127–146 (Edinburgh: T& T Clark, 1993), Williams, *Ambrose of Milan and the End of the Nicene-Arian Conflicts* (New York: Oxford University Press, 1995), T. D. Barnes, "Ambrose and the Basilicas of Milan in 385 and 386: The Primary Documents and Their Implications," *Zeitschrift für antikes Christentum* 4 (2000): 289–299, and Dayna Kalleres, *City of Demons* (Berkeley, CA: University of California Press, 2015), pp. 199–238; for Antioch, see Wendy Mayer, "Antioch and the Intersection between Religious Factionalism, Place, and Power in Late Antiquity," in *The Power of Religion in Late Antiquity*, ed. Andrew Cain and Noel Lenski, pp. 357–368 (Burlington, VT: Ashgate, 2009), and Christine Shepardson, *Controlling Contested Places. Late Antique Antioch and the Spatial Politics of Religious Controversy* (University of California Press, 2014).

During Julian's reign (361–363), dissident bishops were allowed to return to their sees and claim their basilicas.[95] Optatus reports that dissidents resorted to violence to regain control of basilicas:[96]

> You turned many men into exiles from their dioceses when you invaded their basilicas with hired gangs. In so many places that it would take me too long to specify them by name, many of your men engineered bloody slaughters so savage that accounts of the awful deeds were submitted to the secular judges of the time.

Optatus' description continues with a particularly gruesome account of one such attack in Mauretania Sitifensis during the course of which two Catholic deacons were killed. Catholics had barricaded themselves in the Lemellef basilica, and dissidents took to the roof, which they subsequently dismantled, using the tiles to attack the parishioners below.[97] Optatus relates that dissidents destroyed Catholic altars and vessels and fed Catholic sacraments to the dogs. They replaced these symbols of Catholic impurity with

---

[95] Optatus, *de schism. Don.* 2.16, 6.1, 2, 5, 6. See also Ammianus Marcellinus, *Hist.* 22.5.3. The legislation itself is not extant.

[96] Optatus, *de schism. Don.* 2.17.2, tr. Shaw, *Sacred Violence*, p. 150 (SC 412): *De sedibus suis multos fecistis extorres, cum conducta manu venientes basilicas invasistis: multi ex numero vestro per loca plurima quae sub nominibus dicere longum est, cruentas operati sunt caedes et tam atroces ut de talibus factis ab illius temporis judicibus relatio mitteretur.* We have only Optatus' version of these events.

[97] Optatus, *de schism. Don.* 2.18.1–2, tr. Shaw, *Sacred Violence*, p. 154 (SC 412): *Operata est apud loca supradicta in catholicos trucidatio. Memoramini per loca singula qui fuerint vestri discursus. Nonne de numero vestro fuerunt Felix Zabensis et Ianuarius Flumenpiscensis et ceteri qui tota celeritate concurrerunt ad Castellum Lemellefense? Ubi cum contra importunitatem suam viderent basilicam clausam, praesentes iusserunt comites suos ut ascenderent culmina, nudarent tecta, iactarent tegulas. Imperia eorum sine mora completa sunt. Et cum altare defenderent diaconi catholici, tegulis plurimi cruentati sunt, duo occisi sunt, Primus, filius Ianuarii, et Donatus, filius Nini, urgentibus et praesentibus coepiscopis vestris supra memoratis, ut sine dubio de vobis dictum sit: Veloces pedes eorum ad effundendum sanguinem. De qua re Primosus episcopus catholicus loci supra memorati in concilio vestro apud Thevestinam civitatem questus est et querelas eius dissimulanter audistis* (In the places that I mentioned above, there was devised a slaughter of Catholics. Recall your attacks on these individual places. Were not Felix of Zabi and Januarius of Flumen Piscium from among your number? And also the others who hurried to the castellum of Lemellef? When they saw that the church was barricaded against their savagery, they ordered their followers to climb onto the roof, to strip off the roofing tiles and then to hurl them down [i.e. onto the parishioners huddled in the church below]. Their orders were obeyed without delay. When the Catholic deacons defended the altar, many of them were covered in bloody wounds caused by the falling tiles. Two of them, Primus the son of Januarius and Donatus the son of Ninus, died. All of this happened while your bishops, named above, were present and were urging on the attackers. Without doubt it can be said of you, "Their feet hurry to shed blood" (LXX Ps 13.3). Primosus, the Catholic bishop of the place [i.e. Lemellef], made a complaint about this affair at the church council that you held at Theveste, and you actually pretended to listen to his complaints).

their own ritual appurtenances.[98] As discussed in Chapter 2, the dissidents took great efforts to purge these captured basilicas of Catholic impurities, scrubbing and washing them until purity was restored. The violence that dissidents demonstrated toward Catholic material objects was a visible and tangible expression of the hostility between them and their opponents.

The privilege of dissident Christianity did not last. The emperor Valentinian restored Catholic supremacy. As we saw in the case of Bagaï, religious conflict was portrayed as enmeshed with political strife by trotting out examples of military battles staged in religious arenas. This entanglement of religion and politics helps explain the significant role of religion in such conflicts. When tribal disputes erupted into what Rome termed the "revolt" of the Roman cavalry general Firmus, son of Moorish chieftain Nubel, against the emperor Valentinian in 372, the commander besieged the Numidian city of Tipasa.[99] Augustine described Firmus as allying with dissidents in order to betray Catholics.[100] The episode is also mentioned in the *Passio Sanctae Salsae*, a fifth-century martyrology set in the fourth-century Roman harbortown of Tipasa (Tipaza, Algeria).[101]

The martyrology relates how a young fourteen-year-old virgin named Salsa shamed her pagan family by becoming baptized and then destroying the town's bronze serpentine pagan idol (*serpens*) on its festival by hurling its head over the cliff into the sea below.[102] The townspeople were so enraged by her sacrilege that they promptly stoned and stabbed her, throwing her body into the sea.[103] A storm broke out, and the captain of a Gallic vessel anchored at the harbor dreamed that he must rescue the body and give it an honorable burial.[104] As the squall raged, the captain despaired of his life and jumped into the sea, miraculously (*Deo procurante*) saving and being saved by the martyr's body.[105] When the storm subsided, he placed the girl's

---

[98] Optatus, *de schism. Don.* 6.1–2.

[99] "Nuvel," *PCA* 1: 785, PLRE 1: 633–634; "Firmus 3,"PLRE 1: 340, "Firmus 1," *PCA* 1: 457. *Passio Salsae* 13. For a thorough and new understanding of the conflict, see Shaw, *Sacred Violence*, pp. 38–46.

[100] Augustine mentions the case of the Numidian town of Rusicade and Firmus' persecution of the dissident Christians who followed the Cartenna bishop Rogatus for opposing circumcellion violence (*Ep.* 87.10 (CSEL 34A: 406), *Parm.* 1.10 (CSEL 51:38)). See Shaw's discussion of Augustine's artifice for polemical purposes (*Sacred Violence*, pp. 54–58).

[101] Anna Maria Piredda, *Passio Sanctae Salsae. Testo critico con introduzione e traduzione italiana* (Sassari: Edizioni Gallizzi, 2002), p. 37.

[102] *Passio Salsae* 2–7 (ed. Piredda). The deity has been identified as the Punic Eshmun or Aesclepius (Piredda, p. 18), healing gods associated with snakes. See, however, the Punic curse tablet invoking the serpent deity Havat (Cook *NSI* 135).

[103] *Passio Salsae* 9 (ed. Piredda).

[104] *Passio Salsae* 11–12 (ed. Piredda).

[105] *Passio Salsae* 12 (ed. Piredda).

body in a small shrine (*tabernaculum*) so it could receive proper veneration.[106] Salsa became the patron saint of the town. The final two chapters of
the martyrology recount miracles performed through the martyr, the first
of which involves the military commander Firmus.

The hagiographic account describes how Firmus appealed to the martyr
Salsa at her tomb for military victory, but his overtures were rejected and his
petitionary prayers went unheeded. In anger Firmus attacked her *memoria*,
"piercing the slab of the tomb with spears."[107] In disgust, Firmus retreated.
The martyrology attributes Firmus' eventual defeat and death to the martyr's intervention.[108] The portrayal by Augustine and the *Passio* of Firmus as
an enemy of Catholics may overstate or even fabricate the rebel's religious
motivation, yet the fact that Firmus is portrayed as attacking a sacred building suggests that by the time Augustine and the *Passio* author are writing,
such an act had already become symbolic of power and control.[109]

A year after the Firmus revolt, the state was once again embroiled in
sectarian squabbles. Although imperial legislation would not condemn a
"Donatist" until 403 (see the discussion of Crispinus later in this chapter),
the position of non-Catholic Christianity throughout the empire systematically declined over the course of the last quarter of the fourth century.[110]
Dissident bishops did not consider Catholic baptisms to be valid, so they

---

[106] *Passio Salsae* 12 (ed. Piredda): *ad custodiam temporum propagandam, colenda potius quam con-
denda sepelitur.*

[107] *Passio Salsae* 13: ... *percutit iratus scenam sepulcri cuspidibus* ... The attack evokes the piercing
of Christ's side (Jn 19:34). The context for Firmus' appeal is given earlier in the chapter:
*Cereos incendit: extincti sunt nec miscuerunt sacrilegio flammae consensum; calicem, panem ac mero
libavit: effusus est nec passa utriusque creaturae substantia per se sub colore pietatis vota impietatis impleri; et quicquid repetitis precibus temptaverat in exitium civitatis, adverso Deo et martyre
resistente, inefficax remansisse persensit et doluit* (He lit the candles: the flames went out, not
consenting to the sacrilege; [he offered] the goblet and bread, and he poured libation with
wine, but it was spilled; the substance of both species could not bear that vows of wickedness might be fulfilled through him in the guise of faith. He realized then that whatever
harm he tried to inflict with repeated prayers for the fall of the city would be ineffective
because they were opposed by God rejected by the martyr).

[108] The telescoping of the three-year period of time during which Tipasa was under Firmus'
control is a feature of the hagiographic genre. Drijvers points out that the historical
account of the revolt in Ammianus omits chronology, but that most scholars date the revolt
to 372–375 (Jan Willem Drijvers, "Ammianus on the Revolt of Firmus," in *Ammianus after
Julian: the Reign of Valentinian and Valens in Books 26–31 of the* Res Gestae, ed. J. den Boeft,
J. W. Drijvers, D. Den Hengst, and H. C. Teitler, pp. 146–147 (Leiden: Brill, 2007).

[109] The dating (372–429) of the *Passio Salsae* is based on Piredda, *Passio Sanctae Salsae*, p. 37.

[110] Although *Cod. theod.* 16.5.12 of 383, addressed to the Eastern Prefect, forbids heretical
sects from assembly and churchbuilding, either with public or private funds, and arrogates
their immovable property to the state, it omits Donatists from the list. *Cod. theod.* 16.5.21
of 392 more vaguely refers to clergy ordained in *haeretici errores* (heretical falsehoods). The

administered a second baptism to those Christians who entered their con-gregations.[111] In a decree addressed to the African Proconsul, Valentinian and Valens declared that clergy who rebaptized, namely dissident Christians, were "unworthy of the priesthood" (*sacerdotio indignum*).[112] The technique of architectural dispossession was systematically employed to marginalize and disempower such heretics.

In 378 the emperors Valens, Gratian, and Valentinian II promulgated a law addressed to the proconsul of Africa prohibiting "heretical assemblies" from "convening, or from setting up an altar ... whether such assemblies were held in towns or in the country outside the churches where our peace prevails."[113] At the time, the law applied mainly to Manicheans; "Donatists" were still identified as sectarians, not heretics. Yet they would soon be demoted from this former category. In 379, after Theodosius had succeeded Valens, another African law specifically included rebaptism in its enumeration of "heresies."[114] Legal proscriptions against heretics were reinforced by banning their assembly within the Roman urbs. In 388, heretics were barred from "all places, from the walls of the cities, from the congregation of honorable men, from the communion of saints."[115] They could not "presume to assemble

---

dissident bishop Crispinus of Calama appealed the decision, which was upheld by the imperial court in Ravenna and implemented as general law (*Cod. theod.* 16.5.39 dated to 405).

[111] Augustine accused Crispinus of forcibly rebaptizing eighty farmers on his newly acquired estate (*C. litt. Petil.* 2.83.184) (CSEL 52: 114): *Nonne crispinus vester calamensis cum emis-set possessionem et hoc emphyteuticam, non dubitavit in fundo catholicorum imperatorum, quorum legibus nec in civitatibus esse iussi estis, uno terroris impetu octoginta ferme animas miserabili gemitu mussitantes rebaptizando submergere?* (Did not Crispinus of Calama – one of yours – after he had bought property which he held by emphyteusis, unequivocally on a farm of the Catholic emperors by whose laws you were ordered out of the cities, by one attack of ter-ror immersed for rebaptism nearly eighty sorry, muttering souls, with a lament?).

[112] *Cod. theod.* 16.6.1.

[113] *Cod. theod.* 16.5.4, tr. Pharr, modified (ed. Mommsen): *olim pro religione Catholicae sanctitatis, ut coetus haeretici usurpatio conquiesceret, iussimus, sive in oppidis sive in agris extra ecclesias, quas nostra pax obtinet, conventus agerentur, publicari loca omnia, in quibus falso religionis obtentu altaria locarentur. quod sive dissimulatione iudicum seu profanorum improbitate contigerit, eadem erit ex utroque pernicies.*

[114] *Cod. theod.* 16.5.5 (ed. Mommsen): *Quisquis redempta venerabili lavacro corpora reparata morte tabificat, id auferendo quod geminat, sibi solus talia noverit, alios nefaria institutione non perdat. Omnesque perversae istius superstitionis magistri pariter et ministri, seu illi sacerdotali adsumptione episcoporum nomen infamant seu, quod proximum est, presbyterorum vocabulo religionem mentiun-tur, seu etiam se diaconos, cum nec christiani quidem habeantur, appellant, hi conciliabulis damnatae dudum opinionis abstineant.*

[115] *Cod. theod.* 16.5.14, tr. Pharr (ed. Mommsen): *Apollinarianos ceterosque diversarum haeresum sectatores ab omnibus locis iubemus inhiberi, a moenibus urbium, a congressu honestorum, a com-munione sanctorum.*

congregations or many formal churches, either by public or private endowment, within the residences of the cities, the estates, or the villas. ... [A]ny such dwellings, moreover, shall be made subject to the ownership and rights of our treasury."[116] The enforcement of these property dispossession laws would depend on local officials, who were reluctant to stir up trouble.[117] By 390, however, Catholics had repossessed the dissident Basilica Maiorum/ Restituta of Carthage commemorating the martyrs Perpetua and Felicitas, for this is where they held their episcopal council in that same year and where Augustine subsequently preached numerous sermons.[118]

As we have repeatedly witnessed, spatial contestation became violent when legal methods failed to achieve outcomes acceptable to both sides. The dissident bishop of Thamugadi (Timgad), Optatus, was implicated in such a violent attack on a Catholic basilica in Asna in the early 390s.[119] Augustine mentions the incident in a letter to Alypius, relating that dissidents invaded the basilica and smashed its altar.[120] Although Catholics brought formal charges before the proconsul Seranus, either he refused to hear the case or his verdict supported the dissident Church.[121] In 392, an imperial edict mandated that a fine of ten gold pounds be levied against those elites who were guilty of ordaining or being ordained in a heretical church

---

[116] *Cod. theod.* 16.5.12, tr. Pharr, modified (ed. Mommsen): *neque publicis neque privatis aditionibus intra urbium adque agrorum ac villarum loca aut colligendarum congregationum aut constituendarum ecclesiarum copiam praesumat ... eaedem quoque domus ... fisci nostri dominio iurique subdantur ...*

[117] See Shaw, *Sacred Violence*, pp. 537–538.

[118] *Concilium Carthaginense a.* 390 (CCL 149: 12): *basilica perpetua restituta*; Aug. *Serm.* 305A in 401, *Enarrat. Ps.* 55 and *Enarrat. Ps.* 31.2 in the winter of 412–413, *Enarrat. Ps.* 57 in 403, and *Enarrat. Ps.* 72 in 411. See the discussion of Gareth Sears, *Late Roman African Urbanism. Continuity and Transformation in the City*, BAR International Series 1693 (Oxford, England: Archaeopress, 2007), p. 45, citing Liliane Ennabli, *Carthage. Une métropole chrétienne du IVe a la fin du VIIe siècle*, Études d'Antiquités africaines (Paris: CNRS Editions, 1997), pp. 19–20. Located in a cemetery 800 meters outside the city walls, there is no surviving archaeological evidence of this early structure except what was later rebuilt as a monumental basilica after seizure by the Vandals (Leone, *Changing Townscapes*, p. 110).

[119] Aug. *C. litt. Petil.* 2.83.184. See the excellent discussion in Erika T. Hermanowicz, *Possidius of Calama: A Study of the North African Episcopate* (New York: Oxford University Press, 2008), pp. 104–106.

[120] Aug. *Ep.* 29.12 (CSEL 34.1): *apud asnam, ubi est presbyter frater argentius, circumcelliones invadentes basilicam nostram altare comminuerunt, causa nunc agitur, quae ut pacate agatur et ut ecclesiam catholicam decet ad opprimendas linguas haereseos inpacatae, multum vos petimus, ut oretis* (In Asna, where our brother Argentius is a priest, the circumcellions raided our basilica and smashed the altar. The case is now being tried, and we earnestly entreat you to pray that it may be decided in a peaceful way and as becomes the Catholic Church, so as to silence the tongues of belligerent heretics).

[121] See Hermanowicz, *Possidius*, pp. 104–105.

along with the owner of the property in which it took place, and that "the place" (*locus*) be confiscated.[122] Augustine's indignation at the failure of the imperial law to stick to Optatus, and his implication that the dissidents had formally brought charges against Catholics for assault and property destruction, suggest that African officials at this time were still aiming for a balanced approach to this sectarian struggle for power.[123] The function of place in the power struggle and its role in delineating the boundaries of heresy and orthodoxy only increased as legislation against heretics was invoked to adjudicate intra-dissident relations as well as to exclude dissidents as a whole from Catholic unity.

As imperial pressure mounted for schismatics to join the Catholic party, the dissident Church itself was divided by internal conflict.[124] In 392 a deacon in the church of the newly elected dissident bishop of Carthage Primianus by the name of Maximianus won support for his own episcopal candidacy from his fellow deacons. Primianus excommunicated Maximianus when the deacon was bedridden and unable to appear at his own hearing.[125] This strategy pushed Maximianists to the periphery of the city into the more isolated suburbs to hold their assemblies, finding themselves displaced and marginalized.[126] A group of *seniores*, which served as a sort of informal vestry in their congregations, met to consider accusations made against Primianus, which they circulated among the North African bishops.[127] Roman authorities stepped in to adjudicate the property disputes, supporting Primianists on legal grounds, thereby depriving Maximianists of what, in the eyes of the state, was illegally seized church property.[128] In addition to success for the plaintiffs, official Roman intervention in resolving the

---

[122] *Cod. Theod.* 16.5.21. See discussion in Hermanowicz, *Possidius*, pp. 102–108.

[123] This dynamic would change over the course of the ensuing decades.

[124] For a comprehensive, engaging discussion of these events, see Shaw, *Sacred Violence*, pp. 107–140. See also the treatment by Frend, *Donatist Church*, p. 210.

[125] Aug. *Serm.* 2 Ps. 36.19–23 (CCL 38), discussed in Shaw, *Sacred Violence*, p. 110 and Frend, *Donatist Church*, p. 214.

[126] Shaw, *Sacred Violence*, p. 113.

[127] Shaw, "The Elders of Christian Africa," *Mélanges offerts à R. P. Etienne Gareau*, numéro spéciale de *Cahiers des études anciennes*, ed. P. Brind'Amour, pp. 207–226 (Ottowa: Editions de l'Université d'Ottowa, 1982).

[128] This irritated Augustine who would later invoke the Donatist use of the law against the Maximianists to make a case against the Donatists themselves (Aug. *Gaud.* 1.38.51, tr. author and Shaw, *Sacred Violence*, p. 241 (CSEL 53): *neque enim stabunt contra vos maximianistae, quorum quando potuistis basilicas abstulistis, aut stabunt contra vos pagani, quorum certe ubi potuistis templa evertistis et basilicas destruxistis, quod et nos fecimus, aut stabunt adversum vos symphoniaci daemoniorum, quorum tibias et scabella fregistis, quod et nos fecimus* (Of course, the Maximianists will not stand against you, whose basilicas you confiscated when you had the power; either it is the pagans who will be filing complaints against you, people whose temples, whenever

sectarian contest over sacred spaces increased the role that such buildings played in the Christian power struggle. According to Shaw, "the gradual intrusion of state officials into conflicts within the dissident church was caused primarily by disputes over who had property rights to what church buildings and, more precisely, to the basilicas at Carthage in which the supporters of Maximianus were meeting."[129] Maximianists, of course, viewed the situation in precisely opposite terms.

The dissident faction stood its ground in its newly occupied basilicas, only to have its fate eventually reversed.[130] In 393 they called for an ecumenical council in Cebarsussi (Byzacena). Over forty of the fifty-six bishops present rallied to the side of the more rigorous Maximianus and condemned Primianus on charges of misconduct. The edict's introduction censures Primianus for "hiring a mob of desperate men who, after petitions had been filed with the authorities, blocked the doors of the basilicas"; the list of offenses includes having "sent a mob that pillaged the 'houses' of Christians" and "barred the doors of the basilicas with his mob and with state officials so that we could not enter them."[131] The phrase *multitudo perditorum* (mob of desperate men) recalls Julius Caesar's description of loot-hungry and war-thirsty Gauls in the Gallic war, an apt analogy for the council's rhetorical purposes.[132] The mention of private force was intended to convey its illegitimacy and discredit its perpetrators. Conversely, the explicit reference to state involvement in this property dispute illustrates the power of a new, legal strategy and the degree to which the opposition was forced to reckon with it.[133]

The council's excommunication of Primianus resulted in the ordination of Maximianus as the dissident bishop of Carthage. Primianus rejected

---

it was possible, you leveled to the ground and whose places of worship you destroyed – things that we [Catholics] also did. Or is it the musicians of the demons whose flutes and foot-organs you smashed to pieces – something that we [Catholics] also did ...).

[129] Shaw, *Sacred Violence*, p. 113.

[130] 401 Council of Carthage, *Registri ecclesiae Carthaginensis excerpta* 1 (CCL 149: 199).

[131] Aug. *Enarrat. Ps.* 36.2.20, tr. Shaw, *Sacred Violence*, p. 117 (CCL 38: 129): *conducta multitudine perditorum atque impetratis officialibus, basilicarum ianuas obsedissent ... quod supra dictus primianus multitudinem miserit, quae christianorum domos everteret ... quod loca multa, vi primo, dehinc auctoritate iudiciaria usurpaverit.* The context justifies reading *domos* as referring to basilicas (Shaw, *Sacred Violence*, p. 119). See also Aug. *Enarrat. Ps.* 57.15.

[132] Caes. *Bell. gall.* 3.17.4 (ed. Hering): *magna que praeterea multitudo undique ex Gallia perditorum hominum latronum que convenerat, quos spes praedandi studium que bellandi ab agri cultura et cotidiano labore revocabat* (From every corner of Gaul a great throng of desperadoes and brigands had gathered, for whom the hope of plundering and passion for war had pulled them away from the daily work of farming).

[133] Shaw, *Sacred Violence*, p. 119.

the consecration, calling for a counter-council in response. The following spring of 394, a council of 310 Primianist bishops met in Bagaï to excoriate and excommunicate the Maximianists, who refused to attend the proceedings, and to extend a seven-month grace period during which recanters could be reconciled with the Primianist Church.[134] Primianus once again appealed to the Roman government to recover his lost basilicas.[135]

Although Primianus was likely to have obtained an official order to evict Maximianus from the basilica he occupied, he may have also resorted to unofficial tactics to enforce the law, calling on a mob of locals to do his dirty work.[136] Violence erupted and, according to Augustine, the building was destroyed. Since the report comes to us from the biased pen of Augustine, who is motivated to paint dissidents in the worst possible light, its historical veracity is difficult to determine. Augustine's rhetoric, however, reveals just how useful the metaphor of the Christian community as a building was for conveying the symbolism of spatial contestation:[137]

> Why do they have the name of Christ? Because you have posted Christ's title deed, but only to protect your own property. Do not some people do this on their own house? In order to deter some powerful crook from seizing his house, the householder posts the title deed of a powerful person, even though it is a lie. Hoping to hold onto what is his own, he wants

---

[134] Fragments of the council document, as preserved by later authors, are assembled by Maier, *Dossier du Donatisme* vol. 2, pp. 84–91. See discussion and translation in Shaw, *Sacred Violence*, pp. 126–129.

[135] Aug. *Enarrat. in Ps.* 21.2.31.

[136] Aug. *Cresc.* 3.58.64–59.65 (CSEL 52): ... *per iussa iudicum persequendo sedibus expulistis, quid vos per imperatores, qui eosdem iudices mittunt ... numquid et nunc dicturus es: basilicam vel speluncam maximiani populus nullo nostrorum auctore destruxit?* (According to judicial orders you expelled the one being persecuted from his seat. You did this according to the emperors, who dispatched those provincial governors ... Will you now say: "The people themselves destroyed the basilica – or better, cave – of Maximianus, without our authority"?) Frend understands *sedes* as referring to Maximian's "house" (*Donatist Church*, p. 219), but in context the reference is more likely to his basilical complex, or episcopal seat, which is how Shaw reads the passage (*Sacred Violence*, pp. 130–131). Years later, in 417 CE, Augustine would describe this violence in the most graphic of terms; he also would label the bishop Maximianus anachronistically as "Catholic," because the primate later capitulated (Aug. *Ep.* 185.27). Augustine, prone to rhetorical exaggeration, likely overstates the results of the conflict over the Carthage basilica. See the discussion of source reliability in Shaw, *Sacred Violence*, pp. 130–131.

[137] Aug. *Enarrat. Ps.* 21.2.31, tr. Boulding, modified (CCL 93/1B: 71–72): *Et quare habent nomen christi? quia ad defensionem possessionis tuae titulos christi posuisti. Nonne hoc faciunt nonnulli in domo sua? Ne domum ipsius invadat aliquis potens, ponit ibi titulos potentis, titulos mendaces. Ipse vult esse possessor et frontem domus suae vult de titulo alieno muniri, ut cum titulus lectus fuerit, conterritus potentia nominis abstineat se ab invasione. Fecerunt illud, quando Maximianistas damnaverunt. Egerunt apud iudices et concilium suum recitaverunt tamquam titulos*

the forecourt of his house to be protected by someone else's title deed,
so that when it is read an intruder may be frightened off by the great
name written on it and refrain from breaking in. This is what they did
when they condemned the Maximianists. They contested before judges,
and recounted the decisions of their council, as though they were posting
title deeds to make themselves look like bishops. … O you sad, sad house,
if only he whose title deed you bear could possess you! You bear Christ's
name, do not consent to be the possession of Donatus.

The comparison of those baptized in Christ to a building that bears
the title deed of a prominent person dissolves into an excursus on how
Maximianists petitioned the court for basilica jurisdiction and dissident sectarianism. Augustine associates the spatial metaphor for the abstract notion
of Church unity with the material contest over buildings. This rhetorical
strategy of localization punctuates the entire sermon.

After an extensive series of legal proceedings lasting three years,
Primianists won verdicts from the proconsul to confiscate Maximianist
basilicas in Membressa (Medjez al-Bab, Tunisia), Assuras (Zanfour), and
Musti (El Krib/Hr. Mest).[138] The repossessions did not go smoothly. In the
case of Membressa, the Maximianist bishop Salvius had refused to abandon his basilica. The opposing bishop Restitutus marshaled mob support
from the nearby town of Abitina who drove Salvius out of his basilica and
publicly humiliated him. Salvius' supporters built him another church.[139]
Once again, the rhetoric of the accounts reveals the super-symbolic nature
of the spatial conflict. Salvius' main objective, according to Augustine, was
defending his "episcopal seat," the basilica.[140] The basilica symbolized the

---

ostendentes, ut episcopi viderentur … "O domus misera, ille te possideat cuius titulos habes; Christi
titulos habes, noli esse donati possessio."

[138] Aug. Ep. 51.4, 88.11, Bapt. 2.12.17, Cresc. 3.56.62, 4.5.6, Gaud. 1.39.54, and C. litt. Petil. 1.11
(18).20 (CSEL 52): si iustiores sunt qui patiuntur persecutionem quam illi qui faciunt, idem maximianistae iustiores sunt, quorum et basilica funditus eversa est et militari optati comitatu graviter
agitati sunt et iussiones proconsulis ad omnes eos de basilicis excludendos a primianistis impetratae
manifestae sunt … (If those who suffer persecution are more just than those who exact it,
then more just are those same Maximianists, whose basilica was entirely destroyed and
who were harshly assailed by the military retinue of Optatus, and all of whom the commissioners of the proconsul drove out from the basilicas [which] were openly acquired by
Primianists). See also Aug. Enarrat. Ps 57.15.

[139] Aug. Parm. 3.6.29. Other Maximianists folded under the threat of violence and decided to
join the Primianist camp rather than lose their churches.

[140] Aug. Cresc. 4.49.59 (CSEL 56: 556): nam quia eis pro defendendis ex quantacumque parte sedibus
suis etiam post proconsulis iudicatum turbae sibi faventis fiducia salvius repugnare temptaverat …
(Salvius wanted to defend his episcopal seat the best he could, even after the judgment of
the proconsul, relying on the crowd to support him …).

bishop's authority, which he was not willing to relinquish to the opposition. Furthermore, the language Augustine employs to construe this architectural dispossession highlights the distinction between interiority and exteriority. Passive verbs like *pelli de* (to be driven out of) and *excludi de* (to be thrown out of) reinforced the wedge that Catholics sought to drive between competing Christian factions, despite frequent appeals for unity.[141] Finally, by appealing to the contrast between unlawful seizure and legal possession contained in property law, Augustine distinguishes between those who use illegitimate means to accomplish their ends, namely dissidents, and those who function within the law of the empire, Catholics. Using this logic, unity could only mean that the former capitulate to the latter.

As with Membressa, the Maximianist and Primianist bishops of Assuras were locked in a standoff over the town's basilica in defiance of court judgments which ordered the Maximianist bishop Praetextatus to relinquish his basilica to the Primianist Rogatus.[142] Optatus, the dissident bishop of Thamugadi, intervened to force a reconciliation.[143] Augustine's paraphrase of the court document uses the general term *locus* to refer to the site, as did the imperial code of 392.[144] In another discussion of the events, Augustine employs the poetic technique of synecdoche, using the "altar" to stand for

---

[141] Aug. *Parm.* 3.6.29 (CSEL 51: 141): *si autem dicit nihil aliud impetrasse a proconsule primi- anistas, nisi ut per abitinenses salvius de basilica pelleretur, illos autem sua sponte fecisse quidquid ei postea crudeliter turpiter que fecerunt, cur non sibi dicit sic etiam posse catholicos nihil aliud ab imperatoribus petere, nisi ut isti de basilicis quas nomine sacrilego retinent excludantur, illos autem sua sponte regia potestate et honestate servata in sacrilegos vindicare multo mitius, quam abitinenses nulla imperiali lege, nulla iudiciaria iussione in membressitanum salvium vindicarunt?* (If one says that the Primianists only procured from the proconsul the right to have Salvius driven out of his basilica by the Abitinians, and that these people then perpetrated all these cruel and indecent things against him of their own accord, one must also say that Catholics petition the emperors only for the right to have those who retain the sacrilegious name thrown out of basilicas. It is the emperors themselves who pursued claims against the sacrilegious ones while preserving their royal authority and integrity and without violating the laws of decency much more gently than the Abitinians who lacked the authority of either imperial law or judicial orders in their pursuit of the Membressan Salvius.)

[142] Aug. *Cresc.* 3.56.62.

[143] Aug. *C. litt. Petil.* 2.83.184 and *Cresc.* 3.60.66, discussed in Shaw, *Sacred Violence*, p. 145.

[144] Aug. *Cresc.* 3.56.62 (CSEL 52: 468–469): *quo die clerici et seniores agentes sub Rogato episcopo, qui in locum damnati Praetextati Adsuritani fuerat subrogatus, allegaverunt memorati proconsulis iussionem, cum a foris erant a communione vestra et eiusdem communionis vestrae inimici in iudiciis publicis arguebantur et expellendi de locis Deo summo consecratis tamquam sacrilegi petebantur* (On that day the clergy and elders who had been petitioning on behalf of bishop Rogatus, who had been elected to replace the condemned Assuran Praetextatus in that place, produced the proconsular order. During the whole time that they were outside your communion and were accused of being enemies of your communion, they were making the case in state court that their expulsion from places consecrated to the supreme God was sacrilegious).

the whole basilica.[145] The catch-phrase *altare contra altare* (altar against altar) appears repeatedly throughout his polemical denunciations of religious factionalism.[146] This sectarian conflict was represented as utterly localized, in both senses of being regional as well as spatial. The buildings and their parts represented the opposing parties themselves.

The pattern is repeated in the case of Musti, where the Primianist bishop Peregrinus petitioned the court to enforce his right to the basilica occupied by the Maximianist bishop Felicianus. The court records reflect that not only did the Primianists represent their party as "Catholic," they described the basilica to which they laid claim as a "revered basilica" (*ecclesia veneranda*).[147] They decried the degeneration of the space into a fortress under Felicianus' care, yet they maintained their reverence for the building by calling its walls "hallowed" to "the almighty God." These images offer a glimpse of how the dissidents themselves viewed their religious buildings, and the value of these structures to their users. Not only did the basilicas represent human power and authority, but they represented divine power and authority, which made them even more worth fighting for.

Because violence was both religiously and politically motivated, it is difficult to separate sectarian conflict from the general turmoil of the African

---

[145] Aug. *C. litt. Petil.* 1.10.11, 15.16 (CSEL 52: 13): *felicianum dico mustitanum et praetextatum assuritanum, de quibus interim loquor, qui nominantur inter duodecim maximiani ordinatores et erectores altaris contra eorum altare cui primianus assistit? ... supersunt adhuc in hac vita et in hac provincia, qui se disiunxerunt et a quibus disiuncti sunt, qui altare erexerunt et contra quos erexerunt, qui damnarunt et qui damnati sunt ...* (I am talking about Felicianus of Musti and Praetextatus of Assuras, of whom I am speaking for the moment, who are numbered among the twelve who ordained Maximianus and erected an altar against their altar before which Primianus stands ... There still remains in our lifetime and in this province those who broke away and those they broke away from, those who set up an altar and those against whom they set up ...).

[146] Aug. *Ep.* 43.2.4, 43.6.17, 43.8.24, 76.2, *Ps. c. Don.* 23, 30, 80, 116, *C. litt. Petil.* 1.24.26, *Cresc.* 2.1.2, and 4.7.8.

[147] Aug. *Cresc.* 3.56.62 (CSEL 52): *carthagine in secretario praetorii titianus dixit: peregrinus presbyter et seniores ecclesiae mustitanae et adsuritanae regionis tale desiderium prosequuntur: cum ecclesiae catholicae sanctitatem vir memoriae venerabilis ab errore perfidiae donatus adsereret, in eius nomen et cultum mundi paene totius observantia nutrita coalvit ... inter quos etiam felicianus quidam, qui primo recta sectatus depravationis huius adtaminatione fuscatur, in mustitana positus civitate deo omnipotenti parietes consecratos, [et] ecclesiam venerandam quasi quadam obsessione credidit retinendam* (Titianus [the Maximianists' lawyer] said to the praetorian secretary of Carthage: The priest Peregrinus and the elders of the church of Musti and of the region of Assuras present the following petition: Donatus, a man of venerable memory, protected the sanctity of the Catholic Church from the error of false belief ... Among them are a certain Felicianus who first belonged to the right sect and then was tarnished by contact with this corruption. He is stationed in the city of Musti, behind the almighty God's hallowed walls and believes the venerable church is protecting him as a sort of fortress.)

provinces during the 397–398 revolt of Gildo, launched after he had risen to the imperial position of *magister utriusque militae* and his patron Theodosius died.[148] Under the leadership of bishop Optatus of Thamugadi, the Primianists and other dissident Christians who were not caught up in the intra-sectarian struggle backed Gildo, which had earned them his support. According to the account of Augustine, circumcellions attacked Catholic churches along with villas and estates.[149] Orosius briefly mentions a church desecration (*ecclesiam temerare ausus*) by Gildo's brother Mascezil, whom the Roman general Stilicho sent to quell the rebellion.[150] With the defeat of Gildo and the execution of Optatus for insurrection, Catholics stepped up their campaign for ascendancy. Shaw suggests that they exaggerated cases of violence to make their case against dissidents to the imperial court.[151] While this is undoubtedly true, some degree of veracity lay at the heart of Catholic lobbying; as we have seen, sectarian conflict did periodically erupt in violence against persons and property.

This kind of spatial violence prompted emperors Arcadius and Honorius to specify church destruction as a capital offense, and to enlist the "*apparitores,* called local police (*stationarii*)" to identify offenders from the local population.[152] Although the law qualifies the affected *ecclesia* as "Catholic," three facts support the view that dissidents were included in this general term and were, therefore, also entitled to legal protection from violence. First, as we have already seen, the context of late fourth-century North African intra-dissident conflicts makes clear that the government was willing to intervene in their basilica property disputes. Second, when violence affected both sides, the court hesitated to impose punishment. As Shaw argues, "there was a deep reluctance on the part of secular court

---

[148] For a thorough analysis, see Shaw, *Sacred Violence*, pp. 42–49.

[149] Aug. *C. litt. Petil.* 2.83.184 (CSEL 333): *ipsa ecclesia Catholica solidata principibus Catholicis imperantibus terra mari que armatis turbis ab optato atrociter et hostiliter oppugnata est. quae res coegit tunc primo adversus vos allegari apud vicarium seranum legem illam de decem libris auri, quas nullus vestrum adhuc pendit, et nos crudelitatis arguitis. quid autem mansuetius sit, quam ut coercitione damnorum tanta vestra scelera multarentur?* (The Catholic Church herself, though strengthened by the orders of Catholic heads ruling by land and sea, was violently and inimically assaulted by armed mobs under Optatus. It was this that first compelled them to charge you before the official Seranus that the law which imposes a fine of ten pounds of gold (which to this day none of you have ever paid) should be applied to you, and yet you accuse us of barbarity. But what lighter punishment could you incur for crimes of such magnitude than a monetary fine?)

[150] Orosius, *Hist.* 7.36.13.

[151] Shaw, *Sacred Violence*, pp. 141–145.

[152] *Cod. theod.* 16.2.31 addressed to the praetorian prefect of Illyricum, Italy and Africa, dated to April 25, 398.

administrators to become involved."[153] The most salient example of the court's attitude is the case of Crispinus, the dissident bishop of Calama, who escaped charges associated with his circumcellions' attacks on the Catholic bishop of his town, Possidius, and was ultimately brought up on heresy charges.[154] Third, it was not until this case of Crispinus in 403 that a court fined any dissident the ten gold pounds for heresy required by laws promulgated in 392 and 395.[155] From this point forward, dissenting Christians were potentially subject to imperial legislation against heretics, including those which denied them right of assembly and allowed confiscation of their ritual sites.[156]

Between 401 and 404, Catholic bishops met three times to discuss the problem of Christian dissention, which condemned the violence and culminated in a proscription against those termed "Donatists." Dissidents did not easily submit. In 403, the Catholic bishop of Bagaï, Maximianus, petitioned the court to repossess his basilica located on an estate.[157] Having obtained a favorable judgment, Maximianus attempted to seize the basilica and was nearly killed when dissidents attacked. The basilica was destroyed in the conflict.[158] A similar incident broke out in Thubursicu Bure. Dissident violence caused the death of the father of the resident Catholic bishop, Servus Dei.[159] Shaw notes that "the presence of procurators [at the takeover] is significant,

---

[153] Shaw, Sacred Violence, p. 513.

[154] Aug. Cresc. 3.47.51 (CSEL 52: 459): exhibitus igitur crispinus et, quod se esse proconsuli quaerenti negaverat, facillime convictus haereticus decem tamen libras auri … intercedente Possidio non est conpulsus exsolvere (Crispinus was then presented, having himself denied being what he to the proconsul investigating him, was easily convicted of heresy; nevertheless, on the intercession of Possidius, he [Crispinus] was not forced to pay the ten gold pounds). See the discussion in Shaw, Sacred Violence, pp. 513–514 and 534–535.

[155] Possidius, the Catholic bishop who filed the charges, records the incident in the fourth decade of the fifth century. See Possid. Vita Aug. 12.5, tr. Shaw, Sacred Violence, p. 527 (A. A. R. Bastiasensen, Vite dei Santi vol. 3, Scrittori greci e latini (Milan: Fondazione Lorenzo Valla/Mondadori, 1975), p. 158): Et praeceptus est Crispinus, qui iisdem Donatistis in Calamensi civitate et regione episcopus fuit, praedicatus scilicet et multi temporis et doctus, ad multam teneri aurariam publicis legibus contra haereticos constitutam (It was ordered that Crispinus, who was bishop of these same Donatists in the city and region of Calama, a much-vaunted man, advanced in years, and very learned, should be subjected to the penalty assessed in gold that had been established in the public laws against heretics). The laws Possidius refers to are Cod. theod. 16.5.21 of 392, and Cod. theod. 16.10.10 of 395.

[156] Cod. theod. 16.5.4.

[157] Augustine also describes the incident on two separate occasions (Cresc. 3.43–47 and Ep. 185.27). See discussion in Shaw, Sacred Violence, pp. 527–528.

[158] Aug. Brev. coll. 3.11.23 (CCL 149A: 288) and Don. 17.22 (CSEL 53: 118–119). See Shaw, Sacred Violence, p. 543.

[159] Aug. Cresc. 3.43.47, as discussed in Shaw, Sacred Violence, p. 543. As Shaw points out, it is quite interesting that Augustine refers to the site as merely locus, "place." His usage concurs with the archaeological evidence suggesting that locus had come to stand for locus sanctus.

because it suggests that both sides were accustomed to taking such property disputes before the civil courts."[160] Indeed, such reliance on property laws to settle power disputes was dependable; these cases required no special precedent, since property laws had been on the books for centuries.[161]

Yet property and personal injury laws did not produce the outcome Catholics sought. In 404, they petitioned the Ravenna court with a series of property and other claims against dissident Churches; imperial legislation followed suit. In February of 405, the emperors revoked the pro-dissident legislation of Julian, excluding "Donatism" from the "one catholic worship" and threatening to prosecute dissident violence to the full extent of the law.[162] Having made this public declaration, the emperors tried to use persuasion for enforcement. In March of that year, they issued an edict of Catholic unity that obliged schismatics to join the Catholic Church and allowed the state to occupy and seize stubbornly dissident basilicas.[163] The imperial proscription of dissidents in an edict addressed to the North African Proconsul referred to them not as schismatics but "heretics," like Jews and pagans.[164] This redefinition drove yet another rhetorical wedge between the two warring Christian parties.

By the end of the year, the emperors had lost patience: dissident Christians were threatened punishment with the full force of the law.[165] It is at this late stage of the conflict that "Donatism" acquired the legal designations of *haereticus* and *superstitio* rather than the earlier term *secta*. Imperial legislation banned assemblies of heretics, which now included dissident Christians. In 407, the emperors ordered the African proconsul to extend amnesty to any dissident Christian willing to capitulate to the Catholic "party" (*pars*).[166] In 409, emperor Honorius reiterated to his administrators in North Africa the position of the dissidents as laid out in the earlier legislation of 405:[167]

The Donatists and the rest of the vain heretics and others who cannot be converted to the worship of the Catholic communion, that is, the Jews

---

[160] Shaw, *Sacred Violence*, p. 522.

[161] See, for example, Ulpian's discussion of *dominium et possessionem* (*Dig.* 41. 2.17.1, ed. Mommsen and Krüger) and Gaius' explication of *res sacrae* and *res publicae aut privatae* (*Inst.* 2.3, ed. Seckel et Kuebler = *Dig.* 1.8.1pr).

[162] *Cod. theod.* 16.5.37–38: *una sit Catholica veneratio.* Theodosius coauthored the latter law.

[163] *Cod. theod.* 16.5.38–39, 16.6.4, and commanded to be posted throughout Africa in March as 16.11.2, interpreted by Shaw, *Sacred Violence*, p. 434. For the delegations that helped to procure the legislation from the court at Ravenna, see pp. 550–551.

[164] *Cod. theod.* 16.5.39.

[165] *Cod. theod.* 16.5.39.

[166] *Cod. theod.* 16.5.41.

[167] *Sirm.* 14, tr. Pharr: *Et ne donatistae vel ceterorum vanitas haereticorum aliorumque eorum, quibus catholicae communionis cultus non potest persuaderi, iudaei adque gentiles, quos vulgo paganos*

and the gentiles who are commonly called pagans, shall not suppose that the provisions of the laws previously issued against them have diminished in force.

The order failed to achieve its desired outcome, so Catholic bishops persuaded the state to convene a Church council in Carthage in 411 to address dissident intransigence.[168] The imperial authority intervened in the Donatist–Catholic controversy yet again – this time without proximate political pretext – when it sent the tribune and notary Marcellinus to preside over the 411 council of bishops at Carthage, which endorsed Catholic dominance.[169] The council purported to consider the claims to legitimacy of both parties. Marcellinus proclaimed in favor of the Catholics.[170]

Law was one thing, enforcement another. From 412–414, Catholic bishops convinced the western emperors to order the use of military coercion to oust dissident bishops from their churches and to exile those who refused to join the Catholic "unity" Church.[171] The use of state force caused some dissident Christians to become more entrenched. Appealing to the strong North African history of martyrdom, bishop Gaudentius of Thamugadi in the dissident stronghold of Numidia locked himself and his congregation in his basilica and threatened to burn it and the people along with it rather than acquiesce to official demands that he hand it over to the state.[172] The

---

appellant, arbitrentur legum ante adversum se datarum constituta tepuisse, noverint iudices universi praeceptis earum fideli devotione parendum et inter praecipua curarum, quidquid adversus eos decrevimus, exequendum.

[168] Gesta Coll. Carth. 1.1 (CCL 195).

[169] Gesta coll. Carth. 1.4 (SC 195: 563–569): Inter imperii nostri maximas curas, catholicae legis reverentia aut prima semper aut sola est (Among the greatest concerns of our empire, the first and only concern has always been reverence of Catholic law), per the discussion in Shaw, Sacred Violence, p. 543.

[170] Shaw, "African Christianity," pp. 4–34.

[171] Cod. theod. 16.5.54. See the discussion of Augustine's infamous role in the state's decision to use violence in Gaddis, Religious Violence, pp. 141–148.

[172] Aug. Gaud. 1.1, tr. Shaw, "State Intervention," p. 874 (CSEL 53: 201): gaudentius donatistarum tamugadensis episcopus cum se ipsum in ecclesia quibusdam sibi adiunctis perditis incendere minaretur, viro spectabili tribuno et notario dulcitio, cui piissimus imperator leges suas exsequendas cura perficiendae unitatis iniunxit, agenti, ut oportebat, cum furentibus mansuete ... (Gaudentius, bishop of the Donatists at Thamugadi, was threatening to burn himself alive in his church along with some of the demented persons who were attached to him. The vir spectabilis, tribune and notary, Dulcitius, to whom the most pious emperor had given the task of enforcing his laws for the sake of bringing Unity to a completion, was acting with gentleness (as was only right, of course) towards these madmen.) This scenario is remarkably similar to the stand-offs Ambrose faced in Milan but, as Shaw points out, the closer one was to the Roman capital, the less likely a situation was to escalate to the point of violence (p. 880).

bishop's letter of 419 or 420 CE to the Catholic tribune Dulcitius describes the importance of his church in terms of ritual holiness and religious truth; it was "a church which in the name of God and of his Christ … has always been crowded in worship of the truth."[173] The church's symbolic value was delineated in the course of the standoff. Although Dulcitius clearly construed Gaudentius' letter as a threat to burn down his own church, Augustine explains what the bishop supposedly meant: "Let it not be said that the great work, the Lord's house, where the name of God and his Christ was often invoked by you, was torched by the religion you established there."[174] Viewed as "the Lord's house," the structure had acquired significance beyond merely a gathering place for dissident Christians. To Augustine, the fact that the building was a Christian worship space took precedence over its heretical ownership.[175]

The understanding that the building was inviolable in-and-of-itself explains how Catholics could seize and seamlessly reuse dissident churches; it also parallels the Catholic understanding of baptism, which was regarded as valid regardless of whether the priest who performed the rite was Catholic. Dissidents, on the other hand, rejected baptisms performed by Catholics and required rebaptism, much as they had scrubbed the Catholic basilicas they appropriated. Differences over the innate purity of basilicas likely continued to divide Catholics from dissidents, whom Augustine charges with having "burned Catholic churches."[176] For the dissident

---

[173] Aug. *Gaud.* 1.6.7, tr. Shaw, "State Intervention," p. 875 (CSEL 53: 204): *in hac autem ecclesia, inquit, in qua dei nomen et christi eius … in veritate semper est frequentatum …* Shaw dates the composition to 419 (p. 853), while Gaddis dates it a year later (*Religious Violence*, p. 139).

[174] Aug. *Gaud.* 2.11.12 (CSEL 53: 268): *neve tantum opus, domus domini, ubi a te saepius dei et christi eius invocatum nomen est, per religionem tuam ibidem constitutam concrematum esse dicatur.*

[175] "Dulcitius 2," PCA p. 330.

[176] Aug. *Gaud.* 1:22:25 (CSEL 53: 223): *si catholicorum domus donatistae non diripuissent, si catholicas ecclesias non incendissent, si catholicorum codices sanctos in ipsa incendia non misissent, si catholicorum corpora non immanissimis caedibus afflixissent, si catholicorum membra non praecidissent, si oculos non extinxissent, si denique catholicos non crudeliter occidissent, hanc solam nos a vobis gravissimam persecutionem perpeti verissime diceremus, quia videmus vos insensatos et tabescimus, quia infirmatos et infirmamur, quia scandalizatos et urimur, quia perditos et lugemus. haec mala vestra, quae vos in aeternum interitum mittunt, amarius nos persequuntur quam illa, quae a vobis nostris corporibus vel rebus vel domibus aut basilicis inferuntur. minus persequimini, cum in nos saevitis, quam cum vos peritis* (If Donatists had not plundered Catholic houses, if they had not burned Catholic churches, if they had not consigned Catholic holy books to that same fire, if they had not inflicted Catholic bodies with monstrous beatings, if they had not severed Catholic limbs nor put out their eyes, finally, if they had not cruelly killed Catholics, then we could truly complain about only the harshest persecution you made us suffer: by seeing your idiocy we are consumed! Your weakness weakens us, your stumbling trips us up, your being killed makes us mourn! These evils of yours, that cast you into eternal

bishop Gaudentius, however, if his church could not be used for dissident rites then it was as good as destroyed, whether or not he actually torched it. The building had come to represent his particular type of Christianity to the exclusion of other expressions of religious identification.

Legal prohibitions progressively restricted the ritual arenas available to Donatists. Beginning with public assemblies, then extending to renovated private house churches, then to *omnes loci* (all places), space was incrementally marked as "off-limits."[177] Imperial laws helped to create a symbolic order of social networks in which dissident Christians were portrayed as losing control over their ritual environment. By finally barring them from any kind of sanctioned assembly, this legislation denied heretics a legitimate space in which to perform their ritual practices. The imperial enforcement of these laws against heretics deprived them of control over their ritual environments. The extent of this loss of control, however, varied regionally depending on whether a Catholic sympathizer politically controlled the area.[178]

Legislation put forth an image of Catholic dominance. The act of reserving public, and eventually private, space for Catholic/Orthodox Christianity created the impression of its being the only sanctioned *religio*. As the self-designation indicates, Catholics promoted the idea that they were the only theologically "correct" and universally practiced form of Christianity. By using the words *error* and *haeresis*, the edicts created a structure in which non-Catholic Christians were depicted as outside the norm. By setting up Catholics as the standard, non-Catholics were portrayed as actively choosing to dissent. This symbolic order legitimated the social order by concretizing it in space. The legal code asserted and reinforced the Catholic alliance with imperial power while severing any political relationship, or tolerance, that might have once existed between the state and non-Catholics.[179]

In a sermon delivered on the birthday of Cyprian, either at the end of the fourth or early fifth century, Augustine depicted the Donatist martyrs as excluded from the company of the true martyrs:[180]

perdition, persecute us more bitterly than those things which you inflicted on our bodies, our property, our houses, or our basilicas. You persecute us less by raging against us than by your own destruction (deaths)).

[177] *Cod. theod.* 16.5.4. This same strategy of displacement was employed earlier against Manichaeans and other heretics (see *Cod. theod.* 16.5.3, 16.5.7.3, and 16.5.11).

[178] Consider the example of the Donatist vicarius of Africa, Flavianus, who chose not to enforce the anti-Donatist legislation (Frend, *Donatist Church*, p. 200).

[179] For a thorough analysis of the tolerant attitude of the state during the earlier part of the fourth century, see James J. O'Donnell, "The Demise of Paganism," *Traditio* 35 (1979): 45–88.

[180] Aug. *Serm.* 313E.2 (PLS 2: 616): *Haeretici autem et Donatistae, qui se ad Cyprianum falso iactant pertinere … si martyrium, non se praecipitarent. Non est omnino discipulus Christi, non*

The heretics and also the Donatists, who falsely cast themselves as belonging to Cyprian ... if martyrs, they would not throw themselves [off cliffs]. He is surely not one of Christ's disciples; nor is he one of Cyprian's deputies.

He went on to exclude dissident Christians from the Christian community altogether: "The Donatists aren't false Christians, they're quite simply not Christians at all."[181] Augustine portrayed the social exclusion of Donatists from the group of individuals he identified as the Church to be a logical result of the symbolic exclusion of Donatist martyrs from the company of martyrs in his cosmology. This symbolic order enabled Catholics to imagine a Donatist-free Church. With the help of soldiers loyal to a Catholic imperium, they were able, for a short time, to enact this order. By seizing dissident sacred sites, Catholics could symbolize their difference from and victory over non-Catholics. Dissidents were described as "heretics," engaged in a "carnal binge" "at the very time when we were doing this ... spiritual celebration."[182] The Donatist church down the street, Augustine pointed

---

est comes Cypriani. Brown and Kunzelmann date the sermon to 410, yet Hill proposes the time leading up to the rebellion of Gildo and the activities of the Donatist bishop Optatus of Thamugadi (397, quelled in 398), suggesting the dates 395, 396, or 399.

[181] Aug. Serm. 313E.4, tr. Hill (PLS 2: 617): Donatistae enim non falsi Christiani, sed omnino Christiani non sunt.

[182] Aug. Ep. 29.11, tr. Teske (CSEL 34.1): et quoniam in haereticorum basilica audiebamus ab eis solita convivia celebrata, cum adhuc etiam eo ipso tempore, quo a nobis ista gerebantur, illi in poculis perdurarent, dixi diei pulchritudinem noctis comparatione decorari et colorem candidum nigri vicinitate gratiorem. ita nostrum spiritalis celebrationis conventum minus fortasse futurum fuisse iucundum, nisi ex alia parte carnalis ingurgitatio conferretur, hortatus que sum, ut tales epulas instanter appeterent, si gustassent, quam suavis est dominus; illis autem esse metuendum, qui tamquam primum sectantur, quod aliquando destruetur, cum quisque comes efficiatur eius rei, quam colit, insultarit que apostolus talibus dicens: quorum deus venter, cum idem alio loco dixerit: esca ventri et venter escis; deus autem et hunc et illas evacuabit. nos proinde oportere id sequi, quod non evacuatur, quod remotissimum a carnis affectu spiritus sanctificatione retinetur. atque in hanc sententiam pro tempore cum ea, quae dominus suggerere dignatus est, dicta essent, acta sunt vespertina, quae cotidie solent, nobis que cum episcopo recedentibus fratres eodem loco hymnos dixerunt non parva multitudine utriusque <sexus> ad obscuratum diem manente atque psallente (And since we heard that the customary banquets were being celebrated by the heretics in their basilica, for they were still drinking at the very time when we were doing this, I said that the beauty of the day stands out in comparison with the night and that the color white is more pleasing by reason of its nearness to black. So too, our gathering with its spiritual celebration would perhaps have been less pleasing if the carnal binge did not stand in contrast with it, and I exhorted them constantly to desire such feasts as ours if they had tasted how sweet the Lord is. I warned that those who pursue as primary what will at some point perish must be afraid, since each of us becomes a companion of what he loves, and the apostle mocked such people when he said, "Their god is their belly" (Phil 3:19), for the same apostle said in another passage, "Food is for the belly, and the belly for food, but God will destroy both the one and the other" (1 Cor 6:13). Therefore, we must follow what is not destroyed, but

out to his audience, was engaged in the sensually indulgent behaviors of feasting, dancing, and singing, while they, the Catholics, celebrated the feast of eucharist, read scripture, and sang hymns of praise. What Donatists did in their ritual space was carnal, what Catholics did, spiritual. Catholics distinguished themselves from Donatists and, by separating themselves physically into a distinct arena, achieved not only differentiation, but promoted their triumph. This strategy is apparent in Augustine's Good Friday sermon in the year 397 and his letter to the African tribune Bonifatius written in 417. His sermon accuses heretics of "attack[ing] the Church which they can see perfectly well."[183] The letter employs the metaphor of a decrepit house to describe the demise of dissident churches, concluding that "the Catholic will stand in opposition to the heretic."[184]

Eventually, Catholic bishops advocated spatial reconciliation as a way to work out their yearned-for "unity," even though this unity envisioned dissidents capitulating to Catholicism and dissident basilicas coming under Catholic jurisdiction:[185]

> Each one of us could in turn occupy the higher position with his companion in honor, united with him like a visiting bishop seated with him as a colleague. We grant this honor to both of them, alternating between their basilicas and each anticipating the other in showing mutual deference …

If "unity" could be achieved, space would be the vehicle for expressing its intangible reality in visible, material form.

Serious conflicts continued to plague Roman North Africa. In 413, the African *comes* and then consul, Heraclian, rebelled and attempted to

---

what is kept most distant from the longing of the flesh by the sanctification of the Spirit. And after I had said what the Lord was so good as to suggest along those lines for the time, vespers, which are daily celebrated, were completed, and as we left with the bishop, the brothers sang a hymn, with no small crowd of both men and women remaining and singing until the darkness fell).

[183] Aug. *Serm.* 218B.2, tr. Hill (*Sermons* pt.3 vol. 6, p. 192) (Morin Guelf. 2: 451 = *MiAg* 1): … *isti, quam vident, eius ecclesiam oppugnant.*

[184] Aug. *Ep.* 185(8).33–34, (9).41, tr. Teske (CSEL 57): *sic ergo non stabit haereticus adversus catholicum, qui accepit labores eius, quando praevaluerunt leges catholicorum imperatorum, sed stabit catholicus adversus haereticum, qui abstulit labores eius, quando praevalebant furores impiorum circumcellionum.*

[185] Aug. *Ep.* 128.3 from "Aurelius, Silvanus, and all the Catholic bishops" to Marcellinus, the imperial commissioner sent to oversee the 411 episcopal conference of the two parties, tr. Teske (CSEL 44): *poterit quippe unusquisque nostrum honoris sibi socio copulato vicissim sedere eminentius sicut peregrino episcopo iuxta considente collega. hoc cum alternis basilicis utrimque conceditur, uterque ab alterutro honore mutuo praevenitur* … If this procedure was not amenable to the two congregations, two new (Catholic) bishops were to be elected to preside in each basilica.

pose as emperor.[186] He attacked Italy, but was forced to retreat to Africa, where he was killed along with his supporters, one of whom was the comes Marcellinus.[187] In 429, the Vandals began their conquest of North Africa, which would have dire consequences for Catholics. In a reversal that hindsight might deem poetic justice, the Vandals used the well-developed strategy of displacement against their non-Arian Catholic opponents.

Archaeological Evidence of Internecine Spatial Contestation

Neither Augustine nor any other source reveals the outcome of the standoff between Gaudentius and imperial militia discussed earlier in this chapter. Although eleven Christian churches have been identified in excavations of Thamugadi, only six have been dated to the period of the Gaudentius standoff.[188]

Two of these are cemetery churches. The most likely candidate for the building discussed by Augustine, however, is in the "Western Monastery" complex, identified by Gareth Sears as #22, "Donatist Complex," on the map (Figure 3.3). The complex contains a house with a mosaic identifying a certain "Priest of God, Optatus" (*sacerdote dei Optato*), a church measuring 63 m x 22 m, as well as an ornate baptistery.[189] This Optatus has been identified with the bishop Optatus who supported the Gildo revolt.[190] Sears observes that the enormous structure "situated above the town of Thamugadi would undoubtedly have dominated the city, as it was built on land that rose ten to twenty metres above the rest of the town."[191] Sears suggests that the siting of the complex "may have been an ideological statement about the strength and power of Donatism over the city as a whole and in comparison to its rival Christian sect …."[192] The complex's physical prominence, along with its symbolism, made it a visible and significant target for the state's dislocation efforts.

Another archaeological artifact illustrates how Catholics displayed their triumph over the dissident Christians in their newly acquired ritual

---

[186] Orosius, *Hist.* 7.42.10–14, Zosimus 5. 37. 6, Jerome, *Ep.* 130. 7. 7–8.
[187] Orosius, *Hist.* 7.42.16, who attributes the count Marinus' execution of Marcellinus to either jealousy or bribery.
[188] Isabelle Gui, "Timgad" in *Basiliques chrétiennes d'Afrique du nord*, vol. 1, pp. 263–286.
[189] AE 1967: 582a; Sears, *Late Roman African Urbanism*, p. 62.
[190] PCA "Optatus 2," pp. 797–801.
[191] Sears, *Late Roman African Urbanism*, p. 107.
[192] Sears, *Late Roman African Urbanism*, p. 107.

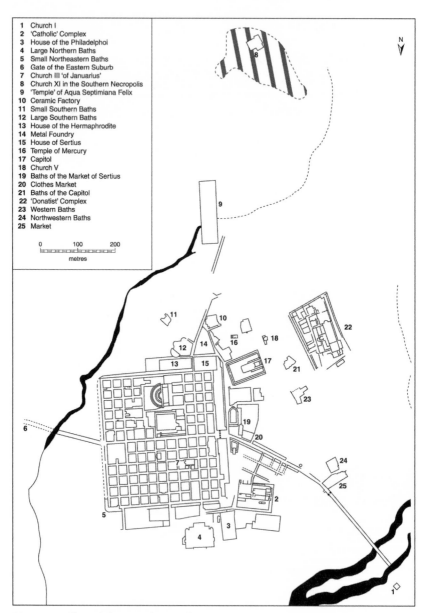

1 Church I
2 'Catholic' Complex
3 House of the Philadelphoi
4 Large Northern Baths
5 Small Northeastern Baths
6 Gate of the Eastern Suburb
7 Church III 'of Januarius'
8 Church XI in the Southern Necropolis
9 'Temple' of Aqua Septimiana Felix
10 Ceramic Factory
11 Small Southern Baths
12 Large Southern Baths
13 House of the Hermaphrodite
14 Metal Foundry
15 House of Sertius
16 Temple of Mercury
17 Capitol
18 Church V
19 Baths of the Market of Sertius
20 Clothes Market
21 Baths of the Capitol
22 'Donatist' Complex
23 Western Baths
24 Northwestern Baths
25 Market

Figure 3.3 Plan of Thamugadi. Gareth Sears, *Late Roman African Urbanism. Continuity and Transformation in the City*, *BAR International Series* 1693 (Oxford:Archaeopress, 2007), fig. 15, p. 161. Image from G. Sears, reproduced with permission.

spaces. An inscription from Donatus' home town of Mascula (Khenchela) in Numidia (Algeria) attests to the ongoing contest for spatial control.[193] Mascula was the see of both dissident and Catholic bishops, increasing the likelihood of direct competition between the two groups. A plaque (49 cm x 20 cm, 21 cm depth) sealed by plaster over a two-meter-deep trough about 70 cm square thought to be from a martyrium dating to the late fourth/ early fifth century is dedicated to a martyr named "Julian," probably killed in fourth-century violence between Catholics and dissident Christians (Figure 3.4).[194] No martyrium has been excavated, but the initial archaeological report posited the existence of one based on the wall, column, corbel, and pilaster remains.[195] The last word of the martyr inscription has been effaced and rechiseled with the letters "KATL," probably an abbreviation for *katholicus*, to replace what Yvette Duval has suggested may previously have been a dissident Christian formula in order to "authenticate the relics of Julianus."[196] With a single stroke, an inscription recorded the result of a complex series of events and conveyed to its audience that it was Catholics who finally controlled the space. Architectural dispossession was not the end of the story. By use of a palimpsestic strategy, the rhetoric of spatial supersession was inscribed in stone for subsequent generations to see.

Sectarian spatial contestation did not subside with the Vandal invasion. In 427–428 CE, Africa was in the midst of a rebellion against Rome, led by its *comes* Bonifatius. Taking advantage of the chaos of the abating civil conflict, the Germanic tribes entered Africa through the Straits of Gibraltar at the end of 428.[197] Within the year, they had moved across the plains, plundering towns as they moved toward Carthage.[198] The capital withstood their assault (until Geiseric reattacked in 439).[199] The Germanic tribes turned coastward to Portus Magnus after pillaging Tassacora. Whether their conquest included the former Roman military camp of Alamiliaria is subject

[193] Duval, *Loca Sanctorum* I, #79 = Diehl ILCV 1.2059 = CIL 8.23325.
[194] The inscription was transcribed by M. Durili in *Recueil des Notices et Mémoires de la société archéologique de la province de Constantine* 43. Ser. 4. Vol. 12. 1909 (Constantine, Algeria: Imprimerie D. Braham, 1910), p. 296.
[195] Jaubert, "Khenchela," *Recueil des Notices* 43, p. 296.
[196] Duval, *Loca Sanctorum* I, pp. 166–167.
[197] A. H. Merrills, "Introduction," p. 3 and Andreas Schwarcz, "The Settlement of Vandals in North Africa," in *Vandals, Romans, and Berbers. New Perspectives on Late Antique North Africa*, ed. A. H. Merrills, pp. 49–57 (Burlington, VT: Ashgate Publishing Ltd., 2004), pp. 50–52, contesting the usual dating of May 429, which is based solely on the ancient testimony of Hydatius.
[198] Schwarcz, "The Settlement of Vandals," p. 52, citing Ludwig Schmidt, *Geschichte der Wandalen* (Munich: C. H. Beck, 1942 (orig. Leipzig: Teubner, 1901)), pp. 60ff.
[199] Schwarcz, "The Settlement of Vandals," p. 53.

Figure 3.4 Martyr Dedication from Mascula. Late fourth/early fifth century. Photo from Y. Duval, *Loca Sanctorum* vol. 1, fig. 79, enhanced by author.

to conjecture, given that the extant sources do not mention the town. In the third century, Alamiliaria served as the garrison station for Caesarea, the provincial capital.[200] There is some disagreement about the process whereby Christians laid claim to the Roman camp, but by the early fifth century, a Christian basilica had been dedicated on the site.[201] A map of the excavation shows the location of the basilica built into the East fortification wall of the former camp (Figure 3.5). At some point over the course of the

[200] Stéphane Gsell, *Fouilles de Bénian (Alamiliaria)* (Paris: Ernest Leroux, 1899), p. 10.

[201] Pierre Salama argues, however, that the army did not abandon its post until well into the fourth century, in which case Alamiliaria would have been taken over at the earliest in the late fourth century ("Occupation de la Maurétanie Césarienne occidentale sous la Bas-Empire romain," in *Mélanges d'archéologie et d'histoire offerts à A. Piganiol* vol. 3, ed. Raymond Chevalier, pp. 1291–1311 (Paris: S. E.V. P. E. N., 1966), cited by N. Duval, p. 1089.)

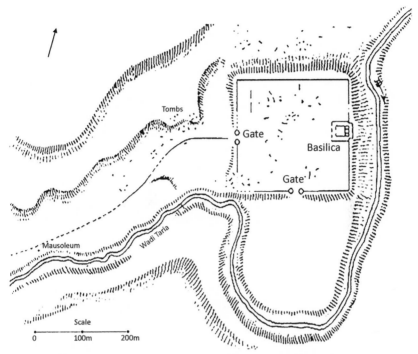

Figure 3.5 Alamiliaria (Mauretania). Stéphane Gsell, *Fouilles de Bénian (Alamiliaria)* (Paris: Ernest Leroux, 1899), fig. 2, adapted by author. Reprinted by permission.

fourth century, the city became predominantly Christian. Christian presence in the region dates back at least to Tertullian, who mentions the evangelization of indigenous Mauri and Gaetuli tribes. Nearby Caesarea and Tipasa produced Christian epitaphs dating to the early fourth century.[202] The oldest dated North African basilica (324 CE), was built about 100 km away in Castellum Tingitanum (Orléansville).[203]

The Vandal war persisted until 435, when King Geiseric signed a treaty with Rome. Sources suggest that with their newfound control of Mauretania Sitifiensis, Numidia, and part of Proconsularis, the Arian Vandals sporadically persecuted Catholics.[204] After the siege of Carthage in 439 the Vandals invaded all of Africa, forcing Rome to sign another treaty with

---

[202] Gsell, *Bénian*, p. 17.
[203] CIL 8.9708 = ILCV 1821: *basilicae fundamenta posita*.
[204] Schwarcz, "The Settlement of Vandals," p. 53, based on Prosper, *Chron.*, n. 1327 year 337, and drawing largely on Christian Courtois, *Les Vandales et l'Afrique* (Paris: Arts et Métiers Graphiques, 1955), p. 170. Concerted efforts, however, did not begin until the 484 Council of Carthage.

Geiseric in 442. From 442 until the death of Roman emperor Valentinian III in 455, the Vandals controlled Proconsularis, Byzacena, Tripolitania, and parts of Numidia. After 455 until the Byzantine conquest in the following century, the Vandals ruled all of North Africa.[205]

The Catholic bishop Victor of Vita (in Byzacena) describes the Vandal assault as particularly focused on sacred spaces, namely "churches and basilicas of the saints, cemeteries and monasteries."[206] In particular Victor cites Geiseric's seizure of the episcopal see, the Basilica Restituta, and the two Carthaginian basilicas associated with Cyprian, the Mensa Cypriani (Bir Ftouha) and the Basilica Mappalia.[207] It is also likely that Vandals seized basilicas throughout their newly acquired territory as, for example, in the case of the Basilica Maiorem in Hippo which contains Vandal epitaphs.[208] Catholics resorted to performing the liturgy in their houses, a well-established strategy that had already been used by other outlawed religious groups.[209]

---

[205] Schwarcz, "The Settlement of Vandals," pp. 53–54, drawing on Christian Courtois, *Les Vandales et l'Afrique* (Paris: Arts et Métiers Graphiques, 1955), pp. 172–175 and Schmidt, *Geschichte der Wandalen*, pp. 60ff.

[206] Victor Vitensis, *Hist. Pers.* I.1, tr. John Moorhead, *Victor of Vita. History of the Vandal Persecution*, Translated Texts for Historians 10 (Liverpool: Liverpool University Press, 1992) (CSEL 7: 4): *Praesertim in ecclesiis basilicisque sanctorum, cymiteriis vel monasteriis sceleratius saeviebant, ut maioribus incendiis domos orationis magis quam urbes cunctaque oppida concremarent.* Victor dates this round of dispossession (along with the exile of Catholic bishops) to early in the reign of Geiseric, while he dates the Arian persecution of Catholics to the latter part of Geiseric's reign (after his conquest of Rome in 455) and sporadically to subsequent kings (*pace* Victor Vitensis, *Hist. Pers.*). For other references to basilica confiscation and closures, see *Hist. Pers.* I.3 (9), I.4 (14), I.5 (15–16), I.6 (18), III.13 (41), III.17 (51), IV.1 (3.2), IV.2 (3.7–8, 14), IV.3 (3.15–16), IV.5 (3.20), IV.16 (3.53), IV.19 (3.67 – citing Lam 1.10).

[207] Victor Vitensis, *Hist. pers.* I.5, tr. Moorhead 1.15–16 (CSEL 7: 8): *ilico ecclesiam nomine Restitutam, in qua semper episcopi commanebant, suae religioni mancipavit … duas egregias et amplas sancti martyris Cypriani, unam ubi sanguinem fudit, aliam ubi eius sepultum est corpus, qui locus Mappalia uocitatur* ([H]e immediately delivered the church called Restituta, in which the bishops had always had their throne, over to his own religion … two unusual and spacious ones dedicated to the holy martyr Cyprian, one where he shed his blood and the other where his body is buried, at a place called Mappalia). Victor's claim that *universas quae intra muros fuerant civitatis* (all the churches … inside the walls of the town) were seized would have only included the Carthagena church, and perhaps the undated Dermech 1–3 and the Rotunda Martyrium, whose date is debated (Ennabli, 1997, p. 6 and 2000: 34–38). Victor's exaggerated tone is part of his rhetorical effect.

[208] G. G. Koenig, "Wandalische Grabfunde des 5. Und 6. Jhs," *Madrider Mitteilungen* 11 (1981): 299–360; p. 341, cited in Moorhead, p. 8n18.

[209] Victor Vitensis, *Hist. pers.* V.6, tr. Moorhead 3.29 (CSEL 7: 87): … *verum etiam publice mysteria divina in domo una congregati celebrare coeperunt* ([T]hey also began to celebrate the divine mysteries in public, gathering together in a house). The use of "public" in a domestic context gives modern readers some sense of the complexity of ancient spatial perceptions (see Andrew Wallace-Hadrill, "Housing the Dead: The Tomb as House in Roman Italy,"

While Victor puts this architectural dispossession in the broader context of the kind of general property destruction associated with conquest, he characterizes the Vandal onslaught as especially anti-Catholic: "[T]hey burned houses of prayer with fires greater than those they used against the cities and all the towns."[210] Throughout his account of Vandal, Arian, and Mauri (or "Moor") persecution, Victor describes the destruction of the late antique landscape: "the former beauty of the towns cannot be deduced from what they look like now."[211] The examples he cites are specific landmarks of Carthage, from where he is writing.

Archaeological evidence neither supports nor confirms Victor's claim about the odeon, theater, and the "temple of Memoria" (which archaeologists call the "circular monument").[212] However, the "Via Caelestis," recently described by the popular British archaeologist Sean Kingsley as the "Carthage's very own Rodeo Drive – adorned with mosaics, columns, and pagan temples flowing down to the Mediterranean," became crowded with new construction during the Vandal period.[213] Physical evidence shows that public buildings like these were reused for manufacturing purposes and their streets crowded with new residences.[214] The redesign of the city was likely motivated by economic interests and increased population density.[215] Yet Victor, using the well-established rhetoric of spatial supersession, attributes what he perceives as "urban decline" to religious animosity of Arian Vandals toward Nicene (homousion) Romans.[216]

---

in *Commemorating the Dead. Texts and Artifacts in Context*, ed. Laurie Brink and Deborah Green, pp. 39–77 (New York: Walter de Gruyter, 2008), pp. 47–48; Harry O. Maier, "The Topography of Heresy and Dissent in Late-Fourth-Century Rome," *Historia: Zeitschrift für Alte Geschichte* 44.2 (1995): 232–249 citing *Cod. theod.* 16.5.20, 16.5.53, and 16.5.40.1, 5).

[210] Victor Vitensis, *Hist. Pers.* I.4.

[211] Victor Vitensis, *Hist. Pers.* I.3 (1.4.3), tr. Moorhead (CSEL 7: 5): ... *pulchritudinem parietum solo aequabant, ut nunc antiqua illa speciositas civitatum, nec quia fuerit prorsus appareat.*

[212] Leone, *Changing Townscapes*, pp. 105, 158–159, although the odeon and theater were no longer in use by the time of the Vandal conquest.

[213] Sean Kingsley, *God's Gold: A Quest for the Lost Temple Treasures of Jerusalem* (New York: HarperCollins, 2007: 2008), p. 223; Henry Hurst and Z. Ben Abdallah have proposed that the Via Caelestis was the harborside promenade at the southernmost point of the city (opposite the Roman "lungomare") located at the base of a series of ascending terraces whose uppermost court contained the Temple of Caelestis (*The Sanctuary of Tanit at Carthage in the Roman Period: A Re-interpretation*, Journal of Roman Archaeology Supplementary Series 30 (Portsmouth, RI: Journal of Roman Archaeology, 1999), p. 96; see also figure 18, p. 32).

[214] Andrew H. Merrills and Richard Miles, *The Vandals* (Malden, MA: Wiley-Blackwell, 2010), pp. 153–154.

[215] Leone, *Changing Townscapes*, pp. 39–41.

[216] Victor collapses race (ethnicity) and religion in interesting, even innovative, ways. He writes that Arians persecuted Vandals attending a Catholic church "whether female or

Victor's observation has led some modern scholars to attribute church damage, architectural decline, and violence in late antique North Africa to the Vandals.[217] Even Victor himself, with his anti-Vandal bias, admits that the early part of each Vandal reign was generally "mild and moderate."[218] Some of these chronological errors have been corrected by redating, as in the case of the hunting mosaic from Bordj-el-Djedid in Carthage formerly identified as Vandal and now dated to the mid-third century; others by rereading "destruction" as reconstruction, as is the case with the harbors of Carthage.[219] Despite this archaeological ambiguity, there is evidence that violence continued between dissident Christians and Catholics "under the cover of invasion," as suggested by Susan Raven.[220] A series of basilica funerary inscriptions from the previously discussed town of Alamiliaria has been interpreted as evidence of Catholic–dissident violence.[221] What little is left of the basilica architecture gives no indication of its sectarian affiliation at any point in its history, yet the inscriptions may allow a schematic chronology.[222]

In 434 CE, "traditores" killed a fifty-year-old consecrated virgin, enabling her to receive the crown of martyrdom. Following the incident, a

male who looked like one of their race" (*Hist. Pers.* II.4, tr. Moorhead (CSEL 7: 27): *Qui videntes feminam vel masculum in specie suae gentis* ...), that these "barbarians" sought to "darken the brightness and nobility of the Roman name ... [and] desire not a single one of the Romans to live" (*Hist. Pers.* V.18, tr. Moorhead (CSEL 7: 102–3): *barbari ... semper cupiunt splendorem et genus Romani nominis nebulare; nec ullum Romanorum omnino desiderant vivere*), and that the "Moors" (*Mauri*) were "pagans" who offered "many forbidden and sacrilegious sacrifices" (*Hist. Pers.* I.11, tr. Moorhead (CSEL 7: 16): *multa apud gentiles inlicita sacrificiorum sacrilegia* ...).

[217] For example, see W. H. C. Frend, "From Donatist Opposition to Byzantine Loyalism: The Cult of Martyrs in North Africa 350–650," in *Vandals, Romans and Berbers*, ed. A. H. Merrills, pp. 259–270; p. 265. However, archaeological reassessment of the period rejects this typology (since Christian Courtois, *Les Vandales et l'Afrique* (Paris: Arts et Métiers Graphiques, 1955)).

[218] *Hist. Pers.* II.1, tr. Moorhead (CSEL 7: 24): *mitius et moderatius*.

[219] Irving Lavin, "The Hunting Mosaics of Antioch and Their Sources. A Study of Compositional Principles in the Development of Early Mediaeval Style," *Dumbarton Oaks Papers* 17 (1963): 179–286, pp. 233–240; Mattingly and Hitchner, "Roman Africa," p. 210. A summary of the revised dating of mosaics can be found in Aicha Ben Abed, "L'Afrique au Ve siècle à l'époque vandale: nouvelles données de l'archéologie," in *Carthage, l'histoire, sa trace et son écho. Les Musées de la ville de Paris, Musée du Petit Palais, 9 mars-2 juillet 1995*, ed. Alain Daguerre de Hureaux, Aicha Ben Abed Ben Khader, Jean-Jacques Aillagon, Claude Lepelley, and Mustapha Khanoussi, pp. 308–315 (Paris: Paris-Musées, 1995).

[220] Raven, *Rome in Africa*, p. 196.

[221] Duval, *Loca Sanctorum* I, p. 411.

[222] The authors suggest that the altar had once been placed in the enclosure in front of the apse and subsequently relocated on a platform opposite the apse, following the same development as in the church near Kelibia in Tunisia (Gui, Duval, and Caillet, *Basiliques chrétiennes*, p. 8). Perhaps the earlier position can be associated with the Donatist occupation, and the latter with the Catholic. Otherwise, archaeologists note the absence of architectural features by which to distinguish Donatist from Catholic basilicas.

group of Christians either began constructing or refurbished a substantial basilica dedicated to their new martyr, who was buried in a crypt just beyond the apse, with an inscription that read:[223]

> Memoria of Robba, consecrated to God. Sister of Honoratus, bishop of Aquae Sirenses, crushed in the mutiny/schism of the *traditores*, she earned the dignity of martyrdom. She lived 50 years and gave up the ghost on the 8th day of the calends of April in the provincial year 395.

Interpretation of the events leading to the martyr's demise is complicated by the adjacent burials. The two northernmost tombs belong to a bishop and his sister, a consecrated virgin, who both died within three months of each other in the year 422. The presence of wooden coffin and bone fragments in the tombs along with their size (2.1 m long x 1.55 m wide x 1.8 m deep) indicates primary, rather than secondary, inhumation.[224] Two other notables, priests, who died within months of Robba's death, are buried on either side of her. The priest's epitaphs allude to no special circumstances associated with their deaths. At least five years later (the date is fragmentary), another bishop of Alamiliaria died and was buried immediately to the north of Robba. Two epitaphs, with no evidence of remains, lie in the basilica narthex: that of a deacon who died in 439 and a bishop who lived or was laid to rest "in faith and unity" at some unknown date.[225] Another priest who died in 446 was buried in the southernmost tomb of the crypt.

I have adapted the excavator's plan to show the location of the tombs within the church (Figure 3.6). Y. Duval, following Gsell, suggested that Robba was a dissident Christian, because her brother who is named in the inscription was identified as such from the record of the 411 Council of Carthage.[226] This would suggest that the reference to "traditor" in Robba's *memoria* refers to Catholics, following the tradition of dissidents employing that epithet disparagingly.[227] Because the martyrium honored Robba, the

---

[223] Gsell's original excavation report dating the construction to between 434 and 439 CE is questioned by Gui, Duval, and Caillet, who propose a date before the takeover (*Basiliques chrétiennes*, p. 8). ILCV 2052: mem. Robbe, sacre dei, germane | Honor[ati A]que Siren(sis) epsi, cede | tradi[torum] u[e]xata meruit digni | tate martiri. Uixit annis L et red | |didit spm die 8ll kal. Apriles pro. CCCXCV.

[224] Gsell, *Bénian*, p. 21.

[225] Gsell, *Bénian*, p. 42.

[226] "Honoratus 10," PCA p. 568. His Donatist identity is reported in the minutes of the 411 Council of Carthage.

[227] For a recent refutation of the Donatist identity of the Alamiliaria basilica and inscription, see J. Divjak and W. Wischmeyer, "Eine donatistische Märtyrerin oder Opfer der Wirren der Vandaleninvasion. Die Grabanlage von Ala Miliaria (Benian/Algerien)," *Mitteilungen*

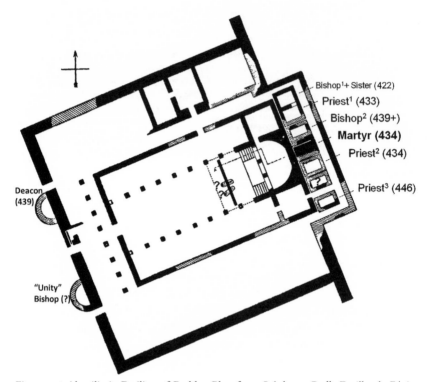

Figure 3.6 Alamiliaria Basilica of Robba. Plan from Stéphane Gsell, *Fouilles de Bénian (Alamiliaria)* (Paris: Ernest Leroux, 1899), fig. 3, with author's annotations. Reprinted by permission.

basilica was considered dissident. Gsell argued that the use of "unity" in the narthex bishop's epitaph identified him as Catholic, because that was the group's motto throughout the fourth and fifth centuries.[228] The date of the Catholic bishop's death is extrapolated from that of the latest burial in the crypt (446), since its position in the narthex suggests an effort to distinguish it from the crypt burials. Therefore, at some point after 446, the basilica

zur christlichen Archéologie 6 (2000): 48–56. As the editors of *L'Année Épigraphique* point out, Divjak and Wischmeyer's argument relies on unfounded assumptions about the age difference between Robba and her brother Honoratus (named in the inscription) and the use of "trado" in Victor of Vita I.2.5 with a different nuance from that used in Donatist writings and the inscription as an epithet for the enemy (*AE Afrique* Vol. 2000 (2003): p. 685, #1804).

[228] Gsell, *Bénian*, p. 42. The assumption that "faith and unity" are Catholic has been recently challenged (Dominique Raynal, *Archéologie et histoire de l'Église d'Afrique: Uppenna II* (Toulouse, France: Presses Universitaires du Mirail, 2005), p. 766).

must have passed from dissident to Catholic hands.[229] That there was a late-fourth-century Catholic resurgence in Alamiliaria can be inferred from the record of Vandal king Huneric's 484 Christian Council in Carthage, which was overseen by a Catholic bishop from Alamiliaria, Mensius, with no dissident or Arian counterpart listed in attendance.[230]

If the accepted interpretation of "traditor" in the martyr inscription is correct, then Robba's death was the result either of a failed attempt by Catholics to take over the dissident basilica, or a successful attempt by dissidents to wrest it from Catholic control.[231] Although the inscriptions on the four earlier tombs next to which Robba is buried give no indication of the occupants' religious identifications, their proximity suggests they shared sectarian affiliation, which would argue in favor of the first hypothesis.[232] Whichever hypothesis is correct, there undoubtedly was a struggle between two Christian sects over the basilica.

Architectural dispossession is not the only phenomenon observable in the archaeological record. There may also be evidence that the rhetoric of spatial supersession was employed epigraphically, as we saw in the case of the Julian inscription from Mascula (Khenchela). At some point, the martyr's dedicatory inscription became partly effaced (Figure 3.7). Duval proposed that pilgrims wore away the writing by touching the inscription or that the stone was damaged in the course of later reuse.[233] Yet the placement of the effacement seems too coincidental for such an explanation; the names of the martyr and her brother, the epithet "traitors," and the martyr's status ("martyrdom") are the precise terms that have been erased. To wit, John Pollini has explored how the effects of weather obscure signs of intentionally inflicted damage.[234] I therefore

---

[229] Gui, Duval, and Caillet, *Basiliques chrétiennes*, p. 8. The evidence for dissident Christianity in Mauretania at this time period is inferred from a response by Pope Leo in 458 to a query from a Norbonne bishop who wanted to know how to handle refugees fleeing Mauretania who had been baptized in different "sects," which Frend interprets as including "Donatists" (*Donatist Church*, p. 305; Leo, *Inquis.* 18 (PL 54: 1209): I: *De his qui ex Africa vel de Mauritania venerunt, et nesciunt in qua secta sint baptizati, quid circa eos debeat observari?* R: *Non se isti baptizatos nesciunt, sed cujus fidei fuerint qui eos baptizaverunt se nescire profitentur: unde quoniam quolibet modo formam baptismatis acceperunt, baptizandi non sunt; sed per manus impositionem, invocata virtute Spiritus sancti, quam ab haereticis accipere non potuerunt, catholicis copulandi sunt*).

[230] "Mensius 1," PCA p. 747, citing *Notitia., Maur. Caes.*, 33 (CSEL 7: 124).

[231] Gui, Duval, and Caillet, *Basiliques chrétiennes*, p. 8.

[232] Gui, Duval, and Caillet, *Basiliques chrétiennes*, p. 8.

[233] Duval, *Loca Sanctorum* I, p. 409.

[234] Pollini, "The Archaeology of Destruction. Christians, Images of Classical Antiquity, and Some Problems of Interpretation," in *The Archaeology of Violence: Interdisciplinary Approaches*, ed. Sarah Ralph, pp. 241–267 (Albany, NY: State University Press of New York, 2013), p. 252.

Figure 3.7 Robba Martyr Dedication. Louvre Museum Ma 3348. Photo ©Mai 2009/ Musée du Louvre/Daniel Lebée-Carine Déambrosis. Reproduced with permission.

propose that, along with the architectural dispossession documented by the sequence and placement of epitaphs in the basilica, Catholics strategically erased parts of the martyr monument. In this way, the Roman tradition of *damnatio memoriae* continued to serve as a weapon of the Catholic arsenal in the dissident conflict of North Africa. The erasures were left in place for all to see, as perpetual reminders of the dishonored martyr's fall from grace, bringing to mind the memory of that which was no longer visible. Erasing the dissident presence from the church's dedicatory inscription would have transformed the space from a dissident church into a Catholic one in such a way as to display the eviction and erasure of its prior occupants, reversing the triumphalism of the original martyrium. The effaced Robba inscription, like the palimpsestic Julian dedication, attests to an epigraphic use of the rhetoric of spatial supersession in intra-Christian conflict.

Also during the Vandal period there is some indication that the church of Castellum Tingitanum (el Asnam/Orléansville), about 150 km from the Robba basilica, changed from dissident to Catholic hands. The 411 Council of Carthage records only the dissident bishop Severinus from the town, while the 484 Council of Carthage records only the Catholic bishop Petrus.[235] The basilica underwent structural alterations in 475 to add a counter-apse (not unusual in North African architecture) to accommodate the burial of bishop Reparatus, which sealed off the original eastern entry.[236] Possible footings of a *ciborium* are found at the western end of the nave, while chancel bases are found only at the eastern apse.[237] This suggests that the renovation reoriented the church from facing west to east, and that the original placement of the altar (shaded) was moved from the center of the nave into the new apse (shaded; Figure 3.8).

The sectarian affiliation of the bishop Reparatus whose epitaph adorns the central medallion of the new apse is unknown, but as far as we know, the orientation of the basilica remained westward from then on.[238] It is intriguing to consider whether the structural reorientation of the basilica was a result of spatial contestation. Did the prevailing sect feel the need to face a different direction than its predecessor?[239] The initial placement of the altar reflected the Constantinian tradition, which persisted in North Africa well into the fifth century.[240] Did the altar's relocation reflect the desire of fifth-century Catholics to conform their interior design to the emerging western Catholic practice of placing the altar in the apse over remains of saints?[241] Further research may produce answers to these intriguing questions; in the meantime, the basilica's inscriptions remain the primary source for interpretation.

[235] *Gesta Coll. Carth.* 1.180 (CCL 195: 822) and *Notitua., Maur. Caes.*, 75 (CSEL 7: 230); "Severinus 2," p. 1070 and "Petrus 5," p. 872, PCA. This identification rests on the location *Castellanus* being identified with Castellum Tingitanum.

[236] Gui, Duval, and Caillet, *Basiliques chrétiennes*, p. 13. This apse was elevated 1 m in order to accommodate a crypt containing two tombs of unknown occupants.

[237] Gui, Duval, and Caillet, *Basiliques chrétiennes*, p. 14.

[238] "Reparatus 4," p. 962, PCA. He is thought to be buried in the crypt below.

[239] Dominique Raynal suggests that the strategy of re-orientation might demonstrate changes in basilica possession (*Archéologie et histoire de l'Église d'Afrique: Uppenna II* (Toulouse, France: Presses Universitaires du Mirail, 2005), p. 768). While it would be very convenient if radical architectural adaptation incontrovertibly reflected such power shifts, it might just as easily reflect other major changes, such as demographic, economic, or aesthetic. This minimalist conclusion heeds Krautheimer's caution that "Donatist or Arian Vandal structures can be distinguished from orthodox Catholic churches only if demarcated by a distinctive religious inscription" (*Early Christian and Byzantine Architecture* (Baltimore, MD: Penguin Books, 1965: 1975), p. 140).

[240] Krautheimer, *Architecture*, p. 188.

[241] Krautheimer, *Architecture*, p. 101. Although some of Krautheimer's observations about Africa have been rejected by recent scholars, his general observations are still relevant. See also Yasin, *Saints and Church Spaces*, pp. 151–157.

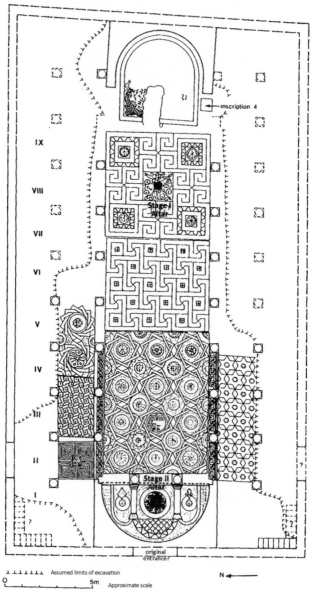

Figure 3.8 Basilica plan of Castellum Tingitanum. From Gui, Duval, and Caillet, *Basiliques chrétiennes d'Afrique du nord*, vol. 2. *Illustrations* (Paris: Institut d'Études Augustiniennes, 1992), pl. 14. Annotated by author. Reproduced by permission.

Architectural Dispossession, Spatial Supersession, and Sectarian Conflict

The evidence discussed in this chapter, both literary and archaeological, attests to persistent spatial conflict between the various sects of North African Christians. As Christians and non-Christians associated specific spaces with this or that type of Christian ritual and its objects, these spaces came to represent particular groups' meanings and memories. The increasing connection of these buildings to the concept and word *ecclesia* made them symbolic, and not just collateral, targets in the conflicts between Christian groups over which was the *true* Church. This "perceptual-symbolic quality" of conventicula, basilicas, and martyria rendered them effective vehicles for negotiating religious authority and political power on a tangible and visible stage. The more these spaces were perceived as special, holy, or sacred, the more they became privileged arenas for confrontations between Christian factions. Boundaries between various groups that were abstract and even abstruse found physicalization in the battle over basilicas and shrines. In this manner, architectural dispossession emerged as a strategy deployed early on in the disputes between dissidents and Catholics, and later among the various splinter groups that subsequently developed.

When writers on both sides represented their views of these conflicts, they employed the rhetoric of spatial supersession to interpret Christian architectural dispossession as the triumph or persecution of the true Church, depending on whose side they were on and which group had the upper hand at the time about which they were writing. This rhetoric relied on an increased valuation of ecclesiastical buildings that derived from their growing association with communal identification, as did the phenomenon of architectural dispossession it utilized. By identifying religious spaces as arenas in which religious triumphalism was negotiated and performed, a new kind of colonialism was born. What allowed this rhetoric of spatial supersession to spill over to non-Christians, that is, to so-called pagans and Jews, is the subject of the next two chapters.

4

CHRISTIAN SUPERSESSION OF
TRADITIONAL ROMAN TEMPLES

For the most part, north African Christians and non-Christians lived together in peace. Regarding interreligious relations, Anna Leone has recently concluded that "religion was not ... a source of friction in late antique North Africa ... [I]n the majority of cases it is possible to draw a picture of tolerance."[1] She convincingly demonstrates that "there is no clear evidence of the intentional destruction of temples."[2] Why, then, did Christian writers employ a triumphalist narrative to interpret the changes that they observed in their late antique landscape? In the case of the intra-religious struggle between dissidents and Catholics discussed in the previous chapter, we saw that the rhetoric of spatial supersession was put to the service of creating and reinforcing group identifications as well as produc-ing their difference. The place meanings and symbolism of religious sites made them especially powerful arenas for contesting authority. In that con-text, architectural dispossession provided a recognizable demonstration of force by one person or group against another, exhibiting the kind of clear boundaries and jurisdiction that the more amorphous group identifications lacked. Violence displayed the taking of sides in a way that merely attend-ing religious rites did not; it exposed the paramount question of collective identification: "Which side are you on: Are you for us or against us?" These allegiances may not have been stable over the course of a person's lifetime, yet at the moment when violence occurred, participants and observers could justifiably distinguish one side from the other. Enclosed architectural forms such as basilicas and visually recognizable memorials both clarified and provoked the questions of collective identification and sociopolitical

---

[1] Leone, *The End of the Pagan City. Religion, Economy, and Urbanism in Late Antique North Africa* (Oxford: Oxford University Press, 2013), pp. 235, 237.

[2] Leone, *Pagan City*, p. 237.

and economic control. The rhetorical strategy of spatial supersession proved equally useful for producing difference and asserting victory in the context of Christian relations to non-Christians. This chapter delineates how some Christian writers perceived the changes in their built environment through this providentialist lens, construing them as a process of "Christianization." How and why images of temple closure, seizure, and even conversion (into churches) in Christian discourse, including imperial law, were interpreted as symbolizing Christian victory in the "war" on paganism is the subject explored in this chapter.

Christians and Traditional Roman Religion

Before the epithet *pagani*, Christians had applied another derogatory designation to practitioners of traditional Roman religion, *superstitio*. As analyzed by Michele Salzman, this term only acquired the legal meaning of erroneous, illicit religion with the decrees of Constantius in response to Julian's support of traditional rites.[3] For two centuries prior to this legislation, however, Christian polemicists had described traditional Roman rites using the biblical category of idolatry, branding them with the epithet *superstitio*.[4] Superstition acquires the negative connotation of "aberrant" by contrast with *religio,* or proper worship. Salzman concludes that "in these late fourth and early fifth century codes, superstitio is reserved for the wrong beliefs and rites of pagans and more frequently, especially in the early fifth century, to Christian heretical groups and Jews."[5] *Superstitio* was another weapon in the rhetorical arsenal for the war against non-Christians.

The presence and influence of non-Christians aroused Christian anxiety about boundaries that is in some ways analogous to the Christian intra-religious experiences reviewed in the previous chapter. Peaceful coexistence did, in fact, present a problem from the perspective of certain outspoken Christian leaders, who were worried about the harmful effect that non-Christians might have on their congregations. As early as 388, Augustine replied to an accusation launched by Faustus of Milevis, a

---

[3] Salzman, "'Superstitio' in the 'Codex Theodosianus' and the Persecution of Pagans," *Vigiliae Christianae* 41. 2 (June 1987): 172–188, p. 181.
[4] In North African writers: Tert. *Nat.* 2.9, 2.17, *apol.* 1.38.4, *Marc.* 2.18, *idol.* 14, Lact. *Inst.* 1.1.23, 1.22.1, 2.9.11, 4.28.11 et al.; Aug. *Retract.* 1.13, *Confess.* 4.1., *civ. dei.* 16.12, 10.32. Salzman cites writings from elsewhere: Firm. Mat. *Math.* 1.7.31, 3.13.7, 6.15.12, 6.25.2, 8.25.8, 8.26.8, 8.29.1, 8.29.4, 8.30.2–3, 8.30.5, 8.31.7 and *Err. Prof. Rel.* 2.1, 6.1, 12.1, 12.7, 13.3, 17.4, 18.1, 20.1, and Ambrose *epp.* 17.16, 18.17.
[5] Salzman, "Superstitio," p. 182.

Manichean teacher, that Christians were merely a "schism of the gentiles," a "pagan" sect:[6]

> Do not attempt to marshal against me those who, while professing the name of Christian, neither understand nor manifest the nature of the faith they profess. And do not bring up the throng of ignoramuses who, even in the true religion, are either superstitious or so succumbed to sensuality that they have forgotten what they promised to God. I know that there are many who worship tombs and pictures. I know that there are many who drink to excess over the dead, and who, at the funeral banquets, bury themselves along with the buried, and call their gluttony and drunkenness by the name of religion. I know that there are many who in words have renounced this world, yet choose to be weighed down by worldly cares and rejoice in their burden. It is not surprising that in such a great multitude of people you should be able to discover some whose lives you can condemn, and by so doing seduce them away from the security of the Catholic faith. Yet you are hard-pressed to produce from among your small number even one of those you call Elect who keeps the precepts which, in your unreasonable superstition, you seek to defend.

It was, in fact, the *recent* influx of Roman aristocrats into the Church, "who in words have renounced this world," that created Augustine's problem. Although these converts identified themselves as *Christiani*, they did little to modify their traditional practices.[7] Their claim of similarity, that Christian practice was no different from that of pagans, challenged Catholic uniqueness. To differentiate correct practice from those of these "ignoramuses," Augustine portrays them as tomb- and picture-worshippers. He claims that

---

[6] The term "paganus," however, does not appear in Augustine until 400, in *Faust*. 20.4. On the development of the term, see James O'Donnell, "Paganus," *Classical Folia* 31 (1977): 163–169; Aug. *Mor. eccl.* 1.34.75, tr. Donald A. Gallagher, FC 56 (CSEL 90, 6.7: 80): *Nolite mihi colligere professores nominis Christiani necque professionis suae vim aut scientes aut exhibentes. Nolite consectari turbas imperitorum, qui vel in ipsa vera religione superstitiosi sunt vel ita libidinibus dediti, ut obliti sint quid promiserint deo. Novi multos esse sepulcrorum et picturarum adoratores. Novi multos esse qui cum luxuriosissime super mortuos bibant et epulas cadaveribus exhibentes super sepultos seipsos sepeliant et voracitates ebrietatesque suas deputent religioni. Novi multos esse qui renuntiaverunt verbis huic saeculo et se omnibus huius saeculi molibus opprimi velint, oppressosque laetentur. Nec mirum est in tanta copia populorum, quod non vobis desunt, quorum vita vituperata decipiatis incautos et a catholica salute avertatis, cum in vestra paucitate magnas patiamini angustias, dum a vobis exigitur vel unus ex his quos electos vocatis, qui praecepta illa ipsa custodiat, quae irrationabili superstitione defenditis. Sed et illa quam vana sint, quam noxia, quam sacrilega et quemadmodum a magna parte vestrum atque adeo paene ab omnibus vobis non observentur, alio volumine ostendere institui.*

[7] Salzman demonstrates that North African aristocrats did not convert in substantial numbers until after Valentinian II, beginning in 393 CE (*The Making of a Christian Aristocracy: Social and Religious Change in the Western Roman Empire* (Cambridge, MA: Harvard University Press, 2002), p. 93).

they make the mistake, often attributed to idolators, of confusing the material object with that which it signifies.[8]

This tack must have proved fruitful, since Augustine uses it again in his correspondence with the grammar instructor Maximus from Madauros in the early 390s concerning an outbreak of attacks on temples. The attacks provoked a riot in which several of the Christian perpetrators were killed.[9] Maximus claims that temples have been forsaken for venerating the tombs of the slain: "The funerary monuments of these men, as if the matter is to be regarded as worthy of memory, are crowded by mobs of stupid louts who have abandoned the traditional temples and who have forgotten the worship of the spirits of their ancestors ...."[10] Augustine responds to the charge defensively, distancing himself and his fellow Catholics from the very Christians Maximus mocks: "You should know that Catholic Christians, who have founded a church (i.e. community) in your town, venerate none of the dead."[11] Dissidents might engage in tomb-worship, he protests, but not Catholics.

Augustine also accuses Maximus and the ancient Romans of having "constructed temples that they imagined should be venerated."[12] He goes on to construct a homology between neglect of the temples and neglect of the Roman gods.[13] He construes the place value of these traditional structures as equivalent to the value of the deities whose cultic images resided within them. Collapsing the distinction between the object of worship and the space in which that worship took place was a polemical move. This conflation also aligned dissident practices with those of pagans. His audience extended beyond the individual correspondent, since the letters were collected and publicly circulated.[14] By portraying his opponents'

---

[8] For example, Deut 4:28, Jeremiah 1:16, 2 Kg 17:12, Ps 31:6, Acts 19:26.

[9] Maximus apud Aug. *Ep.* 16 and Aug. *Ep.* 17. See discussion in Brent Shaw, *Sacred Violence. African Christians and Sectarian Hatred in the Age of Augustine* (New York: Cambridge University Press, 2011), pp. 235–243. Augustine later distances himself from these incidents by blaming them on circumcellions, but this may be a defensive strategy in anticipation of a property destruction indictment (Aug. *Parm.* 1.10.16).

[10] Maximus apud Aug. *Ep.* 16.2, tr. Shaw, *Sacred Violence*, pp. 237–238 (CSEL 34.1): *horum busta; si memoratu dignum est, relictis templis, neglectis maiorum suorum manibus stulti frequentant ...* Maximus mocks their Punic names to deride their social location and forge common cause with a fellow man of letters, Augustine.

[11] Aug. *Ep.* 17.2 (CSEL 34.1): *scias a christianis catholicis, quorum in vestro oppido etiam ecclesia constituta est, nullum coli mortuorum. ...*

[12] Aug. *Ep.* 17.2 (CSEL 34.1): *... templa fecerunt et colenda censuerunt.*

[13] Aug. *Ep.* 17.2 (CSEL 34.1): *quae si neglegis, romanos deos neglegis ...*

[14] Shaw, *Sacred Violence*, p. 237, based on Paolo Mastandrea, *Massimo di Madauros (Agostino, Epistulae 16 e 17)* (Padua: Editoriale Programma, 1985), pp. 33–34.

perceptions of space in these particular ways, Augustine was able to produce group identifications, affinities, and distinctions.

The problem was how to distinguish Catholics from these others, as Augustine would present it in his marathon New Year's day sermon of 404 or 405: "You're segregated from the nations, after all, when you mix physically with the nations, but differ in your style of life."[15] As increasing numbers of the aristocracy came into the Church, the need arose to create an identification that sharply distinguished their previous ways of life (still practiced by those family members who did not convert) from their new identifications as Christians.

Festivals, such as the calends of January, posed particular challenges. Augustine promotes fasting as a counter-practice to New Year's feasting in one of his longest sermons on record, preached on January 1, 404 or 405.[16] In this sermon, estimated at three hours, he contrasts "the *feast* of nations which is taking place today" with the "*fast* at this time."[17] By preaching for such a prolonged period, he did his best to keep the congregation in

---

[15] Aug. *Serm.* Dolbeau 4 = 198.2, tr. Hill (F. Dolbeau, *Augustin d'Hippone. Vingt-six sermons au peuple d'Afrique*, Collection des Études Augustiniennes, Série Antiquité 147 (Paris: Institut d'Études Augustiniennes, 1996), p. 367): *Segregaris enim de gentibus, mixtus corpore gentibus, dissimili vita.*

[16] He admonished his congregation not to overly indulge when breaking the fast (Aug. *Serm.* Dolbeau 4 =198.9, tr. Hill, modified): *Nec ipsos dies festos christianorum, quomodo ebriosi, sic celebretis, quamquam ieiunia propter sacramentum laetitiae relaxari debent. ... Stultum est et irreligiosum inde velle placere martyribus. ...* (And don't celebrate the Christian festival days like drunks do, though the fast must be eased just after eucharist with joyful ceremony. ... It's sheer folly, as well as being irreligious, to wish to win the favor of the martyrs). According to Tilley, the custom of fasting prior to receiving the eucharist was not widely adopted in North Africa until the end of the fourth century. See Tilley, "The Body of Christ and the Body of the Believer: Eucharistic Fasting in Roman North Africa," paper delivered at the Annual Meeting of the American Academy of Religion, November 22, 1998, accessed at http://augustine.villanova.edu/devotion-and-dissent/topics/eucharist-and-other-ritual-meals/body-christ-and-body-believer-eucharistic-fasting-roman-nort/ on July 3, 2014.

[17] Aug. *Serm.* Dolbeau 4 = 198.1, 6, tr. Hill, modified: *sollemnitas gentium quae fit hodierno die; hoc tempore ieiunare.* ... Hill's rationale for dating this sermon to 404 is that in the year 405, January 1 fell on a Sunday, which would have precluded it from being a "fast day" (Hill, 3.11: 229). But, as Tilley points out, the practice of fasting on the Lord's Day prior to eucharist would have required putting off first meal, *prandium*, from 11:00 A.M. until *sero*, or late afternoon (Tilley estimates 3:00 P.M.). See Aug. *Serm.* Dolbeau 4 = 198.6, tr. Hill, modified: *Quid enim magnum est hoc tempore ieiunare, tam parvo die sero prandere* (Is it such a big deal, after all, to fast at this time, to eat first meal on such a short day at late day?) The author of the *Peri Pascha*, traditionally attributed to Melito of Sardis, invokes the same contrast (566–573). For a thorough analysis of the Melito text, see Stuart George Hall, *Melito of Sardis: On Pascha and Fragments*, Early Christian Texts (Oxford: Clarendon Press, 1979) and Lynn H. Cohick, *The Peri Pascha Attributed to Melito of Sardis: Setting, Purpose, and Sources*, Brown Judaic Studies 327 (Providence, RI: Brown University Press, 2000).

the church and out of the streets, where New Year's celebrations were taking place.[18] He also tried to prevent Christians from engaging in the eating and drinking that accompanied the day's festivities by declaring a fast day, a day to refrain from eating. Thus Augustine attempted to differentiate the Christian experience of January 1 from the traditional Roman *kalendae Ianuarii* that was still observed by many Christians with their Roman traditionalist friends and family.

In this climate of concern over boundaries of religious identification, these Christians employed the same strategies they found useful in negotiating their intra-Christian battles for framing interreligious relations. Unlike the ritual arenas in which Roman religion took place, most notably the imperial cult, basilicas provided visible, physical boundaries for distinguishing members of its group from nonmembers, and various degrees of membership within the group.[19] Public Roman sacrifices, particularly at Capitolia, were performed in plain sight; altars stood in front of temples for all to see. Ceremonies at more remote locations entailed processions that were also visible to participants and observers alike. By contrast, the main ritual event of Christian liturgy, the eucharist, was performed within an enclosed space so that those deemed ineligible to witness and participate in the event could be kept out. Not only were catechumens led out of the space at this point in the liturgy, but anyone else who doorkeepers (*ostiarii*) were instructed to bar from entering could be physically kept apart from the group of worshippers.[20] Because of their usefulness in keeping people in or out, basilica walls were exploited by North African Church leaders for constructing and

---

[18] Both John Chrysostom and Maximus of Turin lodge similar complaints against their congregations and refer to the counter-ritual of fasting (*De Lazaro*, discussed in Christine Shepardson, *Controlling Contested Places: Late Antique Antioch and the Spatial Politics of Religious Controversy* (Berkeley, CA: University of California Press, 2014), p. 183; and *De calendis Ianuariis* (*Serm.* 63, 98).

[19] This may be one of the reasons why Christians chose the basilica rather than some other architectural form for their ritual arenas.

[20] For the role of the *ostiarius*, see Aug. *Enarrat. Ps.* 103. 4.10, tr. Hill, *The Works of Saint Augustine* (3rd Release). Electronic Edition. Sermons, (94A–147A) on the Old Testament, vol. III/4, ed. Boniface Ramsey, Past Masters (Charlottesville, VA: InteLex Corporation, 2001) (CSEL 95/1: 199–200): ... *si exercens datam potestatem volentes intrare vel exire perturbet secundum modum potestatis quem accepit a domino.* ... *Et tamen, fratres mei, ostiarius ille ... potest aliquid facere nesciente domino suo et turbare aliquem illo non iubente. Iste autem nec ad illam ianuam positus est, qua intramus ad deum* (While exercising the power given him, this servant then harasses people who want to enter or depart. It is real power that he wields, in the measure conferred on him by his master ... All the same, brothers and sisters, the doorkeeper ... can do things without his master's knowledge or trouble someone without his master's authorization. But the devil is not stationed at the doorway through which we enter into God).

enforcing a variety of social boundaries being negotiated over the course of the fourth and early fifth centuries.

It is often assumed that Christianity displaced traditional Roman and indigenous religious practice over the course of the fourth century. This conclusion arises from mistakingly construing triumphal claims by fourth-century Christian authors as factual reports and assuming that the Theodosian legal code, compiled by an imperial commission from 429 to 437, accurately reflects the situation on the ground at the time when the Code claims specific laws were promulgated. Recent evaluations, however, taking a broader body of evidence into consideration, have revealed a more complex and attenuated process of displacement. Particularly in North Africa, the link between converting buildings and populations emerged decades after Christian schismatic groups had already been vying for spatial control and political power. What caused Christian authors to train their sights on the non-Christian, "pagan" population, extending the narrative of internecine conflict beyond the walls of Christian churches?

Christian use of spatial mapping to distance themselves from non-Christians was well established, as we saw in Chapter 2. Tertullian had warned his readers to stay away from arenas, amphitheaters, and theaters.[21] Christians elsewhere also launched a rhetorical campaign against traditional Roman and North African religion. They employed the well-worn technique of radical dualism to cast "pagans" and dissident Christians as enemies of the true "unified" (i.e. Catholic) Church. Temples were sites where the status of the battle against paganism could apparently be measured. Bishops meeting in Elvira around 300 CE issued their first canon excommunicating Christians who entered temples, places they regarded as polluted by idols.[22] Writers like Eusebius and Optatus took this rhetoric a step further

---

[21] Tert. pace *Spect.*

[22] Canon 1, Elvira. See Alan Cameron, *The Last Pagans of Rome* (New York: Oxford University Press, 2011), p. 61, who identifies this as "canon 56." *Placuit ut quicumque post fidem baptismi salutaris adulta aetate ad templum idoli idolaturus accesserit, et fecerit quod est crimen principale, nec infinem eum ad communionem suscipere* (It is decided that any adult who approaches a temple of an idol as an idolater and commits this "principal crime" (see Tert. *Idol.* 1) after receiving the assurance of saving baptism is not to be admitted into communion [with the Church] even at death). *Cod. Vat. lat.* 1341, fol. 56rb, has a variant text: *Placuit inter eos qui post fidem baptismi salutaris, adulta aetate, ad templum idololatraturus accesserit, et fecerit, quod est crimen principale (quia est summum scelus), placuit, nec in fine eum communionem accipere* (J. D. Mansi, *Sacrorum conciliorum nova et amplissima collection* vol. 2, cols. 5–6). A more recent critical and superior version of the text has been published by Eckhard Reichert, *Die Canones der Synode von Elvira*, Ph.D. diss., Zur Erlangung des Grades des Doktors der Theologie am Fachbereich Evangelische Theologie der Universität Hamburg, 1990, p. 75: *Placuit inter eos qui post fidem baptismi salutaris adulta aetate ad templum idolaturus accesserit et fecerit, quod*

with spatial supersessionism. They heralded the pre-Julian Christian era as already triumphant, boasting that temples had been eviscerated and lay fallow, deprived of their cultic apparatus. Optatus believed that Julian's reign marked only a temporary reversal, to be undone by nothing less than divine intervention.[23] He understood the reprieve extended by emperor Julian to "pagans" as part and parcel of that ruler's toleration of dissident Christians.[24] This juridical alliance was cast as revealing a natural affinity between the two opposition groups: they were both aligned with Satan. It therefore seems almost natural that the spatial strategy used to fight dissidents would be marshaled against those devoted to traditional Roman religion.[25]

The spatial boundaries that demarcated these battle lines could only be maintained in the imagination. Even for Christians, the temples and shrines that populated Roman North African towns and cities were "embedded in the everyday culture."[26] According to Claude Lepelley, public spaces, where many temples were situated, formed a kind of neutrality zone where citizens negotiated their "communal values."[27] Public funds helped to maintain the monumental structures that served as cultural icons, and private donations accounted for any new construction that emerged during this period of shifting landscape.[28] Although the largesse of North African aristocrats displayed in new church construction offered a new avenue for private euergetism, the traditional municipal donations for urban maintenance

---

est crimen capitale, quia est summi sceleris, placuit nec in finem eum communionem accipere (It is decided that any adult who approaches a temple of an idol as an idolater and commits this capital crime, that is of the highest sin, after receiving the assurance of saving baptism is not to be admitted into communion [with the Church] even at death).

[23] Optatus, *de schism. Don.* 2.17.3, tr. Shaw, *Sacred Violence*, p. 150 (SC 412): *Sed intervenit et occurrit iudicium Dei ut ille qui vos iamdudum redire iusserat iusserat, imperator profanus et sacrilegus moreretur, qui persecutionem vobis provocantibus iam miserat aut mittere disponebat* ... (But the judgment of God intervened and confronted you, causing the death of that profane and sacrilegious emperor who by his command had allowed you to return, and who, in answer to your appeals, had already unleashed a persecution against us – or was getting ready to unleash one).

[24] Optatus, *de schism. Don.* 2.16.2, tr. Edwards (SC 412): ... *eadem voce vuobis libertas est reddita, qua voce idolorum patefieri iussa sunt templa* (Freedom was restored to you [Donatists] by the same voice that commanded the idols' temples to be opened). See also Aug. *Ep.* 148, 166. The law is not preserved, but is referred to in *Cod. theod.* 16.5.37 dating to 405.

[25] The same strategy can be found regarding other Christian heretics as well as Manichaens (see *Cod. theod.* 16.5.3, 16.5.7.3, 16.5.40.7, 16.5.62, 16.5.64, and 16.5.65.3).

[26] Shaw, *Sacred Violence*, p. 198.

[27] Claude Lepelley, "Le lieu des valeurs communes. La cité terrain neutre entre païens et chrétiens dans l'Afrique romaine tardive," in *Idéologies et valeurs civiques dans le monde romain: Hommage à Claude Lepelley*, ed. Hervé Inglebert, pp. 271–285 (Paris: Institut d'études augustiniennes, 2002), p. 278.

[28] *Cod. theod.* 16.10.8 dated to 382.

preserved temples along with other municipal buildings.[29] In this climate, the number of traditional Roman cultic structures sharply declined over the course of the fourth century, most likely due to economic and social vicissitudes.[30] Leone estimates, however, that "only 5 per cent [of temples] appear to have been transformed and reused for religious purposes."[31] Even more rarely were these monuments targeted by Christian zealots aiming to Christianize their environment.

Contradicting the facts on the ground, Christian bishops portrayed themselves as fighting an apocalyptic war against idolatry, applying biblical language to their contemporary situation. While Tertullian, Cyprian, and Arnobius had expressed the usual sort of antagonism toward temples and their cult statues in the pre-Constantinian era, none of them suggested that Christians destroy these contemporary manifestations of "idolatry." Over the course of the fourth century, however, some Christians came to see themselves as battling this modern idolatry, which came to be known derisively as "paganism." Augustine urged country landowners to attack pagan shrines, quoting Deuteronomy 7:1 and 7:5: "'you shall pull down their altars ... cut down their groves, and break in pieces all their signs.' When you have received lawful authority, do all this."[32]

Unlike the intra-religious conflicts discussed in Chapter 3, Christian anxiety about traditional Roman religion was essentially unilateral, as Alan Cameron has persuasively argued: "[w]hile late antique Christians certainly saw themselves as engaged in a battle with paganism, what is much less clear is whether pagans saw themselves fighting a battle against Christianity."[33] Cameron meticulously dismantles "the idea that the aristocracy of Rome spearheaded a 'pagan revival' at the end of the fourth century, culminating in a pagan 'last stand' defeated at the battle of the river Frigidus."[34] His evidence includes the controversy surrounding the removal of the altar of Victory from the Roman Curia and concomitant cessation of public funding for state cults, the rededication inscriptions of the Magna Mater temple in Rome, the dialogue in Macrobius' *Saturnalia* between three priests

---

[29] Lepelley, *Les cités de l'Afrique romaines au Bas-Empire* I (Paris: Études Augustiniennes, 1979), p. 111.

[30] Lepelley, "Le lieu des valeurs communes," p. 272.

[31] Leone, *Pagan City*, p. 66.

[32] Aug. *Serm.* 62.11.17, tr. Hill (PL 38: 422): "*aras eorum*," inquit, "*destruetis, lucos eorum comminuetis, et omnes titulos eorum confringetis.*" *Cum acceperitis potestatem, hoc facite.* See the discussion in Leslie Dossey, *Peasant and Empire in Christian North Africa* (Berkeley, CA: University of California Press, 2010), p. 287.

[33] Cameron, *Last Pagans*, p. 10.

[34] Cameron, *Last Pagans*, p. 4.

of the state cults, and Christian antagonism toward traditional Roman literature. Cameron shows that close historical scrutiny reveals the altar of Victory episode to have been driven principally by political and economic concerns, rather than religiously motivated; the Magna Mater association turns out to be "a sort of upper-class freemasonry" rather than a pagan revival; the priestly dialogue is a complete fabrication rooted in Macrobius' Christian agenda; and Christian authors' hostility to Roman civil culture reveals their own asceticism, despite their having been classically educated and their own writing being deeply infused with classical quotations and allusions.[35]

Although it is unlikely that practitioners of traditional Roman religion understood themselves as fighting against burgeoning Christianity, it is absolutely clear that sacred space came to play a decisive role in Christian representations of their relationship to their "pagan" milieu as a "battle." Christians used architectural enclosures to delineate boundaries between themselves and others. When faced with the challenge of monitoring these boundaries, group leaders found that violence was a useful tool for recruiting group members to police each other. To enlist folks in the task of boundary-patrol, leaders appealed to conscience and loyalty, with mixed results.

As they had done in the case of internal schism, bishops turned to state authorities to assist their policing efforts with legitimate force. Through proscription of sacrifices and fiscal neglect of cults and their buildings, the imperial court did its part in contributing to the demise of traditional Roman religion.[36] As Shaw has thoroughly demonstrated, this effort was only undertaken in earnest in the reign of Theodosius the Great:[37]

> For most of the post-Constantinian period, the western imperial court evinced no committed interest in aggressively seeking the deliberate and destructive repression either of non-Christians or of deviants from the true Christian community. The court vacillated back and forth on such issues, pushed by Christian lobbying, but mostly pulled by its own interests ... This mixed and mobile background changed dramatically with Theodosius' ascent to the throne in 379.

Within a decade of the Madauros episode, the incident in the dissident basilica of Thamugadi discussed in Chapter 3 prompted Augustine

---

[35] Cameron, *Last Pagans*, Altar of Victory: pp. 39–51, 75–89, 337–343; Magna Mater: pp. 4, 144–147; Macrobius: pp. 231–272, 390–395; Christian hostility: pp. 399–420.
[36] *Cod. theod.* 16.10.2 of 346 CE; 16.10.19, dated to 407; and *Cod. theod.* 16.10.20, dated to 415.
[37] Shaw, *Sacred Violence*, p. 223.

to fully admit Catholic involvement in destroying temples. In a letter to the dissident bishop he declares:"Either it is the pagans who will be filing complaints against you, people whose temples, whenever it was possible, you leveled to the ground and whose places of worship you destroyed – things that we Catholics also did."[38] What had changed from the time of the Madauros episode to the one at Thamugadi? In 399 CE, the western emperors passed laws sanctioning the removal of traditional cult statues from shrines throughout North Africa.[39] Whether Catholics had been involved in such activity previously or not, their bishops now felt emboldened not only to admit this publicly but to incite such activity from their pulpits.[40]

Bishops were prone to exaggeration, however. Shaw has shown how "Christian preachers in Africa ... tended to over-represent the force of the law."[41] Imperial edicts repeatedly mandated a more orderly and systematic process of dismantling the temple cults, while Christian sermons and treatises emphasized their demise through acts of violent destruction.[42] Bishops overstated legal claims in order to goad their congregants into taking matters into their own hands by mobilizing violent gangs to attack pagan temples.[43] Yet Church leaders also invoked imperial action and legislation to create the appearance of supremacy and to bolster their supersessionist claims. By construing the demise of temples as part of systematic efforts to destroy paganism, they created a climate of combat, a clash of civilizations. Incendiary rhetoric proved to be an effective tool in escalating the battle for the hearts and minds of the North African populace.

Roman Attacks on Churches

The reaction of local Roman officials to restrictive imperial legislation and subsequent inaction could itself be violent, as the riots of Calama, Numidia in the opening days of June 408 illustrate. Christians clashed with traditional Roman practitioners, who retaliated by attacking the Christian church. The events and their aftermath took place against the backdrop

---

[38] Aug. *Gaud.* 1.38.51, tr. Shaw, *Sacred Violence*, p. 241 (CSEL 53): *aut stabunt contra vos pagani, quorum certe ubi potuistis templa evertistis et basilicas destruxistis, quod et nos fecimus.*

[39] *Cod. theod.* 16.10.17, 18 and Aug. *Serm.* 62.18.

[40] The 399 CE attack on the Hercules statue in Sufes is one such example, not discussed here because it did not entail full-scale building vandalism. See Shaw, *Sacred Violence*, p. 249.

[41] Shaw, *Sacred Violence*, p. 227.

[42] Shaw, *Sacred Violence*, pp. 226–230.

[43] Shaw, *Sacred Violence*, p. 228.

of roiling political instability in the western imperial capital of Ravenna. Emperor Honorius struggled over various military and political failures with his former guardian, now *magister officiorum* (overseer of the central civil administration) and father-in-law, the Roman general Stilicho.[44] The dissention reached a head in August of 408 when the emperor had the general executed after he refused to retaliate against the instigators of a military mutiny that nearly claimed Honorius' life.[45] This instability generated uncertainty among African authorities about whether and how to enforce imperial edicts.[46]

The ten-day conflict resulted in the stoning, looting, and burning of the Calama basilica. The riots were sparked initially by Christian reactions to public displays during the calends of June's traditional Roman festival, and subsequently by the civil court's failure to intervene against revelers and the ensuing violence.[47] The perpetrators escaped civil punishment.

Augustine's description of the church attacks is far more detailed than his cursory mention of the single Christian death that resulted, as Catherine Conybeare has noted.[48] The bishop devotes twenty-one times fewer words to the killing of "one of the servants of God (*unum servorum dei*)" than he does to the rest of the events.[49] Although Conybeare suggests that the reason for this imbalance is that "he is clearly averse to describing in detail acts of violence," other evidence suggests the motive for Augustine's brevity may be more calculated.[50] Nectarius, the Calama noble who appealed to

---

[44] Meaghan McEvoy, *Child Emperor Rule in the Late Roman West, AD 367–455* (New York: Oxford University Press, 2013), pp. 153–186. "Stilicho," PLRE 2: 1033.

[45] Zosimus *Hist. nov.* 5–34.

[46] Johannes Hahn, "The Challenge of Religious Violence: Imperial Ideology and Policy in the Fourth Century," in *Contested Monarchy: Integrating the Roman Empire in the Fourth Century AD*, ed. Johannes Wienand, pp. 379–404 (New York: Oxford University Press, 2015). Also see David Hunt, "Christianising the Roman Empire. The Evidence of the Code," in *The Theodosian Code: Studies in the Imperial Law of Late Antiquity*, 2nd ed., Jill Harries and Ian Wood, pp. 143–158 (London: Bristol Classical Press, 2010), p. 151 and Shaw, *Sacred Violence*, p. 538.

[47] Aug. *Ep.* 90.8 (CSEL 34.2): *grando lapidationibus reddita est, qua transacta continuo tertiam lapidationem et postremo ignes ecclesiasticis tectis atque hominibus intulerunt.* See Shaw, *Sacred Violence*, pp. 251–259 for a comprehensive treatment of the incident. Shaw points out that while Christian leaders must have been aware of what Augustine refers to as "recent legislation [*recentissimas leges*, namely] … *Cod. theod.* 16.10.19 issued in November 407, but not actually posted in Carthage until 5 June 408," others in Calama were undoubtedly surprised to learn that their festivities could be construed as illegal (p. 259 n. 199).

[48] Catherine Conybeare, "Making Space for Violence," *Journal of Late Antiquity* 6.2 (Fall 2013): 203–215, p. 205.

[49] Aug. *Ep.* 91.8 (CCL 31A).

[50] Aug. *Ep.* 91.8 (CCL 31A).

the bishop of Hippo to convince Roman officials to extend mercy to the city's nobility in their sentencing, remarks: "I think it is more grievous to be stripped of one's assets than to be slain."[51] Minimizing death, or characterizing it as collateral damage in the course of attacks on sacred space degrades the value of human life while simultaneously raising the value of certain property or acknowledging its higher worth.[52] This place attachment might aptly be called "oikodomiaphilia," to adapt Yi-Fu Tuan's term "topophilia."[53]

The oikodomiaphilia exhibited in the initial exchange of letters between Augustine and Nectarius during the summer of 409 may be due to the fact that, until very recently, attacks on churches had only been punishable by long-standing property laws.[54] It is only in January of the same year – in response to post-Calama petitions – that imperial legislation defined assaults on Catholic clergy and their churches as distinct types of public crimes perpetrated by heretics, Jews, and "Gentiles, commonly called pagans."[55] Categorizing these crimes as "public" empowered the state, not merely the victim, to file complaints and extended punishment beyond monetary compensation. Despite the apparent forcefulness of the edict, it was received with confusion and suspicion by African officials, who again delayed enforcing imperial directives. This disarray was due in no small measure to the political turmoil at the imperial court in the wake of Stilicho's demise. The African court's inaction inspired new rounds of violence and entreaties to the imperial court.[56]

The edict preserved in Sirmondian constitution 14 singled out African bishops and their churches for protection and defined offenses committed

[51] Nectarius, apud Aug. *Ep.* 103.3 (CSEL 34.2): *gravius esse spoliari facultatibus quam occidi.* "Nectarius," PAC: 776–779. The identification of Nectarius as non-Christian has been convincingly challenged by James J. O'Donnell, *Augustine: A New Biography* (New York: Ecco, 2005), pp. 185–188; Hermanowicz, *Possidius*, pp. 166–168, Neil McLynn "Pagans in a Christian Empire," in *A Companion to Late Antiquity*, ed. Philip Rousseau and Jutta Raithel, pp. 572–587 (Chichester, UK: Wiley-Blackwell, 2009), p. 587, and Éric Rebillard, *Christians and Their Many Identities in Late Antiquity, North Africa, 200–450 CE* (Cornell University Press, 2012, Kindle edition), Kindle locations 1941–1974, who concludes that when writing to Augustine, Nectarius activates his Romanness while downplaying his identity as a Christian catechumen because it is not relevant to the issue at hand (Kindle location 1968).
[52] Conybeare, "Making Space," p. 212.
[53] Tuan, *Topophilia: A Study of Environmental Perception, Attitudes, and Values* (Englewood Cliffs, NJ: Prentice-Hall, 1974), p. xii. Domephilia, which signifies attachment to one's home, is not to be confused with domophilia.
[54] *Const. Sirmond.* 14 = *Cod. theod.* 16.2.31 (SC 531).
[55] *Const. Sirmond.* 14 = *Cod. theod.* 16.2.31 (SC 531): *gentiles, quos vulgo paganos appellant.*
[56] Aug. *Ep.* 97, addressed to Stilicho's replacement, Olympius.

against them specifically as *sacrilegia*.[57] Although the reclassification is generally viewed by scholars as a triumph for Augustine and the other Catholics who petitioned the court in the aftermath of the violence of 407–408, the decision also presented a quandary for Augustine and his fellow bishops.[58] While the full power of the state could now (theoretically) be brought to bear on anti-Catholic offenses, such crimes, if perpetrated by other Christians, should ideally be adjudicated internally, within the Church.[59] This was apparently the case with the Calama episode; some who Augustine calls "Christians" had joined non-Christians in looting the church.[60] Those looters who subsequently activated their Christianness apparently escaped civil punishment because they sought repentance according to ecclesiastical procedure and had been forgiven; those who could or would not identify as Christian were subjected to the stringency of civil authority, requiring what Augustine calls "correction" (*emendatio*).[61] Augustine promised

---

[57] *Const. Sirmond.* 14, tr. Shaw, *Sacred Violence*, p. 799 (SC 531: 526): *Ut, si quisquam in hoc genus sacrilegii proruperit, ut in ecclesias Catholicas inruens sacerdotibus et ministris vel ipsi cultui locoque aliquid importet iniuriae, quod geretur, litteris ordinum, magistratuum et curatoris et notariis apparitorum, quos stationarios appellant, deferatur in notitiam potestatum, ita ut vocabula eorum, qui agnosci potuerint, declarentur. Et si per multitudinem commissum dicitur, si non omnes, possunt tamen aliquanti cognosci, quorum confessione sociorum nomina publicentur* (If any persons break out into these types of sacrilegious acts and in the course of invading Catholic churches they do any kind of harm to the priests [i.e. bishops] and to their assistants, to the worship itself or to the place of worship, what happens shall be brought to the notice of the authorities. This must be done by means of reports made by the town senates, by the municipal magistrates and curators, and by the reports of the officials who are called stationarii, so that the names of those who have been identified can be published. If the act is reported to have been committed by a mob, then, if not all of them, at least some of them can be identified and, through confessions of these persons, the names of their accomplices can be made known).

[58] See most recently Maria Victoria Escribano Paño, "Bishops, Judges and Emperors: *Cod. theod.* 16.2.31 / *Cod. theod.* 16.5.46 / Sirm. 14 (409)," in *The Role of the Bishop in Late Antiquity: Conflict and Compromise*, ed. Andrew Fear and José Fernández Urbiña, pp. 105–126 (New York: Bloomsbury Academic, 2013), pp. 115–116, Shaw, *Sacred Violence*, p. 276, Hermanowicz, *Possidius*, pp. 186–187, and Sigrid Mratschek, "*Te velimus … consilii participem.* Augustine of Hippo and Olympius – a Case Study of Religious–Political Cooperation in the Fifth Century," in *Studia Patristica* 38. *St Augustine and His Opponents, Other Latin Writers*, papers presented at the thirteenth International Conference on Patristic Studies held in Oxford 1999, ed. M.F. Wiles and E.J. Yarnold, pp. 224–232 (Leuven: Peeters, 2001).

[59] Aug. *Ep.* 100.2 (CCL 31A): *causas ecclesiasticas insinuare vobis nemo praeter ecclesiasticos curat* (no one presides over cases involving the Church finding their way to you except ecclesiastical authorities).

[60] I therefore reject Rebillard's equivocation that "the celebrants **might** well have included both Christians and non-Christians" (Rebillard, *Christians and Their Many Identities*, Kindle location 2054, emphasis added).

[61] Aug. *Ep.* 104.8–9.

Nectarius that he had importuned the local authorities to pardon non-Christian offenders.[62] Christian morals demanded it.[63]

Augustine explained that this double standard was justifiable, since repentance was a closed religious system of reciprocity and, unlike forgiveness, could not be extended unilaterally to non-Christians:[64]

> This is the reason why we believed that the sorrow of repentance was fruitful for those Christians, when they confessed and asked forgiveness, who had been involved in that sin either by not going to the rescue of the church about to be burned or by taking something from those most criminal robberies.

What motivated these looters to activate their Romanness when attacking the Calama basilica yet their Christianness in the aftermath of this conflict as it was navigating the civil courts? Perhaps civic pride and *romanitas* inspired their participation in the festivities and they were caught up in the consequent basilica-looting. It is possible that the opportunity to escape civil punishment, precisely the concern Nectarius addressed in his letters, spurred their confessions within Church auspices. It may also be that these Christians were dissident Christians who joined the attack on the Catholic basilica out of religious opposition, but were later reconciled to the Catholics in order to avoid the kind of steep fines against heretics that had been imposed by the governor in a previous internecine conflict at Calama in 403.[65]

Augustine crafted the hair-splitting distinction and boundaries on the basis of the perpetrators' functional identification as Christians (or not). His strategy reproduced and reinforced, in legal terms, the boundary between Christians and non-Christians (as well as Catholics and non-Catholics) that we have seen was produced repeatedly in North African Christian (Catholic) literature and ritual arenas. This distinction extended to victims as well: "whatever is perpetrated against the association of Christians by impious and grace-less people is certainly more grievous and brutal than if

---

[62] Aug. *Ep.* 104.16. Augustine's claim is verified by *Ep.* 100.2, addressed to the African proconsul Donatus, a fellow Christian ("Donatus 24," PAC 309–310).

[63] Aug. *Ep.* 100.1 (CSEL 34.2): *pro lenitatis christianae consideratione* (out of consideration for Christian leniency).

[64] Aug. *Ep.* 104.9, tr. Teske (CSEL 34.2): *hinc est, quod christianis confitentibus atque deprecantibus, qui delicto illo fuerant implicati vel non succurrendo arsurae ecclesiae vel de sceleratissimis rapinis aliquid auferendo, paenitentiae dolorem fructuosum esse credidimus eis que ad correctionem sufficere existimavimus...*

[65] The incident and relevant legislation are discussed in Chapter 3.

the same crime were committed against others."[66] The parties to this spatial conflict thus employed structural parallelism between spatial boundaries and human bodily boundaries to produce the difference between Catholic Christians and those outside the group.

At the same time that laws proscribed the kind of traditional Roman rituals displayed in the streets of Calama on the calends of June, imperial legislation also aimed to protect desacralized temples from Christian zealotry, and state funding continued to provide nonsacrificial spectacles and feasts (*voluptates* and *convivia*).[67] Imperial legislation thereby exhibits a certain degree of ambivalence; emperors were yanked in opposite directions by their allegiance to traditional elites on the one hand and on the other by their desire to appease influential Christian bishops.[68] They were caught between maintaining some measure of cultural stability and containing the spontaneous eruptions of violence perpetrated by zealous Christians.[69] Even after 399, inscriptions attest to the continued maintenance of temple structures, if only for architectural, rather than ceremonial, purposes.[70] Unlike the cities of Alexandria, Gaza, or Constantinople, no exorbitant tales of spectacular temple destructions survive from North Africa.[71] As is the

---

[66] Aug. *Ep.* 100.1 (CCL 31A): *quicquid mali contra Christianam societatem ab hominibus impiis ingratisque committitur, profecto gravius est et atrocius, quam si in alios talia committantur ...*

[67] *Cod. theod.* 16.10.17, 18 from Arcadius and Honorius to Apollodorus, proconsul of Africa. As late as 409 CE, Augustine could still rail against these (*Enarrat. Ps.* 80; 102, 103.1–4, 146, and 147, cited in Lepelley, *Les cités de l'Afrique* I, p. 110). The concern persisted, as witnessed by the sermon of Quodvultdeus dated to 439 (*Sermo de tempore barbarico* I.1, PL 40: 700, discussed in Lepelley, *Cités de l'Afrique* I, p. 110).

[68] *Cod. theod.* 16.10.7, dated to December 381 and *Cod. theod.* 16.10.8, dated to November 382, both addressed to officials in the eastern empire. Shaw interprets *Cod. theod.* 16.10.8 as a reaction to the overzealous response to the earlier law by "freelance Christian enforcers" (*Sacred Violence*, p. 224). In addition to the cultural and aesthetic forces militating against such radical measures, it is likely that political considerations were also at work.

[69] See *Cod. theod.* 16.10.17 and 16.10.18.

[70] Lepelley, *Les cités de l'Afrique* I, p. 295, citing CIL 8.23968–9 (discussed in this chapter at note 114), which refurbished the walls and portico of a temple, elements visible only from the exterior. For the concept of the artistic significance of cult statues in the case of Osrhoene, see *Cod. theod.* 16.10.8, tr. Saradi-Mendelovici: *in qua simulacra feruntur posita artis pretio quam divinitate metienda* (in which images are reported to have been placed which must be measured by the value of their art rather than by their divinity). See the discussion in Helen Saradi-Mendelovici, "Christian Attitudes toward Pagan Monuments in Late Antiquity and Their Legacy in Later Byzantine Centuries," *Dumbarton Oaks Papers* 44 (1990): 47–61.

[71] Although it is likely that this absence is due to the lack of such events, there is simply no evidence on the basis of which we can either affirm or deny the possibility that such accounts and their architectural remains once existed but have simply disappeared in the shifting sands of history.

case with other locales throughout the empire, brief literary references to churches that were formerly temples and scant archaeological evidence of such spatial replacement provide a picture of sporadic, rather than systematic, change.[72]

Rhetorical Supersessionism Meets Architectural Dispossession

Although the discourse of spatial supersession preceded architectural dispossession, the two became mutually reinforcing. Rhetoric proliferated as temple dereliction, destruction, decommissioning, and appropriation increased. In turn, the language of those who sought to eliminate places for pagan worship was fortified by their occurrence. An episcopal council of Carthage decreed in 401 CE that temples and their statues be completely destroyed.[73] Emperors Theodosius and Honorius eventually bowed to this pressure by ordering the removal of cult statues, confiscation of temples (in 407 CE), and abolition of traditional priesthoods (in 415 CE).[74] Honorius'

[72] See, for example, the shrine of Babylas in Daphne (Chrysostom, *De s. Babyla*, analyzed in Shepardson, *Controlling Contested Spaces*, pp. 58–91).

[73] *Concil. Carth.* 16 June 401 = *Reg. Eccl. Carth. Excerpt.* 58, tr. Riggs and Cameron (CCL 149: 196): *Instant etiam aliae necessitates a religiosis imperatoribus postulandae: ut reliquias idolorum per omnem Africam iubeant penitus amputari – nam plerisque in locis maritimis atque possessionibus diversis adhuc erroris istius iniquitas viget – ut praecipiantur et ipsa deleri, et templa eorum, quae in agris vel in locis abditis constituta, nullo ornamento sunt, iubeantur omnimodo destrui* (There remain still other requirements to be sought from the most pious emperors: that they should command the remaining idols throughout all Africa to be utterly destroyed, for in a number of coastal areas and in various rural estates the wickedness of such error flourishes, and that they should direct both the idols themselves to be utterly destroyed and their temples which have been set up in rural parts or remote sites without identification), David Riggs, "The Continuity of Paganism between the Cities and Countryside of Late Roman Africa," in *Urban Centers and Rural Context in Late Antiquity*, ed. T. S. Burns and J. W. Eadie, pp. 285–300 (East Lansing, MI: University of Michigan Press, 2001), p. 293 and Cameron, *Last Pagans*, p. 784.

[74] *Cod. theod.* 16.10.19.pr-3, tr. Mirow and Kelley (Arcadius, Honorius, and Theodosius, from Rome, 15 November 407): *Post alia: Templorum detrahantur annonae et rem annonariam iuvent expensis devotissimorum militum profuturae. Simulacra, si qua etiamnunc in templis fanisque consistunt et quae alicubi ritum vel acceperunt vel accipiunt paganorum, suis sedibus evellantur, cum hoc repetita sciamus saepius sanctione decretum. Aedificia ipsa templorum, quae in civitatibus vel oppidis vel extra oppida sunt, ad usum publicum vindicentur. Arae locis omnibus destruantur omniaque templa in possessionibus nostris ad usus adcommodos transferantur; domini destruere cogantur. Non liceat omnino in honorem sacrilegi ritus funestioribus locis exercere convivia vel quicquam sollemnitatis agitare. Episcopis quoque locorum haec ipsa prohibendi ecclesiasticae manus tribuimus facultatem; iudices autem viginti librarum auri poena constringimus et pari forma officia eorum, si haec eorum fuerint dissimulatione neglecta* (After another: the annual income shall be withheld from temples and shall be allocated to the yearly account for the benefit of our most dedicated soldiers.

decommissioning of temples, described later by the bishop of Carthage, Quodvultdeus, likely entailed merely the temple "closings" and the warehousing or destruction of their idols.[75]

Despite their exuberant campaign against "paganism," North African bishops did not advocate destroying all shrines; those sites in the countryside should be demolished only if they lacked "artistic value."[76] Nonetheless, the decommissioning of temples, especially when reallocated as churches, provided them with the kind of concrete, visible, and lasting proof they had adduced in their rhetorical constructions of Christian victory. Emperors were finally legislating the episcopal vision of a world where paganism had been defeated and replaced by Christianity, lending legal imprimatur to the kind of assaults that had previously been perpetrated illegally. Orators latched onto these examples to illustrate that the battle had been won, as it were, on the ground. As Augustine would write in a letter to the citizens of Madaura after the decree of Honorius:[77]

> Images, if any even now stand in temples and shrines, which have received or do receive any worship of pagans, shall be torn from their foundations, since we know that this has been very often decreed by repeated ordinance. The buildings themselves of the temples, which are in cities or towns or outside of towns, shall be dedicated to public use. Altars in all places shall be destroyed and all temples within our holdings shall be dedicated to public use. The proprietors shall be forced to destroy them. It shall not be lawful at all to hold banquets in places polluted with blood in order to honor sacrilegious rites or to celebrate any sort of ritual), Matthew C. Mirow and Kathleen A. Kelley, "Laws on Religion from the *Theodosian* and *Justinianic Codes*," in *Religions of Late Antiquity in Practice*, ed. Richard Valantasis, pp. 263–274 (Princeton, NJ: Princeton University Press, 2000), p. 272; and *Cod. theod.* 16.10.20.pr (Honorius and Theodosius, from Ravenna, August 30, 415).

[75] Quodvultdeus, *Liber de promiss.* 3.38.44 (SC 102): *Honorius etiam theodosii minor filius christiana religione ac devotione praeditus templa omnia cum suis adiacentibus spatiis ecclesiis contulit simulque eorum simulacra confringenda in potestatem dedit* (The same Honorius, the younger son of Theodosius, out of devotion to the Christian religion, similarly transferred to his jurisdiction all temples together with their adjacent gathering places and gave the authority to shatter their images).

[76] Béatrice Caseau, "The Fate of Rural Temples in Late Antiquity and the Christianisation of the Countryside," *Recent Research on the Late Antique Countryside*, ed. William Bowden, Luke Lavan, and Carlos Machado, *Late Antique Archaeology* vol. 2 (Brill, 2004), pp. 105–144, p. 130. Also see the discussion by Saradi-Mendelovici, "Christian Attitudes," p. 52.

[77] Aug. *Ep.* 232. 3, tr. Teske, modified (CCL 57): *Videtis certe simulacrorum templa partim sine reparatione conlapsa partim diruta partim clausa partim in usus alios commutata ipsa que simulacra vel confringi vel incendi vel includi vel destrui atque ipsas huius saeculi potestates, quae aliquando pro simulacris populum christianum persequebantur, victas et domitas non a repugnantibus sed a morientibus christianis et contra eadem simulacra, pro quibus christianos occidebant, impetus suos leges que vertisse et imperii nobilissimi eminentissimum culmen ad sepulcrum piscatoris petri submisso diademate supplicare. Haec omnia divinae scripturae, quae in manus omnium iam venerunt, ante longissima tempora futura esse testatae sunt; haec omnia tanto robustiore fide laetamur fieri, quanto maiore auctoritate praedicta esse in sanctis litteris invenimus.* Dating follows Paolo Mastandrea, *Massimo di Madauros*

You certainly see the temples of idols in part fallen down in disrepair, in part destroyed, in part closed, and in part turned to other uses. You certainly see that the idols are either broken or burned or shut away or destroyed. You certainly see that the powers of this world, which were at one time persecuting the people of the Christians in defense of their idols, have been defeated and subdued by Christians – not by Christians fighting back but by Christians dying. And you certainly see that those powers have turned their attacks and laws against those same idols for which they once killed Christians and that the supreme head of the most renowned empire lays aside his diadem and offers supplication at the tomb of Peter the fisherman.

Of the four methods that Augustine lists by which traditional Roman temples could meet their end – neglect, destruction, closure, and repurpose, he hones in on the middle two, the intentional causes, to make his point: paganism's days were numbered and Christianity was on the rise. Orators like Augustine perceived the gradual desacralization of temples and the rise of Christian basilicas as Christian displacement. The changing landscape provided them with "evidence" of Christian triumphalism and the defeat of what they repeatedly portrayed to their audiences as the Church's chief opponent, "paganism." Augustine continued to express optimism about the demise of pagan worship in his sermons: "Do you not see his [the Devil's] temples falling into ruins, his images shattered, his priests turning to God?"[78] The bishop conceived of history as proleptically proclaiming Christian victory.

The thrill of victory suffered a setback in 410, however, with the Visigoth sack of Rome. North Africa received refugees fleeing the devastation, and Christians found themselves blamed for the city's fall. Christian opponents taunted that "Christian times" had brought the destruction of the empire's crown jewel.[79] Augustine devoted over a decade of his writing

---

(*Agostino, Epistulae 16 e 17*), (Padua: Editoriale programma, 1985), pp. 81–88. Augustine attributes this particular spate of temple attacks to the circumcellions, whom Shaw describes as "brutish lower elements of the local population, probably mainly rural workers, many of whom still bore Punic names like Miggin, Namphamo, and Saname ... These barbarous men viewed the attacks on pagans and their sacred cult places as a virtuous duty. There must have been armed resistance to them, since members of the Christian gangs were injured and some of them had died in the attacks" (Shaw, *Sacred Violence*, p. 238).

[78] Aug. *Serm.* 15A.6, tr. Hill (*Sermons*, pt. 3, vol. 1, pp. 336–337), dated to 410 CE (CCL 41: 208): *Non videtis templa eius cadere, simulacra confringi, sacerdotes eius ad deum converti?* (cited in Shaw, *Sacred Violence*, p. 259).

[79] Aug. *Serm.* 81.9 (PL 38): *ecce, inquit, christianis temporibus roma perit* ("Now you see," he says, "Rome is ruined in Christian times").

career to producing an apology to refute these accusations and shore up the faith of wavering Christians, *The City of God*. Orosius assisted him in the effort by writing *Seven Books of History against the Pagans*, which compared the Christian defeat of pagans to the triumph of the Israelites over the Egyptians.[80] The fall of Rome had to fit into this narrative arc. In order to achieve this, Orosius interprets the death in 408 of Stilicho and his son Eucherius as divine punishment for plotting the fall of Rome by supporting pagans and opening the gates of the city to the barbarians.[81] Their support of pagans was displayed by restoring temples and destroying churches. Orosius thereby turns on its head the accusation pagans had lobbed against Christians in the wake of the fall; to him, looking with apologetic, providentialist hindsight, it was the return to paganism – as expressed through ritual buildings – that brought down the city. And thus the myth of "pagan resurgence" was born.[82]

Following the same line of argument, Augustine, in his own apologetic work, *The City of God*, claimed victory for Christianity in the spatial realm. He cited a singular event in the city of Carthage as proof:[83]

> What we do know is that right here in the city of Carthage, the most renowned and eminent city in Africa, on the fourteenth day before the Kalends of April [March 19], Gaudentius and Jovius, *comites* of the Emperor Honorius, destroyed the temples of the false gods and smashed their idols.

Despite Augustine's totalizing interpretation of post-410 events, this episode is better placed in 399 CE with the promulgation of legislation regarding pagan temples and cult images.[84]

The rhetoric of spatial displacement continued to be a prominent feature of late Roman Christian discourse. In a guest sermon delivered by

---

[80] Orosius, *Hist.* 7.27.14, tr. A. T. Fear, *Orosius. Seven Books of History Against the Pagans* (Liverpool: Liverpool University Press, 2010, p. 368) (CSEL 5): *Ibi Aegyptiorum vasa pretiosa Hebraeis tradita sunt: hic in ecclesias Christianorum praecipua paganorum templa cesserunt* (There the precious vessels of the Egyptians were given to the Hebrews; here, the most glorious pagan temples became Christian churches).

[81] Orosius, *Hist.* 7.38.5. Orosius goes so far as to label them "pagan," which Burns rejects as aspersion (Thomas S. Burns, *Barbarians Within the Gates of Rome: A Study of Roman Military Policy and the Barbarians, ca.375–425 A.D.* (Bloomington, IN: Indiana University Press, 1995), pp. 220–221.

[82] See Cameron, *Last Pagans*.

[83] Aug. *Civ. Dei*, 18.54 (CCL 48: 655): *Interim, quod scimus, in civitate notissima et eminentissima Carthagine Africae Gaudentius et Iovius comites imperatoris Honorii quarto decimo Kalendas Aprilis falsorum deorum templa everterunt et simulacra fregerunt* (as cited in Shaw, *Sacred Violence*, p. 227.

[84] *Cod. theod.* 16.10.17, 18. See discussion earlier in this chapter.

Augustine in the *Basilica Honoriana* of Carthage in 417 CE, he implied that the site was formerly a temple: "'For we,' the apostle says, 'are the temple of the living God, as God has said, I will live in them and walk' [2 Cor 6.16]. The idols that were here knew how to be fixed in a place, but they did not know how to walk."[85] The name of the basilica suggests that it had been funded by the emperor Honorius for Catholics.[86] Some scholars have understood Augustine to be referring to a temple seizure, since he mentions "idols that were here (*hic*)."[87] Yet others reject this explanation.[88] No additional references or archaeological finds exist to help decide the point. It is true that *hic* usually refers to an immediate locus. However, "right here" might just as well refer more generally to the city as a whole, especially when one considers that Augustine was not native to Carthage and "here" might signify the broader geographic parameters of the city.[89] Regardless of the meaning of Augustine's allusion, his contrast between the "fixed" idols and the "living God" within the broader context of the sermon makes clear his providentialist interpretation of historical events: a new age was dawning.

Another rhetorical feature of this sermon is that Augustine uses the building of God's temple in Jerusalem from Psalm 95/6 as a metaphor for the growth of Christianity in the Roman empire. For the bishop of Hippo, Christian expansion was a zero-sum game; its success required the demise of paganism: "So let us hear this architect [Christ], constructing some new

---

[85] Aug. *Serm.* 163 (Gert Partoens, "Le sermon 163 de saint augustin. Introduction et édition," *Revue Bénédictine* 115 (2005): 251–285, pp. 251–253): *Nos enim, sicut dicit apostolus, templum dei vivi sumus; propter quod dicit deus, inhabitabo in illis, et deambulabo. Quae autem hic simulacra fuerunt, figi noverant, ambulare non noverant*, cited in Shaw, *Sacred Violence*, p. 233.

[86] Ennabli, *Métropole chrétienne*, p. 31: "Le nom de la basilique semble venir de sa construction sous le règne d'Honorius (395–423), à son instigation et grace sans doute à son aide financière, ce qui lui aurait valu ce patronage" (The name of the basilica seems to derive from its construction during the reign of Honorius (395–423), at his initiative and probably thanks to his financial support, which would have earned him the patronage).

[87] Shaw, *Sacred Violence*, pp. 233–234.

[88] Ennabli, *Métropole chrétienne*, p. 31, no. 13, and Partoens, "le sermon 163 de saint augustin, p. 252: "D'ailleurs, n'aurait-il pas été étrange qu'Augustin, qui aimait tant fustiger la vénération que vouaient ses contemporains à la Dea Caelestis, n'en ait pas fait mention au cours d'un sermon prononcé dans son ancien lieu de culte et traitant la transformation de temples païens en sanctuaries chrétiens?" (Besides, would it not have been strange for Augustine, who loved to castigate the veneration that lured his contemporaries to Dea Caelestis, to fail to mention it during a sermon given in her former place of worship and dealing with the transformation of pagan temples into Christian sanctuaries?).

[89] See *hic* with *civitas* in Aug. *Civ. Dei* 15.18 and 22.6.

and tearing down some old.''[90] This motif is not merely a metaphor; it reflects how Augustine and his fellow polemicists portrayed the changing architectural landscape of late antiquity to their audiences. This interpretation of the built environment promoted a cosmology that projected a new social and political role for Christians in the context of empire. Those who chose to activate their Christianness when taking in the scenery could recognize their recent success in the growing number of buildings they could claim as their own.

In the same providentialist vein, Christian opinion-makers interpreted the repurposing of the hillside temple of Caelestis overlooking the Carthaginian port as a pagan defeat. Caelestis, identified with the Roman goddess Juno, was the patron deity of Carthage, a symbol of the *ancien régime*. The temple's repurposing certainly constitutes architectural dispossession, yet whether it was a symbolic action performed in an already defunct site or wholesale takeover was a matter of interpretation, even in the ancient accounts. A close look at the report of the events by Quodvultdeus, bishop of Carthage in the 430s reveals internal contradictions.[91] He first states that the temple had fallen into disrepair due to neglect, making it the ideal place for the then bishop Aurelius to stage a flamboyant display of power:[92]

> In Africa, at Carthage, there was a very big sanctuary of Caelestis, so they said, surrounded by temples of all her deities … When [the temple] had been closed for some time through neglect … the Christians wanted to appropriate it for the use of the true religion, but the pagans protested

---

[90] Aug. *Serm.* 163.6 (ed. Partoens, p. 276): *Audiamus ergo et apostolum, architectum magistri:* Ut sapiens, inquit, architectus fundamentum posui (1 Cor 3:10). *Audiamus ergo istum architectum quaedam nova construentem, quaedam vetera deicientem* (Let us hear, then, his apostle, the architect of the master: 'As a wise,' he says, 'architect, I have laid the foundation.' So let us hear. …

[91] "Quodvultdeus," PAC, pp. 947–949.

[92] Quodvultdeus, *Liber de promiss.* 3.38.44, tr. Henry Hurst, *The Sanctuary of Tanit at Carthage in the Roman Period. A Re-Interpretation,* Journal of Roman Archaeology Supplementary Series 30 (Portsmouth, RI: JRA, 1999), pp. 91–92, slightly modified (CCL 413.3): *Apud africam carthagini caelestis, ut ferebant, templum nimis amplum omnium deorum suorum aedibus vallatum … cum diutius clausum incuria … que populus christianus usui verae religionis vindicare, dracones aspides que illic esse ad custodiam templi gentilis populus clamitabat. Quo magis christiani feruore succensi ea facilitate omnia amoverunt inlaesi qua templum suo vere caelesti regi et domino consecrarent. Namque cum sanctae paschae sollemnis ageretur festivitas, collecta illic et undique omni curiositate etiam adveniens multitudo, sacerdotum multorum pater et dignae memoriae nominandus antistes aurelius, caelestis iam patriae civis, cathedram illic posuit in loco caelestis et sedit. Ipse tunc aderam cum sociis et amicis atque, ut se adulescentium aetas impatiens circumquaque vertebat, dum curiosi singula quaeque pro magnitudine inspicimus, mirum quoddam et incredibile nostro se ingessit aspectui: titulus aeneus grandioribus que litteris in frontispicio templi conscriptus: aurelius*

that there were dragons and poisonous snakes there to guard the sanctuary. This only inflamed the zeal of the Christians and they cleared the site without suffering harm and with such ease as to allow them to consecrate the temple to the truly Celestial King and Lord. Indeed, when the solemn festival of holy Easter was being celebrated and a crowd collected there from all parts in a high state of curiosity, the bishop Aurelius ... placed his seat there in the place of Caeletis, and sat on it. I myself was present ... a remarkable and incredible detail presented itself to our gaze: an inscription in very large bronze letters on the front of the temple, saying "Aurelius the priest dedicated this." Reading this the crowd marveled at the actions which with prophetic spirit God's foreknowledge had brought to this predestined conclusion.

Quodvultdeus depicts Aurelius as taking advantage of the derelict state of the temple to set up his *cathedra* on the site, symbolizing Christian triumph over the goddess Caelestis. This first description is somewhat reminiscent of Ambrose's discovery of the saints Protasius and Gervasius in Milan for the dedication of a new suburban basilica in the previous century.[93] Unlike Ambrose's public performance, however, Aurelius' ceremonial sit-in seems less scripted, even serendipitous.

Quodvultdeus then reports that the temple was later leveled by Ursus during his term as tribune in 421 CE:[94]

And when a false prophecy was circulated by a pagan, as if it had come from the same Caelestis, that the street and temples would again be given back to the ancient ritual of worship, He, that God whose prophetic utterances

---

pontifex dedicavit. Hunc legentes populi mirabantur praesago tunc spiritu acta quae praescius dei ordo certo isto fine concluserat. See the discussion in R. P. C. Hanson, "The Transformation of Pagan Temples into Churches in the Early Christian Centuries," *Journal of Semitic Studies* 23 (1978): 257–267, pp. 262–263 and Leone, *Pagan City*, pp. 32–33. "Aurelius 1," PCA 1: 105–127.

[93] Ambrose, *Ep.* 77/22. See discussion in Neil McLynn, *Ambrose of Milan: Church and Court in a Christian Capital*, The Transformation of the Classical Heritage 22 (Berkeley, CA: University of California Press, 1994), p. 212, and Zangara, "L'*inventio* dei martiri Gervasio e Protasio," *Augustinianum* 21 (1981): 119–133. The basilica was also identified as the *Basilica Apostolorum* by Nazaro Spieser, "Ambrose's Foundations at Milan and the Question of Martyria," tr. Featherstone, in *Urban and Religious Spaces in Late Antiquity and Early Byzantium*, Variorum Collected Studies Series 706 (Burlington, VT: Ashgate, 2001), p. 2.

[94] Quodvultdeus, *Liber de promiss.* 3.38.44, tr. Hurst (CCL 413.3): *Cum que a quodam pagano falsum vaticinium velut eiusdem caelestis proferretur, quo rursus et via et templa prisco sacrorum ritui redderentur, ille, ille verus deus cuius prophetica vaticinia nesciunt omnino mentiri nec fallere, sub constantio et augusta placidia quorum nunc filius valentinianus pius et christianus imperat, urso insistente tribuno, omnia illa templa ad solum usque perducta agrum reliquit, in sepulturam scilicet mortuorum.* For Ursus, see PAC, "Ursus (3)," p. 1236. Historians debate the date of Ursus' tribunate (See, for example, Hanson, "Pagan Temples," who dates it to 418).

know neither falsehood nor deception, in the time of Constantius and Augusta Placidia, whose son the pious and Christian Valentinian now rules, through the agency of the tribune Ursus, razed all those sanctuaries to the ground and left just their sites for the burial of the dead.

If the temple had been adapted by Aurelius into a church before 421, it is doubtful that Ursus would have subsequently demolished it.[95] Leone concludes that sometime before it was razed and its grounds designated as a cemetery, Aurelius used the occasion of Easter "to represent the power of the Church over the pagan community through [the] symbolic action" of occupying the abandoned temple.[96] This interpretation is certainly consonant with the theme of the holiday, the triumph of Christ over death and the devil.

Further evidence supporting this view can be found in the possible concurrence of Easter with the *fercula* festival for Berecynthia (Cybele), which Augustine associates with Dea Caelestis. The Caelestis festival culminated in a ceremonial washing of the cult statue on March 27.[97] For Nicene Christians, the date of Easter varied between March 22 and April 25. If the two festivals coincided that year, Aurelius might have taken it upon himself under the aegis of *ecclesiasticae manus* to preempt a cultic revival later validated by a pagan "prophecy."[98] Doing so would have foiled any attempts by his congregants to expand their Easter festivities to include the once public, familiar *fercula* ritual. We have already discussed the Christian practice of including pagan rites in their celebrations as addressed by Augustine's New Year's Day sermons.[99] Quodvultdeus' description of the crowd as having

---

[95] Hanson, "Pagan Temples," p. 263. Even if it fell into dissident hands, it is highly unlikely that the state would have destroyed the building rather than evicting its occupants, following the pattern we have seen in the previous chapter.

[96] Leone, *Pagan City*, p. 33.

[97] Aug. *Civ. Dei* 2.4, Ovid, *Fasti* 4.340, and the Philocalian calendar of 354 CE (Duncan Fishwick, "The Cannophori and the March Festival of Magna Mater," *TAPA* 97 (1966): 193–202). Easter dates were not standardized. Rome and Alexandria's celebrations could be held a month apart (Eduard Schwartz, *Christliche und jüdische Ostertafeln* (Berlin: Weidmann, 1905), pp. 50–58).

[98] *Cod. theod.* 16.10.19.3, which was not promulgated in Africa until June 5, 408. Bayliss interprets *ecclesiasticae manus* as "subject to the orders of the church," from the law granting clergy the authority to prevent pagan ritual assemblies (R. Bayliss, *Provincial Cilicia and the Archaeology of Temple Conversion* (Oxford: Archaeopress, 2004), p. 19, citing *Cod. theod.* 16.10.19.3 dating to 407/408). As Shaw points out, this law was not posted in Carthage until June 5, 408, which contributed to the violence at Calama on June 1 of that year (Shaw, *Sacred Violence*, p. 256).

[99] See, for example, Aug. *Serm.* Dolbeau 4.9 = 26D.9 = 198.9. Other examples include March 7, the birthday of martyrs Perpetua and Felicitas and the feast of *Junonalia*; June

"collected there" suggests that Aurelius' stunt was more of an ad hoc public performance than a formal, well-planned property confiscation.

Quodvultdeus similarly interprets the actions of the tribune Ursus supersessionistically: a Christian cemetery *replaces* the central shrine of Carthage. His symbolic interpretation, however, does not bear up to archaeological scrutiny. Scholars' initial classification of the sanctum-turned-cemetery as exclusively Christian has been convincingly overturned based on a reevaluation of the fifth–seventh-century terracotta figurines and other small objects found there.[100] It is most likely that Ursus leveled the derelict temples to accommodate the growing demand for intra-mural burials. Quodvultdeus' interpretation of the building's bronze dedication as a miracle foretelling the episcopacy of Aurelius is explained as the donor inscription put up by Marcus Aurelius as *pontifex*. The eagerness shared purportedly by those in attendance to see a miracle in a dilapidated inscription shows just how willing Christians were to interpret whatever text or event they encountered providentially, and to adapt them to their religious messages.[101] Quodvultdeus concludes his description of the Caelestis temple incident by asserting that the downfall of pagan worship, which had been predicted in ancient times by the Greek prophet Hermes Trismegistus, had come to pass.[102]

Augustine also comments on the fate of the Caelestis temple in his sermon on Psalm 98 delivered in Carthage possibly in 411 CE. He puts the biblical imagery to work in helping his audience interpret their physical surroundings. Augustine invokes the topographical image of the Caelestis temple on the "mount" and its stone idols to convey Christian victory, for these idols (made with hands) have been vanquished by the metaphorical "stone

24, the birth of John the Baptist and the feast of *Fortis Fortunae* (the summer solstice); and December 25, the birth of Jesus and the *Natalis Invicti* (the birth of the "unconquered sun" or winter solstice).
[100] Hurst, *Sanctuary of Tanit*, pp. 87–88. For its identification as Christian see, for example, Shaw, *Sacred Violence*, p. 234.
[101] For the proposal that the dedication was from the second-century emperor Marcus Aurelius, see Hurst, *Sanctuary of Tanit*, p. 92.
[102] Quodvultdeus, *Liber de promiss.* 3.38.44 (CCSL 60): *Doluit haec futura hermes ille trismegistus et maerens inter cetera scripsit dicens: "tunc terra ista sanctissima, sedes delubrorum atque templorum, mortuorum erit cadaverum que plenissima"* (Hermes Trismegistus was upset about this future event and lamenting in the course of other things he wrote, saying "Then shall that holiest land, the place of sanctuaries and temples, be overflowing with the dead and corpses"). Augustine quotes the same Hermetic passage in his defense of martyr veneration in *Civ. Dei* 8.26.1, 25. Lactantius, Augustine, and Quodvultdeus considered the pseudonymous author of the Hermetic corpus to be an ancient pagan prophet.

from the mountain made without hands (*lapis de monte sine manibus*)," namely Christer:[103]

> No craftsman will ever again assemble the idols that Christ has smashed. ... "Exalt the Lord our God, and worship at his holy mount, for the Lord our God is holy (Ps 98:6)." ... This stone cut out of the mount without hands (Dan 2:34, 45) has crushed all the kingdoms of the world: we see all the kingdoms of the earth crushed by that stone. ... Which were the kingdoms of the earth? The kingdoms of idols, the kingdoms of demons, now shattered. ... So consider what sovereignty this Caelestis [sc. Goddess of the Skies] used to enjoy here at Carthage. But where is the kingdom of this Caelestis now? The stone hewn from the mount without hands has shattered all the kingdoms of earth.

Unlike Quodvultdeus, Augustine seems to have no personal knowledge of events surrounding the temple destruction. More likely he is relying on second-hand information (likely supplied by Quodvultdeus himself). Equipped with information about the local situation, the visiting Bishop of Hippo appeals to his Carthaginian audience's familiarity with their city's landscape. At a time when Christians were fending off accusations of having caused the fall of Rome, he constructs a triumphalist perceptual symbolism by mapping the biblical narrative of God's conquest of idolatry onto that landscape.

Unfortunately there are no additional sources explaining why the tribune Ursus might have destroyed the dilapidated sanctuary. Some scholars have been puzzled by the creation of a cemetery within the city walls, perhaps still offensive to Roman sensibilities.[104] Yet the evidence of a growing number of urban burials in areas of the city that had been abandoned suggests that the urban landscape was changing, and that space within the walls was at a premium.[105] In addition to demographic shifts, these changes may be the result of

---

[103] Aug. *Enarrat. Ps.* 98.2 and 98.14, my translation (lines 2–5) and tr. Shaw, *Sacred Violence*, p. 234 (CCL 39: 1379 and 1391–1392): *Idola quae fregit Christus, numquam iterum faciet faber ... Exaltate dominum deum nostrum, et adorate in monte sancto eius, quoniam sanctus dominus deus noster. ... Lapis iste praecisus de monte sine manibus, confregit omnia regna terrarum: videmus confracta ab illo lapide omnia regna terrae. ... Quae erant regna terrae? Regna idolorum, regna daemoniorum fracta sunt. ... Regnum Caelestis quale erat Carthagini! Ubi nunc est regnum Caelestis? Lapis ille fregit omnia regna terrarum, lapis praecisus de monte sine manibus.* The term "not made with hands" (Greek: ἀχειροποίητον) was already associated in the earliest Christian writings with supersession, but of Judaism rather than traditional Greek or Roman religion, in Mark 14:58, 2 Cor 5:1, and Hebrews 9:24. Supersessionism of the latter, labeled "idolatry," can be found in the books of Maccabees.

[104] Hurst, *Sanctuary of Tanit*, p. 93.

[105] Leone, *Changing Townscapes*, pp. 201–203, 206.

economic decline or political realignments. Whatever motives the tribune and his imperial patrons may have harbored, North African bishops perceived these changes in religious terms and purveyed their interpretations to their audiences. Through their rhetoric of spatial contestation, these ancient spin doctors shaped public perception of space. Rather than construing the reallocation of space in pragmatic or materialist terms, they saw it as a sign of God's favor.

Architectural Dispossession: The Archaeological Record

Archaeological evidence has helped identify the utilitarian dimensions of the transformation of the built environment in late antiquity.[106] In his analysis of temple conversion in provincial Cilicia, Richard Bayliss summarizes this research succinctly:[107]

> The 4th century does appear to us today as an age of opportunism and small-scale industrialization, characterized by a widespread decline in the maintenance of public works, the reuse of building materials, and the encroachment of private concerns into public spaces.

Many factors, such as natural disasters, population relocation, and declining cultic attendance, contributed to the abandonment and reuse of temples and their building materials, among which the growth of Christianity was only one.[108] The reuse of temples, their land, and/or their spolia for theaters, civil basilicas, warehouses, necropoli, dwellings, museums, walls, aqueducts, roads, workshops, and bridges occurred in imperial North Africa and continued through the late antique period.[109]

---

[106] Bryan Ward-Perkins, *From Classical Antiquity to the Middle Ages. Urban Public Building in Northern and Central Italy, AD 300–850*, Oxford Historical Monographs (New York: Oxford University Press, 1984) and "Re-using the Architectural Legacy of the Past, *entre idéologie et pragmatisme*," in *The Idea and Ideal of the Town Between Late Antiquity and the Early Middle Ages*, ed. G. P. Brogiolo and Bryan Ward-Perkins, pp. 225–244 (Leiden: E. J. Brill, 1999); J. H. W. G. Liebeschuetz, "The End of the Ancient City: A Center of Administration and a Way of Life," in *The City in Late Antiquity*, Leicester-Nottingham Studies in Ancient Society, ed. J. Rich, pp. 1–49 (New York: Routledge, 1992); N. Duval, "Église et temple en Afrique du nord: note sur les installations chrétiennes dans les temples a cour a propos de l'église dite de Servus a Sbeitla," *Bulletin archéologique du Comité des travaux historiques et scientifiques* NS 7 (1971): 265–296; F. W. Deichmann, "Frühchristliche Kirchen in antiken Heiligtümer," *Jahrbuch des deutschen archäologischen Instituts* 54 (1939): 105–136; Richard Brilliant and Dale Kinney, ed., *Reuse Value: Spolia and Appropriation in Art and Architecture from Constantine to Sherrie Levine* (Burlington, VT: Ashgate, 2011); Sears, *Late Roman African Urbanism;* and Leone, *Changing Townscapes.*
[107] Bayliss, *Provincial Cilicia*, p. 32.
[108] Sears, "Fate of Temples," p. 239.
[109] Sears, "Fate of Temples," pp. 237–242.

Although temple-church conversions may have been a factor in the reconfiguration of the urban landscape, they were neither as dominant nor as widespread as literary sources suggest. After structures like dwellings, baths, theaters, civil basilicas, military installations, libraries, shops, warehouses, factories, porticoes, stoas, bridges, and propylaea, "classical temples ... were the last buildings to be converted" into churches.[110] Jean-Michel Spieser, in his survey of Greece, concludes that "churches were not installed in temples, or on the site of temples already destroyed or in ruins, until a much later period when this probably no longer had any clearly anti-pagan significance."[111] Elsewhere I have demonstrated that for the West, this period likely coincided with Justinian's deliberate, systematic campaign to seize places of non-Christian assembly and convert them to churches in the sixth century.[112]

The late fourth- and early fifth-century churches built on or of former temples attested by the archaeological record are, therefore, the exception rather than the rule. During this period, temples were more likely to be preserved than destroyed or reused: "[E]pigraphic evidence for North Africa in particular has found that the upkeep of temples by pagan communities was not an uncommon phenomenon even late in the fourth and early in the fifth centuries."[113] Sears has shown that, for the second half of the fourth century (363–395), temples constitute 7.8 percent of North African building restoration inscriptions, such as the reconstruction of a temple in Hr. Morabba in Proconsularis in the 380s.[114] Particularly in North Africa, where pagan elites embraced Christianity later than in other western regions of the empire, traditional worship continued well into the fifth century.

---

[110] Jan Vaes, "Riutilizzazione cristiana di edifici dell'antichità classica. Un atlante. Christian Reutilization of the Buildings of Classical Antiquity: An Atlas," Il territorio secolarizzato/ The Secularized Territory, ed. Pierluigi Nicoli, Lotus International 65 (1990): 16–39, p. 23.

[111] Jean-Michel Spieser, "The Christianization of Pagan Sanctuaries," tr. J. M. Featherstone, in Urban and Religious Spaces in Late Antiquity and Early Byzantium, Variorum Collected Studies Series 706 (Burlington, VT: Ashgate, 2001), p. VI:13, originally published as "La christianisation des sanctuaries païens en Grèce," in Neue Forschungen in griechischen Heiligtümern (Tübingen: Ernst Wasmuth, 1976): 309–320.

[112] Lander, "Inventing Synagogue Conversion: The Case of Late Roman North Africa," Journal of Ancient Judaism 4.3 (2013): 401–416.

[113] Michael Milojevic, "Retrofit Ecclesia: A Non-Conforming Building Type," Byzantinische Forschungen 24 (1997): 343–366, p. 344.

[114] Sears, "Fate of Temples," pp. 232–233 and 236; CIL 8.23968–9: Ad indictum b[eatissimorum tem]porum dd[dd(ominorum) Augggg(ustorum)]q(ue) nost]rorum Valentin[iani The]odosi Arcadi [et Maximi ---] | quibus Romanum [nomen confirmatur et] moenia r[ecidiva consurgunt por]ticum cum aed[e vetus]tate conlapsam Co[---] | restituit dedicante V[---]adio pro[consule Africae et sa]cri audito[ri cognitore] insist(ente) [---], published

The fact that temples were still being maintained and used even after their idols and altars had been removed reveals cracks in the rhetorical project of North African bishops. A letter written in 398 to Augustine by a certain Publicola, often identified as the Roman senator and father of Melania the Younger, Valerius Publicola, inquired whether it was acceptable for a Christian to consume water and food procured from temple property. The letter is even more interesting if we accept Danuta Shanzer's recent identification of Publicola as a wealthy Jewish landowner in the process of converting to Christianity, since it would show that Jews shared Christian concerns about "pagan demons" lurking in religious spaces:[115]

> If there is a well or a spring in an idol temple which is still cared for, but nothing (sc. nothing contaminating) was done in said well or spring, ought a Christian to draw water from it and drink? ... Ought a Christian knowingly to buy vegetables or other produce from a garden or estate belonging to idols and their priests and eat it?

Publicola's anxiety reveals that even at the close of the fourth or early fifth century, when the letter was written, temples were still "cared for" (*colitur*). Augustine's reply, which cites the authority of 1 Cor. 10:26 as a prooftext, admits this:[116]

> But if what is grown in the fields is consecrated to an idol or offered in sacrifice, it must then be reckoned among the food offered to an idol. We

in Ari Saastamoinen, *The Phraseology of Latin Building Inscriptions in Roman North Africa*, Commentationes Humanarum Litterarum 127.2010 (Helsinki: Societas Scientiarum Fennica, 2010), p. 564, with discussion pp. 59–60. Based on Barnes' chronology, the proconsulate of V---adius dates to either 384/385, 386/387, or 387/388 (Barnes, "Proconsuls of Africa: Corrigenda" *Phoenix* 39.3 (1985): 273–274, p. 274).

[115] Publicola apud Aug. *Ep.* 46.14, 18, tr. Shanzer, slightly modified (CSEL 34.2): *si in templo, quod colitur, idoli puteus ibi sit vel fons et nihil ibi factum sit in eodem puteo vel fonte, si debet haurire aquam inde Christianus et bibere? ... Si de horto vel de possessione idolorum vel sacerdotum eorum debet Christianus sciens holus emere vel aliquem fructum et inde edere?* (Shanzer, "Who was Augustine's Publicola?" *Revue des Études Juives* 171.1–2 (2012): 27–60). Also see the discussion in Lepelley, "La diabolisation du paganisme et ses conséquences psychologiques: les angoisses de Publicola, correspondant de saint Augustin," in *Impies et païens entre Antiquité et Moyen Âge*, ed. L. Mary and M. Sot, pp. 81–96 (Paris: Picard, 2002); and B. Caseau, "Religious Intolerance and Pagan Statuary," in *Archaeology of Late Antique 'Paganism'*: 479–502, p. 484. Kalleres thoroughly analyzes the Christian fear of demons in *City of Demons.* The Jewish fear is well-documented in Rachel Neis, *The Sense of Sight in Rabbinic Culture. Jewish Ways of Seeing in Late Antiquity* (New York: Cambridge University Press, 2013).

[116] Aug. *Ep.* 47.4, tr. Teske (CSEL 34.2): *sed si illud, quod in agris nascitur, consecratur idolo vel sacrificatur, tunc inter idolothyta deputandum est. cavendum est enim, ne, si putaverimus non vescendum holere, quod nascitur in horto templi idoli, consequens sit, ut existimemus non debuisse apostolos apud athenas cibum sumere, quia civitas erat minervae eius que numini consecrata.*

must, after all, beware that, if we think that one should not eat a vegetable that was grown in the garden of the temple of an idol, it does not follow that we think that the apostle [Paul] ought not to have taken food among the Athenians because it was the city of Minerva and consecrated to her godhead. I would answer this same thing concerning a well or a fountain that is in a temple. It really disturbs me more, however, if something from the sacrifices is thrown into the fountain or well.

We recall that this correspondence was exchanged before the imperial legislation against temples of 407 was promulgated. Archaeological evidence, in fact, suggests that "it is only with the Byzantine conquest in the 6th c. that widespread destruction of temples took place, for the incorporation of their masonry into fortifications, or for the conversion of their remains into Christian churches."[117]

The tangle of rhetoric and archaeological interpretation plagues modern scholarship as much as it did ancient discourse. Friedrich Deichmann published the most extensive treatment of architectural dispossession of temples by churches in 1939.[118] Influenced by the triumphalist rhetoric of late antique literary sources, these nineteenth and early twentieth-century archaeologists dated some churches built on former temple sites about one century too early. First R. P. C. Hanson and later Gareth Sears reevaluated much of this evidence.[119] Sears has challenged the early dating of the New Temple-church at Tipasa and the temple-church at Mactar.[120] The temple-church in the Vetus Forum of Leptis Magna has recently been re-excavated by Karl-Uwe Mahler and has been re-dated to the period of Justinian's reconquest in the middle third of the sixth century.[121] Considering the temple conversions dated by a majority of scholars to fourth–fifth century, our analysis will be confined to the temple of Ceres-church at Thuburbo Maius, church I at Thamugadi, the temple of Asclepius-church at Djebel Oust, and church III (so-called Basilica of Servus) at Sufetula.

---

[117] Sears, "Fate of Temples," p. 229.

[118] F. W. Deichmann, "Frühchristliche Kirchen in antiken Heiligtümern," *Jahrbuch des Deutschen Archaiologichen Instituts* 54 (1939): 105–136.

[119] Hanson, "Pagan Temples."

[120] Sears, "Fate of Temples," pp. 251–252.

[121] Note that preliminary findings led to the conclusion that "the church was built almost entirely of spolia. Most of them come from the buildings in the forum" (Karl-Uwe Mahler, "The Church in the Old Forum of Leptis Magna. A Preliminary Report," in *For the Preservation of the Cultural Heritage in Libya: A Dialogue among Institutions: Proceedings of Conference, 1–2 July 2011,* ed. Serenella Ensoli and Fabrizio Serra, pp. 49–53 (Garda, VR, Italy: Studio Bibliografico Bosazzi, 2012), p. 51). Unembellished limestone blocks were reused from the adjacent, defunct Magna Mater temple, while more decorative elements were taken from the Arch of Trajan, which had fallen into disrepair.

Temple of Ceres-church at Thuburbo Maius

The city of Thuburbo Maius in Proconsularis (El Fahs, Tunisia) received its status as a *municipium* under the emperor Hadrian and later, under Commodus, became a *colonia*. Its name indicates Berber origins, and early settlement remains attest to a period of Punic occupation.[122] The Temple of Ceres, located about 200 m south east of the forum, dates to the economic boom experienced during the period spanning the last quarter of the second century to the mid-third century CE. The city center gradually declined until, in the fifth century, the forum area was refitted with small dwellings and oil presses.[123] A church adapted from the Ceres Temple has been dated to the late fourth century or early fifth century on stylistic grounds of its mosaics and *ad sanctos* burials.[124] Two of the tombs, found in the choir and courtyard of the church, have been dated to the mid-fifth century.[125] The church reused several of the temple walls and colonnades but reversed the temple's southwestern orientation, adding a synthronos in the sixth century. Also in this later period, the temple's cella was refitted as a cruciform baptistery (Figure 4.1).[126] The date of the city center's decline coincides with the church's construction, suggesting that the temple had been abandoned and had fallen into disrepair before Christians seized the

---

[122] Aïcha Ben Abed, *Tunisian Mosaics: Treasures from Roman Africa*, Conservation and Cultural Heritage (Getty Conservation Institute, 2006), p. 62.

[123] Stephen Roskams, "The Urban Transition in the Maghreb," *Early Medieval Towns in the Western Mediterranean: Ravello, 22–24 September 1994*. Documenti di archeologia 10, ed. Gian Pietro Brogiolo (Mantua: Editrice S.A.P., 1996): 43–54, p. 48.

[124] M. A. Alexander, A. Ben Abed-Ben Khader, M. Ennaifer, and M. Spiro, *Corpus des mosaïques des Tunisie. 2.2: Thuburbo Majus, les mosaïques de la région des grands thermes* (Tunis: Institut national d'archéologie et d'arts, 1985), p. 55.

[125] Andrew Merrills and Richard Miles, *The Vandals* (Malden, MA: Wiley-Blackwell, 2010), p. 83. The mosaic epitaph of Arifridos is too fragmentary to reconstruct anything but his name, that he lived to at least twenty years old, and that he was interred during the ides of November (ILCV 2652). See Philipp von Rummel, "Les Vandales ont-ils porté en Afrique une vêtement spécifique?" in *La Méditerranée et le monde mérovingien: témoins archéologiques. Actes des XXIIIs Journées internationales d'archéologie merovingienne, Arles, 11–13 octobre 2002*, ed. Xavier Delestre, Patrick Périn and Michel Kazanski, pp. 281–291 (Aix-en-Provence: Assoc. Française d'Archéologie Mérovingienne, 2005). However, competing interpretations of the sartorial remains as either late Roman or Vandal complicate the dating (Merrills and Miles, *Vandals*, p. 272 note 4). A dissenting view is proposed by Alexandre Lézine, who dates the epitaphs, and hence the church, to the sixth century (Alexandre Lézine, *Thuburbo Maius* (Tunis: Société Tunisienne de Diffusion, 1968), pp. 24–25, cited in Leone, *Pagan City*, p. 71). Leone also dates the mosaic floor to the beginning of the sixth century (*Changing Townscapes*, p. 250).

[126] Noël Duval, "Église et Temple en Afrique du Nord. Note sur les installations Chrétiennes dans les temples à cour à propos de l'église dite de Servus à Sbeitla," *Bulletin archéologique du Comité des travaux historiques et scientifiques*. n.s.7 (1971): 265–296, as summarized in Milojevic, "Retrofit Ecclesia," p. 352.

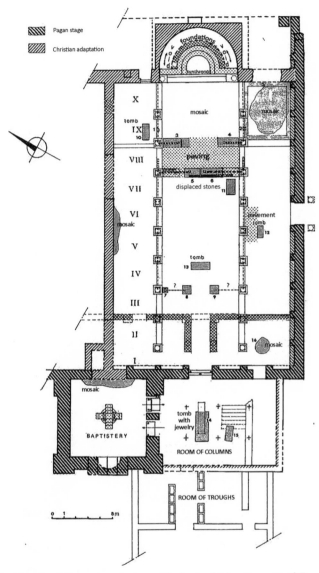

Figure 4.1 Temple of Ceres-church plan at Thuburbo Maius. From Noël Duval, "Église et Temple en Afrique du Nord. Note sur les installations Chrétiennes dans les temples à cour à propos de l'église dite de Servus à Sbeitla," *Bulletin archéologique du Comité des travaux historiques et scientifiques. New Series* 7 (1971): 265–296, fig. 11. BnF. Reproduced with permission.

opportunity to reconstruct a moderately sized (15 m x 30 m) church on the site. Leone assigns the initial church construction to the Vandal period, situating it within the broader pattern of architectural reuse evident during that time: "[B]uildings were reused because they were free, and easy to change."[127] Rather than understanding the Thuburbo temple-church as evidence of late Roman architectural dispossession, then, most recent assessments regard the transformation of this Roman temple into a Christian church as belonging to the Vandal and Byzantine period of reuse of defunct or dilapidated Roman structures. Therefore, it does not contribute to our understanding of late Roman architectural dispossession.

Church I at Thamugadi (Timgad, Algeria)

Emperor Trajan established the colony of Thamugadi (Timgad, Algeria) in 100 CE. The city prospered until the fourth century, when economic hardship forced civic leaders to default on their munificences.[128] Christianity flourished, as evidenced by the presence of wealthy Christian clergy in the *ordo* and the eleven basilicas constructed over the course of the fourth through sixth centuries.[129] The church under consideration is located southeast of the city center, near the gate to the road to Lambaesis, in the northwestern part of the Christian necropolis (#1 on the plan, Figure 3.3, in the previous chapter).[130] The irregularly shaped apsidal church, measuring 28.6 m x 36.43 m, contains three aisles of five bays, separated by two rows of supports (Figure 4.2).[131] Two elements suggest that the church, like most others in North Africa, memorialized its special dead: a pillared crypt was built under the apse and one of the two sacristies; and a sarcophagus containing a handful of children's bones was buried beneath a paved surface enclosed by a chancel located toward the middle of the nave, to the right of the longitudinal axis.[132] The mid-twentieth-century excavator Marcel Christofle surmised that an altar had once stood in the chancel, subsequently suggesting to archaeologist and historian Paul-Albert Février that this was a martyrological commemoration. That an exterior door or courtyard provided visitors with direct access to the crypt via two adjoining

---

[127] Leone, *Changing Townscapes*, pp. 154, 208–209, 211.
[128] *Cod. theod.* 6.22.2.
[129] Sears, *Late Roman African Urbanism*, pp. 60–61.
[130] Gui, Duval, and Caillet, *Basiliques chrétiennes d'afrique du nord*, vol. 1, p. 263.
[131] Gui, Duval, and Caillet, *Basiliques chrétiennes*, p. 264.
[132] Gui, Duval, and Caillet, *Basiliques chrétiennes*, p. 265.

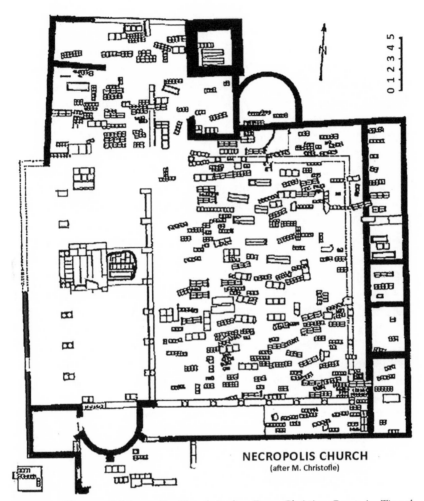

Figure 4.2 Thamugadi Necropolis Church I plan. From Christian Courtois, *Timgad. Antique Thamugadi* (Algiers: Imprimerie Officielle, 1961), p. 65.

rooms without going through the church proper suggests that, in addition to functioning as a memorial, the church may have also served as a pilgrimage site, albeit on a much smaller scale than other such churches (like Carthage's Damous El Karita, first built at the turn of the fifth century but substantially expanded and refurbished twice in the next two centuries, and the sixth century Bir Ftouha).[133]

---

[133] Heimo Dolenz, *Damous El Karita* (Vienna: Wien Österreichisches Archäologisches Institut, 2001); Susan Stevens, Angela V. Kalinowski, and Hans VanderLeest, *Bir Ftouha: A*

Although the retrofit nature of the building's architectural design (particularly of the building's façade) made Gui "wonder whether the church had not been installed in a temple," we must recall that the church is located over 900 meters (0.56 miles) from the city center. Such a remote location raises questions about what kind of temple would have been located on such a site, and what possible significance building a church on top of it might have had. If it had served as a processional temple in one of the city's annual civic festivals, its appropriation as a church might have been tremendously meaningful to both pagan and Christian residents of Timgad. We could imagine the kind of supersessionist rhetoric invoked by fourth-century Christian authors trumpeting the architectural transformation in religiopolitically triumphalistic terms. If, on the other hand, the building was a less significant feature of both the late antique landscape and ritual, then perhaps the renovation attracted little attention and was regarded like any number of the other architectural adaptations occurring during this era of urban transformation. Unfortunately no additional evidence exists to help decide this question. In the face of insufficient evidence, however, scholars are not justified in assuming the first theoretical scenario presented previously as the default pattern merely because a few Christian authors described the Christian–pagan relationship in adversarial, victorious terms. The phenomenon is sufficiently rare for us to reconsider it as the default when we encounter archaeological strata of a church on top of an earlier temple structure in this pre-Byzantine period of late antiquity, as the remaining examples from Djebel Oust and Sbeitla demonstrate.

Temple of Asclepius-church Djebel Oust

A baths complex at Djebel Oust, a hot springs at the foot of the Zaghouan mountain located 38 km southwest of Carthage on the road to Bulla Regia, contains a temple to Asclepius that was adapted into a church.[134] Although the temple cella containing the natural spring was refurbished into a baptistery, the quadrafoil mosaic and synthronos indicate a Byzantine date. The western sanctuary, however, may date to the fifth century (Figure 4.3). The two rooms on either side of the apse may have been used for baptismal purposes prior to the construction of the southern baptistery. This choice

Pilgrimage Church Complex at Carthage, JRA Supplementary Series 59 (Portsmouth, RI: Journal of Roman Archaeology, 2005).
[134] Duval, "Église et Temple," pp. 290–292. See also Leone, *Pagan City,* pp. 71–72, who has redrawn Duval's figure with the compass inadvertently reversed.

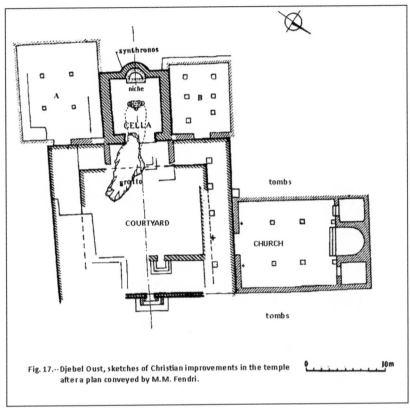

Fig. 17.--Djebel Oust, sketches of Christian improvements in the temple after a plan conveyed by M.M. Fendri.

Figure 4.3 Plan of Temple of Asclepius-church Djebel Oust. From Noël Duval, "Église et Temple en Afrique du Nord. Note sur les installations Chrétiennes dans les temples à cour à propos de l'église dite de Servus à Sbeitla," *Bulletin archéologique du Comité des travaux historiques et scientifiques. New Series* 7 (1971): 265–296, fig. 17. BnF. Reproduced with permission.

of location may have resulted from an initial avoidance of the Asclepian spring and reluctance to "Christianize the healing water."[135] As we saw with Augustine's correspondence with Publicola, Christian aversion to sites associated with pagan gods relied on their active usage. Unlike temples which, once relieved of their statues were no longer actively venerated, natural phenomena, like springs, presented no such obstacles to continuing worship. On the one hand, as we have seen, such an undertaking could symbolize the demise of the old traditional cults and the success of the newer Christian worship. Conversely, some Christians perceived the old space to

[135] Duval, "Église et Temple," p. 292.

be haunted by demons of the old cults, for such demons were thought to cling particularly tenaciously to their prior residence. The rhetoric of spatial supersession worked to help assuage such anxieties so that the necessary task of construction could forge ahead unencumbered by this ambivalence. By the sixth century, however, such inhibitions are no longer evident.

Church III (so-called Basilica of Servus) at Sufetula

Located in the high steppes region of Tunisia, at the junction of highways leading from the northern plains to the southern oases and from the low steppes and the sahel to the mountains of the interior, Sufetula (Sbeitla, Tunisia) in the province of Byzacena was established, or already extant, during the rule of Vespasian.[136] The city, whose entrance is marked by a triumphal gateway, contained a forum, capitolium, amphitheater, and baths. Church III is situated on the street to the forum, about 50 m east of the Arch of Antoninus. It was built inside a former third-century temple dedicated to an unidentified deity. Tunisian archaeologist Fathi Bejaoui dates the building to "the end of the Byzantine period" based on the iconography of the four stone sarcophagi found in the apse, one of which bore the name of a presbyter by the name of Servus.[137] The new church reused the temple's external *temenos* wall and was repositioned to a north-west orientation.[138] Like the church at Thuburbo, this structure also refashioned the temple *cella* into its baptistery (Figure 4.4).[139] By this late date, the end of the Byzantine period, it is highly unlikely that the church's adaptation of the temple site indicates any forcible seizure or hostile transformation. Repurposing of abandoned buildings was a common urban practice in the late antique and Byzantine periods. It was at that time, for example, that the gateway complex was adapted into a citadel. In fact, the church of Servus was not the first Christian building in Sufetula to reuse previous Roman construction. In the fourth century church IV, located adjacent to the Capitolium, was built using an earlier porticoed monument.[140] It is quite

[136] *The Princeton Encyclopedia of Classical Sites*, ed. Richard Stillwell, William L. MacDonald, and Marian Holland McAllister, (Princeton, NJ: Princeton University Press, 1976), electronic edition at perseus.tufts.edu.

[137] Fathi Bejaoui, "Nouvelles données archéologiques à Sbeïtla," *Africa* 14 (1996): 37–64, p. 40; *AE* 1912: 295 = *ILCV* 1:1185.

[138] Duval, "Église et Temple," as summarized in Milojevic, "Retrofit Ecclesia," p. 351.

[139] Duval, "Église et Temple," as summarized in Milojevic, "Retrofit Ecclesia," pp. 351–352.

[140] Bejaoui, "Sbeïtla," pp. 43, 47.

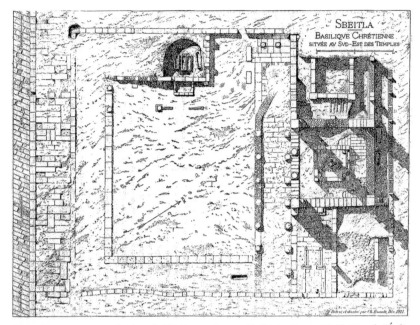

Figure 4.4 Drawing of Church III Excavation at Sufetula. From Noël Duval, "Église et Temple en Afrique du Nord. Note sur les installations Chrétiennes dans les temples à cour à propos de l'église dite de Servus à Sbeitla," *Bulletin archéologique du Comité des travaux historiques et scientifiques. New Series* 7 (1971): 265–296, fig. 4. BnF. Reproduced with permission.

likely, therefore, that the Servus church was yet another in a series of mundane transformations of the shifting landscape that reflected the gradual changes of late antiquity.

Conclusion

Christian reuse of temples conformed to the general urban program of late antiquity. As Lepelley has demonstrated, economic pressures – particulary in the provinces – inspired Roman legislation that repeatedly instructed governors to favor restoration and renovation over new construction.[141] The same economic and legal constraints governed Christian building choices, yet reuse created problems for Christians who still perceived temples as "kingdoms of idols [and] kingdoms of demons."[142] As we have seen, in

---

[141] Lepelley, *Les cités de l'Afrique* I, p. 62.
[142] Aug. *Enarrat. Ps.* 98.14 (CCL 39: 1392): *Regna idolorum, regna daemoniorum.*

most cases these temples had lain derelict for some time before they were refurbished as churches. The Christian narrative of hostile takeover, therefore, was not a journalistic report of events as they had transpired. Quite the contrary: it was a new narrative formulated to reconstruct persistent perceptions of sacred space and allow Christians to accept refurbished temples as appropriate sites for their holy purposes. This narrative introduced the conception that a temple had to be deconsecrated, or destroyed, before it could be used for Christian rites.[143]

Yet the narrative did more than that: it also addressed those Christians who clung to their traditional Roman religious practices and values. Jan Vaes has emphasized the continuity of those sites that were adapted from temple to church: "they constituted an already familiar setting for the Christianized population."[144] On an experiential level, this continuity represented a seamless transition for a population that was used to congregating at these particular locations for worship. All the more reason for their clergy to interpret the architectural adaptation as spatial supersession, as the defeat of the old gods by the new: to exorcise the perception of demons from the former religion and to dispel any misconceptions the populace might have entertained that their Christian practices were merely, so to speak, "old wine" in "new wineskins." Construing architectural displacement as symbolizing the battle between Christianity and paganism, as a clash of opposites, with Christianity triumphant, worked to drive pagan notions of sacred space out of the church and replace former place meanings with new ones. These new place meanings, shared by those who lived them, drew from the well of biblical symbolism and long-established rhetorical traditions of spatial supersessionism. Like a cleaver that both separates and binds, the providentialist, triumphal narrative was part of a rhetorical program that sought to theologize the shifting landscape of the late antique North African city and assuage Christian anxieties about distinguishing themselves from their religious "others." If practitioners of Roman traditional religion represented Christians' internal, fraternal "others," as their own former identifications or family members, Jews represented Christians' religious, fraternal "others"; slightly more distant, yet perhaps more threatening because of their ancestral claim to the Old Testament. The next chapter examines this Jewish–Christian spatial relationship.

---

[143] Vaes, "Riutilizzazione cristiana," p. 23.
[144] Vaes, "Riutilizzazione cristiana," p. 23.

5

CHRISTIAN SUPERSESSION
OF SYNAGOGUES

I T IS OFTEN CLAIMED THAT, beginning in the fourth century, attacks on synagogues throughout the Roman empire became increasingly frequent.[1] The recorded incidents in North Africa are fewer when compared with the evidence from the northern and eastern Mediterranean. This may be due to the paucity of evidence rather than historical reality. There are no extant literary works produced by Jews of late Roman North Africa. Perhaps due to the dearth of evidence as well, scholarly treatment of the topic of Jewish–Christian relations in North Africa has suffered from tendencies to generalize from other Jewish experiences across the Roman empire and from overreliance on literary sources, which are both Christian and numerous. This chapter explores North African Jewish perceptions of worship space as expressed in archaeology, as well as examples of architectural dispossession and literary accounts of spatial supersession.

Synagogues as Holy Spaces

The earliest evidence for North African synagogue buildings is found in the Christian literary corpus.[2] Noting the caveats of using such polemical material, nevertheless it is useful for establishing Christian perceptions of Jewish worship space and what might have motivated their attacks on such sites.[3] Like the word *ecclesia*, the word *synagoga* refers originally to

[1] See, for example, Amnon Linder, *The Jews in Roman Imperial Legislation* (Detroit, MI: Wayne State University Press, 1983: 1987), pp. 73–74. Some of the material presented in this chapter was previously published in the *Journal of Ancient Judaism* 4.3 ("Inventing Synagogue Conversion").
[2] Thesaurus Linguae Latinae *synagoga*.
[3] See especially Karen B. Stern, *Inscribing Devotion and Death: Archaeological Evidence for Jewish Populations of North Africa* (Boston, MA: E. J. Brill, 2008), pp. 25–31.

a community and subsequently to the building where it gathered. The earliest writers use the word either in the former sense or to refer to New Testament-era synagogues, with some notable exceptions: Tertullian describes contemporary synagogue structures that have been dispersed among the gentiles as devoid of the Holy Spirit, in contrast to both the ancient Jerusalem temple and Christ; the third-century North African poet Commodianus accuses pagans of hedging their bets by attending rites in synagogues as well as Roman temples; and an early-fifth-century letter from Hippo attributed to Augustine appealing to dissident Christians for solidarity against Jews notes that Jews do not read the letters of Paul in their synagogues.[4] As was the case of the anti-dissident materials discussed

---

[4] Tert. *Adv. Jud.* 13.15, tr. Geoffrey D. Dunn, *Tertullian* (New York: Routledge, 2004), p. 69 (CCL 2: 1388): *Indubitate non recipiendo christum, fontem aquae vitae, lacus contritos coeperunt habere, id est synagogas, in dispersione scilicet gentium, in quibus iam spiritus sanctus non immoratur, ut in praeteritum in templo commorabatur ante adventum christi, qui est verum dei templum* (Without doubt, by not receiving Christ, the fountain of the water of life (Rev. 21.6), they have begun to possess worn-out troughs – that is, the synagogues among the scattering of the Gentiles. The Holy Spirit does not now remain in them, as it used to dwell in the temple in the past, before the coming of Christ, who is the true temple of God); Commodianus, *Instructiones* 1.24 "Inter Utrumque Viventibus" (CCL 128: 19): *Quid in sinagoga decurris saepe bifarius? / Ut tibi misericors fiat, quem denegas ultro? / Exis inde foris, iterum tu fana requiris; / Vis inter utrumque vivere, sed inde peribis* ("To Those Who Live In-between:" Why do you, bet-hedger, race down frequently to the synagogue? So that the one whom you wantonly deny might act mercifully toward you? After that you go out to the forum, again you seek temples; You want to live between the two, but thus you will die). My dating of Commodianus is from Jean-Michel Poinsotte (*Commodien. Instructions*, Collection des Universités de France (Paris: Les Belles Lettres, 2009), p. xv), but there is no scholarly consensus due to the paucity of evidence; some scholars date him to the fifth century (following Heinrich Brewer, *Kommodian von Gaza. Ein Arelatensischer Laiendichter aus der Mitte des fünften Jahrhunders* (Paderborn: F. Schöningh, 1906), pp. 1–28); Aug. *Unit. eccl.* (= *Ad catholicos de secta Donatistarum*) 6.11 (CSEL 52: 243): *quid ad haec dicitis? an iudaeorum nobis cum perversitate contenditis, ut dicatis in solo populo nato ex carne abrahae intellegendum semen abrahae? sed iudaei paulum apostolum non legunt in synagogis suis, quem vos legitis in conventiculis vestris. quid ergo dicat apostolus audiamus – quaerimus enim iam quemadmodum intellegendum sit semen abrahae* ... (What do you say to this [Gen 22.16–18]? Do you struggle with the stubbornness of the Jews against us, and would you declare that the "race of Abraham" should be understood as only people born of the flesh of Abraham? But the Jews do not read the apostle Paul in their synagogues, which you read in your conventicles. Therefore, let us hear what the Apostle says, for now we are explicating how the "race of Abraham" should be understood). The author goes on to quote Galatians 3:15 concerning the gentiles being covenanted in by Christ to receive god's biblical promises. Stern's discussion of Commodianus, *Instructiones* 1.37 in *Inscribing Devotion* (p. 27) disregards this reference to the synagogue when asserting: "Commodian makes no mention here of synagogues – the buildings to which one would expect reference if the offenders in question were attracted to both Judaism and Christianity." While it is true that the particular passage she discusses does not include such a reference, the passage from 1.24 cited earlier demonstrates that Commodianus had the synagogue in mind.

in Chapter 3, counter-reading against these authors' biases allows us to draw some tentative conclusions.[5]

It is likely that Tertullian portrays synagogues as lacking the divine presence in order to counter non-Jewish perception of synagogues as holy, where they could find the presence of God.[6] Commodianus may compare the synagogue to pagan sanctuaries because some North Africans perceived them both as providing access to the divine powers that bestowed blessings and were therefore willing to patronize both. These readings are only tentative, however, because there are no Jewish literary sources to corroborate them, and because the term *synagoga* is not uniquely Jewish, as Augustine acknowledges in his sermons on the Psalms:[7] "It is true that 'Asaph' means 'synagogue,' which is a 'congregation' or 'assembly,' and that name is more often used for the nation of the Jews, but one can also call this *ecclesia* a congregation, just as the earlier people is also called an *ecclesia*."[8]

Archaeological evidence, though appallingly meager, supports this perception of the synagogue as a special, revered place. Excavators of Roman North Africa have only identified two synagogues, the second of which is uncertain, at Naro (Hammam Lif, Tunisia), and Lepcis Magna (Khoms, Libya).[9] Just as Christian architectural dispossession and the concomitant

---

[5] See Charles Bobertz, "'For the Vineyard of the Lard of Hosts as the House of Israel': Cyprian of Carthage and the Jews," *Jewish Quarterly Review* 82 (1991): 1–15; Paula Fredriksen, "Excaecati Occulta Justitia Dei: Augustine on the Jews and Judaism," *Journal of Early Christian Studies* 2 (1995): 299–324, and *Augustine and the Jews* (New York: Doubleday, 2008).

[6] Compare the anti-synagogue preaching of John Chrysostom (Christine Shepardson, "Controlling Contested Places: John Chrysostom's Adversus Iudaeos Homilies and the Spatial Politics of Religious Controversy," *JECS* 15.4 (Winter, 2007): 483–516 and Shepardson, *Controlling Contested Places. Late Antique Antioch and the Spatial Politics of Religious Controversy* (University of California Press, 2014), pp. 92–128).

[7] Augustine's response to the Pelagian Julian of Eclanum's eight-volume critique of the bishop of Hippo's Catholic orthodoxy includes a quotation about public eating and Christian (orthodox) debates staged "in the forum or in meeting places (*synagogae*)" (*C. Iul.* 4.37, tr. Hill (I/25, p. 416) (PL 45: 1356): *comede igitur in foro, aut in synagogis, in quibus disputationes tuae personant ...*).

[8] Aug. *Enarrat. Ps.* 78.3 (CCL 39): *quamquam enim Asaph synagoga interpretetur, quae est congregatio, idque nomen usitatius insederit genti Iudaeorum, tamen et ecclesiam istam posse dici congregationem, et illum veterem populum dictum esse ecclesiam.* See also *Enarrat. Ps.* 73.1, 77.3, and 81.1.

[9] Other synagogue locations draw on synagogue titles in epitaphs. See, for example, Edmond Frezouls for Volubilis, near Meknes, Morocco ("Une synagogue juive atteste à Volubilis," *Acta of the 5th International Congress of Greek and Latin Epigraphy, 1967* (Oxford: Blackwell Publishers, 1971), pp. 287–292), to which Hirschberg adds a bronze lamp decorated with a *menorah* motif, possibly in the Rebat Museum (Haim Zeev Hirschberg, *A History of the Jews in North Africa: From Antiquity to the Sixteenth Century* vol. 1 (Leiden: E. J. Brill, 1974), p. 52). John Lund posits the existence of a synagogue at Carthage on the basis of lamps decorated with the menorah motifs (Hayes types I and II,

rhetorical production of spatial supersessionism relied for their power on place meanings of and attachments to Christian sites, a similar relationship may be cautiously discerned in the case of synagogues. Although the changing perception of Christian spatial valuation could be easily traced through literary and material remains, there is no comparable body of evidence for the Jewish context. Rather, the dedicatory inscription of the one excavated synagogue at Naro offers merely a glimpse of how North African Jews might have regarded their synagogues. We must rely on a comparison of this space to other North African buildings, on other North African Jewish inscriptions, as well as on non-Jewish literature for general conclusions.[10]

As noted in the Introduction, archaeological evidence is not only sparse but poorly excavated and ill-preserved. The interpretive challenges of the Naro synagogue excavation are thoroughly summarized by Stern and will not be repeated here.[11] Like other worship spaces in late antique North Africa dating to the fourth through sixth centuries, the synagogue developed in stages from a residential building, to an assembly hall, than to an audience-chamber.[12] Recent scholarship dates the well-known dedicatory mosaic to this final phase of construction, namely the sixth century.[13] The identification of the inscription as Jewish is justified not only by its reference to the building as "synagogue," but by its use of the menorah symbol associated with Jews throughout the Mediterranean in its medallions' iconography (Figure 5.1).

The menorah is also used in North African Jewish epitaphs and oil lamps from elsewhere.[14] Although the menorah may not be an exclusively Jewish symbol, it does appear in contexts where it seems to be adding meaning and value to the objects it adorns.[15] The fact that North African Jewish

Deneauve VIIB, VIIIB and XIA; "A Synagogue at Carthage? Menorah-lamps from the Danish Excavations" *JRA* 8 (1995): 245–262; *Karthago: Die Ergebnisse der Hamburger Grabung unter dem Decumanus maximus*, Hamburger Forschungen zur Archäologie 2 (Mainz: Philipp von Zabern, 2007), p. 614).

[10] Stern, *Inscribing Devotion.*

[11] Stern, *Inscribing Devotion*, pp. 193–197, 201–202, 216–218.

[12] Stern, *Inscribing Devotion*, pp. 203–216.

[13] J.-P. Darmon, "Les mosaïques de la synagogue de Hammam Lif: un reexamen du dossier," in, *Fifth International Colloquium on Ancient Mosaics* (Bath, England, on September 5–12, 1987), vol. 2, ed. Peter Johnson, Roger Ling, and David J. Smith, pp. 7–29, *JRA Supplementary Series* 9 (Portsmouth, RI: Journal of Roman Archaeology), and Stern, *Inscribing Devotion*, p. 195. This contradicts earlier scholarship which dated it to the fourth century (e.g. James B. Rives, *Religion and Authority in Roman Carthage. From Augustus to Constantine* (Oxford University Press, 1995), p. 216).

[14] Le Bohec no. 20, 23, 24, cited in Stern, *Inscribing Devotion*, p. 10, n. 11 and p. 263; Rachel Hachlili, *Ancient Jewish Art and Archaeology in the Diaspora* (Boston, MA: Brill, 1998), p. 374.

[15] Stern, *Inscribing Devotion*, pp. 273–274, 306; Steven Fine, "When is a Menorah 'Jewish'?: On the Complexities of a Symbol During the Age of Transition," in *Age of Transition: Byzantine*

Figure 5.1 *Revue archéologique. La Mosaïque de Hammam-Lif. Inscription de la grande salle*, 1884. Ser. 3, vol. 3, pl. IX, X (Paris: Ernest Leroux, 1883–1884). Brooklyn Museum Libraries. Wilbour Library of Egyptology. Reprinted with permission.

epitaphs sometimes picture *menorot* along with an incense shovel, a sacrificial implement used in the Jerusalem temple, as well as a palm branch and ram's horn, ritual objects once associated with the temple but thought to have carried over into synagogue worship, suggests that temple images conveyed esteem to the sites they adorned. Steven Fine maintains that synagogue holiness derives from the holy things they contained, most notably the Scriptures.[16] This sensibility is strikingly similar to dissident Christian views of worship space, as we saw in Chapter 2, where Christians went to great lengths to protect their Scriptures from Roman authorities because the texts were regarded as sacred. Although the limitations of our evidence prevent us from concluding definitively that such attitudes prevailed among North African Jews, the evidence we do have suggests that these views are highly likely. The particular Naro dedication supports a perception of the synagogue as a privileged, distinctive space.

Although the Latin text of the mosaic presents some interpretive difficulties, the dedication can be construed as: "Your servant Iulia NaP tiled (this mosaic) for the sacred synagogue of Naro, for the sake of her salvation, from her own coffers."[17] Most pertinent to our discussion is the use of *sancta* to modify *sinagoga*.[18] Like the contemporaneous church inscriptions

Culture in the Islamic World, ed. Helen C. Evans, pp. 34–53 (New Haven, CT: Yale University Press, 2015).

[16] Steven Fine, *This Holy Place* (Notre Dame, IN: University of Notre Dame Press, 1997), p. 33.

[17] Stern, *Inscribing Devotion*, p. 240: Sancta[m] Sinagoga[m] Naron pro salut[e] su[a] ancilla tua Iulia NaP de suo prop[r]i[o] tesselavit. Note that Stern's transcription unnecessarily adapts the grammar of the original Latin to Classical forms, and therefore is an interpretation rather than an actual transcription. This adaptation is not necessary, since there are examples of "pro" taking the accusative in other inscriptions (e.g. *Inscr. Grut.* 4.12; 46.9; *Inscr. Orell.* 2360, listed in Lewis and Short, s.v. "pro"; *Corpus Cultus Equitis Thracii – Ccet: Moesia Inferior*, ed. Nubar Hampartumian and Manfred Oppermann, #64b, dated 152 CE; and AE 1949: 122).

[18] See Stern's discussion of the difficulties associated with this term (*Inscribing Devotion*, pp. 222–223).

that describe basilicas in the same way, this adjective, combined with the expense of the synagogue's construction and ornamentation (explicitly mentioned in the inscription), reflects the dedicant's regard for the building's privileged status, its place meaning, and place attachment.[19] This place meaning and place attachment are corroborated by small finds at Naro, such as decorated building fragments and clay lamps, and the synagogue's other two donor inscriptions, one of which dedicates an entire room for synagogue implements (*instrumenta*).[20] The perceptual-symbolism of North African synagogues included temple memory, salvation vehicle, sacred storage, and ritual arena.

Attitudes toward Synagogues in Roman Legislation

Polemical portraits of synagogues, like those of Tertullian and Augustine previously discussed, were rooted in Christians' need to distinguish themselves from Jews.[21] These literary representations have led generations of

---

[19] The absence of any earlier North African inscriptions bearing the term "synagogue" with an adjective that reveals fourth-century Jewish attitudes toward worship space raises the question whether the Hammam Lif inscription might reflect the influence of later Byzantine aesthetics. However, as early as the second-century BCE, in nearby Alexandria, an inscription refers to the area in which the synagogue stood as a "sacred precinct" (ὁ ἱερὸς περίβολος), and in Arsinoë-Crocodilopolis, a documentary papyrus designated the land on which a synagogue stood as "sacred land" (ἱερὰ γῆ; JIGRE 9 (= CIJ 2.1433) and CPJ 1.134, discussed in Aryeh Kasher, "Synagogues as 'Houses of Prayer' and 'Holy Places' in the Jewish Communities of Hellenistic and Roman Egypt," in *Ancient Synagogues: Historical Analysis and Archaeological Discovery*, ed. Dan Urman and Paul V. M. Flesher, pp. 205–220 (Leiden: E. J. Brill, 1995), p. 216. The longstanding attitude of Egyptian Jews toward their synagogues and their use for Jewish political purposes made them prime targets of Alexandrian violence, as reported by the statesman-philosopher Philo who experienced it first-hand (*In Flaccum* 48). Philo describes the worship areas of the ascetic contemplative community of Therapeutae as σεμνεῖα (revered places) and as ἱερά (holy places), the same word used to describe God's word and law (λόγος and νόμος); Philo, *Contemp.* 25, 32; *Spec.* 2.23 and 3.119, for example. See the discussion of Celia Deutsch, "The Therapeutae, Text Work, Ritual, and Mystical Experience," in *Paradise Now: Essays on Early Jewish and Christian Mysticism*, ed. April DeConick, pp. 287–312 (Atlanta, GA: Society of Biblical Literature, 2006), pp. 295–296). Drawing on the ritual theory of Catherine Bell, Deutsch has shown that the production and use of texts as ritual objects both required structured space and conveyed holiness to the arenas where such activities took place. Aryeh Kasher has argued that the sanctity of Egyptian synagogues derived from their functional resemblance to the Jerusalem temple as houses of worship, i.e. prayer and Torah-reading ("Synagogues as 'Houses of Prayer', p. 206).

[20] CIL 8.1247b and 8.12547c.

[21] To see this dynamic of differentiation through the technique of sexual slander, see Susanna Drake, *Slandering the Jew: Sexuality and Difference in Early Christian Texts* (Philadelphia, PA: University of Pennsylvania Press, 2013).

modern scholars "to presuppose that the traditions of anti-Judaism so characteristic of late Roman Christian rhetoric translated, as it did in the later
medieval and modern periods, into active and generalized anti-Semitism," as
Paula Fredriksen has duly noted.[22] Rather, Fredriksen proposes that, when
read correctly, these very polemical sources attest to "the vitality of habitual contacts, both social and religious, between Christians and Jews ...."[23]
The example she highlights, Augustine's legal judgment in the case of the
Jew Licinius, shows how, more than any tradition of religiously hostile rhetoric, the everyday lives of North Africans were influenced by centuries-old
Roman social norms of conventional coexistence.[24]

Unlike other parts of the empire, where some Christians trumpeted their
conversion of Jews, North Africa seemed preoccupied with other interreligious dynamics. This situation is illustrated by the difference between
how the relics of the protomartyr Stephen were received in Palestine and
Minorca as opposed to North Africa. According to an encyclical written
around 415, the relics were discovered in Jerusalem through an apparition
of the Jewish sage Gamaliel in a series of dreams to a Christian priest.[25]
After reporting the location to the bishop and patriarch of the holy city,
the unearthing of the relics was accompanied by an earthquake, miraculous
healings, and great ceremony, then subsequently distributed throughout the
Mediterranean.[26] The letter also characterizes Stephen as the first warrior
in "the Lord's wars against the Jews."[27] The relics of this warrior against the
Jews arrived in Spain and North Africa. In Minorca, according to a letter
circulated in 418 by the island's bishop, Severus, the protomartyr's relics
incited the miraculous conversion of some 540 Jews and the refurbishing of
their fire-damaged synagogue into a church.[28]

---

[22] Paula Fredriksen, *Augustine and the Jews*, p. 98.

[23] Fredriksen, *Augustine and the Jews*, p. 101.

[24] Fredriksen, *Augustine and the Jews*, p. 352.

[25] *Epistola Luciani ad omnem ecclesiam de revelatione corporis Stephani Martyris primi et aliorum* (PL 41: 807–818).

[26] The encyclical transformed Gamaliel, identified in Acts 22:3 as the teacher of Paul, into a devout, model Christian. *Epistola Luciani* 3 (PL 41: 809): *Ego Gamaliel compatiens Christi ministro, et festinans habere mercedem et partem cum sancto viro in fide ... Et hunc ego Gamaliel quasi persecutionem pro Christo passum ...* (I am Gamaliel, suffering with the service of Christ, eager for a reward and a portion with the holy man in faith ... And I Gamaliel suffered this as persecution for Christ ...).

[27] *Epistola Luciani* 6 (PL 41: 813): *... qui primum adversum Judaeos dominica bella bellavit ...*

[28] *Epistula Severi* in Scott Bradbury, *Severus of Minorca: Letter on the Conversion of the Jews*, Oxford Early Christian Texts (New York: Oxford University Press, 1996). On the stoning of Stephen (Acts 7:54–60), see Shelly Matthews, *Perfect Martyr: The Stoning of Stephen and the Construction of Christian Identity* (New York: Oxford University Press, 2010).

Unlike Palestine and Minorca, North Africa's reaction to the miracles associated with the newly imported relics did not focus on their conversionary effect on Jews. Around 423, the relics of Stephen were brought from Palestine to Africa under the direction of Euodius, bishop at Uzalis.[29] Events which clergy deemed to be authentic and attributed to the work of the martyrs were recorded in writing and subsequently read aloud in church.[30] By 423/424 Augustine oversaw a transport of Stephen relics from Hippo to the diocese of bishop Quintilianus by two consecrated women: the widow Galla and her daughter Simpliciola, a consecrated virgin.[31]

Completely unrelated to their association with Jews, the growing fervor over the relics was not universally accepted. According to Augustine, Aurelius in Carthage had not implemented the practice of recording the miracles, despite the circulation of the encyclical letter by Severus.[32] The reaction of Euodius' congregation to the public reading of the Severus letter in 425, although enthusiastic, prompted the bishop to conclude: "But all this is said to show the faithful in some way that it is not by chance but by a particular arrangement of God that the relics of St. Stephen were assured to arrive among us, who are greater sinners."[33] The Jews of the encyclical served as merely goads to Christian faith; they were mentioned nowhere else. Rather, Euodius emphasized miracles of healing, liberation, revelation, restored property, and demon-eviction. Even where North African Christian congregations were regaled with the miraculous Minorca tale, as far as we can tell, the message they were encouraged to take away from the story had nothing to do with Jews.

---

[29] Delehaye, "Les premiers 'libelli miraculorum,'" *Analecta Bollandiana* 29 (1910): 427–434, p. 428. Euodius recorded the miracles that occurred at Uzalis in *De miraculis sancti Stephani protomartyris* (PL 41: 833–854; see the critical edition: *Les Miracles de saint Étienne. Recherches sur le recueil pseudo-augustinien* [BHL 7860–7861] *avec édition critique, traduction et commentaire*, ed. Jean Meyers, Hagiologia. Études sur la Sainteté en Occident. Studies on Western Sainthood 5 (Turnhout: Brepols), 2006).

[30] Delehaye, "Libelli miraculorum," p. 432.

[31] Aug. *Ep.* 212. "Galla," PCA 1: 519; "Simpliciola,"PCA 1: 1085. "Quintilianus," PCA 1: 942 (no location is given).

[32] Augustine expressed indignation that Aurelius did not report miracles that were happening in Carthage (see the case of the noblewoman Innocentia, *civ. Dei* 22.8). It is curious that, at Augustine's apparent insistence, she only recounted her healing to a group of fellow elite women and not in a more public arena. Perhaps Aurelius did not approve of such publicity, and Augustine was deferring to his authority.

[33] *De miraculis sancti Stephani* 1.2 (PL 41: 835): *Verum haec dicta sint, ut commendare fratribus aliquo modo possemus, quam non utcumque et temere, sed divina dignatione ad nos quantumlibet homines peccatores, sancti Stephani reliquiae videantur pervenisse.* Shaw draws a similar conclusion (*Sacred Violence,* p. 619).

The archaeological record, as much as it allows, reveals a similar dynamic among Jews and Christians. Stern devotes significant discussion to relations between Jews and non-Jews insofar as they can be discerned from epitaphs and the remains of the synagogue at Hammam Lif.[34] Although Stern's primary purpose is to demonstrate that Jews employed largely the same motifs and language as their non-Jewish contemporaries, she notes other dimensions of their social relations throughout her analysis.

Stern introduces her study of North African Jewry by discussing a famous picture of a lamp from the Gammarth catacombs sketched by its excavator depicting a robed figure with a cross-shaped staff surrounded by a serpent atop an overturned menorah (Figure 5.2). By entertaining several alternative interpretations of the image to the ones proposed by previous scholars, Stern shows that assumptions about Jewish–Christian relations gleaned from polemical texts are unhelpful in interpreting the archaeological record.[35] Yet the absence of Jewish literature from Roman North Africa requires the current investigation to rely solely on non-Jewish literature and scant archaeological evidence.

Roman legislation provides a useful literary medium through which to view perceptions and treatment of synagogues. Considering that synagogue legislation is the type of late Roman law best categorized as case law (occasioned by particular circumstances that elicited government response, often taking the form of a "rescript"), this body of evidence suggests that the North African provinces experienced notably fewer synagogue disturbances than their northern and eastern counterparts, since there are no such laws promulgated there specifically.[36] The repetition of laws protecting

[34] Stern, *Inscribing Devotion*, pp. 51–144, 193–253.

[35] Stern, *Inscribing Devotion*, p. ix, citing E. R. Goodenough, *Jewish Symbols in the Greco-Roman Period* (New York: Pantheon Books, 1953), vol. 2 p. 201, vol. 3 p. 957; Marcel Simon, *Recherches d'histoire judéo-christienne* (Paris: Mouton, 1962), figs. 3–4; Claudia Setzer, "Jews, Jewish Christians, and Judaizers in North Africa," in *Putting Body and Soul Together: Essays in Honor of Robin Scroggs*, ed. Virginia Wiles, Alexandra Brown and Graydon Syder, pp. 185–200 (Valley Forge, PA: Trinity Press International, 1997), p. 198; and Rachel Hachlili, *The Menorah, The Ancient Seven-armed Candelabrum. Origin, Form and Significance* (Leiden-Boston-Köln: Brill, 2001), fig.VII-4, L 7.15. Also see Fine, "Menorah," pp. 47–48.

[36] John F. Matthews, *Laying Down the Law: A Study of the Theodosian Code* (New Haven, CT: Yale University Press, 2000), pp. 13, 17–18. When general laws were sent to provincial magistrates, they were adapted to fit the local situation (A. Linder, "La Loi romaine et les juifs d'Afrique du nord," in *Juifs et Judaisme en Afrique du Nord dans l'Antiquité et le Haut Moyen-age. Actes du Colloque International du Centre de Recherché et d'Études Juives et Hébraiques et du Groupe de Recherches sur l'Afrique Antique, 26–27 Septembre, 1983*, ed. Carol Iancu et Jean-Marie Lassere, pp. 57–64 (Montpellier: Université Paul Valéry, 1985), p. 58). The absence of synagogue protection laws does not correlate with

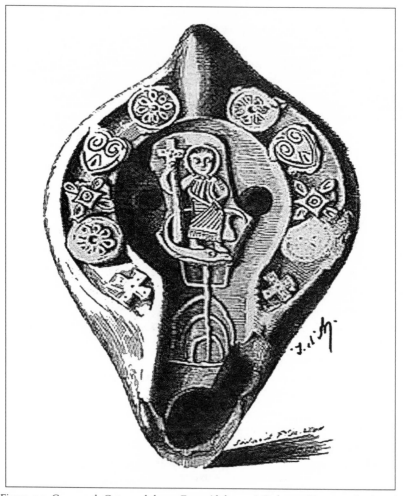

Figure 5.2 Gammarth Catacomb lamp. From Alphonse J. Delattre, *Gamart ou la nécropole juive de Carthage* (Lyon: Imprimerie Mougin-Rusand, 1895), p. 40.

synagogues from vandalism beginning in 393 have suggested to previous scholars that attacks on Jewish houses of worship escalated throughout the entire empire, including North Africa.[37] However, recent specialists of

the absence of strife. *Cod. theod.* 16.8.5 of October 335 addresses attacks on (or by) Jews who converted to Christianity ("La Loi romaine," p. 57); several laws issued between 335 and 535 attempt to prevent Jewish proselytism ("La Loi romaine," p. 60); and a law of 409 indicates that some Jews have joined other disgruntled religious groups in their attacks on North African Catholics (*Const. Sirm.* 14).

[37] See, for example, Levine, *Ancient Synagogue*, p. 211 and Leonard Rutgers, "The Synagogue as Foe in Early Christian Literature," in *"Follow the Wise:" Studies in Jewish History and Culture in Honor of Lee I. Levine*, ed. Zeev Weiss, Oded Irshai, Jodi Magness, and Seth Schwartz, pp. 449–468 (Winona Lake, IN: Eisenbrauns, 2010).

Roman law have noted that such repetition reflects more specific historical circumstances, and such generalizations are unwarranted.[38] Fergus Millar has noted:[39]

> Given this restricted regional focus, it therefore needs to be stressed also that, with minimal exceptions, all the "laws" issued by Late Roman Emperors were in fact letters written to officials holding office in particular regions. Especially after the division of 395, it also makes a fundamental difference whether the "law," or letter, concerned was issued from Italy (Rome or Ravenna) or from Constantinople. The consolidation of these laws into a single series in the Theodosian Code of 437 created an illusion. In reality there were two separate, but loosely related, spheres of legislation.

All of the synagogue legislation is promulgated in the form of *epistulae* issued on the occasion of particular legal complaints in specific locales. While each might carry the force of general law, it did not necessary apply universally throughout the empire.[40] The law of 393 (*Cod. theod.* 16.8.9) issued by emperors Theodosius, Arcadius, and Honorius was addressed to a particular *comes*, Addeus, for the Eastern dioceses. Similar correspondence between the same parties (*Cod. theod.* 1.7.2 in Augustamnia, Egypt) addressed the specific circumstance of Addeus overturning a ruling of the (inferior) Egyptian provincial governor. The same emperors had to issue another letter that very day to clarify that their assessment of the particular circumstance in Egypt should be applied generally throughout the empire (*Cod. theod.* 1.5.10). By contrast the synagogue protection law of 397 (*Cod. theod.* 16.8.12) issued by co-emperors Arcadius and Honorius was not a general law; it was addressed to the prefect of Illyricum (Dacia and Macedonia).

Co-emperors Honorius and Theodosius II issued the greatest number of synagogue laws. The 412 law (*Cod. theod.* 16.8.20) was addressed to the

---

[38] Matthew, *Laying Down the Law*, pp. 16–18.

[39] Millar, "Christian Emperors, Christian Church and the Jews of the Diaspora in the Greek East, CE 379–450," *Journal of Jewish Studies* 55.1 (Spring 2004): 1–24, ⌐ 4.

[40] Jill Harries and Ian Wood, *The Theodosian Code* (Ithaca, NY: Cornell University Press, 1993), p. 6. Linder notes that occasionally laws addressed to the East applied to the West, but the evidence he uses to support this claim (*Cod. theod.* 12.1.158 dating to 398) was promulgated to clarify to the local Jewish population in Apulia and Calabria (Italy) that they were not exempt from curial duties as they imagined (Linder, "La Loi romaine," pp. 57–64, p. 59). He also maintains that Honorius thereby revoked the Asian law (*Cod. theod.* 16.8.13 of 397), which he claims applied generally in the empire, for the West, but Jewish confusion more likely stems from the fact that the original law issued by Constantine in 330 (*Cod. theod.* 16.8.4), which the law of 397 seems merely to recapitulate, was a universal law addressed to Jewish leaders throughout the empire, while the 397 law addressed to the eastern praetorian prefect, only applied to the East.

praetorian prefect of Italy. Linder notes that "this might represent the government's reaction to the seizure of a Jewish synagogue in Edessa and its conversion to a church in 411/412," but then the *epistola* would have likely been addressed to the Eastern prefect under whose jurisdiction Edessa fell.[41] The 415 law (*Cod. theod.* 16.8.22) is addressed to the praetorian prefect of the East. It marks a policy novum by prohibiting new synagogue construction and requiring the demolition of those *in solitudine* if it could be done peacefully.[42] Pharr translates *in solitudine* as "in desert places," while Linder translates "in deserted places,"[43] referring to isolated or remote locations.[44] Linder's reading echoes the reference in Honorius' law regarding the decommissioning of traditional Roman temples "which are ... outside of towns."[45] An *epistola* addressed to Philippus, the praetorian prefect of Illyricum (*Cod. theod.* 16.8.21), and dated by Linder to 420 reiterated the 397 law promulgated by the previous administration. The repetition might have been necessitated by either the succession of a series of prefects and the emergence of a different disposition toward synagogues, or by some particular incident of synagogue desecration.

More is known about the legislation of February 15, 423 (*Cod. theod.* 16.8.25) addressed to the Eastern praetorian prefect, Asclepiodotus, the empress Eudocia's uncle. The edict refers to a previous law, which the compendium editors Godefroy and Mommsen interpret as a reference to 16.8.9, criminalizing attacks on Jewish assemblies and prohibiting synagogue vandalism in the name of Christianity (*sub christianae religionis nomine*), but according to Linder refers to 16.8.21, which protects Jews from physical and verbal abuse whether in their synagogues or in their homes.[46] Because 16.8.9 is addressed to the same diocese as this law, it is more likely the one being cited. The law of February 423 differs from both of the earlier laws, however, in that it mentions "synagogues arrogated to churches" (*synagogae ... ecclesiis vindicatae*).[47]

---

[41] Linder, *Jews in Roman Imperial Legislation*, p. 263.
[42] *Cod. theod.* 16.8.22: *Nullas condi faciat synagogas et si quae sint in solitudine, si sine sedition ossint deponi, perficiat* ... The same phrase appears in D. 47.10.7.8 Ulp. 57 in reference to assaults perpetrated out of public view.
[43] Clyde Pharr, *The Theodosian Code and Novels, and the Sirmondian Constitutions, The Corpus of Roman Law = Corpus Juris Romani I* (Princeton, NJ: Princeton University Press, 1952), p. 470; Linder, *Jews in Roman Imperial Legislation*, p. 269.
[44] See, for example, Jerome *Adv. Jovianianum* 2.9 (PL 23: 298).
[45] *Cod. theod.* 16.10.19.pr-3: ... *quae* ... *extra oppida sunt* ... The full text is given in Chapter 4.
[46] Linder, *Jews in Roman Imperial Legislation*, p. 289.
[47] *Cod. theod.* 16.8.25, ed. Mommsen, pp. 893–894, discussed in Linder, *Jews in Roman Imperial Legislation*, pp. 287–289.

Sometime probably within the next couple of months, the emperor Theodosius II entertained a complaint by Jews at the imperial court which he referred to as "pathetic supplications" (*miserabiles preces*), prompting him to reissue the February law again in April.[48] Two months later, the emperor reiterated synagogue protection, revoking the suggestion in the February law that "old ones shall be seized from them."[49] Asclepiodotus, the Praetorian prefect of the East to whom the law was addressed, apparently enforced the protections, for the Syrian monk Simeon Stylites wrote a letter to Theodosius II in which he accused the emperor of being a "friend, comrade, and protector of the faithless Jew."[50] Although Simeon claims that Theodosius II revoked the favorable legislation and dismissed Asclepiodotus for his betrayal of the Church in 425, the next legislation on synagogues of 438 or 439 does not reflect a policy change but merely maintains the status quo, prohibiting new construction and sanctioning synagogue repairs.[51]

Although scholars repeat the claim of Syriac specialist François Nau that this series of synagogue protection laws was issued in reaction to the destruction of Palestinian synagogues by the Mesopotamian monophysite monk Barsauma, Günther Stemberger has convincingly demonstrated the flaws in this argument.[52] With the exception of Illyricum, however, none of these laws are addressed to the western provinces. There are seven laws addressing issues besides synagogues concerning Jews in Africa, so this absence cannot be explained by a general silence in the legal sources.[53] Nor is there a dearth of laws addressed to North African magistrates; the preponderance of such *epistolae* collected in the Theodosian code indicates that

---

[48] *Cod. theod.* 16.8.26, tr. Linder, *Jews in Roman Imperial Legislation*, p. 291.

[49] *Cod. theod.* 16.8.27, tr. Linder, *Jews in Roman Imperial Legislation*, p. 297: ... *nec auferendas sibi veters pertimescant*.

[50] *Vita Sym. syr.* 130–31 (TU XXXII: 4, 174–175), tr. Kenneth Holum, *Theodosian Empresses: Women and Imperial Dominion in Late Antiquity*, Transformation of the Classical Heritage (Berkeley, CA: University of California Press), p. 125.

[51] *Novella*, 3, *CJ* 1.9.18, promulgated as universal laws (*hac victura in omne aevum lege* "shall stand forever").

[52] Günter Stemberger, *Jews and Christians in the Holy Land*, tr. Ruth Tuschling (Edinburgh: T & T Clark, 2000), pp. 310–312.

[53] 1. *Cod. theod.* 16.8.3 (on Jewish curial service, promulgated throughout Constantine's jurisdiction, 321 CE); 2. *Sirm.* 4 = *Cod. theod.* 16.9.1, 16.8.5 (banning Jewish circumcision of non-Jewish slaves and prohibiting Jewish persecution of former Jews to Christianity, 335 CE); 3. *Cod. theod.* 12.1.158 (repealing Jewish exemption from curial liturgies, 398 CE); 4. *Cod. theod.* 16.8.17 (404 CE, rescript of revocation of *Cod. theod.* 16.8.14, which banned patriarchal tax collection); 5. *Cod. theod.* 16.5.44 (Jews disturbing Christian worship, 408 CE); 6. *Sirm.* 14 (fragments preserved in *Cod. theod.* 16.2.31, 16.5.46 (Jews disturbing Christian worship, 409 CE); 7. *Cod. theod.* 16.2.46 and 16.5.63, fragments, addressed to the African proconsul, of *Sirm.* 6 (banning Jews from imperial administration and legal profession, 425 CE), from Linder, "La Loi romaine," pp. 57–59.

the legal compilers had ample access to African archives.[54] The most logical conclusion, then, is that North African synagogues were targeted less than those in other regions of the empire.

Laws protecting Jewish property from Christian violence suggest that synagogue attacks could be perceived and portrayed as gratuitous, provoked, or retaliatory. In a famous letter of 388 CE regarding the attack on a synagogue in Callinicum (Raqqa, Syria), Ambrose argues that the attack be viewed as retribution for Jewish attacks on churches during Julian's reign.[55] The role of Jews in the 414–415 CE riots of Alexandria, which targeted religious arenas, and their subsequent expulsion revived the specter of Jewish aggression.[56] Oded Irshai argues that the Alexandrian riots are structurally analogous to the Christian-celebrant riots in Calama in 408 (discussed earlier in Chapter 4): both cases were incited by ethnic, political, and religious tensions and, in both cases, the state declined involvement.[57] The two episodes are dissimilar in one important way, namely, the role of Jews. In contrast to Alexandria, Jewish–Christian rivalry in North Africa left a much more subtle trace in the written record.

In the fifth century, edicts group Jews together with those whom the state had already depicted as enemies of the catholic ("universal") Church.[58] A decree addressed to the African proconsul mandates punishment of Jews along with heretics and Donatists who attack Catholic worship.[59] Linder points out that legislation from this period through the sixth century uses a

[54] Linder, "La Loi romaine," p. 58.
[55] Ambrose, Ep. 74.5. For discussion of this incident see Sizgorich, Violence and Belief, pp. 81–84.
[56] Socrates Hist. Eccl. 7.13.
[57] Irshai, "Christian Historiographers' Reflections on Jewish-Christian Violence in Fifth-Century Alexandria," in Jews, Christians, and the Roman Empire. The Poetics of Power in Late Antiquity, ed. Natalie B. Dohrmann and Annette Yoshiko Reed, pp. 137–153 (Philadelphia, PA: University of Pennsylvania Press, 2013), pp. 144–149.
[58] Linder, "The Legal Status of the Jews," in The Cambridge History of Judaism: Volume 4, The Late Roman-Rabbinic Period, ed. Steven T. Katz, pp. 128–173 (New York: Cambridge University Press, 2006), pp. 149–151.
[59] Cod. theod. 16.5.44 dated 408 CE, tr. Shaw, Sacred Violence, p. 276 (ed. Mommsen): Donatistarum haereticorum iudaeorum nova adque inusitata detexit audacia, quod catholicae fidei velint sacramenta turbare. Quae pestis cave contagione latius emanet ac profluat. In eos igitur, qui aliquid, quod sit catholicae sectae contrarium adversumque, temptaverint, supplicium iustae animadversionis expromi praecipimus (The new and unusually daring actions taken by the Donatists, the heretics, and the Jews have revealed that they wish to throw into disorder the sacraments of the Catholic faith. You must beware lest this disease should become entrenched and spread more widely by contagion. Against those persons who attempt to do anything that is contrary to and opposed to the Catholic sect, we order that punishments of a just measure must be executed). Also see Cod. theod. 16.8.26 (423 CE) and Cod. theod. 16.10.24 (423 CE). Cod. theod. 16.5.63 of 425 CE, addressed to the North African proconsul

cluster of negative epithets to describe Jews and their religion.[60] The cluster includes Jews in the rhetoric of spatial contestation that had previously characterized intra-Christian and Christian–"pagan" relations. This discourse thereby created and reinforced perceptions of Jews as socially, theologically, and politically separate from, or even opposed to, Christians. It also laid the groundwork for the physical marginalization of their communal structures.

Synagogues as Sites of Architectural Displacement: The Archaeological Record

Of the three North African synagogue excavations reported, synagogue authority Rachel Hachlili includes only Lepcis Magna among a list of synagogues converted into churches.[61] Lepcis Magna (Khoms, Libya) was a Carthaginian trading city refurbished by emperor Septimius Severus (193–211).[62] The Severan forum became the civil center during an urban renewal program the emperor sponsored for his birthplace that built a new harbor, colonnaded street, basilica, and temple.[63] The "synagogue" (highlighted in gray) was adapted from the civic basilica (Figure 5.3). The southern side-room of the basilica was refurbished in the fifth century with an eastward-facing niche where an exterior door had been, a raised seat adjacent to the niche, and a set of side benches along three of the walls (Figure 5.4). This late antique phase of reconstruction took place when the city was in decline.[64] In fact, before the building was adapted into a church, the area had been flooded, depositing over a foot of sand on top of the marble floor.[65] When the building was converted to a church in the sixth century, a barrel-vaulted masonry ceiling replaced the earlier timber roof and the floor was raised. This latter renovation suggests that the Byzantine architects attempted to protect the new structure from the kind of flooding that had damaged the earlier building.

Georgius, groups all heresies, schisms, and breaches of faith with pagans and uses the word *sacrilegium* to describe their *superstitio*. Jews, pagans, and heretics are also grouped together (*Cod. theod.* 16.5.46, 16.8.26).

[60] Linder, "Legal Status," pp. 149–151.
[61] Hachlili, *Ancient Jewish Art*, p. 93.
[62] John Bryan Ward-Perkins, *Roman Imperial Architecture* (New Haven, CT: Yale University Press, 1994), p. 371.
[63] *The Princeton Encyclopedia of Classical Sites*, ed. Richard Stillwell, William L. MacDonald, and Marian Holland McAllister (Princeton, NJ: Princeton University Press, 1976).
[64] John Bryan Ward-Perkins, "Excavations in the Severan Basilica at Lepcis Magna," *Papers of the British School at Rome* 20 (1952): 111–121, p. 118.
[65] Ward-Perkins, "Excavations in the Severan Basilica," p. 111.

LEPCIS MAGNA:
SEVERAN FORUM AND BASILICA

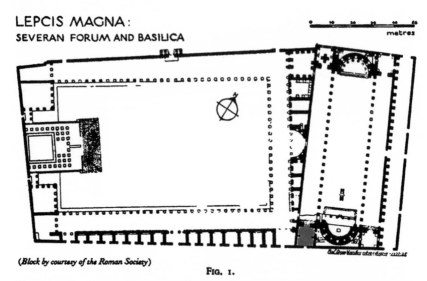

(Block by courtesy of the Roman Society)

FIG. 1.

Figure 5.3 The Severan Forum and Basilica of Lepcis Magna. From John Bryan Ward-Perkins, "Excavations in the Severan Basilica at Lepcis Magna," *Papers of the British School at Rome* 20 (1952), fig. 1. Reproduced with permission.

The precise historical circumstances under which these structural adaptations transpired eludes modern interpreters. The archaeological record does not give a clear picture of the means by which this structure – if it was a synagogue – became a Byzantine church. Evidence supporting architectural dispossession is both legal and literary. At the request of the episcopal Council of Carthage of 535, emperor Justinian addressed a decree to African Prefect Salomon that synagogues be "converted in form to churches."[66] Grouped with Arians, dissident Christians, pagans, and other heretics, Jews were legally denied the right of public assembly.[67] While it is tempting to apply this law to the archaeological remains of Lepcis Magna, it is more

---

[66] Linder, *Jews in Roman Imperial Legislation*, pp. 381–389, Novella 37 (ed. Schöll and Kroll, pp. 244–245): *Sed neque synagogas eorum stare concedimus, sed ad ecclesiasrum figuram eas volumes reformari* (Yet we do not grant that their synagogues shall stand, but want them to be converted in form to churches). See also Linder's discussion (p. 74).

[67] Linder, *Jews in Roman Imperial Legislation*, pp. 381–389, Novella 37 (ed. Schöll and Kroll, pp. 244–245): *Neque enim Iudaeos neque paganos neque Donatistas neque Arianos neque alios quoscumque haereticos vel speluncas habere vel quaedam quasi ritu ecclesiasticofacere patimur, cum hominibus impiis sacra peragenda permittere satis absurdum est* (We do not suffer the Jews, the pagans, the Donatists, the Arians, or all other heretics either to have caves or perform as though in an ecclesiastical rite, for it is perfectly absurd to permit impious men to deal with sacred matters). The use of *speluncae* to refer to illegitimate places of assembly alludes to Jer 7.11and Mk 11.17 (with parallels).

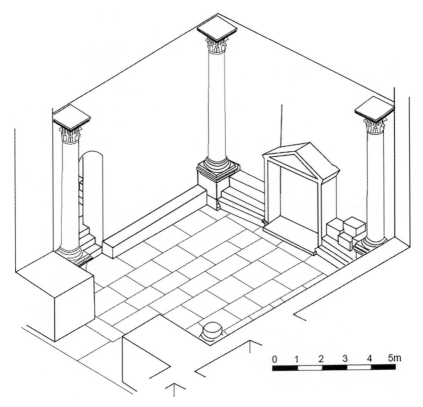

Figure 5.4 Fifth-century reconstruction of southern side-room of Severan basilica, Lepcis Magna. Author's CAD drawing based on John Bryan Ward-Perkins, "Excavations in the Severan Basilica at Lepcis Magna," *Papers of the British School at Rome* 20 (1952), plate 29.

likely that the site, regardless of whether it was a synagogue, experienced decline by the forces of nature rather than malevolent human action.[68]

Synagogues and Spatial Supersession: The Literary Record

While the archaeological evidence for North African synagogue dispossession is scanty and highly equivocal, literary evidence is more forthcoming. The most often-cited literary evidence of architectural dispossession for North African Jews is the *Passio Sanctae Salsae*, which relates the conversion

---

[68] Nonetheless, Hachlili includes this site among "Synagogues Converted into Churches" (Hachlili, *Ancient Jewish Art*, p. 93).

into a church of a synagogue in the Roman harbortown of Tipasa (Tipaza, Algeria), discussed in Chapter 2.[69] In describing the site of the serpent-dragon temple, the third chapter of the martyrology relates:[70]

> But in that dragon [serpent-headed idol] the devil was worshiped; to him they offered libations, and to this wretched one they brought votives and abominable sacrifices. I rejoice that an improvement has completely changed the nature of that place. Where not long ago a temple of the Gentiles had been erected, afterwards – in that very place – the devil built a synagogue of the Jews. But now it is better that the quarter turned (*migravit*) to Christ instead, so that in the place where twin blasphemies prevailed before, now the Church shall triumph in honor of the martyrs.

The adverb "that very place" (*ibidem*) is used locatively; it points to a particular location. The author essentially invites his audience, in an *ekphrastic* exercise, to conjure up where the martyrdom occurred and where the former pagan temple and subsequent synagogue stood. The place is identified as a general area, or quarter (*vicus*) of the city, so it is possible that the temple and synagogue coexisted on the site. This proximity may have prompted the author to describe them as "twins" (*gemina*). Most commentators interpret the text, however, as referring to successive structures.[71] If the term "Jews" here is meant literally, and not as a derogatory reference to sectarian Christians, then the linkage of temple and synagogue echoes

---

[69] Marcel Simon, *Verus Israel: A Study of the Relations between Christians and Jews in the Roman Empire (AD 135–425)*, tr. H. McKeating (Vallentine Mitchell & Co. Ltd., 1948; 1996), p. 225; Jean Juster, *Les Juifs dans l'Empire romain. Leur condition juridique, économique et sociale.* 2 vols. (New York: Burt Franklin, 1914), I: 462; James Parkes, *The Conflict Between the Church and the Synagogue* (Philadelphia, PA: Jewish Publication Society, 1934; 1961), p. 187; Haim Zeev Hirschberg, *A History of the Jews in North Africa: From Antiquity to the Sixteenth Century* Vol. 1 (Leiden: E. J. Brill, 1974), p. 70; and Levine, *Ancient Synagogue*, p. 298. Following Frezouls, Hirschberg mentions that a contemporaneous incident in "Caesarea" was recorded in the *Acta Marcianae* (a virgin from the Roman harbor town of Rusuccur (Tigzirt, Algeria)), but the hagiographic account only mentions an *archisynagogos*, not a synagogue (Frezouls, "Une synagogue juive," p. 288; *Acta Marcianae* 4; cf. Paul Monceaux, *Histoire Litteraire*, III, p. 156). Parkes consigns this tale to the realm of "myth, bordering on farce" (p. 144). Both Caesarea and Tipasa are located in the province of Mauretania Caesariensis.

[70] *Passio Salsae* 3 (ed. Piredda): *Sed in dracone illo diabolus colebatur: huic libamina, huic vota et sacrificia miseri infanda celebrabant. Gaudeo sane conditionem loci illius feliciori proventu fuisse mutatam. Ubi enim dudum templa fuerant instituta gentilium, postmodum ibidem diabolus synagogam constituit Iudaeorum; sed nunc meliore vice migravit ad Christum, ut in loco in quo gemina regnabant ante sacrilegia, nunc in honore martyris triumphet Ecclesia.*

[71] See most recently Gareth Sears, *Late Roman African Urbanism. Continuity and Transformation in the City*, BAR International Series 1693 (Oxford: Archaeopress, 2007), p. 68.

the pairing of Jews and "pagans" in imperial legislation.[72] The characterization of the transformation as "turned to Christ" supports the view that the account has in mind literal Jews.

By describing the synagogue as a "blasphemy" (*sacrilegium*), the author of this martyr account employs language and ideology used in Roman law. The Latin *sacrilegium* contains both sacred and secular nuances, since such crimes were considered offenses against both God and state.[73] The term is first applied to synagogues in legislation of 353, which bans Christian conversion (*efficio*) to Judaism and attendance at their "blasphemous assemblies."[74] By describing the relationship of the Church to the Synagogue as "triumph" (*triumpho*), the author employs rhetoric from the realm of heresy and battle. By using such rhetoric, the account conveys the divinity (*ad Christum*) and rightness (*meliore*) of spatial supersession, simultaneously absolving Christians of any potential wrongdoing regarding temple and synagogue property-destruction and conveying the divine right of the Christianization of space.[75]

The narrative omits the circumstances by which the pagan temple became a synagogue, but it is clear that the martyr's burial shrine cannot have been located at the same site, because she was buried immediately after the festival celebrating the pagan deity housed there.[76] By the time the

---

[72] In that case, Tipasa would not even constitute a literary case of Jewish synagogue conversion. I am grateful to Oded Irshai for suggesting to me that the text might use the eponym "Jews" metaphorically (see also Parkes, *Conflict*, pp. 300–303).

[73] See *Cod. theod.* 2.8.18 for an example of the former and 6.29.9 for the latter.

[74] *Cod. theod.* 16.8.7 (*sacrilegis coetibus aggregetur*). Dating follows Linder, *Jews in Roman Imperial Legislation*, p. 151.

[75] For the former motive I am indebted to the suggestion of Ross S. Kraemer, who made the connection to the portrayal of the fire that consumes all but the walls of the Minorca synagogue in the *Epistula Severi* 13.13 as mysterious and spontaneous. In that account, the fact that the Christian mob had just looted the synagogue (despite the author's protestations to the contrary) suggests that the fire may have been caused by arson and that the account may have been written, among other reasons, to deflect suggestions of Christian impropriety (which incurred serious legal consequences).

[76] The events described by the *Passio Salsae* have been compared to the account mentioned by the sixth-century Greek historian, Procopius of Caesarea, of a Jewish temple conversion in Boreum (Tripolitania, modern Bu Grada, Libya, over 2,000 km west of Tipasa) after the Jewish residents were forcibly converted to Christianity during the reign of emperor Justinian (527–565). The events described by bishop Severus from the island of Minorca in 418, discussed at the beginning of this chapter, took place closer by, about 400 km north of Tipasa into the Mediterranean. Yet there is no evidence to either warrant or deter a comparison between the Tipasa narrative and those of Boreum and Minorca (Procopius, *Aed.* 6.2.21–23, cited in Linder, *Jews in Roman Imperial Legislation*, p. 388 n10; see also Günter Stemberger, *Judaica Minora: Teil II: Geschichte und Literatur des rabbinischen Judentums* (Tübingen: Mohr Siebeck, 2010), p. 114). Although scholars take Procopius' use of the word ναός to refer

account was composed in the early fifth century, there must have been two sites venerating the saint: one at which her martyrdom took place and one where she was buried (as in the case of Cyprian of Carthage). Some have suggested that the former was located in the center of town, while the latter was probably located by the harbor.[77]

Unfortunately the archaeological record offers no evidence for a synagogue. To date, no inscriptions have been identified in connection with the Tipasa Jewish community described in the Salsa martyrology. Although some scholars identify a church near the forum with the synagogue, others believe that the synagogue should be located on the promontory of the forum as described by the martyrology, which has yielded no such ruins.[78] The archaeologist Grandidier suggested in 1897 that the urban basilica on the martyrdom site associated with the synagogue was destroyed due to the cliff's erosion.[79] A column capital bearing a menorah depiction and dating to the fourth or fifth century, thought by some to be from Tipasa, was discovered in Rouaiha, Algeria, about 200 km southwest of Tipasa (Figure 5.5).[80]

The martyrdom narrative's claim that the site of the pagan shrine vanquished by the young girl Salsa became a synagogue before it was transformed into a church raises questions about the transformation. Under what circumstances would this have been possible? In North Africa, pagan temples, like synagogues, were protected by law until the fifth century. The martyrology makes no claim to intentional destruction. There are no human actors in the description at all; just the devil, the synagogue, Christ, and the Church. Perhaps the author casts the transformation as an apocalyptic battle because it was not caused by human beings. It may have been

---

to a synagogue, the fact that the Jews date this building to the age of King Solomon suggests it may be pre-Roman and therefore indeed a temple like that built by Onias in second-century BCE Leontopolis or the one built in sixth-century BCE Elephantine.

[77] Paul Monceaux, *La vraie legende dorée. Relations de martyre* (Paris: Payot, 1928), p. 301, cited in Piredda, *Passio,* p. 15. Remains of the cemetery basilica are dated to the late fourth/early fifth century. An inscription attributing the church's renovation to patron bishop Potentius is dated to the mid-fifth century ("Potentius 2," PCA 1: 898, r. ca. 446).

[78] A. Ballu, "Travaux de fouilles et de consolidations effectués en 1920 par le Service des Monuments historiques: Tipaza," *Recueil des notices et mémoires de la Société archéologique historique et géographique de Constantine* 54 (1922–1923): 2–8, pp. 6–7, and C. Courtois, "Victorinus et Salsa. Note d'Hagiographie tipasienne," *Recueil des notices et mémoires de la Société archéologique historique et géographique de Constantine, Livre du Centenaire, 1852–1952,* 68 (1953): 109–119, cited in Le Bohec, *Les sources archéologique,* p. 26 n. 21; Piredda, *Passio,* p. 15.

[79] O. Grandidier, "Tipasa. Ancien évêché de la Maurétanie Cesarienne, I," *Bulletin de la Société d'Archéologie du Diocèse d'Alger* 2.6 (1897): 183–225, cited in Piredda, *Passio,* p. 15.

[80] For the Tipasa claim, see Stern, *Inscribing Devotion,* p. 196.

Figure 5.5 "Judeo-Berber" Menorah Capital. Photo from Pierre Cadenat, "Chapitaux Tardifs du limes de Maurétanie césarienne dans la région de Tiaret," *Antiquités africaines* 14 (1979): fig. 13, p. 247. Reproduced with permission.

collateral damage in the conflict of the Roman cavalry general Firmus, mentioned earlier in the martyrology, or a casualty of natural disaster. The circumstances of its writing, in the wake of the Visigothic sack of Rome, might have also fueled such inflamed rhetoric.[81]

This line of inquiry exceeds the bounds of our evidence, intriguing though it may be. We must be content to conclude that the narrator, whatever the archaeological reality, wants his audience to believe that the church currently located on the martyrdom site replaced both a synagogue and temple that previously stood there, and that this spatial supersession was both divinely ordained and a symbol of Christianity's victory over both Judaism and traditional Roman religion.

Summary

This chapter began with a survey of Christian and Jewish attitudes toward the synagogue as a structure. By reading against the grain of polemical Christian authors and analogous reasoning using archaeological evidence,

[81] Based on the martyrology's heretical stance toward Donatists and its equivalence with paganism, the account was likely written between 410 and 429 (Piredda, *Passio*, p. 37).

we concluded that synagogues were perceived as powerful spaces by both Jews and Christians. Jews construed this power as holiness, while polemicizing Christians characterized it as demonic. As places of divine power and sites of communal euergetism and organization, protected by imperial legislation, synagogues accrued multiple layers of significant place meanings to the people who used them and the social context in which they were situated. These advances did not square with the providentialist lens through which certain Christian leaders came to view history. In the case of North African synagogues, the rhetoric of supersession, which had served them well in intra-religious conflicts, was employed to interpret their built environment as the triumph of the Church over the Synagogue. Not only did this drive a wedge between Christians and Jews, it affirmed, even proved, the Church's triumphant claim every time these Christians passed or entered the building that was said to have replaced Jewish worship space. By concretizing the abstract notion of supersessionism in the spatial realities of Christians' everyday lives, Christian authors relocated the Christian-Jewish debate from the ideational to the physical realm. Although actual architectural dispossessions seem to be less prevalent in North Africa than elsewhere in the empire, insofar as our evidence permits, the landscape as *perceived* and *interpreted* by leading North African Christians told a more adversarial story.[82]

---

[82] Salient examples of architectural dispossession can be found in Antioch, discussed by Shepardson, *Controlling Contested Places*.

CONCLUSION: RITUAL SPATIAL CONTROL, AUTHORITY, AND IDENTIFICATION

CHRISTIANS, AND MOST LIKELY JEWS, increasingly came to view their places of worship and burial as holy over the course of the third and fourth centuries, as demonstrated by the literary and material evidence reviewed in the previous four chapters. Use of the term *sacra* or *sancta* in connection with their community's buildings, their inscriptions, or their memorials, demonstrates a growing identification of holiness with tangible objects, most notably sites. Generation after generation, leaders and worshippers imbued these sites with layers of symbolic meaning, so that they became "super-symbols," charged with power that was not only significant to their users, but discernible to outside observers as well. With this increased valuation of space, or localization of religious identification, competition over holy sites in late antique North Africa emerged first among Christians, then between Christians and non-Christians, namely Roman traditionalists and Jews. The strategy of localization employed was two-pronged, consisting of both the rhetorical technique of spatial supersessionism and the physical tool of architectural dispossession.

As so-called Catholics sought to distinguish themselves from other Christian groups, and those dissident groups carved out their character in opposition to Catholics, sacred space served as both a literal and symbolic arena in which to perform conflict and display shifting identifications. The idea of using space to distinguish between different groups with conflicting religious commitments had already been employed by Tertullian in the second century to delineate various "pagan" places for Christians to avoid. This imaginal map continued to inform how Christians perceived their lived environment. As Christians began building their own monumental structures, whether martyria or basilicas, their identification with their own buildings became increasingly pronounced. The earliest sources about the

North African schism include conflict between Catholics and dissidents over ritual space, such as the violent incident in the Sicilibba basilica.

As the winds of political power shifted back and forth over the course of the ensuing century, control over sacred sites alternated between Catholics and dissidents. As each group vied for power and carved out distinct ways for group members to self-identify and be identified by nongroup members, commentators interpreted the battle over ritual space providentially, as symbolizing a cosmic struggle between Christ and his adversaries; they conceived of control over these sites as nothing less than universal triumph. As this rhetoric of spatial supersession took hold among its audience, architectural dispossession was extended to non-Christian spaces: first to traditional Roman shrines and temples, and then to Jewish synagogues.

Initially the separation of competing groups into distinct spaces helped to reify their differences, forcing those who may have not embraced the distinction for their own self-definition to make a concrete choice about which building they would frequent and which building they would claim as their own. The "lived experience" of these spaces, to use Lefebvre's typology, created and reinforced sectarian differences. Such distinctions allowed Augustine's episcopal audience to conjure up an actual building filled with people when he referred to the churches of those he deemed heretics and schismatics as "their congregations."[1] Eventually Christian leaders coupled this physical division with a rhetoric of supersession in an attempt to create the perception that the visible, tangible landscape bore witness to Catholic victory.

Legal prohibitions progressively restricted the ritual arenas available to dissident Christians. Rhetorical strategies, like invoking epithets such as *superstitio* and *praecipitates*, then *error* and *haeresis*, created the impression that these other Christians were not only beyond the pale; they were outside the fold. This symbolic arrangement was concretized in spatial terms both rhetorically, by attaching delegitimizing labels to dissident spaces, and physically, by seizing dissident spaces and reinscribing them as Catholic. Periodically, the power dynamic was reversed, and by the Vandal conquest, a new group of Christians joined the battle over sacred space.

What caused this originally internal spatial rhetoric to spill over into adjacent religious communities was Christian leaders' growing anxiety over interreligious boundaries. As increasing numbers of the aristocracy came into the Church, the need arose for Christians to sharply distinguish the

---

[1] Aug. *Fid. symb.* 10.21 (CSEL p. 27): *nam haeretici et schismatici congregationes suas ecclesias vocant.*

dispositions and behaviors used to identify them as Christian from their previous traditionally Roman religious ways (still practiced by those family members who did not convert). Rebillard noted that church-going was "the most obvious way to make public one's Christianity," of "expressing Christian membership."[2] Buildings, therefore, were the primary locus for Christian identification.

The forging of a new, imperial Christian identification relied not only on differentiation from but triumph over both traditional Roman religion and Judaism; the distinction of space lent a tangible dimension to an otherwise abstract notion, a notion that was particularly alien to a religious worldview that was accustomed to aggregating and translating unfamiliar deities and customs rather than excluding them from its worship.[3] Whether replacing a synagogue or a temple, the image of a church built on top of an earlier religious building evoked the kind of triumphal image that drew from military visual idiom. As a prevalent symbol of Roman supremacy, the gesture of superimposition proved to be a powerful weapon in the rhetorical arsenal of late antique North African Christians.

Despite the fact that, or perhaps because, Christians and Jews seemed to coexist in relative harmony, some Christians nevertheless chose to portray the transformation of the Tipasa synagogue into a church in triumphalist language. Using the rhetoric of architectural supersessionism that had been deployed in their intra-Christian conflict, these writers found such imagery useful for delineating their theology of replacement in concrete terms. Unfortunately, in the case of synagogues, the archaeological record is too sparse to determine the relationship between this rhetoric and the technique of architectural dispossession. As in the case of the Lepcis Magna synagogue, it is more likely that transformation resulted from environmental rather than human processes.

At the dawn of the Vandal invasion, displacement was proving to be an effective strategy in the Catholic bid for power. With state support, dissident Christians and Roman traditionalists were eventually pushed to the periphery of ancient towns. Catholics took over sites like Mascula, where they obliterated a dissident inscription and replaced it with their own. They also targeted venerable martyr shrines, such as the one at Vegesela

---

[2] Éric Rebillard, "Religious Sociology: Being Christian," in *A Companion to Augustine*, ed. Mark Vessey, pp. 40–54 (Malden, MA: Blackwell Publishing, 2012; 2015), p. 44, and *Christians and Their Many Identities in Late Antiquity, North Africa, 200–450 CE* (Cornell University Press, 2012, Kindle edition), Kindle location 1588.

[3] For an interesting if controversial summary of this view of traditional Roman religion, see Jan Assmann, *Moses the Egyptian. The Memory of Egypt in Western Monotheism* (Cambridge, MA: Harvard University Press, 1997), pp. 1–22.

and the Basilica Maiorum/Perpetua Restituta of Carthage, and defunct Roman sanctuaries, like the Ceres temple at Thuburbo Maius. Ironically, the Vandals' intolerance of Catholics would lead the new conquerors to deploy the same strategy of architectural dispossession to weaken their religious adversaries.[4]

During the greater century from Constantine to Honorius, North African Christians learned and deployed an important strategy in their new acquisition of and struggle for political power: the use of sacred space. As Christians became increasingly spatially focalized, they invested their houses of assembly with perceptual-symbolic meanings for which the term "holiness" was short-hand. This transformation of perceptual-symbolic meaning made these spaces ideal targets for negotiating group relations and boundaries. With increasing awareness of the power of buildings, both as places to perform religious identification and to display wealth and political influence, spatial contestation helped to concretize the more abstract process of delineating religious differences. The rhetorical strategy of interpreting shifts in the changing late antique landscape in these same terms of spatial contestation proved sufficiently useful to deploy against non-Christians as well. In the Byzantine period, this strategy continued to serve the interests of Christian building policies. The rhetoric of spatial supersession, therefore, aided the phenomenon of architectural dispossession; indeed, this reimagining laid the groundwork for later widespread dispossession. Tension between the imperial respect for property and Christian desire to materially eradicate traditional religion continued into the fifth century, yet it was not until the Byzantine reconquest of North Africa under Justinian that this tension was resolved in favor of Christianity.[5]

Further Observations

Although the dynamic studied in this book drew on ancient examples, the phenomenon of architectural dispossession still afflicts the world today. On February 23, 2006 a *New York Times* headline read, "Blast at Shiite Shrine Sets Off Sectarian Fury in Iraq." The attack on the Askariya Shrine in Samarra, 60 miles north of Baghdad, destroyed the shrine's golden dome.

---

[4] Arian Vandals destroyed or confiscated Catholic property (Victor Vitensis, *Hist. Pers.* 1.1–4).
[5] Leone attributes the Byzantine spate of temple reuse to "the re-monumentalization of North African cities that occurred immediately after the Byzantine conquest" (Anna Leone, *The End of the Pagan City. Religion, Economy, and Urbanism in Late Antique North Africa* (Oxford, 2013), p. 81). Also see Shira Lander, "Inventing Synagogue Conversion: The Case of Late Roman North Africa," *Journal of Ancient Judaism* 4.3 (2013): 401–416.

According to the *Times*, the attack "ignited a nationwide outpouring of rage and panic that seemed to bring Iraq closer than ever to outright civil war."[6] The article went on to quote a fifty-year-old government employee as saying "I would rather hear of the death of a friend than to hear this news."[7] This response may shock a twenty-first-century American audience. Some might wonder, "In what universe of values does the worth of a building outweigh that of human life?" Others may ask, "What was it about that particular site that elicited such an impassioned response?" Or perhaps this response was a hyperbolic exclamation of grief, a rhetorical flourish uttered in the heat of the moment. Yet it may call to mind the comment of Nectarius regarding the Calama basilica attack: "I think it is more grievous to be stripped of one's assets than to be slain."[8]

The dynamics revealed in the Askariya Shrine incident and its aftermath are surprisingly not unique. The attack erupted in the context of sectarian conflict, an internal rivalry between two branches of Islam. Yet equally violent and symbolic attacks are regularly launched by one religious group against another. Religious buildings mean more to their builders, users, and observers than reasoned explication admits; impassioned laments and actions suggest that people ascribe to these buildings deep and multiple levels of meaning. The stated reason for attacking religious sites might be that they symbolize a religious group's collective identification and power, yet the Iraqi government employee's reaction suggests that they are of *greater* value than the human beings to whom they owe their existence. Associated with age-old stories, rites, and meanings, these places symbolize what their users regard as defining their collective identification and most cosmologically significant. In the final analysis, it is the practices of spatial supersession and architectural dispossession discussed in this book that produced and reproduced a context in which place could be perceived as more important than human life.

I have chosen to end this book with examples from our own time, far beyond the chronological and religious parameters of this study, to highlight the fact that what makes headlines today is not so very different from what caught people's attention in antiquity. Although these headlines were taken from a modern case, dramatic examples of how religious adherents exploit each other's sacred spaces for ideological purposes are not new. Spatial violence rivets our gaze no less now than in ancient times.

[6] Robert F. Worth, "Blast at Shiite Shrine Sets Off Sectarian Fury in Iraq," *New York Times* February 23, 2006: A1(L). InfoTrac Newsstand. Web. June 24, 2011.
[7] Worth, "Blast at Shiite Shrine Sets Off Sectarian Fury in Iraq."
[8] Nectarius, apud Aug. *Ep.* 103.3 (CSEL 34.2): *gravius esse spoliari facultatibus quam occidi.*

The centrality of space in religious conflicts like those in late antique North Africa serves as a caution even to those who live in a society where church and state are legally separate. Perceptual-symbolic value deeply embeds such buildings in people's imagination and fosters profound emotional attachments to them. To the people who use these buildings as their ritual arenas and share the structural symbolism with which they are imbued, these spaces hold significance that may even exceed that of human life. Such deeply held place attachment explains how someone could assert: "I would rather hear of the death of a friend than to hear this news."[9] This book has investigated ancient examples of religious leaders willing to die rather than relinquish their sanctuaries, and of people willing to kill in order to seize or destroy them.

Such cases still abound. In the contemporary United States and Europe, religious buildings are regularly defaced with hateful slogans and symbols, and are occasionally the targets of vandalism and willful destruction. Throughout the African countries of Mali, Egypt, and Libya, militants of the radical Salafi group Ansar Dine ("Defenders of the Faith") have destroyed shrines of Sufi saints, whose worship is not only considered forbidden by their interpretation of Islamic law but whose graves must remain separate from worship spaces for reasons of purity.[10] Although regularly condemned by political, humanitarian, and cultural organizations such as UNESCO, this spatial violence will continue as long as sacred spaces hold such perceptual-symbolic value and meaning to their builders and users.

The violence of architectural dispossession derives its perceptual-symbolic value, its place meanings, and attachment from the symbolic meaning of the buildings themselves. Having become a symbol, spatial violence can be invoked as a powerful and influential rhetorical strategy for performing identification and cultivating a climate of conflict. As a symbol, spatial violence remains perpetually available for assigning new meanings and representing even more than the original builders, users, and destroyers might have intended. Those new meanings could potentially be even more destructive than the original destruction in provoking hostility and conflict.

Our observations about late antique North Africa suggest that society is continually engaged in the process of mapping its shifting ideologies onto the spaces it reconstructs, and is in turn continually reshaped by its spatial production. How Christians encountered and reshaped the spaces of others

---

[9] Worth, "Blast at Shiite Shrine Sets Off Sectarian Fury in Iraq."
[10] *The New York Times* Reuters, "Islamist Militants in Mali Continue to Destroy Shrines," published July 1, 2012; accessed August 12, 2013.

whom they materially bumped up against – namely Roman traditionalists and Jews – reveals aspects of their ideas about those others that are not always evident in literary texts. The reconfigured lived environment was perceived by its occupants anew, reshaping their attitudes toward the others whose spaces had been reconfigured. These architectural transformations gave rise to new constructions of self and other, insider and outsider, which refashioned the Roman self as Christian and recast the other as Jewish and "pagan."

As we have seen throughout this book, space is the medium through which human beings experience and express their existence. As Martin Heidegger observed, built space is how human beings dwell, or live in a particular time and place.[11] Since this built environment is produced by social factors, we should expect that buildings will continue to serve as useful tools in all types of human conflict because of the social processes involved in their construction, their material role in everyday life, and their perceptual-symbolic meanings. Analysis of the contestation over sacred spaces and places, both material and ideational, built and imagined, helps illuminate the dynamics of religious conflict and social transformation that continues to punctuate human history.

---

[11] Martin Heidegger, "Bauen Wohnen Denken (Building, Dwelling, Thinking)," tr. Albert Hofstadter, *Basic Writings*, ed. David F. Krell (New York: Harper & Row, 1977, 1993 (originally 1951)), pp. 353–363.

INDEX